# THE NOBEL PRIZE WINNERS

## Physics

# THE NOBEL PRIZE WINNERS

# Physics

Volume 1
1901–1937

*Edited by*
FRANK N. MAGILL

SALEM PRESS
Pasadena, California   Englewood Cliffs, New Jersey

*037795°6*

PHYSICS

**Library of Congress Cataloging-in-Publication Data**
The Nobel Prize winners: physics/edited by Frank N.
Magill. p. cm.
Includes bibliographies and indexes.
Contents: v. 1. 1901-1937—v. 2. 1938-1967—v. 3. 1968-
1988.
1. Physicists-Biography. 2. Nobel prizes.
[1. Physicists-Biography. 2. Nobel prizes]
I. Magill, Frank Northen, 1907-      .
QC15.N63      1989      530'.092'2-dc19      89-6409
[B]
[920]
ISBN 0-89356-557-1 (set)
ISBN 0-89356-558-x (volume 1)

# PUBLISHER'S NOTE

THE NOBEL PRIZE WINNERS: PHYSICS is the second set in a series that will cover the Nobel laureates in all award areas: Literature, Physics, Chemistry, Physiology or Medicine, Peace, and Economic Sciences. This series is one of the few reference works in English to offer comprehensive coverage of the winners and of the speeches and commentary attendant on the Prize. Organized by subject, it is accessible to library users.

Volume 1 opens with a complete "History and Overview" of the Nobel Prize in Physics by R. Baird Shuman of the University of Illinois at Urbana-Champaign. He covers Alfred Nobel's creation of the award and its subsequent implementation and administration by the Nobel Foundation and the Royal Swedish Academy of Sciences. Next, the selection procedure and the growth in the award's value are discussed. The second half of the article reviews the history of the physics prize, examining each decade's laureates, their work, and trends in the award's bestowal. In his conclusion, Dr. Shuman compares the physics prize with the other awards and comments on its social and political context.

A time line appears after the overview essay; it lists, in tabular form, essential information about the Nobel laureates in physics: names, dates of birth and death, award years, nationalities, and the areas of physics with which they are most closely linked. The articles are arranged chronologically, beginning with Wilhelm Röntgen, the recipient of the first prize, in 1901, and ending with Leon M. Lederman, Melvin Schwartz, and Jack Steinberger, the winners in 1988.

To provide the reader with some historical perspective, each article is preceded by a listing of the winners in the other disciplines for the same year. A photograph of the laureate appears on the left-hand page facing the opening of the article.

The essays, which average 3,500 words in length, follow a standard format designed for quick access to information. Ready-reference listings at the start of each article give the laureate's name, places and dates of birth and death (if applicable), and areas of concentration within physics. A brief description of the individual's impact on physics and why he or she won the award appears in italics. This statement may take its cue from the Nobel Foundation's official award citation, but it does not duplicate it; rather, it speaks from a late twentieth century perspective.

The text of each essay is broken into five sections. *The Award* contains three: "Presentation," a synopsis of the speech delivered by the award's presenter, a member of the Royal Swedish Academy of Sciences; "Nobel lecture," an overview of the laureate's address describing the prizewinning work; and "Critical reception," a survey of the popular and professional responses to the Academy's choice. A *Biography* sketches the major events of the laureate's life, and the *Scientific Career* section, constituting roughly one-third to one-half of the article, traces his or her professional life, highlighting important research, experiments, and publications. Finally, the *Bibliography* has two parts: The "Primary Bibliography" lists the laureate's principal works, by genre, through 1988; the "Secondary Bibliography"

v

lists works about the laureate and is annotated, providing readers with criteria for choosing sources for further study.

A comprehensive index includes the names of the winners and other principal personages; titles of important works mentioned in the articles; key terms, theories, experiments, and discoveries; and the names of important laboratories and institutions. The laureates are also indexed under their nationalities and under their areas of concentration, to help the reader interested in locating all the winners from a particular country or branch of physics. A complete alphabetical list of the laureates appears in the front matter of each volume.

### Acknowledgments

The articles appearing in these volumes, written by experts in their respective fields, are signed, and a complete listing of the contributors and their academic affiliations is included in the front matter of volume 1. Without the efforts of these many fine academicians in physics and the history of science, the compilation of this reference work would not have been possible.

The editors also wish to acknowledge the ongoing cooperation of The Nobel Foundation in providing historical and current information. Permission to reprint all the photographs of the physics laureates reproduced in these three volumes has been kindly provided by the copyright holder, © The Nobel Foundation.

# CONTRIBUTORS

Stephen R. Addison
*University of Central Arkansas*

Carl G. Adler
*East Carolina University*

Arthur L. Alt
*College of Great Falls*

Bulent I. Atalay
*Mary Washington College*
*University of Virginia*

Theodore P. Aufdemberge
*Concordia College*

Harry E. Bates
*Towson State University*

Thomas W. Becker
*Webster University*

Richard P. Benton
*Trinity College*

Beatrice Birchak
*University of Houston—Downtown*

Jeanie R. Brink
*Arizona State University*

Alan Brown
*Livingston University*

Christopher Burawa
*Arizona State University*

Byron D. Cannon
*University of Utah*

Dennis Chamberland
*National Aeronautics and Space Administration*
*Kennedy Space Center*

Allan D. Charles
*University of South Carolina at Union*

Victor W. Chen
*Chabot College*

Charles A. Dranguet, Jr.
*Southeastern Louisiana University*

David G. Fenton
*Connecticut College*

Robert J. Forman
*Saint John's University, New York*

C. George Fry
*Saint Francis College*

Kostas Gavroglu
*Harvard University*

Richard K. Gehrenbeck
*Rhode Island College*

Douglas Gomery
*University of Maryland*

Gregory A. Good
*West Virginia University*

Hans G. Graetzer
*South Dakota State University*

Mark S. Gulley
*New Mexico Military Institute*

Mikael Hard
*Gothenburg University*

Robert M. Hawthorne, Jr.
*Unity College in Maine*

James R. Hofmann
*California State University, Fullerton*

Ruth H. Howes
*Ball State University*

Shakuntala Jayaswal
*University of New Haven*

Charles S. Kraszewski
*Pennsylvania State University—University Park*

Alexis Latner
*Rice University Library*

Leon Lewis
*Appalachian State University*

Clarice F. Lolich
*Oklahoma State University*

## NOBEL PRIZE

James Charles LoPresto
*Edinboro University*

Mark R. McCulloh
*Davidson College*

Paul Madden
*Hardin Simmons University*

V. L. Madhyastha
*Fairleigh Dickinson University*

Robert G. Melton
*Pennsylvania State University—University Park*

Ellen F. Mitchum
*The Space Center*

Margaret C. Morrison
*University of Minnesota*

Nancy J. Nersessian
*Princeton University*

Robert J. Paradowski
*Rochester Institute of Technology*

Caroline G. Porcari
*University of South Carolina*

N. A. Renzetti
*California Institute of Technology*
*Columbia University*

Charles W. Rogers
*Southwestern Oklahoma State University*

Joseph Rosenblum
*University of North Carolina at Greensboro*

Marc Rothenberg
*Smithsonian Institution*

Roger Sensenbaugh
*Indiana University, Bloomington*

Gilbert Shapiro
*University of California, Berkeley*

Martha Sherwood-Pike
*University of Oregon*

R. Baird Shuman
*University of Illinois at Urbana-Champaign*

Sedgwick Simons, Jr.
*University of Houston—Downtown*

Genevieve Slomski
*Independent Scholar*

Clyde J. Smith
*Centenary College*

Ralph B. Snyder
*University of Connecticut*

Katherine R. Sopka
*Four Corners Analytic Sciences*

M. F. Soto
*Bernard M. Baruch College*
*City University of New York*

Joseph L. Spradley
*Wheaton College*

Grace Marmor Spruch
*Rutgers University, Newark*

Lulynne Streeter
*Independent Scholar*

Peter J. Walsh
*Fairleigh Dickinson University*

Louis Winkler
*Pennsylvania State University—University Park*

# CONTENTS

## NOBEL PRIZE

# ALPHABETICAL LIST OF PRIZE WINNERS

# NOBEL PRIZE

# NOBEL PRIZE

## NOBEL PRIZE

# THE NOBEL PRIZE WINNERS

## Physics

**ALFRED NOBEL**

# THE NOBEL PRIZE IN PHYSICS
## History and Overview

Since its inception in 1901, the Nobel Prize has been the premier international award for people in the fields of chemistry, physics, physiology or medicine, and literature. A fifth prize, the Nobel Peace Prize, which can be awarded to individuals or, unlike the other Nobel Prizes, to organizations, reflects perhaps better than the others the inherent intent of Alfred Bernhard Nobel (1833-1896), who established the prizes.

The inventor of dynamite and smokeless gunpowder, Nobel was a man of great intelligence and social conscience as well as great wealth. He had business interests throughout the world and could legitimately be called an internationalist. Nobel held more than 350 patents, many of them immensely profitable. He waived his royalties on the production of dynamite in favor of taking a share of the profits of virtually every major explosives factory in the world. Nearing the end of his life, Nobel, unmarried and childless, realized that the world might remember him only as an inventor who had helped make modern warfare possible. By establishing the Nobel Prize, he also established himself in the memories of future generations as a man who had encouraged peace and human welfare rather than as the man who had produced materials that propelled warfare into a new dimension.

The Nobel Prize has become a standard against which all similar awards are measured. Throughout the years of its existence, the money that accompanies the prize has increased substantially, although some other awards, such as the so-called MacArthur genius awards, come close monetarily to matching the Nobel Prize. Nevertheless, the intangible values of being named a Nobel laureate in any of the five areas are incalculable. Clearly, the Nobel Prize has retained its prestige through the decades in part because it is an international award that receives worldwide publicity, but also because of the limited number of people who can be honored by receiving it.

The Nobel Foundation has strongly resisted efforts to expand the prize into areas other than those stipulated in Nobel's will, even though donors have frequently offered to subsidize similar prizes bearing the Nobel name in such areas as mathematics, art, architecture, and music. The Foundation justifies its action by arguing that, if the number of recipients expands dramatically, the award will become inflated and will have less meaning and prestige than Nobel intended.

The only major deviation from Nobel's will that the Foundation has approved to date came in 1968, when it permitted the Bank of Sweden to endow the Prize in Economic Sciences in Memory of Alfred Nobel to commemorate the Bank's tercentenary. This prize, first awarded in 1969, is made immediately after the others each year on December 10, the anniversary of Alfred Nobel's death. It has assumed fully the status of the other Nobel Prizes and is, like those in chemistry and physics, awarded by the Royal Swedish Academy of Sciences.

*Alfred Nobel's Last Will and Testament*

Alfred Nobel's last will and testament, dated November 27, 1895, slightly more than a year before his death, superseded his will of 1893 and differed from it substantially. Although the earlier will contained intimations of the direction the later will would take, it referred only generally and subsidized quite minimally awards to people who had made important, original discoveries that broadened the scope of knowledge and advanced the cause of human progress. After relatively small charitable bequests and bequests to servants and friends, it awarded the bulk of Nobel's enormous estate to members of his family. This early will, nevertheless, sowed the seed that was to germinate and blossom into the Nobel Prizes as they are known today.

Upon his death in 1896, Nobel left an estate equivalent to $9 million. Accounting for inflation, the estate had an estimated value well in excess of $100 million in 1988. The will that disposed of this estate left small bequests to servants and friends and somewhat larger bequests to family members. The bulk of the remaining estate was to be invested in safe securities, the income from which was to be used for the establishment of four awards to be made annually, one each in the fields physics, chemistry, literature, and physiology or medicine to the individuals who had, during the preceding year, done the most in their fields to benefit mankind. A fifth prize, designated for the person who has made the greatest contribution to friendship among nations, to disarmament, or to arms limitation, is the Nobel Peace Prize, available to organizations as well as to individuals.

Nobel signed his will, a deceptively simple holograph document, in the presence of four witnesses at the Swedish Club in Paris on November 27, 1895. The portion of the document that establishes the prizes consists of only two paragraphs. It stipulates that the prizes shall be awarded without regard to the recipients' nationalities. It further states that the awards in physics and chemistry shall be made by the Swedish Academy of Sciences, those in literature by the Stockholm Academy (which became the Swedish Academy), those in physiology or medicine by the Royal Institute in Stockholm (which became the Karolinska Medico-Surgical Institute), and those in peace by the Norwegian Storthing (Parliament). The last stipulation necessitates two awards ceremonies, one in Oslo, Norway, for the bestowal of the Peace Prize, now awarded by the Norwegian Nobel Committee, and one in Stockholm, Sweden, for the bestowal of the remaining prizes.

The will, reflecting Nobel's distrust of lawyers and his tendency to entrust responsibility fully to people who worked closely with him, appoints as executors Ragnar Sohlman and Rudolph Lilliquist. Sohlman, twenty-six years old at the time of Nobel's death, assumed the greater responsibility of the two executors and is directly responsible for bringing about the fulfillment of Alfred Nobel's dream, working against difficulties that a regiment of lawyers would have found daunting.

*Implementing the Nobel Bequest*

Ragnar Sohlman realized that Nobel's will might easily be successfully contested by disgruntled relatives whose share of the estate had been dramatically reduced by the will of 1895. They could reasonably be expected to argue that Nobel had left the bulk of his enormous estate to fund prizes that did not exist and that were to be administered by organizations that had not been approached in advance to see whether they would be willing and able to assume the responsibility for awarding the prizes.

In some ways, the vagueness of the will is among its chief strengths. As Nobel stipulated the provisions of his bequest, he allowed room for interpretation, leaving details of implementation to those who would administer the estate and, eventually, the prizes. The vagueness allowed for reinterpretation to meet changing social conditions. Sohlman's chief task was to reach some accord with Nobel's family so that they would not contest the document. Fortunately, one of the heirs, Nobel's nephew Emmanuel, a wealthy businessman living in Russia, was supportive of his uncle's desire to establish the prizes set forth in the will, and he encouraged a dejected and pessimistic Sohlman to persist in following Nobel's wishes, reminding him that in Russia an executor is looked upon as the soul's messenger.

Sohlman won the battle to have the will registered and probated in Karlskoga, near Bofors, Sweden, which, he argued, was Nobel's legal residence at the time death overtook him in his villa at San Remo, Italy. Sweden had more to gain from Nobel's will than any other country in which it might have been probated; but for this fortuitous choice, which was affirmed a year after the death, the somewhat casual document would undoubtedly have been overturned.

Eventually, the family agreed not to challenge the will in return for receiving payments from the estate somewhat in excess of those Nobel had originally made to them. In terms of the economy of their day, the Nobel heirs were well provided for. The next daunting task to face Sohlman was that of converting Nobel's vast and scattered holdings into liquid assets without unsettling the world economy. He had to do this before he could establish the Nobel Foundation, which would be charged with overseeing the details of the awards but not of making the awards itself.

Sohlman also had to persuade the institutions Nobel had designated to make the awards to assume this responsibility, and this was no easy task. To complicate an already complicated situation, Sohlman was called up for military service and had to conduct much of the business connected with administering the Nobel estate while he was a conscript in the army. Despite these obstacles, Sohlman moved quickly, confidently, and judiciously, reaching his accord with the Nobel family in 1898. Although he could not turn all of Nobel's holdings into liquid assets for some years to come, he had disposed of enough of them by 1900 that in June of that year, he saw established the Nobel Foundation, an almost miraculous achievement to have been carried out in less than four years after Nobel's death.

## The Nobel Foundation

The Nobel Foundation, presided over by a five-member board, is staffed by approximately a dozen people. Three of its board members were originally appointed by the Swedish Nobel Committee and two were named by the king. As the board has continued to function, its chair has been named by the government and is currently chosen from among the institutions that award the prizes.

The Foundation coordinates and assists in the work of the various committees and academies that make the awards but does not itself make awards or have veto power over the decisions of the committees and academies charged with granting the prizes. The Foundation, established with an original endowment of 31.5 million kronor, has seen its assets grow through the years and now has almost twenty times the resources with which it began.

The endowment would be twice that size except for two factors. First, the Foundation had to pay heavy income taxes for the first forty-six years of its existence. It was not until 1946 that Sweden gave the Foundation tax-exempt status. Second, until 1953, because of Nobel's stipulation that his bequest be invested in safe investments, the Foundation was permitted by law to invest only in government bonds. With the relaxation of this provision and with its tax-exempt status in place, the Foundation has grown richer and the prizes given Nobel laureates more generous than in the first five decades that the award was given.

The Foundation, besides being responsible for handling the endowment's investments, publishes numerous books related to the Nobel Prize and to Alfred Nobel. One of its most important publications is the annual *Les Prix Nobel*, in which are published all the Nobel lectures for each year, as well as a biography of each laureate and details of the award ceremonies. The Foundation handles all of the logistics of the awards, the travel arrangements of recipients and their families, and the social activities that accompany the annual ceremonies.

At times the Foundation has been called upon to interpret Nobel's will in such ways as to make its provisions consistent with changes that have taken place in society. For example, the Foundation, in consultation with the award-making academies and committees, stipulated that prizes may be shared but that no more than three people may share a single prize. The tendency of major research scientists to work collaboratively necessitated this alteration. The Foundation also decided that organizations as well as individuals are eligible for the Nobel Peace Prize.

Because notable researchers must sometimes wait many years before their work is recognized, the Nobel Prize deviates from the provision in the will that prizes be granted for work done in the preceding year. In some fields, the grant is made for specific work rather than for the work of one's career up to the time of the award, as in the case of Albert Einstein, who received the prize for his research in the photoelectric effect, not for his more popularly recognized research in relativity. In other fields, particularly literature, the prize increasingly is granted for the whole of the laureate's production rather than for a single accomplishment, and the Peace Prize is often granted for a lifetime of services and activity rather than for one supreme instance of such performance.

The Foundation provided that if a prize is deferred in a given year, it may be awarded the following year along with the prize for that year. As a result of this provision, Einstein was awarded his Nobel Prize in Physics in 1922, although it was the 1921 prize that he received; Niels Bohr received the 1922 prize in physics, and the official presentations occurred simultaneously on December 10, 1922.

When the Norwegian Parliament found that it could not handle efficiently the task of awarding the Nobel Peace Prize, the Foundation approved the formation of the Norwegian Nobel Committee, whose five members are appointed by the Parliament, to undertake the task. It is understandable that this change had to be made when one considers that, between 1901 and 1903, candidates nominated for the Peace Prize numbered 332.

The Foundation, which is housed in the same building in Stockholm as the Royal Swedish Academy of Sciences, disburses operating funds to the various academies and committees that make the awards, collects nominations and information for the academies and committees that award the prizes, helps to stock their libraries with works relevant to their deliberations, and arranges for translations of works written originally in languages that those making the decisions do not know. It also holds annual Nobel symposia in the sciences and publishes their proceedings.

### The Selection Procedure

As it works to select the ultimate recipients of the prize in physics each year, the Nobel Committee for Physics, consisting of five members assisted by such specialists as it may require, adheres to an undeviating schedule. Three or four months before the prize for one year is awarded, more than a thousand letters have been sent to former prizewinners, to members of the Royal Swedish Academy of Sciences, and to key people in higher institutions and in appropriate professional organizations in the United States, France, West Germany, Italy, the Soviet Union, the Netherlands, Belgium, Italy, and Switzerland soliciting nominations for the following year. Letters sent in the early autumn of one year request nominations for the following year's prizes.

In order for nominations to be considered, they must be in hand by January 31 of the next year. It is usual for the Royal Academy to receive up to more than two hundred nominations a year for each award in the sciences, although, because of duplicate nominations, the actual number of nominees is likely to be about one hundred. Nominations may be made only by those invited to make them, and their identity is not made public. Self-nomination is not permitted. Within two weeks after the nominations have been received, the secretary to the committee compiles the official list of nominees, each of whom is accorded serious consideration. The committee members then begin their investigation into the research of each nominee, meeting at least once a week until early spring to pare down the initial list.

Because the time lag between a physicist's making a significant breakthrough and that scientist's receiving an award may be great, some nominees' names recur on the list for as long as several decades, reducing slightly the pressure of investigating each case from scratch. By the end of March or early April, the original list should have been reduced to no more than twenty names, and, on occasion, to half that.

At this point, the committee begins the most intensive part of its work, the bargaining and compromising that will lead eventually to the selection of no more than three winners in cases where the prize is shared. The winnowing process continues until the list has been reduced to five people or groups of people who become the finalists for that year. By late April, that list is decided upon and samples of each candidate's work are distributed for careful, more leisurely perusal over the summer. Official committee meetings end in May and do not resume until late in September.

Shortly after its first fall meeting, the committee must produce its list of finalists and submit it to the appropriate group, numbering about twenty-five people, of the Royal Swedish Academy of Sciences. Each of these groups—one each in physics, chemistry, and economics—votes by secret ballot and ultimately sends its decision, which cannot be appealed or overridden, to the Royal Academy. The members of each committee are sworn to secrecy for a period of fifty years after their deliberations, and through the years this confidentiality has seldom been breached.

Those who have participated in the selection process concede that they cannot with any assurance select the best possible candidate year in and year out because of the difficulty of determining in any absolute way what represents the best. Very strong candidates are passed over; the wisdom of some choices has been debated. It is significant, for example, that Albert Einstein, although he was nominated for the prize in physics almost annually from 1910 onward, was passed over until 1922, at which time he was awarded the prize that had been reserved in 1921—and then he did not receive it for the work in relativity that was to be regarded as his main scientific legacy. Nevertheless, the award committees are consistently mindful of Alfred Nobel's charge that winners be those who have "conferred the greatest benefit on mankind" regardless of nationality, and while some contest whether the choices have consistently been the best possible, few deny that the laureates chosen have, in fact, met the criteria set forth in Nobel's will.

Those to be honored are notified in the last half of October, and the world press is informed of the winners in all six fields. The Nobel laureates except for the winner of the Peace Prize, are fêted in Stockholm during the week before the award is actually given. Usually the Nobel lectures take place on December 8. The awards banquet on December 10 is followed the next day by a formal dinner at the Royal Palace hosted by the reigning monarch.

### The Award

The amount of the Nobel Prize has always been considerable. In 1901, the year of the initial awards, each prize carried a stipend of 150,800 kronor, which was essentially about as much as a typical university professor earned in twenty-five years. The amount increased each decade, but not until the mid-1960's did the award money reach 300,000 kronor. Within another decade, by 1975, the award brought 630,000 kronor, more than twice what it had in 1965. The amount again doubled by 1983, and the 1987 awards each carried a stipend of 2 million kronor, the equivalent of $340,000 in the United States.

Although the amount of each award is substantial, it must be remembered, particularly in the sciences, that because the work being recognized is collaborative, the award is often shared with one or two other people. Forced more frequently than not to share their prizes, most Nobel laureates in physics have found that, although winning the award changes their lives in ways that make serious inroads on their research time, they are better able to attract competitive research money as a result of their laureate status than they were before they received such recognition.

About 67 percent of the income from the Nobel bequest goes directly to the recipients of the prizes. The remainder is spent on the considerable administrative expenses associated with making the awards and subsidizing the other activities of the Foundation.

*The Physics Prize*

Between 1901 and 1988, 133 individuals were awarded 134 Nobel Prizes in Physics (John Bardeen having won the award twice). Of this group, two were women, Marie Curie (1867-1934), who in 1903 shared the award with her husband Pierre (1859-1906), and with Antoine-Henri Becquerel (1852-1908), for her work in radiation; and Maria Goeppert Mayer (1906-1972), who in 1963 shared the award with Eugene Wigner (born 1902) and J. Hans D. Jensen (1907-1973), for her discoveries relating to nuclear shell structure. Marie Curie was again named a Nobel laureate in 1911, when she alone received the prize in chemistry for her work in discovering radium and plutonium, the first person to be honored twice.

When Albert Einstein was passed over for a second Nobel Prize in Physics, it was assumed that no scientist would again be honored twice, particularly if the second prize would be in the same field as the first one. Subsequently, the Red Cross received the Nobel Peace Prize twice, in 1917 and again in 1945. It was not until 1972, however, when John Bardeen (born 1908) shared a prize for his pioneering work in superconductivity, that an individual was twice honored in the same field— Bardeen had shared the 1956 prize in physics for the discovery of the transistor effect and for the invention of the transistor. Linus Pauling (born 1901), who received the 1954 prize in chemistry, also received the 1962 Peace Prize.

Although some people have complained that the Nobel Prizes generally have favored Scandinavians unduly, such has not been the case in physics. Aside from four Swedish and three Danish recipients, the remainder have been from outside Scandinavia, with the largest contingent coming from the United States (50), followed by Great Britain (20), Germany (18), France (8), the Soviet Union (7), the Netherlands (6), Sweden (4), Switzerland (3), Italy (3), Japan (3), Austria (3), Denmark (3), China (2), Ireland (1), India (1), and Pakistan (1).

For various reasons, the prize is sometimes reserved. In such cases, it may be awarded the following year or it may be omitted altogether. In 1916, 1931, 1933, 1940, 1941, and 1942, the prize was not awarded in physics and the prize money was returned to special physics funds and to the main fund. In 1917, 1918, 1921, 1924,

1925, 1928, 1932, and 1943, the prize was reserved but was awarded in the following year, in every instance except 1918 along with the prize for the year in question. From 1916 to 1918, World War I was raging, making it difficult to obtain and explore fully the broad range of nominations from which the committee usually works. The award was withheld from 1940 to 1942 and was reserved in 1943, also war years, for the same reason.

If one can generalize about trends in the bestowal of the prize in physics, it appears that recipients whose work was more theoretical than practical had little chance of winning the prize in the earlier years of the awards, although practical outcomes, such as the invention of the transistor or of the bubble chamber or the holographic method, have marked many of the later awards as well.

People have often wondered why Alfred Nobel excluded mathematics from the fields in which awards would be offered. Gossip has it that in one of his ill-starred love affairs, he lost the woman he loved to one of Europe's most notable mathematicians and that mathematics was specifically excluded so that no possibility would exist that this man would ever be honored with a Nobel Prize. A more likely explanation, however, is that Nobel favored sciences that were more practical than abstract, so that mathematics, essentially an abstract science, did not qualify in his mind for the sorts of awards that he envisioned and wanted to fund.

## 1901-1911

The first decade of the Nobel Prizes was a trial period of sorts, and the awards made in some areas were generally considered unfortunate or bewildering choices. Such was less the case in physics, however, than in some other fields. During the first decade, fifteen awards were made in physics. Much was happening in the field during this period. The Curies were doing their pioneering work with radium, Einstein emerged by the end of the decade as a world-class physicist, Einstein's teacher, Philipp von Lenard, was challenging new frontiers with his work on cathode rays, and Guglielmo Marconi had made his significant contributions to the field of wireless telegraphy. In retrospect, the list of Nobel winners from this decade seems quite illustrious, although some might wonder why Einstein had to wait until 1922 to receive his award and might wonder as well why he was honored for his work in photoelectric effect rather than his better-known work in relativity.

The countries whose scientists were honored during this first decade of the awards were Germany (4), France (4), the Netherlands (3), Great Britain (2), the United States (1), and Italy (1).

## 1912-1920

The decade of World War I saw only nine awards in physics. This dearth was in part the result of the difficulty in getting nominations and information about nominees in the last half of the decade. During this period, the youngest Nobel recipient in physics to date, William Lawrence Bragg, was honored along with his father, Sir William Henry Bragg, for their joint work in analyzing the structure of crystals by the use of X rays. The younger Bragg was twenty-five years old at the time of the award. Several of the awards of this period had to do with the study of radiation or with studying some other areas of physics by using X rays.

Perhaps the most fruitful research designated for an award in the decade was that conducted by Heike Kamerlingh Onnes on how matter is affected by low temperatures, work that won for him the prize in 1913 and that also pointed the way to research in superconductivity that would win the 1972 prize for Bardeen and his colleagues, Leon N Cooper and John Robert Schrieffer.

The 1911-1920 awards were given to scientists from Germany (3), Great Britain (3), the Netherlands (1), Switzerland (1), and Sweden (1). The absence of the United States from this list is attributable at least partially to its geographical isolation that made communication during the war years difficult.

### *1921-1929*

Eleven physicists were honored with the prize in physics in the decade of the 1920's, during which the prize was reserved four times, although in each case it was presented in the following year. The countries of the recipients were Germany (3), Great Britain (2), the United States (2), France (2), Denmark (1), and Sweden (1). The awards for this period show a recognition of the ascendancy of atomic physics and of wave theory.

It appears that the committee had difficulty keeping up in its work during this period. Certainly the scientists honored during the decade did fundamental and pioneering research in their fields. Their number includes Albert Einstein, Niels Bohr, Jean Baptiste Perrin, Arthur Holly Compton (1892-1962), Charles Thomson Rees Wilson, and Sir Owen Willans Richardson—all men who advanced understanding in their fields significantly and, consistent with the terms of Nobel's will, contributed substantially to the benefit of humankind.

In physics more than a field such as literature, the world community of scientists has quite a clear understanding of the work that has the most potent effect upon the discipline. Laureates including Einstein and, more recently, one of the 1988 winners, Leon Max Lederman, have realized well in advance of the actual award that their work had reached the point at which it would necessarily be so recognized. So sure of this was Einstein that three years before he received the award he agreed to make it part of his divorce settlement with his first wife.

### *1930-1939*

In the decade that ended with the beginning of World War II, eleven more prizes were given in physics. With the rise of Nazism, Germany, whose scientists had been well recognized in past decades, produced only one Nobel laureate, Werner Heisenberg, who won the prize that had been reserved in 1932, awarded in 1933, for his work in quantum mechanics. Scientists such as Einstein were fleeing Germany, Italy, and Austria for safer havens.

Perhaps the most significant prize of the 1930's was that awarded to Enrico

Fermi, for work that led to the discovery of nuclear reactions brought about by slow neutrons. Fermi, who left Italy to attend the Stockholm awards ceremony, fled from Stockholm directly to the United States and was to be one of the major contributors to the development of nuclear energy by the splitting of the atom. It was his work in Chicago that led directly to the development of the atom bomb.

The geographical distribution of the awards for this decade is interesting, political considerations apparently showing themselves in the national distribution of the prizes. The United States (3) gained an ascendancy and tied with Great Britain (3) for the greatest number of Nobel laureates. Austria (2), India (1), Italy (1), and Germany (1) completed the list.

### 1940-1949

World War II raged through half of this decade, and only seven awards were made in physics, partly because of the difficulty involved in obtaining nominations and in doing the follow-up research they necessitated, and partly because so many scientists were diverted from their research pursuits to serve their countries in more immediately practical ways. The prize had to be reserved from 1940 through 1942; the money was allocated internally. The 1943 prize was awarded in 1944.

Despite these problems, the United States, which up to that time had produced a total of six Nobel laureates, had the highest number of winners in the decade. Although the raw number was three, it marked a turning point for the United States, whose winners were soon to total more than twice the number of any other country. Interestingly, one of the three U.S. citizens honored during this decade was a naturalized citizen who had fled from Nazi Germany, and one was a naturalized citizen who had fled from Austria.

The awards from 1940 to 1949 ranged from the theoretical, such as Wolfgang Pauli's discovery of the exclusion (Pauli) principle or Hideki Yukawa's prediction of the existence of mesons, to the practical, such as Percy Bridgman's invention of apparatus to produce extremely high pressures or Patrick Blackett's development of the Wilson cloud chamber method. The emphasis, however, was more on the practical than on the theoretical.

During the war-torn 1940's, the distributions of awards among nations was to the United States (3), Great Britain (2), Austria (1), and Japan (1), with the noticeable absence from the list of laureates from the two major Axis countries, Germany and Italy. Some Nobel laureates from Germany were, during this decade, forced by the Nazi government to refuse the prize.

### 1950-1959

If the decade of the 1940's produced few Nobel Prize laureates in physics, the following decade remedied the situation dramatically by honoring twenty scientists with the prize. Three factors account for this substantial increase: First, the Committee felt some pressure to catch up. Second, much of the classified research that scientists had done for their governments during the war could now be made public.

Third, awards in the sciences were increasingly being shared by two or three researchers who collaborated in their research.

In this decade, the United States had three times the number of laureates of the two next highest-ranking nations, Great Britain and the Soviet Union. Of its nine winners, three were born outside the United States and were naturalized citizens. In this decade, every prize except that awarded to Frits Zernike of the Netherlands in 1953 was shared, whereas in the preceding decade, not one of the seven prizes was shared.

Those honored during this decade essentially pursued work that was more practical than theoretical, a situation that could be anticipated in the decade after a major global conflict. Among the achievements recognized were the discovery of the transistor effect, semiconduction, a photographic method of studying nuclear processes, and the statistical interpretation of the wave function.

Honorees were from the United States (9), Great Britain (3), the Soviet Union (3), China (2), West Germany (1), Ireland (1), and the Netherlands (1). Much of Europe and Asia was still recovering from World War II during this decade and the United States, not touched physically by the war, as Germany, Austria, Italy, France, Great Britain, the Soviet Union, and Japan had been, was moving ahead scientifically in ways that these war-torn nations could not.

## 1960-1969

The United States again led the list of Nobel laureates in the decade of the 1960's, capturing ten prizes. A total of seventeen awards was made, and it was clear from the selections that the scientific momentum in the United States, much of it engendered by the war, had not decreased. The numbers are particularly telling when one notes that in the 1960's six of the ten prizes, those in 1960, 1962, 1966, 1967, 1968, and 1969, were not shared.

In this decade, Maria Goeppert Mayer became the first woman to receive a Nobel Prize in Physics for what was essentially theoretical work (as opposed to Marie Curie's work with radium and X rays) that had obvious practical outcomes. The committee generally was more accepting of theoretical work in this decade than it had been previously, honoring Eugene Wigner for his contributions to the theory of the atomic nucleus, Hans Bethe for his theory of nuclear reactions, and Lev Davidovich Landau for his theories about condensed matter.

In this decade, the United States received ten, the Soviet Union three, West Germany two, France one, and Japan one award. Among the winners from the United States, three were born in other countries and were naturalized citizens.

## 1970-1979

The bumper crop of Nobel Prizes in Physics came in the decade of the 1970's, with a total of twenty-five awards, just over half of them to U.S. scientists. The only award that was not shared was the one given to Dennis Gabor in 1971 for his invention of the holographic method.

Precedent was broken in 1972 by awarding John Bardeen his second Nobel Prize in Physics. He modestly contended that he would not have been so honored a second time were it not for the fact that the two collaborators with whom he shared the award, Leon N Cooper and John Robert Schrieffer, had to be honored for the groundbreaking work in superconductivity that the BCS theory represents. Bardeen, despite his self-effacing disclaimers, was the senior researcher in the super-conductivity project.

A great many of the researchers honored during this period were experimenting in the fields of superconductivity and low-temperature physics, which is closely related to it. Although most of the awards were given for work with practical outcomes, the committee still seemed disposed to accord recognition to those doing largely theoretical work, which is essentially what the work of Bardeen and his colleagues was and which is also reflected in the work of laureates Philip W. Anderson, Sir Nevill Mott, and John H. Van Vleck, who were recognized for their theoretical investigation of the electronic structure of magnetic and disordered systems.

During the decade of the 1970's, the laureates were from the United States (13), Great Britain (5), Denmark (2), France (1), Japan (1), Pakistan (1), Sweden (1), and the Soviet Union (1).

### 1980-1988

The data are not all in for the decade of the 1980's. In the nine years for which data are available, nineteen awards have been made in physics, and again the United States took more than half of them. For this period, individual awards were made only in 1982 and 1985. The tendency in this decade has again been to reward research that has practical outcomes, such as the development of laser spectroscopy by Nicolaas Bloembergen and Arthur L. Schawlow or the development of high-resolution electron spectroscopy by Kai M. Siegbahn. If Kenneth G. Wilson's work in developing a theory for critical phenomena relating to phase transitions tends toward the abstract, the 1988 award to Leon Lederman, Melvin Schwartz, and Jack Steinberger—for developing a method through which neutrinos can be fired at other basic particles as a means of determining the atomic structure of those parti-cles—has enormous practical implications for science.

The awards made between 1980 and 1988 went to laureates from the United States (10), West Germany (4), Italy (1), the Netherlands (1), Sweden (1), and Switzer-land (2).

### Conclusions

The Nobel Prize in Physics has not been one of the more controversial prizes among those given. Certainly the awards in peace and in literature evoke more pop-ular response than those in the sciences, where essentially researchers are judged by their peers because the population at large does not understand the intricacies or the implications of the work they are doing.

It is safe to say the awards in physics are less conservatively determined than those in literature—where, for example, many Third World literatures are unavailable in languages that are commonly understood and where some of the most significant progress is made by people such as James Joyce, who was so far ahead of his time that his work was not interpreted satisfactorily during his lifetime. The world of physics is a small, more manageable world than that of literature.

In examining the prizes in physics, one notices interesting population shifts among scientists from politically troubled countries to freer ones: There was a rise in Great Britain and the United States during and immediately following the war years. It is also noteworthy that global conflicts intensify scientific research, as is evidenced by the increase in the number of Nobel laureates in physics in the decades after World War II. Other factors, of course, are at work here. In the United States, for example, a flexible system of free public education has been accessible to most of the populace, and research grants for science have been available in generous quantity both from government and private sources.

Notably absent from the list of laureates in physics are scientists from Latin America, Canada, Australia, New Zealand, the Arab countries, and Africa. Scientific research seems to be centered in Western Europe, the Soviet Union, and the United States, although India and China are beginning to make headway in such research. In some of the geographical areas that have not been contributors to the Nobel pool of laureates, the chief challenge is to provide basic education and subsistence to large, unskilled or semiskilled populations. Scientific research requires facilities and the leisure to pursue research, which often consumes huge quantities of time before it produces any obvious results.

## Selected Readings

Jackson, Donald Dale. "The Nobility of Alfred Nobel." *Smithsonian* 19 (November, 1988): 201-224. Jackson is especially effective in analyzing the reasons that Nobel decided essentially to disinherit his family and establish the prizes for which he is remembered. The article is well written and accurate.

Kaplan, Flora, comp. *Nobel Prize Winners: Charts, Indexes, Sketches*. Chicago: Nobelle, 1941. This volume, now badly dated, provides reliable information about all the laureates from 1901 to 1939, along with charts that show geographical distributions. The book has now been superseded by Tyler Wasson's *Nobel Prize Winners*.

Kostelanetz, Richard. "The Ultimate Prize." *The New York Times Book Review* 86 (September 27, 1981): 3, 31-32. The chief virtue of this article is that it explains clearly and accurately the calendar the Nobel committees must follow as they progress toward making their final decisions. Kostelanetz makes interesting observations about the politics of the Nobel Prize.

Nobel Foundation. *Les Prix Nobel*. Stockholm: Almqvist and Wiksell International. This series, published annually in English and other languages, presents information about all the Nobel Prizes awarded in a given year, as well as biographical sketches of each recipient and a copy of the acceptance speech delivered by each.

Sohlman, Ragnar. *The Legacy of Alfred Nobel: The Story Behind the Nobel Prizes*. Translated by Elspeth Harley Schubert. London: Bodley Head, 1983. Alfred Nobel's will is presented in this book along with a firsthand account by its chief executor of how the will came about and of the difficulties encountered in carrying out its provisions. Sohlman, only twenty-six years old when Nobel died, performed a heroic task in settling the Nobel estate to the point that four years after Nobel's death, the foundation that would oversee the awards was established, and that the following year, the first prizes were awarded.

Steiner, George. "The Scandal of the Nobel Prize." *The New York Times Book Review* 84 (September 30, 1984): 1, 38-39. Despite its sensational title, the article is quite balanced and has a great many positive things to say about the Nobel Prize, although Steiner questions why some giants, particularly in literature, have not been granted Nobel status.

Wasson, Tyler, ed. *Nobel Prize Winners*. New York: H. W. Wilson, 1987. This book, assembled with the help of a blue-ribbon group of consultants, provides superb background material that is accurate, succinct, and current. It then proceeds to present biographical sketches of Nobel winners in all fields from 1901 to 1986. An important resource for one interested in the Nobel Prizes.

Wilhelm, Peter. *The Nobel Prize*. London: Springwood Books, 1983. This profusely illustrated book presents an excellent background of the Nobel Prizes and their founder. An appendix contains a list of all the Nobel awards from 1901 to 1982 with brief biographical details and a summary of why the award was made. Offers a particularly sympathetic view of Ragnar Sohlman, the executor of Alfred Nobel's will.

Zuckerman, Harriet. "After Winning the Prize Is When Trouble Really Starts." *The New York Times* 132, sec. IV (January 2, 1983): 7. This article is an extension of work that Zuckerman has done since she completed her book on the awards to U.S. scientists (below). Although she seems to begin with a conclusion, the article is revealing in what it has to say about the personality cult that has been associated with the Nobel Prizes.

—————————. *Scientific Élites: Nobel Laureates in the United States*. New York: Free Press, 1977. Zuckerman, a sociologist of science, is particularly concerned with the effect that winning the prize has on the laureates. Her study presents a sometimes pessimistic view of the effect that the recognition received by Nobel laureates has on their future work. An interesting study that should be read along with the interviews that Wilhelm includes in his book (cited above).

*R. Baird Shuman*

# TIME LINE

| YEAR | RECIPIENT | COUNTRY | AREA |
|------|-----------|---------|------|
| 1901 | Wilhelm Conrad Röntgen (1845-1923) | Germany | X-radiation |
| 1902 | Hendrik Antoon Lorentz (1853-1928) | Netherlands | electromagnetic theory |
|      | Pieter Zeeman (1865-1943) | Netherlands | electromagnetic theory/magneto-optics |
| 1903 | Antoine-Henri Becquerel (1852-1908) | France | radioactivity |
|      | Pierre Curie (1859-1906) | France | radioactivity/magnetism/crystallography |
|      | Marie Curie (1867-1934) | Poland/France | radioactivity |
| 1904 | Lord Rayleigh (1842-1919) | Great Britain | acoustics/optics |
| 1905 | Philipp Lenard (1862-1947) | Germany | photoelectricity/electrons |
| 1906 | Sir Joseph John Thomson (1856-1940) | Great Britain | particle physics |
| 1907 | Albert Abraham Michelson (1852-1931) | United States | optics/spectroscopy/interferometry |
| 1908 | Gabriel Lippmann (1845-1921) | France | applied mathematical physics |
| 1909 | Guglielmo Marconi (1874-1937) | Italy | radio telegraphy |
|      | Karl Ferdinand Braun (1850-1918) | Germany | wireless telegraphy |
| 1910 | Johannes Diderik van der Waals (1837-1923) | Netherlands | equation of state theory |
| 1911 | Wilhelm Wien (1864-1928) | Germany | thermal radiation |
| 1912 | Nils Gustaf Dalén (1869-1937) | Sweden | engineering |
| 1913 | Heike Kamerlingh Onnes (1853-1926) | Netherlands | low-temperature physics |
| 1914 | Max von Laue (1879-1960) | Germany | X-ray optics |
| 1915 | Sir William Henry Bragg (1862-1942) | Great Britain | radioactivity/X-ray spectroscopy/X-ray crystallography |
|      | Sir Lawrence Bragg (1890-1971) | Great Britain | X-ray crystallography |
| 1916 | Reserved | — | — |
| 1917 | Charles Glover Barkla (1877-1944) | Great Britain | X-radiation/secondary radiation |
| 1918 | Max Planck (1858-1947) | Germany | quantum physics |
| 1919 | Johannes Stark (1874-1957) | Germany | electrical conduction in gases |

| YEAR | RECIPIENT | COUNTRY | AREA |
|------|-----------|---------|------|
| 1920 | Charles-Édouard Guillaume (1861-1938) | Switzerland | metallurgy/metrology |
| 1921 | Albert Einstein (1879-1955) | Germany/ Switzerland/ United States | theoretical physics |
| 1922 | Niels Bohr (1885-1962) | Denmark | atomic structure/ quantum theory |
| 1923 | Robert Andrews Millikan (1868-1953) | United States | electronic charge/ photoelectric effect |
| 1924 | Karl Manne Georg Siegbahn (1886-1978) | Sweden | X-ray spectroscopy |
| 1925 | James Franck (1882-1964) | Germany | atomic physics/ molecular physics |
|      | Gustav Hertz (1887-1975) | Germany | atomic physics/ molecular physics |
| 1926 | Jean-Baptiste Perrin (1870-1942) | France | molecular physics |
| 1927 | Arthur Holly Compton (1892-1962) | United States | X-radiation/optics |
|      | Charles Thomson Rees Wilson (1869-1959) | Great Britain | ionizing particles/ atmospheric electricity |
| 1928 | Sir Owen Willans Richardson (1879-1959) | Great Britain | thermionics |
| 1929 | Louis de Broglie (1892-1987) | France | quantum physics/wave mechanics |
| 1930 | Sir Chandrasekhara Venkata Raman (1888-1970) | India | optics |
| 1931 | Reserved | — | — |
| 1932 | Werner Heisenberg (1901-1976) | Germany | quantum mechanics |
| 1933 | Erwin Schrödinger (1887-1961) | Austria | atomic theory/wave mechanics |
|      | Paul Adrien Maurice Dirac (1902-1984) | Great Britain | quantum mechanics |
| 1934 | Reserved | — | — |
| 1935 | Sir James Chadwick (1891-1974) | Great Britain | atomic physics/nuclear physics |
| 1936 | Victor Franz Hess (1883-1964) | Austria | cosmic radiation |
|      | Carl David Anderson (1905-    ) | United States | particle physics |
| 1937 | Clinton Joseph Davisson (1881-1958) | United States | electron physics |
|      | Sir George Paget Thomson (1892-1975) | Great Britain | electron diffraction |

| YEAR | RECIPIENT | COUNTRY | AREA |
|------|-----------|---------|------|
| 1938 | Enrico Fermi (1901-1954) | Italy | radioactivity/nuclear reactions |
| 1939 | Ernest Orlando Lawrence (1901-1958) | United States | nuclear physics |
| 1940-1942 | Reserved | — | — |
| 1943 | Otto Stern (1888-1969) | United States | quantum physics |
| 1944 | Isidor Isaac Rabi (1898-1988) | United States | nuclear physics |
| 1945 | Wolfgang Pauli (1900-1958) | Austria/United States | quantum mechanics |
| 1946 | Percy Williams Bridgman (1882-1961) | United States | high-pressure physics |
| 1947 | Sir Edward Victor Appleton (1892-1965) | Great Britain | radio physics/ atmospheric physics |
| 1948 | Patrick M. S. Blackett (1897-1974) | Great Britain | nuclear physics/cosmic radiation |
| 1949 | Hideki Yukawa (1907-1981) | Japan | nuclear physics |
| 1950 | Cecil Frank Powell (1903-1969) | Great Britain | nuclear physics/cosmic radiation |
| 1951 | Sir John Douglas Cockcroft (1897-1967) | Great Britain | nuclear physics |
|  | Ernest Thomas Sinton Walton (1903-    ) | Ireland | nuclear physics |
| 1952 | Felix Bloch (1905-1983) | United States | nuclear physics |
|  | Edward Mills Purcell (1912-    ) | United States | nuclear magnetic resonance |
| 1953 | Frits Zernike (1888-1966) | Netherlands | optics |
| 1954 | Max Born (1882-1970) | Great Britain | quantum mechanics |
|  | Walther Bothe (1891-1957) | West Germany | particle physics/ nuclear energy |
| 1955 | Willis Eugene Lamb, Jr. (1913-    ) | United States | quantum electrodynamics |
|  | Polykarp Kusch (1911-    ) | United States | atomic physics/ molecular physics |
| 1956 | William Shockley (1910-    ) | United States | solid-state physics |
|  | John Bardeen (1908-    ) | United States | solid-state physics |
|  | Walter H. Brattain (1902-1987) | United States | solid-state physics |
| 1957 | Chen Ning Yang (1922-    ) | China/United States | particle physics/ statistical mechanics |
|  | Tsung-Dao Lee (1926-    ) | China/United States | particle physics/ statistical mechanics |
| 1958 | Pavel Alekseyevich Cherenkov (1904-    ) | Soviet Union | nuclear physics/ particle physics |

| YEAR | RECIPIENT | COUNTRY | AREA |
|------|-----------|---------|------|
| 1958 | Ilya Mikhailovich Frank (1908- ) | Soviet Union | nuclear physics/ particle physics/ optics |
|  | Igor Yevgenyevich Tamm (1895-1971) | Soviet Union | particle physics/plasma physics |
| 1959 | Emilio Gino Segrè (1905- ) | United States | nuclear physics |
|  | Owen Chamberlain (1920- ) | United States | nuclear physics |
| 1960 | Donald A. Glaser (1926- ) | United States | particle physics |
| 1961 | Robert Hofstadter (1915- ) | United States | nuclear physics |
|  | Rudolf Ludwig Mössbauer (1929- ) | West Germany | gamma radiation |
| 1962 | Lev Davidovich Landau (1908-1968) | Soviet Union | quantum mechanics |
| 1963 | Eugene Paul Wigner (1902- ) | Hungary/United States | atomic theory |
|  | Maria Goeppert Mayer (1906-1972) | Germany/United States | nuclear physics |
|  | J. Hans D. Jensen (1907-1973) | West Germany | nuclear physics |
| 1964 | Charles Hard Townes (1915- ) | United States | quantum electronics |
|  | Nikolay Gennadiyevich Basov (1922- ) | Soviet Union | quantum electronics |
|  | Aleksandr Mikhailovich Prokhorov (1916- ) | Soviet Union | quantum radiophysics/ quantum electronics |
| 1965 | Shin'ichirō Tomonaga (1906-1979) | Japan | quantum electrodynamics |
|  | Julian Seymour Schwinger (1918- ) | United States | quantum electrodynamics |
|  | Richard P. Feynman (1918-1988) | United States | quantum electrodynamics |
| 1966 | Alfred Kastler (1902-1984) | France | optical spectroscopy/ Hertzian resonances |
| 1967 | Hans Albrecht Bethe (1906- ) | United States | nuclear physics/ astrophysics |
| 1968 | Luis W. Alvarez (1911-1988) | United States | high-energy particle physics |
| 1969 | Murray Gell-Mann (1929- ) | United States | particle physics |
| 1970 | Hannes Alfvén (1908- ) | Sweden | plasma physics |
|  | Louis-Eugène-Félix Néel (1904- ) | France | nuclear magnetism |
| 1971 | Dennis Gabor (1900-1979) | Great Britain | electron optics/ holography |
| 1972 | John Bardeen (1908- ) | United States | superconductivity |

| YEAR | RECIPIENT | COUNTRY | AREA |
|------|-----------|---------|------|
| 1972 | Leon N Cooper (1930-    ) | United States | superconductivity |
|      | John Robert Schrieffer (1931-    ) | United States | superconductivity |
| 1973 | Leo Esaki (1925-    ) | Japan | quantum mechanics/ solid-state physics |
|      | Ivar Giaever (1929-    ) | Norway/United States | quantum mechanics/ solid-state physics/ biophysics |
|      | Brian D. Josephson (1940-    ) | Great Britain | quantum mechanics/ solid-state physics |
| 1974 | Sir Martin Ryle (1918-1984) | Great Britain | radio astronomy |
|      | Antony Hewish (1924-    ) | Great Britain | radio astronomy |
| 1975 | Aage Bohr (1922-    ) | Denmark | nuclear physics |
|      | Ben R. Mottelson (1926-    ) | Denmark | nuclear physics |
|      | L. James Rainwater (1917-1986) | United States | structural nuclear physics |
| 1976 | Burton Richter (1931-    ) | United States | particle physics |
|      | Samuel C. C. Ting (1936-    ) | United States | particle physics |
| 1977 | John H. Van Vleck (1899-1980) | United States | magnetism/quantum mechanics/solid-state physics |
|      | Sir Nevill Mott (1905-    ) | Great Britain | solid-state physics |
|      | Philip W. Anderson (1923-    ) | United States | solid-state physics |
| 1978 | Pyotr Leonidovich Kapitsa (1894-1984) | Soviet Union | low-temperature physics/plasma physics |
|      | Arno A. Penzias (1933-    ) | Germany/United States | radio astronomy |
|      | Robert W. Wilson (1936-    ) | United States | radio astronomy |
| 1979 | Sheldon L. Glashow (1932-    ) | United States | particle physics |
|      | Abdus Salam (1926-    ) | Pakistan | particle physics |
|      | Steven Weinberg (1933-    ) | United States | particle physics |
| 1980 | James W. Cronin (1931-    ) | United States | particle physics |
|      | Val L. Fitch (1923-    ) | United States | particle physics |
| 1981 | Nicolaas Bloembergen (1920-    ) | United States | optics/quantum electronics |
|      | Arthur L. Schawlow (1921-    ) | United States | optics/laser spectroscopy |
|      | Kai M. Siegbahn (1918-    ) | Sweden | chemical physics |
| 1982 | Kenneth G. Wilson (1936-    ) | United States | elementary particle theory |
| 1983 | Subrahmanyan Chandrasekhar (1910-    ) | United States | astrophysics |

| YEAR | RECIPIENT | COUNTRY | AREA |
|------|-----------|---------|------|
| 1983 | William A. Fowler (1911-    ) | United States | astrophysics/nuclear physics |
| 1984 | Carlo Rubbia (1934-    ) | Italy | high-energy particle physics |
|      | Simon van der Meer (1925-    ) | Netherlands | high-energy particle physics |
| 1985 | Klaus von Klitzing (1943-    ) | West Germany | condensed-matter physics |
| 1986 | Ernst Ruska (1906-1988) | West Germany | electrical engineering/ electron microscopy |
|      | Gerd Binnig (1947-    ) | West Germany | scanning tunneling microscopy |
|      | Heinrich Rohrer (1933-    ) | Switzerland | scanning tunneling microscopy |
| 1987 | Karl Alexander Müller (1927-    ) | Switzerland | solid-state physics/ superconductivity |
|      | J. Georg Bednorz (1950-    ) | West Germany | solid-state physics/ superconductivity |
| 1988 | Leon M. Lederman (1922-    ) | United States | high-energy particle physics |
|      | Melvin Schwartz (1932-    ) | United States | high-energy particle physics |
|      | Jack Steinberger (1921-    ) | Germany/United States | high-energy particle physics |

# 1901

### Physics
Wilhelm Conrad Röntgen, Germany

### Chemistry
Jacobus Van't Hoff, Netherlands

### Physiology or Medicine
Emil von Behring, Germany

### Literature
Sully Prudhomme, France

### Peace
Jean Henri Dunant, Switzerland
Frédéric Passy, France

# WILHELM CONRAD RÖNTGEN
## 1901

*Born:* Lennep, Prussia; March 27, 1845
*Died:* Munich, Germany; February 10, 1923
*Nationality:* German
*Area of concentration:* X-radiation

*The first Nobel Prize in Physics was awarded to Röntgen in recognition of his discovery of the remarkable penetrating radiation which had come to be known as Röntgen rays, or X rays*

## The Award

*Presentation*

C. T. Odhner, the former Rector of the National Archives and President of the Royal Swedish Academy of Sciences, made the presentation speech for the Nobel Prize in Physics on December 10, 1901, the fifth anniversary of the death of Alfred Nobel. Oscar II was then King of Sweden and Norway. The large hall of the Music Academy was filled with invited guests representing the governments of various nations and the elite of the professions of the Scandinavian countries. The Nobel diploma, the gold medal, and the monetary award were presented by the Crown Prince. The pomp surrounding these first ceremonies set the tone for the years to follow.

Professor Odhner made a short speech in which he acknowledged that the actual constitution of X rays was still unknown, though "rays" was chosen to characterize these phenomena, as they propagate themselves in straight lines as does light. Another decade was to pass before it was established that the so-called Röntgen rays are extremely short-wavelength members of the electromagnetic spectrum, which includes visible light and radio waves. All that could be done in 1901 was to enumerate some of the properties of this strange radiation.

The most striking property of X rays is their ability to penetrate materials that are opaque to visible light. Wood, leather, and cardboard are penetrable by X rays, as are the muscular tissues of animal organisms. Metals, however, cannot be penetrated by these rays. When a foreign body, such as a bullet or a needle, has entered living tissues, its location can be found by illuminating the area with X rays, and taking a shadowgraph of it on a photographic plate. It had also been found that X rays were useful in treating certain severe skin diseases, such as lupus. That they are also capable of damaging normal cells, and must be used with care, was just beginning to be recognized, and was not mentioned in the presentation.

Professor Odhner closed by noting that the medical applications of X rays had already brought great benefit to humankind, thereby meeting Alfred Nobel's criteria for the awarding of the prize "to a very high degree."

*Nobel lecture*

Contrary to the custom which was then being initiated, Röntgen did not give an official Nobel lecture. He spoke a few words in response to the presentation, however, saying that he appreciated immensely the singular honor of the prize and that this recognition would certainly be an effective stimulant to him to greater unselfish activity in science, which he hoped would benefit all humankind.

*Critical reception*

The news of the discovery of X rays created an immediate worldwide journalistic sensation. This scientific achievement was readily understood by laymen, and its potential applications fired the public imagination.

Röntgen's own scientific paper, "Über eine neue Art von Strahlen" ("On a New Kind of Rays"), was published on December 28, 1895, in the proceedings of the Würzburg Physical-Medical Society, a rather obscure journal. It was written in a succinct, clear style that can easily be comprehended by the nonspecialist. On New Year's Day, 1896, copies were mailed to many recognized physicists throughout Europe, along with prints of some of the X-ray photographs that Röntgen had made.

One of the recipients, Professor Franz Exner of the University of Vienna, showed the pictures to guests at his house. One guest was the son of the editor of the Vienna *Presse*, Z. K. Lecher. The *Presse* promptly printed a report about Röntgen's work. By January 6, the news had been repeated in the *Frankfurter Zeitung*, and in the Berlin *Vossische Zeitung* under the headline "A Sensational Discovery." On January 7 the London *Standard* printed the report. Within a few days, newspapers throughout the world, including *Le Matin* (Paris) and *The New York Times*, had reprinted these reports and had begun to make startling speculations on the future applications of Röntgen's discovery.

The popular magazines were quick to follow. London's *Saturday Review*, in its issue of January 11, described in detail the new photographic discovery. France's *L'Illustration* added a detailed description of the discovery of the new "light." *Literary Digest*, of January 25, ran a report on "the photography of unseen substances." Professional journals such as *The New York Medical Record*, *Lancet*, and the *British Medical Journal* for January 11, the *Münchner medezinische Wochenschrift* for January 14, the *Wiener klinische Wochenschrift* for January 16, *Comptes rendus* for January 20, the *Settimana medica* for January 25, and the *Journal of the American Medical Association* for February 15, among others, printed articles on the value of X rays in medicine. Articles also appeared in nonmedical scientific journals: in *The New York Electrical Engineer* for January 8, the *London Electrician* for January 10, *Nature* for January 16, *Il nuovo cimento* for January, and *L'Éclairage électrique* for February 8. At least 994 scientific articles about Röntgen and his discovery were published in the year 1896 alone.

Photography journals also found much of interest to report. The *British Journal of Photography* of January 10 described the "wonder camera of the Würzburg professor." *Photogram* of London had a special February issue titled "The New Light and the New Photography." *Photographic Review* was able to reproduce several X-ray pictures in its March issue.

More detailed articles followed: *Science* in New York published a comprehensive article, "The X-Rays," in its January 31 issue. The lead story in the April, 1896, issue of *McClure's* magazine was based on an interview of Röntgen by the English journalist H. J. W. Dam.

Anticipated applications of the discovery ranged from the medical uses of identifying bone fractures and locating foreign metallic objects to the fitting of shoes. Wild stories circulated: from photographing spirits with X rays to using them to see through women's clothes. There can be no doubt that X rays were firmly implanted in the mind of the general public very quickly after their discovery.

Five years later, the existence and use of X rays had become so commonplace that the news of yet another honor bestowed upon their discoverer aroused little interest in the English-speaking press. Not a single mention of the award of the first Nobel Prize in Physics was to be found in contemporary volumes of either *The New York Times* or *The Times* of London. In a sense, the public had anticipated and responded to the award in advance of its bestowal. The inaugural Nobel Prize in Physics was inarguably appropriate.

## Biography

Wilhelm Conrad Röntgen was born on March 27, 1845, at Lennep in the Prussian Bergische Rhein-Provinz, which later became part of West Germany. He was the only child of Friedrich Conrad Röntgen, a textile merchant, and Charlotte Constanze Frowein Röntgen, a native of Amsterdam. When the boy was three years old, his family moved to Apeldoorn in the Netherlands, thereby losing their Prussian citizenship, and soon after became Dutch subjects.

The young Röntgen attended the primary public school in Apeldoorn. Then he attended the Kostschool, a private boarding school of Martinus Hermann van Doorn. In 1862 he moved to Utrecht and entered a technical school, a small private institution, which was superseded by the Hoogere Burgerschool. He was unfairly expelled from the Hoogere school, accused of having drawn a caricature of one of the teachers, which in fact had been done by another student.

In 1865, Röntgen registered at the University of Utrecht as an irregular student. The following year he moved to Zurich, where a student could enter the Federal Institute of Technology, or Polytechnikum, without a graduation certificate, by passing an examination. He began studies there as a student of mechanical engineering, attending classes taught by Rudolf Clausius, and worked in the laboratory of August Kundt, who succeeded Clausius as professor of physics. Röntgen received his diploma in engineering in 1868 and his Ph.D. in physics in 1869. He continued to work as an assistant to Kundt in Zurich for another year.

While a student in Zurich, Röntgen met Anna Bertha Ludwig, the daughter of an innkeeper who had befriended Röntgen. The two were married on January 19, 1872, at the Röntgen family home in Apeldoorn. They had no children of their own. In 1887 they took Bertha's six-year-old niece, Josephine Bertha ("Bertheli"), into their home, thereafter rearing her as their own child.

In 1870 Kundt accepted the chair of physics at the University of Würzburg, and Röntgen went with him as his assistant. In 1872 Kundt moved to the newly reopened Kaiser-Wilhelms-Universität at Strassburg, and the Röntgens went with him again. Röntgen's parents moved to Strassburg to be near the young couple. In 1874 Röntgen qualified as a lecturer at Strassburg, an official but unpaid member of the university who could earn his living by giving private lessons. Although in 1875 Röntgen accepted a full professorship in physics and mathematics at the Agricultural Academy in Hohenheim, six miles south of Stuttgart, he returned to Strassburg in 1876 as associate professor of experimental physics. Three years later he accepted the chair of physics at the University of Giessen, thirty miles north of Frankfurt.

After having declined invitations to similar positions in the Universities of Jena (1886) and Utrecht (1888), he accepted an offer from the University of Würzburg in 1888. In 1894 he was elected Rektor, or president, of the university. It was after his term as Rektor had ended that he performed the crucial experiments that led to the discovery of X rays.

In 1899 he declined an offer to the chair of physics at the University of Leipzig, but in 1900 he accepted a similar offer to the University of Munich, by special request of the Bavarian government. There he remained for the rest of his life. He died of carcinoma of the intestine on February 10, 1923.

## Scientific Career

Wilhelm Conrad Röntgen made his great discovery at the age of fifty, at the climax of a quarter-century career in experimental physics. He was well-known as a careful, conscientious, painstaking scientist, who was often capable of measuring effects so slight that many of his contemporaries would not have thought the experiments possible. Still, before 1896 Röntgen was not considered one of the outstanding natural scientists of the time. Neither the papers he had published before nor those that he wrote afterward came close to the brilliance of the work dated December 28, 1895, on a new kind of radiation.

The discovery of X rays is a classic example of scientific serendipity: the discovery of something other than the object of the scientific experiment. There is a certain amount of chance involved in stumbling upon the unexpected. But as Louis Pasteur (1822-1895) said, "Chance favors only the mind that is prepared."

Röntgen's Ph.D. thesis at the Polytechnikum in Zurich was titled "Studies About Gases." His first published paper, written during his first sojourn in Würzburg, was on a similar topic: "Über die Bestimmung des Verhältnisses der spezifischen Wärmen bei der Luft" (on the determination of the ratio of the specific heats for air). During the Strassburg period (1873-1879), he produced fourteen more papers. Some of them presented further work on the properties of gases. Others were about electrical discharges, about crystals, and about instrumentation. An important series of experiments done by Kundt and Röntgen together investigated the rotation of the plane of polarization of light in gases. This is an effect which Michael Faraday (1791-1867) had predicted but had never been able to measure.

There were eighteen publications while Röntgen resided in Giessen (1880-1888). The Kerr effect, in which electrostatic fields influence the polarization of light waves passing through crystals, was investigated in Strassburg, and the work was completed in Giessen. Röntgen studied the effects of temperature and pressure on the electrical properties of crystals, and the influence of pressure on the viscosity of liquids and on the compressibility of liquids and solids. He conducted a series of investigations into the absorption of heat in water vapor.

In 1888, Röntgen performed his famous experiments to prove that magnetic effects are produced in a dielectric, such as a slab of glass, when it is moved between two electrically charged plates. This effect had been predicted using theoretical reasoning based on the electromagnetic theory of Faraday and James Clerk Maxwell (1831-1879). Hendrik Antoon Lorentz (1853-1928) dubbed it the "Röntgen current." This result marked an important confirmation of the understanding of electromagnetism. Röntgen's reputation before 1896 rested as much on this experiment as on any of his other work.

In his second Würzburg period (1889-1895), Röntgen published fifteen papers before the discovery of X rays. These works extended the sort of investigations he had begun earlier in his career. There were papers on the properties of liquids and the influence of pressure on various properties. He published descriptions of his apparatus, showing his special inclination for experimental precision. This was an era when physicists, Röntgen among them, might well have concluded that all the basic laws of nature had already been discovered and that nothing remained but to complete the tables listing the properties of materials and extend the precision of measurements to the next decimal place. Röntgen was to be the first to show that this conclusion was shortsighted.

Röntgen published only three papers on the topic of X rays. His life after the discovery became so preoccupied with the clamor that fame brought him that he was forced to leave the development of the field he had created mostly to others. In Munich (1904-1921) he wrote papers about the electrical conductivity of certain crystals, including the influence of X-ray irradiation on these properties. His papers on thermal expansion of cuprite and diamond, and on the effects of temperature and pressure on electrical behavior, hark back to some of his earliest work.

The crucial moments in Röntgen's career took place during November and December of 1895. For seven weeks he was the only person living who knew of the existence of the mysterious penetrating radiation which he called *X-Strahlen*. Röntgen was not the first scientist to produce X rays in his laboratory. Sir William Crookes (1832-1919), for example, had been studying the effects of electrical discharges in evacuated glass tubes for twenty years before Röntgen's historic feat. Crookes had noticed that photographic plates stored in the same room as his discharge tubes tended to become "fogged" (prematurely exposed). He therefore took the precautionary step of removing his unexposed emulsions to another room. That solved the problem of the fogged plates, but it prevented Crookes from making a world-shaking discovery.

Röntgen read an 1893 paper of Philipp Lenard (1862-1947), who had equipped ordinary glass discharge tubes with extremely thin aluminum "windows," through which the negatively charged cathode rays could penetrate into the air outside. The cathode rays penetrated barely an inch into the air, causing it to glow blue-violet, but even that short distance might be enough to enable the investigator to study their properties. Röntgen decided to repeat some of Lenard's work. He purchased a Ruhmkorff induction coil, capable of generating electrical tension of thousands of volts. He equipped his laboratory with a variety of glass tubes, some with the Lenard design, others with heavier solid glass walls all around. He refitted a Raps vacuum pump, to evacuate the tubes. This pump worked by trapping gas molecules in a stream of mercury liquid falling through the apparatus. It required sometimes several days of repeatedly closing valves, lifting the mercury supply, opening valves, and lowering the mercury to obtain a useful vacuum.

With this apparatus, Röntgen repeated what Lenard had done. He added some features of his own: A sheet of paper covered with ground fluorescent crystals served as a more reliable detector of the cathode rays than the dim glow of the air. He fitted a mask of black cardboard around the glass tube, so as not to be distracted by the glows of the residual gases inside the tube. By using higher voltage and better vacuum than Lenard, he hoped to make the cathode rays penetrate farther into the air.

On Friday night, November 8, 1895, Röntgen was ready to begin his next set of experiments. The Lenard tube had developed a leak, so he was using instead a thick-walled tube of the Crookes design. He turned off the lights, drew the curtains, and waited for his eyes to adapt to the dark. Then he started the induction coil and verified that no light was escaping from inside the tube through the black mask he had made.

On a nearby bench, about a meter away from the discharge tube, he noticed a faint flickering in the dark. This was too far away, he knew, for the cathode rays to penetrate through the air. The flickering was correlated with the high voltage. When he turned it off the flickering stopped. He turned the voltage on again, and the flickering returned. He struck a match to see what was flickering. It was the fluorescent screen, which was supposed to glow only when it was close to the cathode ray tube.

In the dark again, Röntgen began moving the screen back and forth in the room. It seemed clear that whatever was causing the glow was coming directly from the glass discharge tube. He turned the screen away from the tube. It still glowed. The "influence," as he thought of it, could penetrate not only a meter of air, but also the thickness of the cardboard screen. He tried other obstacles: a playing card, a whole deck of cards, a book. The mysterious "influence" penetrated them all. Röntgen knew that nothing like this had ever been seen before. What kind of invisible influence was this, that could make the fluorescent screen glow behind the shadow of a thousand-page volume?

In succeeding nights, Röntgen continued to work in the laboratory, afraid to discuss what he was observing with anyone, even his wife. He found that there were some materials that could stop his X rays: steel, but not wood; lead, but not water; bone, but not flesh. At one point, he put his fingers in front of the little screen, and saw the shadow, not of his hand, but of the skeleton inside.

An important breakthrough came when he found that photographic plates could record the rays. Now he could be sure that his eyes, always a problem for the colorblind Röntgen, were not playing tricks on him. Now he could make measurements in the daylight. He would activate his X-ray tube, place the object to be photographed under it, and under that his photographic plate, still wrapped in its light-tight coverings. In this way he took pictures of a set of laboratory weights still inside their wooden box; of the metal parts of his hunting rifle, revealed inside the wooden stock; of the skeleton of a salamander.

On a particularly fateful night, Röntgen asked his wife Bertha down to the laboratory. He told her to place her hand on top of a photographic plate holder and wait for a few seconds while he worked the apparatus. After making the exposure, he went to develop the photograph. There was a picture of the bones of Bertha's hand, her wedding ring clearly visible. Bertha was shocked. Until that moment, nobody had ever seen the skeleton of a healthy living person; skeletons and bones were symbols of death. She retreated to her quarters, never to participate in her husband's experiments again.

By December, 1895, Röntgen realized that it was time to publish his results. During the holiday season, he would be too busy to do any more work. He wrote his manuscript, had it set in print in the local medical-physical journal, and put the copies in the mail. Within weeks doctors were using X rays in their hospitals, manufacturers were using them to locate defects in their products, shoe salesman were using them to fit shoes. Röntgen himself was reluctant to profit from his discovery. He refused to take out a patent on X rays, believing that they should be used freely for the benefit of humanity. He did not accept the appellation "von Röntgen," which would have been a sign of aristocracy. He did, however, accept the Nobel Prize in Physics when the first prize was offered in 1901.

## Bibliography

*Primary*
PHYSICS: "Über die Bestimmung des Verhältnisses der spezifischen Wärmen bei der Luft," *Annalen der Physik und Chemie*, vol. 141, 1870; "Bestimmung des Verhältnisses der spezifischen Wärmen bei konstantem Druck zu derjenigen bei konstantem Volumen für einige Gase," *Annalen der Physik und Chemie*, vol. 148, 1873; "Über das Löten von platinierten Gläsern," *Annalen der Physik und Chemie*, vol. 150, 1873; "Über fortführende Entladungen der Elektrizität," *Annalen der*

*Physik und Chemie*, 151, 1874; "Über eine Variation der Sénarmontschen Methode zur Bestimmung der isothermen Flächen in Kristallen," *Annalen der Physik und Chemie*, vol. 151, 1874; "Über eine Anwendung des Eiskalorimeters zur Bestimmung der Intensität der Sonnenstrahlung," *Wien. Ber.* (2) 69, 1874 (with Exner); "Über das Verhältnis der Querkontraktion zur Längsdilatation bei Kautschuk," *Annalen der Physik und Chemie*, vol. 159, 1876; "A Telephonic Alarm," *Nature*, vol. 17, 1877; "Mitteilung einiger Versuche aus dem Gebiet der Kapillarität," *Annalen der Physik und Chemie*, N.F. 3, 1878; "Über ein Aneroidbarometer mit Spiegelablesung," *Annalen der Physik und Chemie*, N.F. 4, 1878; "Über eine Methode zur Erzuegung von Isothermen auf Kristallen," *Z. Kryst.*, vol. 3, 1878; "Über Entladungen der Elektrizität in Isolatoren," *Göttinger Nachr.*, 1878; "Nachweis der elektromagnetischen Drehung der Polarisationsebene des Lichtes im Schwefelkohlenstoffdampf," *Münch. Ber.*, vol. 8, 1878 (with Kundt); "Nachtrag zur Abhandlung über Drehung der Polarisationsebene im Schwefelkohlenstoffdampf," *Münch. Ber.*, vol. 9, 1879 (with Kundt); "Über die elektromagnetische Drehung der Polarisationsebene des Lichtes in den Gasen," *Annalen der Physik und Chemie*, N.F. 8, 1879 (with Kundt); "Über die von Herrn Kerr gefundene neue Beziehung zwischen Licht und Elektrizität," *Annalen der Physik und Chemie*, N.F. 10, 1880; "Über die elektromagnetische Drehung der Polarisationsebene des Lichtes in den Gasen. 2. Abhandlung," *Annalen der Physik und Chemie*, N.F. 10, 1880 (with Kundt); "Über die durch Elektrizität bewirkten Form- und volumänderungen von dielektrischen Körpern," *Annalen der Physik und Chemie*, N.F. 11, 1880; "Über Töne, welche durch intermittierende Bestrahlung eines Gases entstehen," *Annalen der Physik und Chemie*, N.F. 12, 1881; "Versuche über die Absorption von Strahlen durch Gase, nach einer neuen Methode ausgeführt," *Ber. d. Oberhess. Ges. f. Nat. u. Heilk.*, vol. 20, 1881; "Über die durch elektrische Kräfte erzeugte Änderung der Doppelbrechung des Quarzes," *Annalen der Physik und Chemie*, N.F. 18, 1883; "Bemerkung zu der Abhandlung des Herrn A. Kundt: Über das optische Verhalten des Quarzes im elektrischen Feld," *Annalen der Physik und Chemie*, N.F. 19, 1883; "Über die thermo-, aktino- und piezo-elektrischen Eigenschaften des Quarzes," *Annalen der Physik und Chemie*, N.F. 19, 1883; "Über einen Vorlesungsapparat zur Demonstration des Poiseuilleschen Gesetzes," *Annalen der Physik und Chemie*, N.F. 20, 1883; "Über den Einfluss des Druckes auf die Viskosität der Flüssigkeiten, speziell des Wassers," *Annalen der Physik und Chemie*, N.F. 22, 1884; "Neue Versuche über die Absorption von Wärme durch Wasserdampf," *Annalen der Physik und Chemie*, N.F. 23, 1884; "Versuche über die elektromagnetische Wirkung der dielektrischen Polarisation," *Math. u. Naturw. Mitt. a. d. Sitzgsber, preuss. Akad. Wiss., Physik.-math. Kl.*, 1885; "Über Kompressibilität und Oberflächenspannung von Flüssigkeiten," *Annalen der Physik und Chemie*, N.F. 29, 1886 (with Schneider); "Über die Kompressibilität von verdünnten Salzlösungen und die des festen Chlornatriums," *Annalen der Physik und Chemie*, N.F. 31, 1887 (with Schneider); "Über die durch Bewegung eines im homogen elektrischen

Felde befindlichen Dielektrikums hervorgerufene elektrodynamische Kraft," *Math. u. Naturw. Mitt. a. d. Sitzgsber. preuss. Akad. Wiss., Physik.-math. Kl.*, 1888; "Über die Kompressibilität des Wassers," *Annalen der Physik und Chemie*, N.F. 33, 1888 (with Schneider); "Über die Kompressibilität des Sylvins, des Steinsalzes und der wässrigen Chlorkaliumlösungen," *Annalen der Physik und Chemie*, N.F. 34, 1888 (with Schneider); "Über den Einfluss des Druckes auf die Brechungsexponenten von Schwefelkohlenstoff und Wasser," *Ber. d. Oberhess. Ges. f. Nat. u. Heilk.*, vol. 28, 1888 (with Zehnder); "Elektrische Eigenschaften des Quarzes," *Annalen der Physik und Chemie*, N.F. 39, 1889; "Beschreibung des Apparates, mit welchem die Versuche über die elektro-dynamische Wirkung bewegter Dielektrika ausgeführt wurden," *Annalen der Physik und Chemie*, N.F. 40, 1890; "Einige Vorlesungsversuche," *Annalen der Physik und Chemie*, N.F. 40, 1890; "Über die Dicke von kohärenten Ölschichten auf der Oberfläche des Wassers," *Annalen der Physik und Chemie*, N.F. 41, 1890; "Über die Kompressibilität von Schwefelkohlenstoff, Benzol, Äthyläther und einigen Alkoholen," *Annalen der Physik und Chemie*, N.F. 44, 1891; "Über den Einfluss des Druckes auf die Brechungsexponenten von Wasser, Schwefelkohlenstoff, Benzol, Äthyläther und einigen Alkoholen," *Annalen der Physik und Chemie*, N.F. 44, 1891 (with Zehnder); "Über die Konstitution des flüssigen Wassers," *Annalen der Physik und Chemie*, N.F. 45, 1892; "Kurze Mitteilungen von Versuchen über den Einfluss des Druckes auf einige physikalische Erscheinungen," *Annalen der Physik und Chemie*, N.F. 45, 1892; "Über den Einfluss der Kompressionswärme auf die Bestimmungen der Kompressibilität von Flüssigkeiten," *Annalen der Physik und Chemie*, N.F. 45, 1892; "Verfahren zur Herstellung reiner Wasseründ Quecksilberoberflächen," *Annalen der Physik und Chemie*, N.F. 46, 1892; "Über den Einfluss des Druckes auf das galvanische Leitungsvermögen von Elektrolyten," *Nachr. Ges. Wiss. Göttingen. Math.-physik. Kl.*, 1893; "Zur Geschichte der Physik an der Universität Würzburg," *Würzburg*, 1894, 23 S; "Notiz über die Methode zur Messung von Druckdifferenzen mittels Spiegelablesung," *Annalen der Physik und Chemie*, N.F. 51, 1894; "Mitteilung einiger Versuche mit einem rechtwinkeligen Glasprisma," *Annalen der Physik und Chemie*, N.F. 52, 1894; "Über den Einfluss des Druckes auf die Dielektrizitätskonstante des Wassers und des Äthylalkohols," *Annalen der Physik und Chemie*, N.F. 52, 1894; "Über eine neue Art von Strahlen," *Sitzgsber. physik.-med. Ges. Würzburg*, 1895 (also in *Annalen der Physik und Chemie*, N.F. 64, 1898); "Eine neue Art von Strahlen. 2. Mitteilung," *Sitzgsber. physik.-med. Ges. Würzburg*, 1896 (also in *Annalen der Physik und Chemie*, N.F. 64, 1898); "Weitere Beobachtungen über die Eigenschaften der X-Strahlen," *Math. u. naturw. Mitt. a. d. Sitzgsber. preuss. Akad. Wiss., Physik.-math. Kl.*, 1897; "Erklärung," *Physik Z.*, vol. 5, 1904; "Über die Leitung der Elektrizität im Kalkspat und über den Einfluss der X-Strahlen darauf," *Sitzgsber. bayer. Akad. Wiss., Math.-physik. Kl.*, 37, 1907; "Friedrich Kohlrausch," *Sitzgsber. bayer. Akad. Wiss., Math.-physik. Kl.*, 40, Schluss-H., 26, 1910; "Bestimmungen des thermischen linearen Ausdehnungskoeffizienten von

Cuprit und Diamant," *Sitzgsber. bayer. Akad. Wiss., Math.-physik. Kl.*, 1912; "Über die Elektrizitätsleitung in einigen Kristallen und über den Einfluss der Bestrahlung darauf. Zum Teil in Gemeinschaft mit A. Joffé," *Annalen der Physik*, IV. F. 41, 1913; "Pyro- und piezo-elektrische Untersuchungen," *Annalen der Physik*, IV. F. 45, 1914; "Über die Elektrizitätsleitung in einigen Kristallen und über den Einfluss einer Bestrahlung darauf. Zum Teil in Gemeinschaft mit A. Joffé," *Annalen der Physik*, IV. F. 64, 1921.

*Secondary*

Glasser, Otto. *Wilhelm Conrad Röntgen and the Early History of the Röntgen Rays*. Springfield, Ill.: Charles C Thomas, 1934. This volume is an important reference for all the works that followed. It contains a complete list of publications by Röntgen, as well as a list of books, pamphlets, and scientific papers written about X rays during the year 1896. There is a complete English translation of Röntgen's original paper and of many other contemporary documents. One long chapter is titled "Wilhelm Conrad Röntgen, Scientist and Man"; another, "Personal Reminiscences of Röntgen," was written by Margaret Boveri, the daughter of Röntgen's colleague at Würzburg. The second half of the book concentrates on scientific developments in the early years of röntgenology. Contains many photographs of colleagues and family, buildings, apparatus, papers, and early X-ray pictures.

——————————. *Dr. W. C. Röntgen*. 2d ed. Springfield, Ill.: Charles C Thomas, 1958. This volume focuses on Röntgen's life. Much shorter than the 1934 volume, it contains some of the same material, such as the list of Röntgen's publications, a translation of the original discovery article, and some of his original X-ray photographs.

Nitske, W. Robert. *The Life of Wilhelm Conrad Röntgen, Discoverer of the X Ray*. Tucson: University of Arizona Press, 1971. This book is twice the length of the later Glasser biography and contains more details about Röntgen's life. Some of the material from the earlier Glasser work is restored here, such as the response by contemporary newspapers and magazines to Röntgen's winning the Nobel Prize. Excerpts from many personal letters are reproduced.

Oibner, Bern. *The New Rays of Professor Röntgen*. Norwalk, Conn.: Burndy Library, 1963. A short book, one in a series aimed at interesting students in the careers of great scientists. Interesting and readable.

Shapiro, Gilbert. *A Skeleton in the Darkroom: Stories of Serendipity in Science*. New York: Harper & Row, 1986. Seven narratives designed to illustrate the role of chance in scientific discovery. The title story is an account of Röntgen's experiments with X rays. Not so much a biography, it concentrates on the moment of discovery. Suitable for high school and general readers.

*Gilbert Shapiro*

# 1902

### Physics
Hendrik Antoon Lorentz, Netherlands
Pieter Zeeman, Netherlands

### Chemistry
Emil Fischer, Germany

### Physiology or Medicine
Sir Ronald Ross, Great Britain

### Literature
Theodor Mommsen, Germany

### Peace
Élie Ducommun, Switzerland
Charles Albert Gobat, Switzerland

# HENDRIK ANTOON LORENTZ
## 1902

*Born:* Arnhem, Netherlands; July 18, 1853
*Died:* Haarlem, Netherlands; February 4, 1928
*Nationality:* Dutch
*Area of concentration:* Electromagnetic theory

*Lorentz provided a theoretical explanation of Pieter Zeeman's discovery of the splitting of the lines of a spectrum when a magnetic field is applied to the source of the spectrum by hypothesizing that material bodies contain small charged particles capable of oscillation*

## The Award

*Presentation*

Professor Hj. Théel, President of the Royal Swedish Academy of Sciences, presented the Nobel Prize to Hendrik Antoon Lorentz in December, 1902. The award was given jointly to Lorentz and Pieter Zeeman. In his presentation speech, Théel stated that the search for a connection between the phenomena of light and electricity had long occupied physicists. In recent history, Michael Faraday had tried to detect this connection experimentally; James Clerk Maxwell had formulated, mathematically, an electromagnetic theory of light; and Heinrich Rudolph Hertz had established, experimentally, that electric vibrations propagate with the speed of light. Zeeman took up Faraday's last experimental attempt to show the influence of magnetism on radiation from a light source. His experimental results established that light and electric waves are not only analogous; they are identical. Using his electron theory, Lorentz was able to explain the phenomenon and to predict other effects: in particular, that the split spectral lines are also polarized by the magnetic field, later confirmed by Zeeman. Théel noted that the Nobel Committee applauded this cooperative experimental and theoretical research. He called the Zeeman effect one of the most important scientific advances in recent decades, not only because of its contribution to the electromagnetic theory of light but also for its potential to increase scientists' understanding of the molecular structure of matter and the constitution of spectra.

*Nobel lecture*

Lorentz gave his lecture on December 11, 1902. He began by noting that he and Zeeman had agreed to divide their lectures such that Lorentz would present an overview of electron theory, leaving it to Zeeman to discuss the experiment and more recent experimental results. Zeeman's illness prevented this joint presentation (he would give his Nobel lecture in 1903), and so Lorentz briefly outlined the experiment before proceeding to discuss the background of its theoretical explanation. The lecture focuses on Lorentz's own "theory of electrons," since it was the prevailing electromagnetic theory, and he outlined his major scientific problems and achievements in the area. The style of the lecture is admirably lucid, requiring minimal scientific knowledge on the part of his audience. He organized his discussion around the two cornerstones of his theory: electrons, small subatomic particles, and ether, an invisible, all-pervasive medium once thought by scientists to transmit light and electromagnetic waves.

Lorentz noted that after Faraday's discovery of the rotation of the plane of polarized light by the action of a magnetic source, it became imperative to understand how to fuse the light and the electromagnetic ethers. Maxwell's electromagnetic theory did just that, and Hertz's experimental work not only confirmed that theory but also led to the realization that all electromagnetic waves, from telegraphic to X-ray, are fundamentally the same. Lorentz himself had begun to apply Maxwell's theory to problems in optics long before Hertz's experiments had convinced others of its correctness.

Lorentz explained that although the elastic solid theory of the ether was incorrect, it did contain a useful concept: tiny particles in matter that could be set in motion by light vibrations. He claimed, modestly, that his contribution was "merely to translate the conception of co-vibrating particles into the language of the electromagnetic theory of light." From chemical theory he concluded that the particles must be electrically charged and, thus, that their nature and their relationship to the processes in the ether could be investigated by means of the laws of electromagnetism. These tiny, charged particles provided the basis of his explanation of the Zeeman effect and would later be called "electrons," after their experimental discovery by Sir Joseph John Thomson in 1897.

Lorentz next discussed the ether and his reasons for maintaining that it is stationary and completely permeates all matter. Because ether and matter must exist in the same place, one is led to the idea that the atoms must, ultimately, be local modifications of ether. He recounted the experiments by Augustin-Jean Fresnel, recently repeated by Albert Abraham Michelson and Edward Williams Morley, that showed the velocity of light in moving media to be less than expected. Lorentz's theory had yielded the correct value for the dragging coefficient (the factor by which the velocity differs) without the hypothesis of the actual dragging of ether. At this point in its development, his theory could explain most optical phenomena in moving bodies and was well on its way to explaining all electromagnetic phenomena in terms of the interaction between electrons and ether. Lorentz closed the overview by remarking that Emil Wiechert and Joseph Larmor had obtained similar results with their theories and that Jules-Henri Poincaré had contributed significantly to his theory.

By the time of Zeeman's experiments, the theory of electrons was basically complete and could be used to interpret new phenomena. Lorentz left a detailed explanation of the effect to Zeeman but offered his own humorous summary of his contribution: "A man who has peopled the whole world with electrons and made them co-vibrate with light will not scruple to assume that it is also electrons which vibrate within the particles of an incandescent substance and bring about the emission of light." He concluded his lecture by stressing the need to understand more about the nature of the electron and noting problem areas for his theory, in particular, magneto-optic effects more complex than the simple form of the Zeeman effect he had been able to explain.

*Critical reception*

The awarding of the second Nobel prize for physics sparked little interest in the world press: The most that appeared was a listing of the recipients. The popular and the professional scientific periodicals also failed to carry commentary on the awards, although some had carried articles on the institution of the prizes in 1900 and the first awards in 1901. There was widespread agreement in the scientific community that Lorentz should indeed have received the prize.

The joint award with Zeeman set an important precedent for future awards. In his will, Alfred Nobel had stipulated that the award be given for a "discovery" or "invention" in physics, and it was unclear to the committee whether to include theoretical physicists. By awarding the prize jointly to Lorentz and Zeeman, theorists were established as worthy recipients of the prize if the work for which they were nominated was pertinent to a "discovery."

## Biography

Hendrik Antoon Lorentz was born in Arnhem, in the Netherlands, on July 18, 1853. His father, Gerrit Frederik Lorentz, owned a nursery. His mother, Geertruida van Ginkel, died when Lorentz was four. In school Lorentz excelled in mathematics, science, and languages. He was allowed to be self-directed and to work independently, forming a practice he was to follow most of his life. In 1870 he matriculated at the University of Leiden, and he received his candidate's degree (roughly equivalent to a bachelor's degree) summa cum laude in November of 1871. Since he knew more about electromagnetic theory than his teachers did, he returned to Arnhem in February of 1872 to prepare a doctoral dissertation on his own. He passed his oral examination summa cum laude in 1873 and received his doctorate in 1875.

Between 1872 and 1877, Lorentz was an evening-school teacher in Arnhem. In 1877 he was made a professor at Leiden, having been awarded the first Chair for Theoretical Physics in the Netherlands. Through him Leiden became a center for international scientific research. He left Leiden in 1912 to become curator of the Teylers Stichtung Museum primarily because of the increased access to laboratory facilities this made possible, but he continued to lecture at Leiden. During and after World War I, he worked hard to maintain open communication between scientists of warring nations, and in 1923 he was asked to chair the Committee on Intellectual Cooperation of the League of Nations. Lorentz was also quite active in community projects. Most notably, from 1918 to 1926 he made a significant contribution to the project to build the world's largest dike, enclosing the Zuider Zee.

At the time of his death, Lorentz was a great scientific and cultural figure both at home and abroad. Thousands of ordinary Dutch citizens lined the route of his funeral procession, and representatives of the Dutch government and the international scientific community attended the funeral. In a rare tribute, the Dutch telephone and telegraphic services were suspended across the country for three minutes for the man Albert Einstein, speaking as a friend and a representative of the Prussian Academy of Sciences, called "the greatest and noblest man of our times."

## Scientific Career

Lorentz began his scientific work on a major unresolved problem of Maxwell's electromagnetic theory, the reflection and refraction of light. His dissertation establishes the superiority of that theory for the explanation of optical phenomena. It was an impressive work and won for him the first Chair for Theoretical Physics in the Netherlands when he was only twenty-four years old. He had earlier been offered the Chair for Mathematics at Utrecht, but had declined because he preferred to teach physics.

In his inaugural lecture of 1878, Lorentz set forth what was to be the central problem of his scientific career: how to combine Maxwell's electromagnetic theory with a theory of matter so as to account for all optical and electromagnetic phenomena, especially within moving bodies. His solution to this problem fused together two quite disparate notions: Maxwell's continuous transmission of forces through an electromagnetic field and Sir Isaac Newton's particles that act on one another at a distance. Thus, it is through Lorentz's theory of electrons that the duality of fields and particles enters modern physics.

Lorentz's theory of electrons culminates in a set of lectures delivered at Columbia University in 1906. The construction of the theory spanned nearly thirty years. The first step toward the crucial separation of field and matter was made in his monograph *Voortplantingssnelheid van het Licht en de Dichtheid en Samenstelling der Middenstoffen* (1878; *Concerning the Relation Between the Velocity of the Propagation of Light and the Density and Composition of Media*, 1936). This work also introduced the hypothesis that there could be small positive and negative particles within molecules and that these particles could cause dispersion (the splitting of a light ray into its components by refraction). The particles and the ether are the cornerstones of the first full presentation of his electromagnetic theory in "La Théorie électromagnétique de Maxwell et son application aux corps mouvants" (1892; *Maxwell's electromagnetic theory and its application to moving bodies*). Here the particles interact with one another only through the ether, and are thus transmitted continuously through the ether. The electromagnetic field is a state of the ether, and was to remain so throughout Lorentz's work, even after Einstein dismissed the ether in his special theory of relativity. It is in this paper that Lorentz first introduced what he called a "startling hypothesis," that tiny, charged particles within matter oscillate when struck by light waves. Here, also, the Lorentz force (force with which the ether acts on the particles) was first introduced. The Lorentz force is a non-Newtonian force because it does not obey the law of action and reaction. Finally, in this paper Lorentz develops what were later to be called the "Lorentz transformations," a set of equations for transforming the position and motion of physical systems between reference frame in motion with respect to one another.

Thus, although Lorentz could be characterized as extending classical physics to its limits, he also broke with it in significant ways quite early in his career. With the publication of *Versuch einer Theorie der elektrischen und optischen Erscheinungen in bewegten Körpern* (1895; attempt at a theory of electric and optical phenomena in moving bodies), Lorentz's theory became the most comprehensive and successful electromagnetic theory. He used the theory to explain the Zeeman effect. Over the years he continued to refine and expand the theory of electrons to accommodate more phenomena and new experimental data.

Although he did not do much experimental work, experimental results figured significantly in the construction of Lorentz's theory. The interaction between theory and experiment in his work provides a paradigm of the new style of physics that had emerged in the nineteenth century: theoretical physics. Lorentz adopted the view that electric and magnetic actions are transmitted continuously through the ether after Hertz had detected electromagnetic radiation. Lorentz's daughter, Geertruida De Haas-Lorentz, in *H. A. Lorentz: Impressions of His Life and Work* (1957), recounts that he had tried some experiments to detect electromagnetic waves during his years in Arnhem. The phenomenon of aberration (the apparent displacement of a star as the result of the motion of Earth around the Sun) led him to retain the hypothesis that the ether is everywhere locally at rest, or rigid, even when this hypothesis created major problems for his theory. That the "dragging coefficient" for light in moving media could be derived and refined from his hypothesis of the vibrating particles established Lorentz's theory as the most comprehensive electromagnetic theory. His immediate explanation of the Zeeman effect with the same hypothesis gave his theory even greater credibility.

The experimental result that had the greatest impact on the shape of Lorentz's theory was the Michelson-Morley experiment of 1887. Electromagnetic theory had inherited the problem of the overall motion of the ether from the wave theory of light. Electromagnetic fields produced in a moving ether would differ from those produced in a stationary ether. From the outset, Lorentz had adopted the view that the ether is motionless. In a series of experiments, Michelson and Morley tried to detect the effect of Earth's motion through the ether on the propagation of light. According to classical theory, if the ether did not move along with Earth, but remained stationary, the velocity of light in the direction parallel to Earth should differ from that in the perpendicular direction. The 1887 experiment established conclusively that there is no difference; Michelson and others concluded that the ether must move along with Earth. This result was later bolstered by other experimental results of the same level of sensitivity. Although these results seemed to conflict with Lorentz's hypothesis of a stationary ether, he continued to develop his theory, hoping to find an explanation as he went along. Shortly after writing the

1892 paper, he proposed an explanation: The dimensions of an object change when it is in motion through the ether. That is, Lorentz hypothesized that there is an interaction between uncharged matter and the ether, while previously it had been thought that only charged matter and the ether could interact. In the penultimate formulation of his theory, "Electromagnetische verschijnselen in een stelsel dat zich met willekeurige snelheid, kleiner dan die van het licht, beweegt" (1904; "Electromagnetic Phenomena in a System Moving with Any Velocity Less than That of Light," 1904), he used this hypothesis to account for an even wider range of phenomena. An additional feature, however, put the theory at variance with Newtonian mechanics. The mass of an electron, and of uncharged matter, is not constant, but depends on its state of motion. Einstein was to derive all the results of Lorentz's theory of electrons in a quite different manner in 1905. Although Einstein's theory is now called the "special theory of relativity," until around 1911 it was called the "Lorentz-Einstein theory," with few scientists other than Lorentz and Einstein appreciating the important conceptual differences between the theories.

Most of Lorentz's scientific work focused on electrodynamics. Nevertheless, he did make significant contributions to other areas of physics as well. In the 1880's he worked on the molecular-kinetic theory of heat. He also contributed to the general theory of relativity and quantum mechanics. Lorentz did the only applied work of his scientific career in the last years of his life, when he devised a method for calculating storm surge, a nonperiodic function, in a network of channels and shoals. The engineer on the Zuider Zee project marveled that Lorentz's calculations were so precise, and the method of calculation he devised has since been used on other projects.

For nearly half of his scientific career, Lorentz remained in the Netherlands, seeking no contact with his scientific peers. This changed rather dramatically after 1897, when he attended a scientific conference in Düsseldorf and realized the value of discussion with colleagues equally knowledgeable in physics. He addressed the International Congress of Physics in Paris in 1900, and in 1906 he gave the first of several series of lectures in the United States. His linguistic abilities and his talent for dealing with difficult personalities made him the perfect choice for chairing the first Solvay conference in 1911 and all subsequent conferences until his death.

Lorentz was known to be an excellent teacher and lecturer. After he moved to Haarlem in 1912, he gave many popular lectures as part of his position at the Teylers Stichtung Museum. In his capacity as curator, he also served as the secretary of the Dutch Society of Science. From 1909 to 1921, he was president of the physics section of the Royal Netherlands Academy of Science and Letters. He used this position to encourage international scientific cooperation after World War I, but made little progress. In addition to the Nobel Prize, he received the Royal Society's Rumford and Copley medals, was awarded honorary doctorates from the universities of Paris and Cambridge, and was elected to the German Physics Society and the Royal Society.

Although his theory of electrons did not survive, Lorentz's work shaped the foundations of modern physics. His contemporaries and immediate successors saw the separation of field and matter as his most important achievement: It was essential to the development of both relativity and quantum mechanics. Lorentz pushed classical theory beyond its limits and in so doing exposed the foundational problems modern physics would have to resolve.

## Bibliography

*Primary*

PHYSICS: *Voortplantingssnelheid van het Licht en de Dichtheid en Samenstelling der Middenstoffen*, 1878 (*Concerning the Relation Between the Velocity of the Propagation of Light and the Density and Composition of Media*, 1936); *Beginselen der Natuurkunde*, 1888; "La Théorie eléctromagnétique de Maxwell et son application aux corps mouvants," 1892; *Versuch einer Theorie der elektrischen und optischen Erscheinungen in bewegten Körpern*, 1895; "Electromagnetische verschijnselen in een stelsel dat zich met willekeurige snelheid, kleiner dan die van het licht, beweegt," 1904 ("Electromagnetic Phenomena in a System Moving with Any Velocity Less than That of Light," 1904); *H. A. Lorentz, Abhandlungen über theoretische Physik*, 1907; *Theory of Electrons and Its Applications to the Phenomena of Light and Radiant Heat*, 1909; *Les Théories statistiques en thermodynamique*, 1912; *Lessen in de theoretische Natuurkunde*, 1919-1925 (*Lectures in Theoretical Physics*, 1931); *Problems of Modern Physics*, 1927; *H. A. Lorentz: Collected Papers*, 1935-1939.

*Secondary*

De Haas-Lorentz, Geertruida, ed. *H. A. Lorentz: Impressions of His Life and Work*. Amsterdam: North Holland, 1957. This volume, edited by Lorentz's daughter, commemorates the one hundredth anniversary of his birth. It contains assessments of the man and his work by colleagues (including Albert Einstein) and reminiscences by his daughter. The recollections of his daughter, though sketchy, provide the most extensive information available on Lorentz's private life.

Hirosige, Tetu. "Origins of Lorentz's Theory of Electrons and the Concept of the Electromagnetic Field." In *Historical Studies in the Physical Sciences*, edited by Russell McCormmach, vol. 1. Philadelphia: University of Pennsylvania Press, 1969. This is a highly technical, comprehensive analysis of Lorentz's contributions to the development of the electromagnetic field concept.

McCormmach, Russell. "H. A. Lorentz and the Electromagnetic View of Nature." *Isis* 61 (Winter, 1970): 209, 459-497. The article analyzes the development of Lorentz's electromagnetic theory and discusses its relationship to the program to reduce all mechanical phenomena to states of the electromagnetic ether.

_____, ed. "Einstein, Lorentz, and the Electron Theory." In *Historical Studies in the Physical Sciences*. Vol. 2. Philadelphia: University of Pennsylvania Press, 1970. This article focuses on the work leading up to Albert Einstein's formulation of the hypothesis of light quanta and also discusses Lorentz's main objections to the hypothesis.

Nersessian, Nancy. "Lorentz's 'Non-Newtonian Aether-Field.' " In *Faraday to Einstein: Constructing Meaning in Scientific Theories*. Dordrecht: Martinus Nijhoff, 1984. The chapter traces the development of Lorentz's theory of electrons in nontechnical language. It places his concept of field within the context of the formation of the electromagnetic field from Faraday to Einstein.

——————. " 'Why Wasn't Lorentz Einstein?' An Examination of the Scientific Method of H. A. Lorentz." *Centaurus* 29 (1986): 205-242. The article probes the question of why Lorentz never accepted the special theory of relativity, even though it is formally equivalent to the theory of electrons.

*Nancy J. Nersessian*

# 1902

## Physics
Hendrik Antoon Lorentz, Netherlands
Pieter Zeeman, Netherlands

## Chemistry
Emil Fischer, Germany

## Physiology or Medicine
Sir Ronald Ross, Great Britain

## Literature
Theodor Mommsen, Germany

## Peace
Élie Ducommun, Switzerland
Charles Albert Gobat, Switzerland

P. Zeeman,

# PIETER ZEEMAN
## 1902

*Born:* Zonnemaire, isle of Schouwen, Zeeland, Netherlands; May 25, 1865
*Died:* Amsterdam, Netherlands; October 9, 1943
*Nationality:* Dutch
*Areas of concentration:* Electromagnetic theory and magneto-optics

*Zeeman was able to show the influence of magnetism upon light when he discovered that the lines of a spectrum are split when a magnetic field is applied to the source of light*

## The Award

*Presentation*

Professor Hj. Théel, President of the Royal Swedish Academy of Sciences, made his presentation of the Nobel Prize in Physics at the award ceremonies in December of 1902. The award was given jointly to Zeeman and to the theoretical physicist Hendrik Antoon Lorentz (1853-1928). Professor Théel began by providing some background on earlier investigations into the connection between optical and electrical phenomena. This connection had been one of the problems examined by Michael Faraday (1791-1867), the discoverer of electricity. Faraday had suspected this connection and had devoted experiments to it. It was James Clerk Maxwell (1831-1879), however, who formulated the complete mathematical theory for the electric and magnetic phenomena and also showed that optical phenomena can be regarded as particular manifestations of electromagnetic phenomena. According to this theory, the velocity of electromagnetic waves in space was identical to the velocity of light in space. Twenty years later, in 1887, Heinrich Hertz (1857-1894), in a series of brilliant experiments, succeeded in showing the existence of electromagnetic waves as predicted by Maxwell's theory. Their velocity was found to be that of light. Maxwell's theory was inadequate, however, to explain certain electromagnetic phenomena. Lorentz's contribution to the development of the theory of electromagnetism was to assume that extremely small bodies, later known as electrons, were the carriers of charges in the conductors; a host of previously unexplained phenomena could be explained by the motions of these bodies.

Faraday's last experiment had been an attempt to show that magnetism has a direct effect on the radiation from a source of light and thus to show that light and electrical wave motion were identical in nature—but he could not observe such an effect. Zeeman's experimental work culminated in demonstrating such an effect, by applying a strong magnetic field to a source of light. As a result, the light source's spectral lines (the pattern characteristic of each substance that radiates light, after the light is passed through prismlike devices) were resolved into several components. This discovery was satisfactorily explained by Lorentz's "electron theory." Thus the long-sought connection between the electromagnetic and optical phenomena was explicitly demonstrated by Zeeman's experiments.

Professor Théel closed by noting that the Zeeman effect not only provided strong support for the electromagnetic theory of light but also promised valuable contributions to man's understanding of the molecular structure of matter and the spectra characteristic of each substance.

## Nobel lecture

When Zeeman was awarded the Nobel Prize, he was unable to be present at the ceremony; he delivered his Nobel lecture five months later, on May 2, 1903.

Zeeman began his lecture by relating the relatively brief history of the study of the connection between magnetism and light. Faraday had been the first to observe the effects of magnetism on light. In 1845 he had discovered that the polarization plane of light rotates as soon as it passes through bodies that have been magnetized. It was later suggested by Maxwell that optical phenomena may be a particular manifestation of electromagnetic phenomena. Lorentz developed an explanatory schema of the electromagnetic and optical processes by assuming that they are caused by the vibrations of the electrons, the tiny carriers of the electric charges contained in every substance. In this schema the effect of magnetism on light could be explained in terms of the magnetic forces influencing those vibrations of the electrons that were responsible for the optical phenomena. The last experiment recorded in Faraday's diaries took place on March 12, 1862. Faraday recorded the negative results of his attempt to observe, by means of a spectroscope (a device which, much like a prism, is used for the analysis of light), the effects of magnetism on a light source.

Even Maxwell himself was not optimistic that such an effect could be observed. In 1870 he thought it unlikely that any force in nature could cause even a small change in either the mass or the period of oscillation of the light-radiating particles in a flame. Maxwell's pessimism did not discourage Zeeman. He proceeded to investigate the problem while first thinking about the effect discovered by John Kerr (1824-1907). His discovery was announced at the meeting of the British Association in Glasgow in 1876. He had found that a beam of polarized light is reflected from the pole of an electromagnet. When the magnet is activated the beam becomes elliptically polarized, with the major axis rotated from the direction of the original plane.

In August of 1896, Zeeman was able to see that the spectral lines of a sodium flame were broadened when the flame was placed between the poles of a strong electromagnet. The experiment was repeated and care was taken to make sure that the broadening was not the result of some spurious effect of the experimental apparatus or of the conditions of the experiment. Every time, the same broadening was observed.

One of the results of the electromagnetic theory as developed by Lorentz was that an electron moving in a magnetic field experiences a force that is perpendicular both to its direction of motion and to the direction of the magnetic field. Zeeman showed that Lorentz's theory predicted correctly the observed effects whenever the light rays were along the direction perpendicular to the lines of the magnetic force and along the parallel direction. It became evident that the reason the phenomenon had not been observed earlier was that the observed effect was quite small, and measuring such an effect entailed intricate experimental difficulties.

The theoretical explanation of the broadening of the spectral lines in the presence of a magnetic field is dependent on the ratio of the charge of the electron to its mass. The experimental results furnished the first numerical estimate for this ratio that was $10^7$ in the appropriate units per gram of mass. Furthermore, it was deduced that the charge of the electron was negative.

Not all burning substances showed the same splitting in three components as the sodium flame. There were substances that were split into four, five, six, and even nine lines, and iron showed a whole range of different splittings. It was also found that, contrary to the predictions of the theory, the effect of the magnetic field was not the same for all the lines of a particular substance.

Zeeman concluded his talk by mentioning three different phenomena that had been the object of his recent researches. The first involved band spectra. These are spectra that are caused by the vibrations of many electrons and are the characteristic "signature" of certain substances, much as the line spectra are of other substances. Zeeman could not find any changes in these bands even under the strongest magnetic fields. The second phenomenon involved the prediction by Woldemar Voigt (1850-1919) that weak magnetic forces may alter the symmetry of the split lines. This theory predicted that the two external components of a line split into three lines would have different intensities, and Zeeman was able to observe this effect in the cases of iron, zinc, and cadmium. The third phenomenon involved the establishment of the close connection between the rotation of the polarization plane first observed by Faraday and the magnetic splitting of the spectral lines.

Zeeman closed his Nobel lecture by paying tribute to Lorentz and, at the same time, expressing the significance of his own discoveries:

> . . . firm support has been found for the assertion that electricity occurs at thousands of points where we at most conjectured that it was present. Innumerable electrical particles oscillate in every flame and light source. We can in fact assume that every heat source is filled with electrons which will continue to oscillate ceaselessly and indefinitely.

## Critical reception

Zeeman was awarded the Nobel Prize the second year after the establishment of the prize. The universal recognition of the significance of Zeeman's work is also expressed by the fact that among the people who nominated him was Svante August Arrhenius (1859-1927), perhaps the most influential scientist of Sweden, as well as Albert Abraham Michelson (1852-1931), the famous American physicist who became the first U.S. citizen to receive the Nobel Prize.

The discovery of the electron in 1897 by Sir Joseph John Thomson (1856-1940) brought about dramatic changes in scientists' conceptions concerning the structure of matter. Zeeman's discovery a year earlier of the splitting of the spectral lines and Lorentz's explanation of the phenomenon by using his electron theory contributed decisively to this new conceptualization. In Zeeman's work there was nothing to suggest that the electron found to be the emitter of the sodium spectrum was in any way detached or detachable from the sodium atom. The applied magnetic field merely modified the forces which controlled the electron within the atom. It was Thomson's discovery of the electron and his subsequent work that dealt with "free" electrons.

As a result of Zeeman's work, it became possible to comprehend the structure of many molecules. Nevertheless, Lorentz's theory could not explain the anomalous Zeeman effect, which was the more complicated splitting of the lines. It became possible to explain the effect only after the development of quantum mechanics and the introduction of "electron spin," which is a purely quantum mechanical notion. Hence, the Zeeman effect contributed to the conceptual development of quantum mechanics as well.

## Biography

Pieter Zeeman was born at Zonnemaire, a small island village in the Netherlands, on May 25, 1865. His mother was born Wilhelmina Worst, and his father, Catharinus Forandinus Zeeman, was a clergyman. Pieter attended the local school and then left for Delft to study Greek and Latin, since knowledge of both languages was required for entering the university. At Delft he met Heike Kamerlingh Onnes (1853-1926), who was greatly impressed by Zeeman's passion for performing experiments and by his having read and mastered a large number of classic texts, including Maxwell's *Theory of Heat* (1877).

Zeeman entered the University of Leiden in 1885, where he became a pupil of Kamerlingh Onnes and Lorentz. In 1890 he became assistant to Lorentz and began his study of the Kerr phenomenon: the changes in the plane of polarization of light when it is reflected from the pole of an electromagnet. He received his doctoral degree in 1890 and left for Strassburg, where he worked at the institute of Friedrich Wilhelm Georg Kohlrausch (1840-1910). He returned to Leiden after one year and stayed there until 1897 as a lecturer.

After making the discoveries that would win for him the Nobel Prize, Zeeman was offered a lecturership at the University of Amsterdam in 1897, and in 1900 he was appointed Extraordinary Professor. In 1908 he succeeded Johannes Diderik van der Waals (1837-1923) as director of the physics laboratory. In 1923 a specially built laboratory for the needs of his experimental programs was completed, since known as the Zeeman Laboratory of the University of Amsterdam. The laboratory included a concrete block weighing 250 tons for performing experiments that would be free of the effects of vibrations. Zeeman would remain at the University of Amsterdam until 1935.

In 1892 Zeeman was awarded the Gold Medal from the Dutch Society of Sciences at Haarlem for his work *Mesures relatives du phénomène de Kerr*. The same subject occupied him in his doctoral research. In Strassburg he studied the propagation and absorption of electrical waves in fluids, and he resumed the study of the influence of magnetism on light after he returned to Leiden.

Zeeman received honorary doctorates from the universities at Groningen, Oxford, Philadelphia, Strassburg, Liège, Ghent, Glasgow, Brussels, and Paris and distinctions from numerous academies from around the world, including the French Academy of Sciences, Great Britain's Royal Society, and the National Academy of Sciences in the United States. He was married to Johanna Elisabeth Lebret in 1895; they had one son and three daughters. Zeeman died in Amsterdam on October 9, 1943.

## Scientific Career

Pieter Zeeman discovered the splitting of the spectral lines under the influence of an applied magnetic field while he was at the University of Leiden. All of his subsequent work was performed at the University of Amsterdam, where he stayed almost continuously from the time of his first appointment as a lecturer in 1897 until his retirement in 1935.

Faraday, motivated by his deep belief in the essential unity of all the forces in nature, was the first to attempt to observe any influence of magnetism on light. He searched for any such effect very systematically but could find nothing—mainly because his equipment was not sufficiently sensitive. He was, however, able to observe that a transparent, isotropic medium, when placed in a strong magnetic field, has the power to rotate the plane of polarization of light, when the light moves parallel to the magnetic lines of force. (A body is said to be isotropic if its physical properties are not dependent upon the direction in the body along which they are measured.) Though Zeeman knew of these researches of Faraday, it was through his study of the Kerr effect that he made his discovery. In 1893, he tried to see if the light of a flame would undergo any change if placed in a magnetic field; he was unsuccessful. Then he started studying the phenomenon first discovered by Kerr in 1876.

When a plane-polarized light is reflected from the surface of a polished, nonmagnetic metal, the light will generally be found to be elliptically polarized, and the reflected light cannot be extinguished by the analyzer. If, however, the incident light is plane-polarized either in or at right angles to the plane of incidence, then the reflected light is plane-polarized and can be extinguished by the analyzer. Kerr examined the light reflected from a polished pole of a strong electromagnet, under the conditions that one should expect to receive a plane-polarized light in the reflected beam, and found that when the electromagnet was excited, the reflected light was no longer plane-polarized. Ten years after Hertz had demonstrated the fundamental role of electric and magnetic forces for the propagation of light, Zeeman established their role for the production of light as well.

At the end of the nineteenth century and the beginning of the twentieth, and before the new ideas of quantum physics were accepted by all scientists with equal enthusiasm, various researchers insisted on the mechanical rather than the electromagnetic theory of atoms. Zeeman, in the early stages of his research, was one of those scientists. In his first attempts to explain the phenomenon, he did not even use the words "electron," nor did he consider an electric charge of any kind in connection with his atoms or molecules. He expressed the view whose main proponent was Lord Kelvin (William Thomson, 1824-1907), that the radiation of light from atoms revolving in a molecule could be understood only in terms of the rotation of the atoms. The phenomenon itself, however, forced him to turn to Lorentz's electron theory:

> In this theory it is assumed that in all bodies small electrically charged particles with a definite mass are present, that all electric phenomena are dependent upon the configuration and motion of these "ions" and that light-vibrations are vibrations of these "ions." . . . The said ion, moving in a magnetic field, experiences mechanical forces of the kind above mentioned, and these must explain the variation of the period. Professor Lorentz, to whom I communicated these considerations, at once kindly informed me of the manner in which, according to his theory, the motion of an ion in a magnetic field is to be calculated, and pointed out to me that, if the explanation following from his theory be true, the edges of the lines of the spectrum ought to be circularly polarized. The amount of widening might then be used to determine the ratio between charge and mass, to be attributed in this theory to a particle giving out the vibrations of light.

As soon as the electron was discovered and the charge-to-mass ratio was established, the agreement of this ratio with the ratio of the same quantities as obtained from the analysis of the Zeeman effect with known magnetic intensity lent decisive support to the hypothesis that the electron was indeed a constituent part of the atom and responsible for the emission of light.

Lorentz, to whom Zeeman reported the outcome of his experiments before their publication, saw at once how to interpret these results on the basis of his electron theory. Resolving the motion of the quasi-elastically bound charged particle into a linear vibration in the direction of the field (and, therefore, unaffected by the field) and into two superposed circular motions, executed in opposite directions, in the plane perpendicular to the direction of the field, Lorentz predicted that the light from the edges of the broadened line, if viewed in the direction of the lines of force, should be circularly polarized, and if viewed at right angles to the field, should be plane-polarized. This conclusion Zeeman immediately confirmed.

In his early publications, Zeeman had suggested that it would be possible to verify the already accepted existence of strong magnetic fields on the surface of the Sun by trying to observe the widening of the spectral lines from the Sun. In 1908 he was informed by George Ellery Hale (1868-1938), who was then the director of the Mount Wilson Observatory in Southern California, that spectral lines from the Sun appeared to be affected by its magnetic field.

Zeeman's later experiments involved the study of the velocity of light in moving media. He attempted to measure the velocity of light in moving solids such as crystals and quartz. The glass cannot be made to move continuously like water, because it cannot be made to flow aside, as water can, when it has come to the end of the optical path. It was necessary to use a reciprocating motion of the glass and to observe only during that part of the cycle when it was moving with quite a large velocity in the desired direction. The results were found to be consistent with the special theory of relativity, where the velocity of light was considered to be a universal constant and independent of the velocity of the medium in which it was traveling with respect to an observer.

Zeeman also worked on isotope recognition. In 1934, he was able to identify a new argon isotope of mass 38.

## Bibliography

*Primary*

PHYSICS: *Mesures relatives du phénomène de Kerr*, 1892; *Metingen over het verschij-nsel van Kerr bij polaire terugkaatsing op ijzer, kobalt en nikkel, in 't bijzonder over Sissingh's magneto-optisch phaseverschil*, 1893; *On the Influence of Magne-tism on the Nature of the Light Emitted by a Substance*, 1900; *Doublets and Triplets in the Spectrum Produced by External Magnetic Forces*, 1900; *The Effects of a Magnetic Field on Radiation: Memoirs by Faraday, Kerr, and Zeeman*, 1900 (edited by Exum Percival Lewis); *Zuivere en toegepaste wiskunde*, 1902; *Strahl-ung des Lichtes im Magnetischen Felde*, 1903; *Seismographs and Seismograms*, 1908; *Researches in Magneto-Optics, with Special Reference to the Magnetic Resolution of Spectrum Lines*, 1913; *Magneto-optische Untersuchungen, mit be-sonderer Berücksichtigung der magnetischen Zerlegung der Spektrallinien*, 1914; *Magneto-Optisch Verschijnselen*, 1921; *Verhandelingen van Dr. P. Zeeman over magneto-optische verschijnselen*, 1921 (selected papers).

*Secondary*

Baly, Edward Charles Cyril. *Spectroscopy*. Rev. ed. New York: Longman, 1918. This is one of the classic introductory books on spectroscopy, intended primarily for physical chemists and written after the first developments of quantum me-chanics and before the establishment of wave mechanics in the mid-1920's. The author includes an exhaustive treatment of the Zeeman effect together with the failures to explain the anomalous Zeeman effect in relation to the old quantum theory.

Jammer, Max. *The Conceptual Development of Quantum Mechanics*. New York: McGraw-Hill, 1966. One of the most comprehensive accounts of the development of quantum mechanics and the related conceptual problems. The transition from the old quantum theory to the wave and matrix mechanics of the mid-1920's is treated in a particularly detailed manner, and the attempt to explain the anomalous Zeeman effect is treated in such a context. Includes an exhaustive bibliography of the original papers.

Lodge, Oliver. "The History of Zeeman's Discovery and Its Reception in England." *Nature* 109 (January, 1922): 66-69. This article, written by one of the outstanding British physicists of the late nineteenth century, gives interesting information about parallel attempts in England to observe the effects of magnetism on light.

McGucken, William. *Nineteenth Century Spectroscopy: Development of the Understanding of Spectra, 1802-1897*. Baltimore: Johns Hopkins University Press, 1978. Provides most of the background needed to understand the Zeeman effect, as well as an overview of spectroscopy, whose development could not be reconciled with the development of kinetic theory.

Shinji, Endo, and Sachie Saito. "The Zeeman Effect and the Theory of Electron of H. A. Lorentz." *Japanese Studies in History of Science* 6 (1967): 1-18. This article presents a detailed historical account of the discovery of the Zeeman effect and its relation to the electron theory of Lorentz, for which it was a major challenge. Includes an exhaustive bibliography of the articles by Zeeman and Lorentz related to the effect.

Spencer, J. Brookes. "On the Varieties of Nineteenth-Century Magneto-Optical Discovery." *Isis* 61 (Spring, 1970): 34-51. This article relates the history of the background to the Zeeman effect. The work of Faraday and Kerr are systematically treated.

Watson, E. C. "The Discovery of the Zeeman Effect." *American Journal of Physics* 22 (December, 1954): 633-635. This article reproduces and interprets three stained glass windows that have been installed in the Kamerlingh Onnes Laboratory at the University of Leiden to commemorate the discovery of the Zeeman effect.

*Kostas Gavroglu*

# 1903

### Physics
Antoine-Henri Becquerel, France
Pierre Curie, France
Marie Curie, Poland and France

### Chemistry
Svante Arrhenius, Sweden

### Physiology or Medicine
Niels R. Finsen, Denmark

### Literature
Bjørnstjerne Bjørnson, Norway

### Peace
Sir William Cremer, Great Britain

# ANTOINE-HENRI BECQUEREL
## 1903

*Born:* Paris, France; December 15, 1852
*Died:* Le Croisic, France; August 25, 1908
*Nationality:* French
*Area of concentration:* Radioactivity

*Becquerel's discovery in 1896 of the spontaneous radioactivity of uranium in the form of beta and gamma rays—originally termed "Becquerel rays"—revealed a new atomic property, hence a new property of matter as well as a new source of energy. These revelations led eventually to modern atomic and nuclear physics*

## The Award

*Presentation*

The Nobel Prize in Physics for 1903 was divided between Antoine-Henri Becquerel and Pierre and Marie Curie. The formal presentation of the prize took place in Stockholm on the evening of December 10, 1903, before King Oscar II of the United Kingdom of Sweden and Norway, several members of the royal family, and an assembly of other eminent persons. The presentation speech on the awarding of the prize for physics jointly to Becquerel and the Curies was made by H. R. Törnebladh, President of the Royal Swedish Academy of Sciences, who emphasized how the research of the Curies had built on and supplemented the important discovery of Becquerel to acquire an importance of its own.

Dr. Törnebladh further pointed out that just as the Curies' discoveries of radioactive substances other than uranium—namely, thorium, polonium, radium, and actinium—were linked to Becquerel's work, his serendipitous discovery of radioactivity was linked to the German physicist Wilhelm Conrad Röntgen's Nobel Prize-winning discovery in 1895 that cathode rays produce X rays. Törnebladh also remarked on the importance of the Curies' use of the electroscope, made possible by the discovery of Becquerel rays. He enumerated some of the special properties of the Becquerel rays: how they are like light in some respects but not in others; how they are not homogeneous but are composed of different kinds of rays; and how they make other bodies in their vicinity temporarily radioactive.

*Nobel lecture*

In his Nobel lecture, entitled "On Radioactivity, a New Property of Matter," Becquerel summarized the research that had led to his discovery of the Becquerel rays. Learning that Röntgen's discovery of X rays had come about by the use of luminescent vacuum tubes, his own interest in luminescent materials had become aroused. He had wondered whether all such materials when exposed to light would emit such rays, and had decided to try the commonest examples of uranium salts, uranium nitrate and potassium-uranyl sulphate, to see if they would emit Röntgen rays. On photographic plates wrapped in black paper or protected with an aluminum sheet, he placed sheets of double sulphate of uranium and potassium and exposed the whole to sunlight for several hours. When he developed the photographic plates, he found them fogged: The uranium salts had penetrated the black paper or the screen of metal laid on the plates. At first he thought that his hypothesis had been confirmed—that the phenomenon was the result of solar energy— but he soon realized that it was not caused by any familiar excitation such as light, heat, or electricity, but was an independent, spontaneous phenomenon that was of a "new order." He had discovered the spontaneous radiation of uranium.

Becquerel furnished reproductions of the radiographs he had obtained in his various experiments and stated the significance he drew from them. One print revealed the spontaneity of the uranium-salt radiation; another allowed Becquerel to conclude that the emitted radiation was constant and did not diminish appreciably with time. Further, he noted that the radiation discharged electrically charged materials at some remove. This aspect gave him a second method of measurement that provided him with numerical data as opposed to the photographic method that was largely qualitative. By these methods he found that all uranium salts emitted radiation of the same kind, that this characteristic was atomic and was connected with the element uranium, and that metallic uranium was several times more active than the salts he had used in his original experiment. He also found that charged uranium retains its charge even in an absolute vacuum and that the electrical charges exchanged between charged bodies influenced by the rays result from the conductivity that was imparted to the surrounding gases. He paid tribute to British physicist Ernest Rutherford, who established that this conductivity was equal to the ionization (the process by which neutral atoms lose or gain one or more electrons) caused by other factors. In an important experiment, Becquerel noted that radium radiation was deflected by a magnetic field and that there were two kinds of rays, one highly deflected and the other hardly so. The latter became known as alpha rays (emitted by polonium) and the former as beta rays (highly deflected rays of radium). Gamma rays, not deflected by a magnetic field (emitted by uranium), were soon discovered by Paul Villard. Each of these rays has its own characteristics, measured by deflection in a magnetic field and by penetrability. The alpha rays are barely deflectible and have low penetrability; the beta rays are more penetrating than alpha rays; and gamma rays cannot be deflected by a magnetic field and penetrate farther through matter than either of the others.

In concluding his lecture, Becquerel cited the chemical effects of radiation on certain substances; the physiological effects of radium rays; and the phenomena of emanation (the vapor or gas formed by radioactivity, especially in the cases of radium and thorium, that gets deposited on surrounding bodies), and activation (the excitation of the emanation because of ionization that makes the surrounding bodies temporarily active). In summary, he listed the radioactive substances that had thus far been well established: uranium, thorium, radium, polonium, and actinium. Uranium emits beta and gamma rays, but it does not form an emanation in air, although it does in solution. Thorium and radium give off alpha, beta, and gamma rays as well as an emanation. Polonium does not emit beta rays but does give off alpha and gamma rays. It also loses its activity in a relatively short period. Uranium, thorium, and radium have characteristics that are related to but distinct from barium. Barium is found only in uranium minerals. Radioactive elements give off energy in the common forms of heat, electrical charges, gamma radiation, and chemical reactions. Becquerel's most important statement was a hypothesis for the future: The emission of energy by radioactive substances is the result of a slow modification of their atoms; if man could find a way to effect such a modification, he could release energy in large quantities.

*Critical reception*

The leading newspapers of Great Britain and the United States, *The Times* of London and *The New York Times*, gave but cursory coverage of the Nobel Prizes for 1903. The December 11, 1903, issue of *The Times* of London simply announced the winners of the year's Nobel Prizes, noting that the award for physics had been divided between Becquerel and the Curies. In respect to the merits of the awards, no opinion was offered. In the December 11 issue of *The New York Times*, in a dispatch headed "Nobel Prizes Awarded," most space is devoted to the award for peace given to Sir William Randal Cremer, whose name today is largely forgotten. The prizes given by the Swedish academies, including the prize for physics awarded to Bequerel and the Curies, are listed in another paragraph, the paper erroneously reporting that Becquerel was a Norwegian. In another paragraph these prizes are reported as worth about $40,000 each. In the final paragraph it is clear that the paper is especially pleased that the Curies shared in the physics prize. Of the other recipients they "are now perhaps best known. The discovers of radium have . . . not profited financially from the work as greatly as might have been expected, and their admirers throughout the world will be delighted to hear of this windfall for them." No comment at all is made concerning Becquerel's deserts. One paragraph describes the formal presentation of the various prizes.

The response in the English language press was quite varied. Some newspapers reported the 1903 physics award without judgment; some expressed admiration that the award included a woman; still others were skeptical of the choice of a female prizewinner. The Curies as a married couple, and especially Marie Curie, obviously upstaged the much respected but less colorful Becquerel in the minds of press and public. Even before the award was given, the *Independent* (Chicago) took a male-chauvinistic sideswipe at Marie Curie. In a short article, "Radio-Active Matter," in the issue for January 8, 1903, the writer commented:

. . . Madame Curie appears to be an exception to President Jordan's [D. S. Jordan, then president of Stanford University, California] theory that a woman cannot do great original work. It is a possible hypothesis, however, that the chemico-activity exhibited by this remarkable woman is induced by association with her husband.

There were, however, some more positive reactions. In an article, "The Winners of the Nobel Prize," printed in the *Scientific American Supplement*, dated January 16, 1904, the writer expressed pleasure that Becquerel had shared in the prize because the work of the Curies directly derived from his. "It is, therefore," said the writer, "a rather happy decision to award the Nobel Prize in chemistry [*sic*] to M. Becquerel" as well as to the Curies. Writer Vance Thompson in *Cosmopolitan Magazine* for September, 1906, took much the same view, commenting: "There was a just order in this distribution of awards," for to Becquerel "and his father was due the discovery of uranium, out of which proceeded radium."

Surprisingly, in the December 11 issue of the popular French daily *Le Figaro* no report of the previous day's presentation of the Nobel Prize to three of France's most distinguished citizens appeared at all.

## Biography

Antoine-Henri Becquerel was born in Paris on December 15, 1852, to a distinguished family of physicists. He was educated at the Lycée Louis-le-Grand and then at the École Polytechnique. On completing his studies there, he was married to Lucie-Zoé-Marie Jamin, daughter of a professor of physics at the University of Paris. He finished his formal studies at the École de Ponts et Chaussées.

In 1875, Becquerel entered the Department de Ponts et Chaussées as an engineer. He also began his private scientific investigations and tutored students at the École Polytechnique. His grandfather died in 1878. Several months later his wife died following the birth of their son, Jean. Becquerel became assistant to his father, a professor of physics at the Musée d'Histoire Naturelle. In 1888, he obtained his doctor's degree from the University of Paris. In 1889, he gained membership in the Academy of Sciences. In 1890, Becquerel remarried. In 1892, he succeeded to his father's two chairs of physics, at the museum and at the Conservatoire des Arts et Métiers.

## Scientific Career

Henri Becquerel's father's area of concentration was the study of luminescent substances. Such substances emit radiation, especially visible light, such as in fluorescence and phosphorescence. When Becquerel began his scientific investigations, he continued in his father's footsteps. He was greatly impressed with the work of the British physicist Michael Faraday (1791-1867), especially by the "Faraday effect," which has to do with magneto-optical rotation. Having concentrated his efforts in the area of magneto-optics, he thought that he had deduced the relationship between rotatory magnetic power and the index of refraction. He published his formula in 1875. Later, however, he found that his conception was wrong, because the law for magnetic substances proved to be different from that for diamagnetic ones and also different for dissolved magnetic substances.

Since the Faraday effect had not yet been examined in respect to gases, Becquerel turned his mind in that direction; between 1878 and 1880, he conducted experiments in that area. Although his formula for the rotatory magnetic power of magnetic substances was too general to apply to the different classes of solids that existed or to dissolved magnetic elements, nevertheless it allowed him to imagine what magnitude for gases was to be expected. The result of his experiments was that he demonstrated that gases were "normal," that is, had rotatory power similar to those of solids and liquids. He found, however, that oxygen was an exception, since its magnetic property made it "anomalous." The Dutch physicist Pieter Zeeman, under the direction of his teacher, Hendrik Antoon Lorentz, began to study the spectral series of gaseous elements in the late 1890's. Zeeman coined the words "normal" and "anomalous" to describe the "Zeeman effect," wherein a source of light in an intense magnetic field has spectral lines that are split into more or less complicated multiplets, depending upon the direction of the magnetic field. "Normal" meant that the pattern could be simply explained; "anomalous" meant that the effect might or might not be subject to simple explanation.

As a result of his own study of gases, Becquerel became interested in the effect of a huge thickness of magnetized oxygen on light. To begin his investigation, he studied the action of Earth's magnetic field on carbon disulphide. From this study he deduced the intensity of this field and proposed that such intensity become the standard of the strength of electric current. It has been estimated that Earth's magnetic field extends about 80,000 kilometers above Earth.

Becquerel had discovered radioactivity shortly before Zeeman's discovery. Because he himself had been hoping to observe the Zeeman effect as early as the late 1880's, when Zeeman's discovery was announced, Becquerel allowed himself to become temporarily diverted from his studies in radioactivity. He believed the Zeeman effect corresponded to what he had been looking for unsuccessfully. Therefore, cleverly utilizing sodium vapor, he produced magnetic rotation, the Zeeman effect, and anomalous dispersion. This last phenomenon is an inversion of the expected change in refractive index with a wavelength close to an absorption band. Becquerel conceived of electrons as simply filling the spaces between "ether" and "matter," especially since this conception appeared to support "the vortex theory of magnetism" to which he had committed himself.

After investigating the magnetic properties of nickel and cobalt, Becquerel published his findings in a memoir in 1879. He showed ozone (triatomic oxygen formed in the ozone layer of the stratosphere) to be more magnetic than oxygen itself, and he found that nickel-plated iron became magnetic when heated to redness. He also conducted (with his father) temperature tests of underground soil and verified Jean-Baptiste-Joseph Fourier's 1821 theory of heat conduction. During 1883-1884, he studied the bands of the infrared solar spectrum as well as the spectra of other substances—such as water, the atmosphere, rare metals, and metallic vapors—opening a new field to spectrum analysis.

Becquerel investigated the phosphorescence of uranium salts and their emission spectrum, and he attempted to provide the law of distribution of their absorption bands. He found that the uranium nonphosphorescent salts had absorption bands stemming from the same law as that which controlled the phosphorescent ones. To him this feature indicated that the uranium salts had very unusual molecular structures. He further studied the absorption bands of numerous minerals, taking a special interest in the rare-Earth metal didymium and noting the differences of their variations with the plane polarization of light. He concluded that the absorption of a molecule is not influenced by molecules nearby but that a single molecule acts, as it were, independently. He also held that if a crystal shows absorption bands corresponding to directions other than the axial ones, then this characteristic indicates that other elements are present. Since didymium, formerly considered a single element, was found to be a mixture of the rare-Earth elements neodymium and praseodymium (often found associated with cerium and lanthanum), this occurrence confirmed his prediction. In 1891 he described, for the first time, the phosphorescent spectra of minerals subjected to heat.

Becquerel's association with his father, who was especially interested in phosphorescent substances, and the influence of the "new physics" of the first half of the nineteenth century, with its central theory of the "all-pervading ether," naturally colored Becquerel's perceptions. When he learned that the source of Röntgen's X rays was the spot of light on the wall of the glass vacuum tube that had received the stream of cathode rays (electrons, with a negative charge), he immediately wondered whether this emission was caused by the vibrations which produced the phosphorescence and whether all phosphorescent substances emit similar rays. Although this tentative hypothesis proved false, it did lead to his discovery of radioactivity. If Röntgen can be credited as starting the second scientific revolution (the first having been started by Nicolaus Copernicus), then Becquerel can be credited with taking the next giant stride.

In his "Becquerel Memorial Lecture" of 1912, English physicist Sir Oliver Joseph Lodge compared the novelty of Röntgen's discovery with that of Becquerel, both discoveries, to him, being important discoveries of fact. Although Röntgen's discovery was sufficiently new to astonish the public, the origin, existence, and behavior of X rays could be explained by current theories of physics, once the notion was accepted that rays from a cathode tube consisted of minute electrical charges. Their origin as the result of a stream of electrons striking against something solid was provided for by Lamor's "theory of radiation"; their existence could be explained by considering electrons as "pulses in the ether"; and their immunity to refraction, that is, to being diverted, was accounted for by Hermann von Helmholtz's "theory of dispersion." Yet, said Lodge, in comparing the novelty of the two discoveries, he was obliged "to give the palm" to Becquerel, because "the spontaneous splitting up of atoms, and the consequent expulsion of constituent fragments, was not provided for by any theory. It was a revolutionary fact. . . ."

Following his discovery of radioactivity in 1896, Becquerel found in 1899 that the uranium radiation consisted partly of tiny charged particles. The next year he became aware that the negatively charged particles were identical to those Sir Joseph John Thomson had identified with cathode rays and named "electrons."

Becquerel concluded that these electrons must come from within the atoms. In 1901 he identified this activity as the radioactive part of his compound. Thus he offered evidence for the first time that the atom was not the structureless, faceless thing that John Dalton (1766-1844) had envisioned; on the contrary, it possessed an internal structure related to and associated with electrons.

The consequences of Becquerel's work are to be observed in the development of modern physics, for the year 1900 is conventionally employed by historians of science to distinguish classical physics from the modern physics of the twentieth century. Becquerel's research resulted in a closer look and a more persistent effort to determine the structure of the atom. This search has produced new models of the atom, greater dependence on mathematics, and new special fields of study such as particle physics and nuclear physics. Becquerel's work also laid the foundation for a theory of radioactive disintegration of elements, marking the first human manipulation effecting the change of one element into another. Finally, Becquerel's work revealed the immense quantity of potential energy within the atom. This view prompted the nuclear research that led to the discovery of uranium fission and eventually to the harnessing of nuclear power.

Apart from sharing in the Nobel Prize of 1903, Becquerel received numerous honors following his unique discovery of 1896. In 1897 he was elected president of the Société Française de Physique. In 1900 he was awarded the Rumford Medal by the Royal Society of London. In 1905 the U.S. National Academy of Sciences nominated him for the Barnard Medal, which was presented to him at Columbia University's 151st commencement. The next year Becquerel was elected vice president of the French Academy of Sciences, and he later succeeded to the presidency. In 1907 the Berlin Academy of Sciences conferred on him the Helmholtz Medal, and in 1946 the French government issued a commemorative stamp to celebrate the fiftieth anniversary of Becquerel's discovery of radioactivity.

## Bibliography

*Primary*
PHYSICS: Becquerel's original works consist of more than 150 papers and notes in various reports and journals. Most of these are in French, some are in German, and at least one is in English. His longest work is a *mémoire* he wrote concerning his investigations into radioactivity, "Recherches sur une propriété nouvelle de la matière: Activité radiante spontanée ou radioactivité de la matière," in *Mémoires de l'Académie des sciences, Paris*, vol. 46, 1903. Papers Becquerel published up to 1900 are printed in the Royal Society's *Catalogue of Scientific Papers*, vol. 9, 166-167, and vol. 13, 395-396. His papers on radioactivity are all printed in the *Comptes rendus hebdomadaires des séances de l'Académie des sciences*, and include the following: "Sur les radiations émises par phosphorescence," vol. 122, 1896; "Sur les radiations invisibles émises par les corps phosphorescents," vol. 122, 1896; "Sur quelques propriétés nouvelles des radiations invisibles émises par divers corps phosphorescents," vol. 122, 1896; "Sur les radiations invisibles

émises par les sels d'uranium," vol. 122, 1896; "Sur les propriétés différentes des radiations invisibles émises par les sels d'uranium, et du rayonnement de la paroi anticathode d'un tube de Crookes," vol. 122, 1896; "Émission de radiations nouvelles par l'uranium métallique," vol. 122, 1896; "Sur diverses propriétés des rayons uraniques," vol. 123, 1896; "Sur la loi de décharge dans l'air de l'uranium électrisé," vol. 124, 1897; "Recherches sur les rayons uraniques," vol. 124, 1897; "Influence d'un champ magnétique sur le rayonnement des corps radio-actifs," vol. 129, 1899; "Sur le rayonnement des corps radio-actifs," vol. 129, 1899; "Contribution à l'étude du rayonnement du radium," vol. 130, 1900; "Sur la dispersion du rayonnement du radium dans un champ magnétique," vol. 130, 1900; "Déviation du rayonnement du radium dans un champ électrique," vol. 130, 1900; "Sur la transparence de l'aluminum pour le rayonnement du radium," vol. 130, 1900; "Note sur le rayonnement de l'uranium," vol. 130, 1900, and vol. 131, 1900; "Sur la radioactivité secondaire des métaux," vol. 132, 1901; "Sur l'analyse magnétique des rayons du radium et du rayonnement secondaire provoqué par ces rayons," vol. 132, 1901; "Sur quelques effets chimiques produits par la rayonnement du radium," vol. 133, 1901; "Sur la radio-activité de l'uranium," vol. 133, 1901; "Sur quelques propriétés du rayonnement des corps radioactifs," vol. 134, 1902; "Sur le rayonnement du polonium et du radium," vol. 136, 1903; "Sur une propriété des rayons α du radium," vol. 136, 1903. A more extensive list of papers in a variety of publications is included in *J. C. Poggendorffs biographisch-literarisches Handwörterbuch für Mathematik, Astronomie, Physik mit Geophysik, Chemie, Kristallographie und verwandte Wissensgebiete*, vol. 6, *1923 bis 1931*, edited by Hans Stobbe, first of four parts, 1936. Becquerel's Nobel lecture, entitled "On Radioactivity, a New Property of Matter," is to be found in *Nobelstiftelsen, Physics*, vol. 1, *1901-1921*, 1964.

## Secondary

Badash, Lawrence. " 'Chance Favors the Prepared Mind': Henri Becquerel and the Discovery of Radioactivity." *Archives internationales d'histoire des sciences* 18 (1965): 55-66. A relatively modern view of Becquerel's discovery of radioactivity and an appraisal of his accomplishment as compared to the review and assessment of Sir Oliver Lodge in his famous "Becquerel Memorial Lecture" of 1912.

Dahl, Paul. *Introduction to Electron and Ion Optics*. New York: Academic Press, 1973. A sound introduction to electron and ion optics that can serve as a starting point for readers who wish to delve deeper into electron and ion optical design. Matrix formulation is used in treating electrostatic and magnetic lenses and analyzers, while the concept of beam emittance is used to describe a beam of particles and in treating particle analyzers and particle sources.

Enge, Harald A. *Introduction to Nuclear Physics*. Reading, Mass.: Addison-Wesley, 1966. Although some foreknowledge of elementary wave mechanics is expected of the reader, this text is a well-organized presentation of such topics as the nuclear two-body problem; the ground (or stable) state properties of atoms; shell and collective atomic models; alpha-, beta-, and gamma-ray solid state devices; nuclear reactions; nuclear energy (fission and fusion); and elementary particles. Some appendices review quantum mechanics, focusing on ion beams; there is also a table of nuclides. Selected experiments are described to encourage further understanding of nuclear forces and nucleonic structure.

Lodge, Sir Oliver. "Becquerel Memorial Lecture." In *Memorial Lectures Delivered Before the Chemical Society*. Vol. 2. London: Chemical Society, 1914. An excellent review of the state of physics from Faraday to 1912. Shows Lodge's dissatisfaction with the drift of physics toward materialism and the increasing skepticism of physicists. Presents a fine, detailed description of Becquerel's experiments and a summary of his great accomplishments and their enormous consequences.

Ranc, Albert. *Henri Becquerel et la découverte de la radioactivité*. Paris: Éditions de la Liberté, 1946. The only book-length biography of Becquerel available. According to at least one critic the study is weakened by "padding."

Romer, Alfred. "(Antoine-) Henri Becquerel." In *Dictionary of Scientific Biography*, edited by Charles Coulston Gillespie, vol. 1. New York: Charles Scribner's Sons, 1970. Excellent short account of Becquerel's family background, his education, the drift of his scientific investigations, and his chief accomplishments. The article includes a short but important bibliographical description.

Wheaton, Bruce R. *The Tiger and the Shark: Empirical Roots of Wave-Particle Dualism*. Cambridge, England: Cambridge University Press, 1983. An excellent description of the struggle between wave and particle theorists while the foundations of quantum mechanics were being laid from about the year 1896 to 1925. The struggle concluded after the introduction of Heisenberg's uncertainty principle, which had destructive implications for the traditional theory of causality and gave the *coup de grâce* to the nineteenth century philosophy of determinism.

*Richard P. Benton*

# 1903

### Physics
Antoine-Henri Becquerel, France
Pierre Curie, France
Marie Curie, Poland and France

### Chemistry
Svante Arrhenius, Sweden

### Physiology or Medicine
Niels R. Finsen, Denmark

### Literature
Bjørnstjerne Bjørnson, Norway

### Peace
Sir William Cremer, Great Britain

**PIERRE CURIE**

**MARIE CURIE**

# PIERRE CURIE and MARIE CURIE
# 1903

## Pierre Curie

*Born:* Paris, France; May 15, 1859
*Died:* Paris, France; April 19, 1906
*Nationality:* French
*Areas of concentration:* Radioactivity, magnetism, and crystallography

## Marie Curie

*Born:* Warsaw, Poland; November 7, 1867
*Died:* Sancellemoz, near Sallanches, France; July 4, 1934
*Nationality:* Polish; after 1895, French
*Area of concentration:* Radioactivity

*Building on Antoine-Henri Becquerel's discovery of spontaneous radioactivity in uranium, the Curies observed that thorium also exhibits this property, and they found two elements previously unknown, polonium and radium, both more radioactive than uranium. This activity permitted more careful study of radiation and revealed that the atom is not indivisible*

## The Award

*Presentation*

On December 10, 1903, H. R. Törnebladh, President of the Royal Swedish Academy of Sciences, presented the third Nobel Prize in Physics to Antoine-Henri Becquerel, Pierre Curie, and Marie (née Skłodowska) Curie. Törnebladh began his address by reviewing the work of the first recipient of the Nobel Prize in Physics, Wilhelm Conrad Röntgen, the discoverer of X rays. Röntgen had produced these rays by bombarding substances with cathode rays (an electric current created by high tension electricity in a highly rarefied gas). Becquerel observed that even ordinary light could prompt these emissions, and in the course of his experiments he found that uranium compounds emitted such rays even without stimulation.

The phenomenon of spontaneous radioactivity excited the Curies to seek other materials exhibiting this property, and they soon found that thorium behaved much like uranium. While working with pitchblende, a uranium ore, they noted more radioactivity than expected from the quantity of uranium and thorium; they therefore concluded that other radioactive substances, as yet unknown, must be present, and they succeeded in identifying two of these, thorium and radium; a coworker, André-Louis Debierne, discovered a third, actinium.

Because radium is so much more active than uranium, it allowed scientists to examine radiation more precisely and so determine its various components. Some of its rays behave like X rays and are unaffected by a magnetic or electrical field;

others, behaving like cathode rays, can be bent by such forces. Törnebladh also commented on the Curies' recent discovery that radium emits large amounts of heat in a seemingly spontaneous and constant manner, thus providing a new energy source. He remarked that such findings reveal new information about the very nature of matter and so usher in a new era of science.

The speech concluded with a tribute to the cooperation between the Curies. Their joint efforts showed how husband and wife could support each other in their work and the manner in which people of different nationalities (in this case, French and Polish) could unite to advance the cause of science.

*Nobel lecture*

Speaking for Marie Curie and himself, Pierre Curie delivered the Nobel lecture in Stockholm on June 6, 1905; other commitments had prevented their attending the ceremonies in 1903 and presenting the address at the customary time. The delay of eighteen months allowed Curie to provide a more complete explanation of radioactivity than he would have been able to offer earlier.

The speech, an abstract of lectures that Pierre Curie was presenting at the Sorbonne, contains three parts. The first section reviews the discovery of radium, in essence repeating what Törnebladh had stated in his presentation but emphasizing that the Curies had coined the term "radioactive" and that Marie Curie had established the atomic weight of radium at 225.93 (the accepted weight is 226). As Marie Curie would do in her 1911 address upon receiving the chemistry prize, Pierre was careful to stress the joint nature of their discoveries and to give each partner ample credit.

Pierre then turned to the properties of this new element, some of these discovered by the Curies, some by other researchers around the world. One characteristic, again noted by Törnebladh, is the release of large quantities of heat: One gram of radium gives off one hundred calories each hour and continues to do so over many years. Another trait is the emission of three types of rays: alpha (which resemble positively charged helium atoms), beta (which act like electrons), and gamma (similar to X rays).

Radioactive substances also produce a radioactive gas—what Ernest Rutherford called an "emanation"—and this gas loses its radioactivity over time in an exponential way, so that the activity of radon, the emanation of radium, diminishes by one half every four days, the emanation of thorium loses half its radioactivity every fifty-five seconds, and that of actinium every three seconds. This same exponential decay, though not yet apparent in radium because of its long half-life, is evident in polonium, which loses half its radioactivity in 140 days. The Curies further observed that substances placed near radioactive materials become radioactive themselves. This induced radioactivity decays in the same manner as that of the emanations and polonium. Pierre Curie concluded this portion of his speech by noting that other scientists had found spontaneous production of helium from radium.

The third part of the address considered the revolutionary impact of these observations on the entire range of physical and life sciences. Radium offered a new research tool for physics because of its radiation. Especially useful were the beta rays, because they led to discoveries about the relationship between mass and motion. The realization that radium emits electrically charged particles also over-turned the old notion that matter, at least at the atomic level, is inert; such naturally occurring instability revolutionized the way scientists looked at the atom.

In chemistry, radium fulfilled the ancient dream of the alchemists of changing one element into another. Geologists could use these findings to determine the age of a substance, for radium and uranium always occur together in a fixed ratio, and radioactivity decays at a constant rate. By measuring a mineral's radioactivity, one could thus learn how long it had lain in the earth. Meteorologists might discover that radioactivity plays a role in the production of rain and clouds, and biologists could use radium and radon to cure diseases.

Pierre Curie concluded his address with a note of caution, for he realized that radioactive substances could harm as well as heal. Prolonged exposure could cause death, and the Curies wondered what might happen if such material fell into criminal hands. He likened the discovery to that of Alfred Nobel: Dynamite aided in peaceful projects, such as road construction, but it also killed people in war. Although Curie did not mention the fact in his speech, the French Ministry of Defense had already spoken to him about possible military applications of radium for gunsights and mine safety-catches that would allow for fighting at night. Yet in the early days of the new century, Curie optimistically predicted that more good than bad would result from these scientific advances.

## Critical reception

By 1903, the work of the Curies was already well-known. Journalists, autograph seekers, and the curious generally, as well as scientists, repeatedly visited both their small laboratory and their home. Radium was being used to treat cancer and a variety of other diseases, and the Curies' contribution to medicine was the more highly regarded because of their refusal to patent their discovery or otherwise profit from it. Hence the Swedish Academy's decision seemed expected; most journals and newspapers merely reported it without comment, since the Curies had already become something of a legend. Moreover, in the early awards some detected a Scandinavian bias. *The New York Times* noted that three and a half of the five prizes in 1903 had been awarded to those with Scandinavian ties, including Becquerel. The newspaper's only reservation about the selection in physics concerned the man with whom the Curies had to share the prize; the paper maintained that the Curies deserved it all to themselves.

The Curies' work had already prompted an offer from the University of Geneva (1900) and an invitation from the Royal Institution, London, to deliver a Friday night lecture (June, 1903). The Royal Society had added another tribute in November, 1903, when it awarded the Curies its prestigious Humphry Davy Medal. The Nobel Prize heightened this worldwide recognition. From America came a request that the Curies offer a lecture series, with the Curies naming their price. Telegrams piled up in the laboratory, dinner invitations proliferated, cabaret acts represented the Curies on stage, magazines asked for articles, and an American requested permission to name a racehorse for them. Even France belatedly recognized their achievement. In 1904 the Sorbonne finally created a chair of physics for Pierre, and in 1905 the Académie des Sciences, which had rejected him two years earlier, reversed its decision and voted him a member.

Only a few scientists expressed private reservations about the award. Ernest Rutherford, whose research Pierre Curie cited in his Nobel lecture and who was himself to win a Nobel Prize in Chemistry in 1908, admired the Curies' diligence but believed, with some justification, that they did not fully comprehend the nature of radioactivity or its implications for understanding the atom. Henry Bumstead, an American physicist, wrote that he regarded the Curies' research as less original than Rutherford's, and Bertram Borden Boltwood later remarked that Marie Curie was a fool. Boltwood, who taught at Harvard, was influential in persuading his school not to join Yale, the University of Chicago, Columbia University, the University of Pennsylvania, and numerous other institutions in awarding Marie Curie an honorary doctorate when she came to the United States in 1921. All these men were, however, the Curies' rivals; apart from them, few doubted that the award had been well bestowed.

## Biographies

The younger son of Eugène and Sophie-Claire Curie, Pierre Curie was born in Paris on May 15, 1859. Initially taught at home by his physician father, he entered school at fourteen and two years later received his bachelor of science degree. After taking his *licence* in physical sciences in November, 1877, he became a laboratory assistant to Paul Desains at the Sorbonne. He then assumed the post of director of laboratory work at the École de Physique et Chimie Industrielles, also serving as professor there from 1894 to 1904.

Marie Skłodowska Curie was born in Warsaw, Poland, on November 7, 1867. Her father, Wladislaw Skłodowski, was a schoolteacher with a special interest in physics and mathematics, and her mother, Bronislava Boguska Skłodowska, had also taught but had given up her occupation when her oldest child, Sofia, was born. A precocious child, Marie taught herself to read at the age of four, and she was graduated from high school at the age of fifteen with highest honors.

Already as an adolescent she exhibited a dedication to excellence and a determination to drive herself hard. The price she would pay for such exertion also revealed itself early: Following graduation, she suffered a nervous collapse that required her to spend the next year with an uncle in the countryside, away from books and lessons. When she recovered, she returned to Warsaw and resumed her studies at an underground "Floating University," the regular forms of higher education in Russian-ruled Poland being closed to women. She also began tutoring to raise money that would support her older sister Bronia, who had gone to Paris to pursue a medical degree. In 1891 Marie joined Bronia. Two years later she received a degree in physical sciences from the Sorbonne, finishing first in her class, and in 1894, supported by the Alexandrowitch Scholarship of six hundred rubles from her native Poland, she took a degree in mathematics.

## Scientific Careers

As she was completing her studies at the Sorbonne, Marie Skłodowska was working on a project involving the magnetic properties of steel. A fellow Pole told her about Pierre Curie, who was also investigating the subject, and so the two met in the spring of 1894.

At the age of thirty-five, Pierre already had contributed much to the understanding of crystals and magnetism. Since ancient times, people had observed that certain substances, after they had been burnt, attracted bits of ash and other debris. This phenomenon is called pyro-electricity. Working with his brother Jacques, Pierre discovered that when asymmetrical crystals are compressed or allowed to expand, they emit an electrical charge; they called this property piezoelectricity (from the Greek word meaning "to press"). The Curie brothers thus showed that mechanical energy can be converted into electrical energy.

Gabriel Lippmann, one of Marie's teachers at the Sorbonne (who would himself win a Nobel Prize in Physics in 1908) predicted that the reverse effect would also occur: An electrical charge could distort a crystal's structure, and so electrical energy could be transformed into mechanical energy. Jacques and Pierre Curie demonstrated the accuracy of Lippmann's theory, and they formulated the physical law that all asymmetrical crystals would exhibit piezoelectricity; between 1880 and 1883 the brothers published seven papers on their discoveries. This research not only led to a better understanding of crystals and symmetry but also allowed for applications in such devices as the quartz watch and highly sensitive microphones; during World War I this knowledge provided a means of detecting submarines. Because the amounts of electricity generated by the compression of crystals are minute, the Curies designed more sensitive equipment than had previously been available. One item, the quartz electrometer, would play an important role in the study of radioactivity, and they built the first modern balance, a magnetic scale capable of measuring 0.00001 gram.

Pierre Curie's investigation of crystals ended in 1883, when Jacques moved to Montpellier to become a professor of mineralogy and Pierre assumed a post at the École de Physique et Chimie Industrielles. Although he had little equipment and no laboratory—conducting his experiments in a hallway—he began research into magnetism. His discoveries underlie all modern studies in the field and led directly to Louis-Eugène-Félix Néel's Nobel Prize (1970) for work in this area.

Scientists had identified three different types of magnetism. Ferromagnetic substances, such as iron (hence *ferro*, referring to iron), display a high degree of magnetism. Paramagnetic materials are magnetized in the same direction as iron, but much less strongly. Diamagnetic substances, such as those that are paramagnetic, are weakly magnetized, but in the direction opposite to iron. Curie wondered whether any object could exhibit all three forms of magnetism, and he also examined the effect of heat on these forces. He found that ferromagnetism and paramagnetism are related; both result from the actions of groups of atoms and are affected by heat. The law named for Pierre Curie states that paramagnetism varies inversely with absolute temperature, and the Curie point is that temperature at which ferromagnetic materials become paramagnetic. Diamagnetism, though, does not vary with either temperature or phase (solid, liquid, or gas), because it is a property of the atom.

William Thomson, Lord Kelvin, the doyen of nineteenth century British classical physics, was so impressed with this work that he persuaded the École de Physique et Chimie Industrielles to award Curie a professorship (1894). Curie still had no laboratory or other support for his research, and while the extra money for teaching was welcome, the additional responsibility distracted him from his investigations. In 1895 he belatedly received the Planté Prize for his discovery of piezoelectricity, but he probably would have died largely unrecognized had he not met a twenty-six-year-old Polish student seeking advice and laboratory space in 1894. They were married on July 26 the following year.

At first Marie's research followed Pierre's. She reviewed the magnetic properties of various steels, publishing a thorough account of her findings in 1897, and her initial investigation of radioactivity involved the search for substances other than uranium that spontaneously generate an electrical field. For her project she used Pierre's electrometer because it was sufficiently sensitive to measure minute charges. She soon found that thorium behaved like uranium; Gerhard Schmidt of Germany made the same observation. More important was another discovery which only she made, and she quickly grasped its meaning. Marie Curie noted that moisture, the presence of other elements, and the condition (powdered or solid) of uranium did not affect its radioactivity. Hence she concluded that radioactivity must not be the result of interaction between atoms but characteristic of the atom itself. This realization that the atom is not inert but is subject to change underlies the entire field of nuclear physics. In the 1890's the idea was so revolutionary that even the Curies hesitated to adopt it; as late as 1905 Pierre Curie remarked in his Nobel address that perhaps radioactive elements draw their energy from outside sources, and Lord Kelvin died believing in the inviolability of the atom. Further research by Rutherford, Frederick Soddy, and the Curies themselves would confirm Marie's bold guess.

Marie also noticed that pitchblende and chalcolite, ores of uranium and thorium, were more radioactive than expected based solely on the contents of these two elements. She surmised that one or more unidentified substances must be present, and in April, 1898, Pierre abandoned, temporarily he thought, his work on magnetism and symmetry to assist Marie. On July 18, 1898, the couple issued their first joint publication, "Sur une substance nouvelle radioactive continue dans la pitchblende" (on a new radioactive substance contained in pitchblende), announcing the discovery of a new element, polonium, named for Marie's native country. Five months later, on December 26, they published the news of a second previously unknown radioactive element, radium.

Identifying two new elements, especially two new radioactive elements, captured the public imagination already fascinated with uranium and radioactivity; in the year following Becquerel's initial discovery, almost fifty books and some thousand articles had been published on the subject. The true importance of radium lay, however, in its providing a tool to investigate further the nature of these mysterious forces that Becquerel had observed. Because radium is so much more active than uranium—more than a million times more in its pure state—it was a far better source of emissions. Over the next four years, Marie Curie devoted herself to purifying this new substance while her husband studied its properties. Already in 1899 they observed that nonradioactive substances placed near radium become radioactive for a time, and in 1900 the University of Geneva was sufficiently impressed with the Curies' work to offer Pierre a professorship, a laboratory, and research assistants who would work under Marie Curie's direction.

The offer was attractive, for not only was the Curies' income of 3,600 francs a year embarrassingly small, but also their research facilities were virtually nonexistent. Radium is such a small component of pitchblende—only three parts per million—that to isolate a tenth of a gram of radium chloride Marie had to purify eight tons of ore. This she did in what the German chemist Friedrich Wilhelm Ostwald called "a cross between a stable and a potato cellar." Because of the poisonous fumes produced, she often worked outside, since her so-called laboratory lacked proper ventilation.

Yet to move to Geneva would interrupt the research that was yielding repeated discoveries. Between 1898 and 1902, the Curies published thirty-two papers on the physical, chemical, and biological properties of their newfound element. Jules-Henri Poincaré, the French mathematician, also encouraged the Curies to stay in France by persuading the Sorbonne to offer Pierre a teaching post. At the same time Marie received a part-time lectureship in physics at the École Normale Supérieure de Jeunes Filles at Sèvres.

The added income from this teaching was welcome, but the increased demands on their time was not. They were suffering from radiation sickness, too, although neither they nor their doctors recognized the cause of their fatigue and Pierre's joint pains. Still they persevered, analyzing the alpha and beta rays they observed—Paul Villard later found gamma rays—noting the vast quantities of heat radium produced, seemingly forever. One scientist claimed that the Curies had at last discovered the equivalent of perpetual motion. They also determined that radium and radon killed cancer cells faster than healthy ones, and medical applications of this discovery began immediately.

On June 25, 1903, Marie Curie presented the research she had undertaken for her doctorate. Rarely has a dissertation contained such revolutionary findings: The Swedish chemist Svante August Arrhenius, winner of the 1903 Nobel Prize in

Chemistry, called the discovery of radium the single most important event in chemistry in a hundred years. Recognition was greater abroad than at home. The Royal Society awarded the Curies the Davy Medal, the Swedish Academy gave them the Nobel Prize, scientific societies around the world elected them to honorary membership, but the French Académie des Sciences voted not to admit Pierre Curie.

Even France, though, could not long ignore the Curies' achievement. In 1904, the French parliament at last created a chair of physics for him at the Sorbonne and gave him a laboratory with a small staff to be supervised by Marie; the following year the Académie des Sciences reversed its 1903 decision and admitted Pierre by eight votes. Unhappily, he did not enjoy his triumphs for long: On April 19, 1906, he was run over by a horse-drawn truck and died instantly.

After rejecting a state pension, Marie received her husband's post at the Sorbonne on May 1, 1906, and fifteen years to the day that she had enrolled there, she crossed the university's courtyard to deliver the first lecture ever presented by a female faculty member of that institution. On November 5, 1906, the doors to the hall opened at 1:00 P.M.; at 1:05 P.M. they closed on a room packed with students, scientists, and curious onlookers who strained to hear this small woman begin her talk with the last sentence her husband had spoken at that lecturn. In that month, too, Andrew Carnegie donated $50,000 in 5 percent gold bonds to provide scholarships to students working in Curie's laboratory.

They already had a new project, for in *The Times* of London of August 9, 1906, Lord Kelvin had asserted that radium is not an element but rather a compound of lead and helium. Marie Curie had isolated a radium compound in 1902, but she had not yet purified the metal itself. This she succeeded in doing in 1908, and for her work she received a second Nobel Prize, this time in chemistry, in 1911.

Once more, recognition was greater abroad than in France. In the same year that the Curies had won their first Nobel Prize, the Académie des Sciences had voted to deny Pierre membership. In 1911, the Académie refused to admit Marie; no woman would enter until 1979. The French seemed more fascinated with her private life than her scientific achievements, reveling in accounts of her affair with fellow scientist Paul Langevin. Curie was so devastated by the publicity that she was unable to work for more than a year, recording no entries in her laboratory notebook between October 7, 1911, and December 3, 1912.

Her subsequent work did not produce the dramatic breakthroughs that had marked the early research, but she remained active for the rest of her life. She defined and prepared the standard for radium, appropriately named the "curie"; she served as a permanent member of the Solvay conferences from their inception in 1911; and, despite her selfless refusal to profit from the discovery of radium, she sought, as a member of the League of Nations' Committee on International Cooperation, to secure protection for scientific discoveries and remuneration for those who made them. During World War I she devoted her energy to the wounded, securing twenty radiological cars (called *petites curies*) in France, equipping two hundred military hospitals with X-ray machines, and personally training some 150 radiological nurses who used this equipment to help more than a million soldiers.

Her fame twice prompted Americans to donate a gram of radium, worth $100,000 at the time: the first in 1921 for her Institut du Radium in Paris, the second in 1929 for the Marie Skłodowska-Curie Institute in Warsaw. These gifts permitted further medical, chemical, and physics research. From her Paris facilities came the discovery of francium by Marguerite Perey, analysis of alpha rays by Salomon Rosenblum, and the creation of an artificial radioactive element by Frédéric Joliot and Irène Joliot-Curie. In December, 1935, these two scientists, who had been married a decade earlier, stood before the Swedish Academy in Stockholm to receive another Nobel Prize for the Curie family, this time in chemistry. Thirty years earlier, Pierre had spoken for himself and his wife while Marie sat in the audience. This time Irène Joliot-Curie delivered the acceptance speech for the pair, suggesting that her mother had advanced the cause of women as well as science in proving that research was not an exclusively male preserve.

Marie Curie did not live to see her daughter's triumph. Worn out by years of exposure to radiation, she died of leukemia on July 4, 1934, and was buried with her husband at Sceaux. The woman who had shown that the world is in a constant state of flux was finally at rest.

## Bibliography

*Primary*

PHYSICS: Pierre Curie: *Œuvres de Pierre Curie*, 1908. Marie Curie: *Recherches sur les substances radioactives*, 1903 (*Radio-active Substances*, 1903); *Les Théories modernes relatives à l'électricité et à la matière*, 1906; *Traité de radioactivité*, 1910; *L'Isotopie et les éléments isotopes*, 1924; *Radioactivité*, 1935.

OTHER NONFICTION: Marie Curie: *La Radiologie et la guerre*, 1921; *Pierre Curie*, 1923.

*Secondary*

Curie, Eve. *Madame Curie: A Biography*. Translated by Vincent Sheean. Garden City, N.Y.: Doubleday, Doran, 1938. This biography by the Curies' younger daughter paints a flattering, almost saintly picture of the scientists. Eve Curie offers a firsthand account of her parents' life and balances scientific discussion with revelations about their domestic life. The starting point for subsequent biographers.

Giroud, Françoise. *Marie Curie: A Life*. Translated by Lydia Davis. New York: Holmes & Meier, 1986. Giroud does not attempt a scholarly analysis of the Curies or their work but rather offers a personal appreciation that focuses on Marie Curie's life. Although the emphasis is on the domestic and emotional facets, a good overview of the science is also provided.

Klickstein, Herbert S. "Pierre Curie: An Appreciation of His Scientific Achievements." *Journal of Chemical Education* 24 (June, 1947): 278-282. When Pierre Curie was alive, he tended to eclipse his wife and her achievements; more recently the opposite has occurred. Klickstein recalls Pierre's work, especially his discoveries before he turned his attention to radioactivity. Provides a chronological listing of Pierre's fifty-eight journal articles.

Raven, Susan. "First Great Woman Scientist—and Much More." *The New York Times Magazine* 6 (December 3, 1967): 52-53. For the hundredth anniversary of Marie Curie's birth, Raven presented a summary view of the scientist's life and accomplishments. Contains no new information but includes some telling photographs and provides a good, brief introduction to the woman and her work.

Reid, Robert. *Marie Curie*. New York: Saturday Review Press, 1974. Head of the British Broadcasting Corporation's science department, Reid tells his story simply and accurately. Drawing on private papers and journalistic accounts of the period, he sets the Curies within their scientific and social milieu, highlighting the significance of their discoveries without minimizing their limitations. Well indexed, with a selective but wide-ranging bibliography.

*Joseph Rosenblum*

# 1904

### Physics
Lord Rayleigh, Great Britain

### Chemistry
Sir William Ramsay, Great Britain

### Physiology or Medicine
Ivan Pavlov, Russia

### Literature
José Echegaray y Eizaguirre, Spain
Frédéric Mistral, France

### Peace
Institute of International Law

# LORD RAYLEIGH
# 1904

*Born:* Langford Grove, near Maldon, Essex, England; November 12, 1842
*Died:* Terling Place, Witham, Essex, England; June 30, 1919
*Nationality:* British
*Areas of concentration:* Acoustics and optics

*Lord Rayleigh's investigation of the density of atmospheric nitrogen as compared to nitrogen prepared by other means led to the discovery of the noble gas argon*

## The Award

*Presentation*

Professor J. E. Cederblom, President of the Royal Swedish Academy of Sciences, presented the Nobel Prize in Physics to Lord Rayleigh on December 11, 1904, on behalf of the Royal Swedish Academy of Sciences and the King of Sweden, from whom Lord Rayleigh accepted the prize. Cederblom's presentation speech began with a survey of those who had contributed to the knowledge of the composition and nature of the atmosphere. The presenter continued with a discussion of the surprise that accompanied the discovery of a new atmospheric gas, argon, and lauded the accurate experimentation of Rayleigh. Cederblom then described the tests carried out by Lord Rayleigh and Sir William Ramsay, the 1904 chemistry Nobel laureate, that led to the discovery of argon and the determination of its properties. Cederblom concluded by linking Rayleigh's discovery of argon with Ramsay's discovery of helium.

*Nobel lecture*

Lord Rayleigh presented his Nobel lecture on December 12, 1904. He began by summarizing the investigations which had led him to the discovery of argon, first explaining that Prout's law (that all atomic weights should be simple multiples of the atomic weight of hydrogen) did not stand up to some previous experiments on oxygen. This evidence prompted Rayleigh to consider the redetermination of the densities of the atmospheric gases. He continued his lecture with a description of the way in which such density measurements could be made.

Rayleigh described the particular measurements in nitrogen, commenting that he had prepared the nitrogen used in these measurements in two different ways. Discovering an apparent anomaly in the density of nitrogen, he performed more experiments to verify the density anomaly. He next investigated the way in which nitrogen could be removed from the air to allow the isolation of the unknown gas that appeared to be an atmospheric constituent. Rayleigh then described the way in which he and Ramsay had succeeded in isolating argon from the atmosphere.

Rayleigh continued by discussing the most effective way of extracting argon from the atmosphere and discussed some of its physical properties. His lecture concluded with a discussion of his investigations of other atmospheric gases, on measurements of their compressibilities, and on their behavior at reduced pressures.

The lecture is a good example of Rayleigh's ability to convey scientific information to a general audience, but aside from the novelty of his discussion of the discovery of a new atmospheric gas it contains little of scientific interest. This stands in marked contrast to the bulk of Rayleigh's scientific output, which is regularly consulted by active researchers, especially those who work in acoustics and optics.

## Critical reception

The award of the Nobel Prize to Lord Rayleigh was not a controversial event. Nobel Prizes in physics rarely are; in fact, a hint had been received from Stockholm that were he to be nominated he would be acceptable to the Nobel Committee. The nomination was made by Lord Kelvin, who had in fact been nominated by Rayleigh for the 1904 award. Any controversy associated with the discovery of argon in the atmosphere was long since exhausted, but in 1894, after the initial announcement and before the publication of the 1895 paper, the new atmospheric gas was a highly controversial topic.

*The British Medical Journal* (September 11, 1894) was skeptical. A French satirist is supposed to have christened the new gas "oxfordgen." Professor James Dewar, who at the time was liquefying air, was a skeptic because he could find no evidence of the new gas in his liquefied samples. In fact, in a letter to *The Times* of London, Dewar went so far as to suggest that the experiments carried out by Rayleigh had converted the atmospheric nitrogen into an allotropic form of nitrogen which had a different density. By the end of 1894, *The Times* was openly criticizing Rayleigh and his co-worker Ramsay, but they continued their work. By early 1895 their results had become irrefutable. This did not, however, prevent the *Electrical Review* from calling the discovery a myth in February and April of 1895. Most important, the scientific world was satisfied.

Rayleigh found the experience of this public criticism of his work distasteful. All of his other work had been in more mathematically oriented fields. His feelings on this unwanted attention are best expressed in his own words: "I want to get back from chemistry to physics as soon as I can. The second-rate men seem to know their place so much better." By 1904, when the award was actually made, there was no controversy. In the interim Ramsay had found other noble gases in the atmosphere. Ramsay had even asked Rayleigh to continue with him in their efforts, but Rayleigh declined, preferring to leave chemistry and return to more physically oriented research.

## Biography

John William Strutt, the third Baron Rayleigh, was born on November 12, 1842, at Langford Grove, near Maldon, Essex. His father was John James Strutt, the second Baron Rayleigh, and his mother, Clara Elizabeth La Touche Vicars. Unlike many other English physicists who were ennobled for their contributions to science, Rayleigh was a hereditary peer who achieved fame as a scientist. John William Strutt inherited the title of third Baron Rayleigh in 1873.

Lord Rayleigh's early education, although it included studies at Eton and Harrow, was not systematic, as it was frequently interrupted by illness. His introduction to mathematics came at George Murray's Wimbledon Common school, where he spent his early teens. During this period his interest in science was growing and he performed many schoolboy experiments. In 1857 he went to study at Highstead, Torquay, under the Reverend G. T. Warner. He was to spend four years there before going on to Cambridge. Rayleigh was most interested in mathematics while at Torquay, but he also studied the classics as a prerequisite to entering Cambridge.

Rayleigh had tried to get a minor scholarship to Trinity College, Cambridge, in 1860 but failed. He finally entered Trinity College the following year at the age of nineteen. At Cambridge he became a pupil of Edward J. Routh, the now-legendary Cambridge mathematical tutor. Under Routh, Rayleigh achieved the grasp of practical mathematics that characterizes the body of his work. He went on to become Senior Wrangler in the mathematical tripos of 1865; he was also the Smith's Prizeman. This joint accomplishment established Rayleigh as a scholar and was the highest honor he could have earned as an undergraduate. In the following year he was elected a Fellow of Trinity College. Prior to taking up serious scientific investigation he made a trip to the United States in 1867. In these years he was studying the work of the great physicists such as James Clerk Maxwell.

On his return from America in 1868, Rayleigh began to procure scientific apparatus. He had seen little in his undergraduate career except for that used by George Stokes, the Lucasian Professor of Mathematics, in the course of his lectures. Rayleigh's first investigations were in electricity, the subject of his first paper in 1868. He soon became interested in the problem of color vision and in the acoustical problems to which he was to return often throughout his career. Rayleigh conducted his experimentation at Terling Place, which he would inherit on his father's death. In these years he became acquainted with many of the leading British scientists including Maxwell and Charles Darwin.

Rayleigh was married to Evelyn Balfour, the sister of another distinguished Englishman, the scholar and politician Arthur James Balfour. The marriage forced Rayleigh to resign his Cambridge fellowship, and he prepared to move into a house close to Terling Place.

## Scientific Career

The scientific work of Rayleigh has proved to be of lasting significance. His original papers and books are still consulted by active researchers. The reason for this is that his work usually involved topics of practical importance; entire fields have grown from a single paper by Rayleigh. His great work on acoustics is still regarded as the definitive work on the subject, all subsequent works having mainly been taken up with the technological improvements of the second half of the twentieth century.

In 1871, Rayleigh published one of his most enduringly famous papers. In it he considered the light coming from the sky on a mathematical basis and among other things showed why the sky appears to be blue during the day.

In 1872, Rayleigh developed rheumatic fever, and after a long recuperation he decided to take a trip on the Nile to avoid the English winter. It was while on this trip that Rayleigh wrote much of the first volume of *The Theory of Sound*. Returning to England in May of 1873, he set up the laboratory at Terling Place where he would perform his Nobel Prize-winning work. Rayleigh investigated hydraulics and published many works on fluid mechanics.

*The Theory of Sound* (1878) was well received. Among those sending Rayleigh letters of commendation were his former tutor Routh and British astronomer Sir George Biddell Airy. The work was also well received by the outstanding acoustician of the day, Hermann von Helmholtz. In this period Rayleigh was interested in the construction of devices that could produce the spectrum of light. He contributed to the development of the diffraction grating, a device for separating light into its component colors. His great contribution, however, was to apply photography to the discipline. His technique is still in use today.

In 1879, after Maxwell's untimely death, Rayleigh returned to Cambridge and was elected Cavendish Professor of Physics. Rayleigh had thought that his Cambridge days were over, but Maxwell's death, along with an agricultural depression which reduced his income, resulted in his return. He immediately set about improving laboratory education with the able help of his demonstrators Richard Glazebrook and Sir William Napier Shaw. Under Rayleigh's leadership, Cambridge had its first organized laboratory instruction. It is a model that has been copied throughout England. During his tenure as Cavendish Professor, Lord Rayleigh worked on the establishment of electrical standards. Many of the results of his research were reported at meetings of the British Association, an organization of which he became president. After a five-year tenure during which he had received many honors, Rayleigh resigned the Cavendish professorship and returned to his laboratory at Terling Place in December, 1894.

Terling Place was the site of all Rayleigh's further investigations. The laboratory in which he performed the work that was to win for him the Nobel Prize was the converted loft of a stable. He kept himself well informed of scientific activity by subscribing to many scientific journals. Rayleigh employed George Gordon, his instrument-maker at Cambridge, to prepare his apparatus.

Until his death in 1919, Lord Rayleigh made many fundamental contributions to physics. His output did not decline with age and separation from Cambridge. He was much involved in scientific societies in this period; he was the secretary of the Royal Society of London from 1885 to 1896 and served as president of that organization from 1905 to 1908. In 1887 he was appointed Professor of Natural Philosophy at the Royal Institution. This appointment to the Royal Institution usually involved being allowed access to its laboratories. Rayleigh accepted the position with the understanding that he was free to carry on his researches at Terling Place. The only task that he was required to perform was to give lectures for the general public, which he was pleased to do, giving more than one hundred during his tenure. Lord Rayleigh also took on the many public offices and duties which were expected of him as a peer of the realm.

In the 1880's Rayleigh pursued researches in a wide variety of fields, making contributions to acoustics, optics, and electromagnetic theory. He also began to investigate thermal radiation, the electromagnetic radiation emitted by all objects. Rayleigh contributed to the dissemination of knowledge in this period by writing articles on optics and on the wave theory of light for the ninth edition of the *Encyclopædia Britannica*. In the latter part of this decade Rayleigh became interested in the constituents of matter, and he began to make measurements of the relative densities of the gases found in the atmosphere. He continued these studies into the next decade, and in 1892 he found that the density of nitrogen that he obtained from ammonia was slightly different from the density of the nitrogen that he extracted from the atmosphere. It was for his explanation of this anomaly that he was awarded the Nobel Prize in Physics in 1904.

Rayleigh first suspected that the nitrogen he had prepared from ammonia was contaminated by its other gaseous constituent, hydrogen. He ruled that out by purposely contaminating the atmospheric nitrogen with hydrogen and then passing it through the usual hydrogen-removal apparatus. The next consideration was that the atmospheric nitrogen might be contaminated with oxygen, but again he was able to eliminate this possibility. Rayleigh then announced his initial findings in a letter to the scientific journal *Nature* (September 29, 1892), hoping that someone better trained in chemistry would be able to offer an explanation. One of those who did become interested in this result was Ramsay, the winner of the 1904 Nobel Prize in Chemistry. Thereafter both Rayleigh and Ramsay worked on the problem, and in 1894 a paper on the anomaly was presented to the Royal Society. In 1895, a joint paper announcing the discovery of the new atmospheric constituent, argon, was published in *Philosophical Transactions of the Royal Society*. This discovery was the major achievement which led to Lord Rayleigh's 1904 Nobel Prize; Ramsay received the chemistry prize in the same year for his contributions to the discovery of argon and for his further research into the noble gases of the atmosphere.

In his later years, Rayleigh was also the recipient of many honors apart from the Nobel Prize. In 1902 he was in the first group of recipients of the Order of Merit. In the last decade of his life he was again associated with Cambridge University, being appointed as its chancellor in 1908 and serving in that position until his death in 1919.

## Bibliography

*Primary*
PHYSICS: *The Theory of Sound*, 1878.

*Secondary*

Glazebrook, Richard T. *A History of the Cavendish Laboratory, 1871-1910*. London: Longmans, Green, 1910. The section on the Rayleigh period details the reorganization of the Cavendish laboratory that took place under the guidance of Lord Rayleigh.

Howard, John N., ed. *Applied Optics* 3 (October, 1964). This issue is devoted to Lord Rayleigh's life and work. Especially recommended to technically oriented readers.

Lindsay, Robert Bruce. *Men of Physics: Lord Rayleigh: The Man and His Work*. Elmsford, N.Y.: Pergamon Press, 1970. This volume is one of Pergamon's Men of Physics series. It contains a short biography and an assessment of the scientific career of Lord Rayleigh. The choice of Lindsay, the editor of the *Journal of the Acoustical Society of America*, was most fortunate; he has a lucid prose style and an intimate understanding of major parts of Rayleigh's work. The volume also contains a selection of some of Rayleigh's papers and a complete bibliography of his work.

Sharlin, Harold Isadore. *Lord Kelvin, the Dynamic Victorian*. University Park: Pennsylvania State University Press, 1979. An in-depth biography of Lord Rayleigh's contemporary, Lord Kelvin. The interactions of the two scientists are discussed. This work presents a realistic look at the England of Lord Rayleigh's day and discusses the English educational system in general, with particular reference to Lord Rayleigh's Cambridge.

Strutt, Charles R. *The Strutt Family of Terling, 1650-1873*. London: Mitchell, Hughes, and Clarke, 1939. This book contains a large amount of material on the Strutt family. A copy is available at the Niels Bohr Library for the History of Physics.

Strutt, Robert John, fourth Baron Rayleigh. *Life of John William Strutt, Third Baron Rayleigh*. New York: Longmans, Green, 1924. Rev. ed. Madison: University of Wisconsin Press, 1968. The definitive biography of the third Baron Rayleigh by his son, also a physicist. All biographical sketches of Lord Rayleigh are largely based on this exhaustive volume.

*Stephen R. Addison*

# 1905

### Physics
Philipp Lenard, Germany

### Chemistry
Adolf von Baeyer, Germany

### Physiology or Medicine
Robert Koch, Germany

### Literature
Henryk Sienkiewicz, Poland

### Peace
Bertha von Suttner, Austria

# PHILIPP LENARD
## 1905

*Born:* Pozsony (Pressburg), Hungary; June 7, 1862
*Died:* Messelhausen, Germany; May 20, 1947
*Nationality:* Austro-Hungarian; after 1882, German
*Areas of concentration:* Photoelectricity and electrons

*Lenard devised a method whereby cathode rays can be induced to travel through a "window" in a tube of rarefied gas into the open air, which permits simpler and more sophisticated study of these rays. The close study of cathode rays was an indispensable step in the development of modern physics*

## The Award

*Presentation*

In the presence of the Swedish royal family, the President of the Royal Swedish Academy of Sciences, Professor A. Lindstedt, presented Philipp Lenard with the Nobel Prize in Physics for 1905. Lindstedt's citation included a summary of the research into cathode rays which preceded and inspired Lenard's own, beginning with the discovery of the rays by Johann Hittorf in 1869 and especially noting the work of Heinrich Hertz; Lenard was Hertz's assistant when he began his investigations in 1892.

Lindstedt outlined the discovery of the Lenard window, which permitted the close study of cathode rays, then listed specific discoveries made by Lenard and other physicists which were made possible by the introduction of the window. In Lindstedt's estimation, Lenard's discovery of the window and the scientific advances made possible by it were largely responsible for the development of the theory of electrons, including the description of their properties and their behavior. Lindstedt pointed out that electron theory is of fundamental importance to the understanding of both light and electricity and is indispensable to the development of physics and chemistry.

Lindstedt concluded by lauding Lenard as a pioneer whose discoveries provided inspiration and illuminated the path for other Nobel laureates, including Wilhelm Röntgen and Pierre and Marie Curie.

*Nobel lecture*

Lenard presented his Nobel lecture, titled "On Cathode Rays," on May 28, 1906. He began it with a brief summary of the work of Sir William Crookes on cathode rays, which had inspired his own interest in the subject, and then described the genesis of his research. At Heidelberg in 1883, it occurred to him, Lenard said, that the study of cathode rays and direct experiments with them could be carried out only if the rays could be induced out of the vacuum tube. In trying to devise a way of bringing the rays out of the tube, he had the idea of installing a quartz "window" in the tube through which the rays might pass into the open air. Lenard successfully built the device, but it did not accomplish the purpose for which it had been designed.

In 1892, Heinrich Hertz provided the inspiration that resulted in the first successful separation of cathode rays from the tube in which they were produced. Hertz suggested to his assistant Lenard that a "window" made from aluminum leaf might make possible a determination whether cathode rays were "phenomena in matter or phenomena in ether." Lenard immediately recognized that Hertz's suggestion might permit him to build the device he had envisioned four years earlier.

Lenard went on to describe in considerable detail the many refinements he had added to his device and, through its use, the first experiments he had performed to ascertain the nature of cathode rays. The experiments led him, he explained, to the confirmation of the theory that chemical elements all consist of the same basic materials, in differing amounts. Lenard pointed out that Sir William Ramsay and Ernest Rutherford later verified his hypothesis in their experiments with radium.

He then turned his attention, he said, to the effects of magnetic and electrical fields on cathode rays, in order to determine their nature. Through an ingeniously devised series of experiments, he demonstrated that the rays are actually "streaming electricity," electricity "without material, electrical charges without charged bodies." Lenard's experiments made possible the direct study of electricity, its properties, and its behavior under various conditions.

Next, Lenard turned to the generation of cathode rays through the air. His experiments allowed him to determine that an atom consists of "fine constituents with a great many interstices"; in other words, an atom is not solid. Using cathode rays to map the interior of atoms, Lenard and his associates showed that there are extremely strong electrical forces inside atoms. Further experiments led Lenard to conclude that all matter is made up of nothing more than negative and positive electricity in equal proportions.

Lenard concluded his lecture with a discussion of what he termed "secondary cathode radiation" and electrical conductivity in gases.

*Critical reception*

The American newspapers completely ignored Lenard's winning of the Nobel Prize in Physics. There is no mention of the award in either *The New York Times* or the *Los Angeles Times*. *The Times* of London carried only a short notice on May 28, 1911, which did not even mention Lenard's first name or his university affiliation. The *Paris le temps* was little more informative in a brief story on the same day. The silence of the Western press perhaps reflected the fact that all the recipients in 1905 were from central and eastern Europe: Lenard, Adolf von Baeyer (chemistry), and Robert Koch (medicine), from Germany; Henryk Sienkiewicz (literature), from Poland; and the Baroness von Suttner (peace), from Austria.

Only in Germany was Lenard's prize given attention and the work that earned it for him described in detail. The *Berliner Tageblatt* ran a lengthy article on the day the award was presented to Lenard concerning his research and noting that many of his colleagues in German physics approved of the Academy's choice.

## Biography

Philipp Éduard Anton von Lenard was born on June 7, 1862, in Pressburg, Hungary (now Bratislava, Czechoslovakia). His father was a successful winemaker. His mother died while Lenard was a child, and he was reared by her sister, who eventually married Lenard's father.

At his father's insistence, Lenard pursued the study of the chemistry of wine at the Technische Hochschulen—schools similar to the American agricultural and mechanical colleges—in Vienna and Budapest; he then entered the family business. He worked with his father only until he could save enough money to travel to Heidelberg and enroll in the university there in 1883, where he studied under Robert Bunsen. He attended that university for four semesters and the Free University of Berlin for two more. In 1886 he received his doctorate summa cum laude. Shortly thereafter, he was married to Katharina Schlehner.

During the next twenty-eight years, Lenard held professorships at a number of German universities and became one of the most celebrated physicists in the world, winning many awards and prizes. In 1914 he was caught up in the wave of patriotism that accompanied the outbreak of World War I and developed the extreme nationalism that became a dominant force in his life. During the war, he began corresponding with Johannes Stark, a future Nobel laureate in physics, who shared Lenard's growing antagonism toward what he perceived to be the insidious and degenerate influence of Jews on German society in general and German physics in particular.

After the war, Lenard, along with many other Germans, felt a deep sense of humiliation at the terms of the Treaty of Versailles and evolved a bitter hatred of the Weimar Republic, the government that had signed the treaty and that, in Lenard's estimation, was permeated by Jews. Lenard led an attempt to "cleanse" German physics of Jews in 1920, which resulted in a verbal dual between him and Albert Einstein at a national science conference at Bad Nauheim. As early as 1923, he was attracted to the political movement led by Adolf Hitler.

In 1926, Lenard met Hitler personally for the first time at a party conference of the Nationalsozialistische Deutsche Arbeiterpartei (National Socialist German Workers Party, or Nazis) at Heilbronn. Lenard subsequently became Hitler's personal expert on physics. His denunciation of nuclear physics to Hitler as "Jewish physics" probably retarded German research into the atom bomb, a fortunate outcome for Hitler's enemies.

After the defeat of Germany in 1945, Lenard was not arrested, probably because of his advanced age. (Stark, however, spent four years at hard labor for his support of National Socialism.) Lenard was, however, expelled from Heidelberg and exiled to a meager existence in the village of Messelhausen, where he died on May 20, 1947.

## Scientific Career

Lenard's scientific career actually began before he matriculated at Heidelberg in 1883. Working with his secondary school teacher, Virgil Klatt, Lenard began investigations, which he continued throughout his life, into the nature of phosphorescence. By 1889 he had already discovered the cause of phosphorescence: the existence of minute amounts of bismuth, copper, or manganese in alkaline earth sulfides. During World War II, Lenard published a three-volume account of his scientific research. The whole of volume 2 was devoted to his study of phosphorescence.

Immediately after receiving his doctorate at Heidelberg, Lenard became an assistant there to Gerhard Quincke. After three years in that capacity, he went to England for several months, where he worked in several engineering and electrical laboratories in London. Upon returning to Germany, he spent one semester as an assistant at the University of Breslau; he then accepted a similar position at the University of Bonn in 1891.

At the University of Bonn, Lenard became the assistant of Heinrich Hertz, who had already made significant contributions in the physical sciences, not the least of which was his discovery of electromagnetic waves. Lenard had developed an interest in cathode rays after reading Sir William Crookes's famous paper on the subject during his assistantship to Quincke at Heidelberg, and he had attempted, unsuccessfully, to develop a method of inducing the rays out of the cathode tube and into the open air, where they could be studied directly. In 1892, using a method suggested by Hertz, Lenard succeeded in his quest to make the rays more accessible through the use of what became known as the "Lenard window," a discovery of the utmost importance in the development of several fields of physics. After making his discovery, he qualified as a lecturer at the University of Bonn.

Hertz died, suddenly and prematurely, in 1894. It fell to Lenard to oversee the publication of Hertz's collected works, which greatly reduced the time available for his research. As a result, several other physicists soon caught and passed Lenard in experimentation into the nature of cathode rays. Lenard became involved in several bitter controversies—with Sir Joseph John Thomson, among others—as to who first had discovered and described electrons. In retrospect, Lenard's claim to this important discovery seems to be the most valid.

Lenard's preoccupation with the publication of Hertz's work almost certainly cost him the honor of making another discovery using the Lenard window. In 1895, Wilhelm Röntgen discovered X rays with the help of Lenard's device; this advance won for him the first Nobel Prize in Physics, in 1901. Röntgen did not mention the Lenard window when describing his work, even though it had been indispensable to his discovery. Lenard never forgave Röntgen, and he became increasingly suspicious of fellow physicists thereafter. When Röntgenstrahlen became the standard term for X rays in Germany, Lenard continued to refer to them only as "high-frequency radiation."

In 1894, Lenard accepted a tenured professorship at the University of Breslau in theoretical physics, which permitted him little time for research. He left that position after one year to take a nontenured position as lecturer at the technical high school in Aachen as an assistant to Adolph Wüllner, where he had much more time to devote to his experiments. In 1896 he accepted a tenured full professorship at Heidelberg and in 1898 took a similar position at the University of Kiel. At Kiel, he was also appointed director of the physics laboratory, which he completely rebuilt.

In the new laboratory at Kiel, Lenard made several important discoveries concerning photoelectric fields and the properties of electrons. He showed that as light intensity increases, greater numbers of electrons are freed; even so, he found, the velocity of electrons is not affected by intensity but is determined instead by wavelength. This observation became an integral part of Einstein's hypothesis of light quanta in 1905. In that year, Lenard was honored with the Nobel Prize in Physics because of the "overall importance" and "pioneering nature" of his work.

Lenard succeeded Quincke in 1907 as professor of physics and director of the physics and radiology laboratory at the University of Heidelberg, where he spent the remainder of his career. Under his direction, the university undertook the building of a new laboratory, which was completed on the eve of World War I. In 1935, the university renamed the facility the Philipp Lenard Laboratory. Sometime between 1907 and 1910, for reasons which are still obscure, Lenard was severely criticized by several Jewish physicists, including Einstein, who described one of Lenard's papers as "almost infantile." Einstein also commiserated with another Jewish physicist, an assistant at Heidelberg named Johann Laub, over Laub's being forced to waste his time performing experiments assigned to him by Lenard. This criticism was perhaps the genesis of Lenard's antagonism toward Jewish physicists, which manifested itself during the 1920's and 1930's.

During World War I, Lenard developed a supernationalism that played a major directional role in the remainder of his career. The first overt manifestation of his chauvinism came in the publication of *England und Deutschland zur Zeit des Grossen Krieg* (England and Germany up to the Great War) in 1914. In this book, he accused British scientists of intentionally hiding the work of German scientists from the British public and claiming much of it for their own. (Here, Lenard was undoubtedly thinking of his own dispute with Thomson.) It was during the war, too, that Lenard became a close confidant of Johannes Stark, a future Nobel laureate in physics who shared Lenard's extreme nationalism and who had already shown a pronounced judeophobia.

In 1920, Lenard's political views began to influence his scientific career. He became involved in a public dispute with Einstein, and he agreed to lead a movement of non-Jewish scientists which questioned Einstein's authorship of several theories attributed to him and the verity and usefulness of his relativity theory. In September of 1920, Lenard and Einstein engaged in a verbal battle at a major scientific conference. The result, apparently, was the solidification of Lenard's growing animosity toward Jews.

His opposition to the parliamentary republic and his anti-Semitism were further demonstrated in 1922, when the Weimar government decreed a cessation of work in Germany as a memorial for the assassinated Jewish official Walter Rathenau. Lenard refused to dismiss his classes to honor a Jewish member of a government which he believed had betrayed his country, and Jewish students at Heidelberg stormed his laboratory in protest. Lenard's actions attracted nationwide attention and encouraged the growing *Völkisch* (extreme nationalist) movement by demonstrating that members of the intellectual elite of Germany shared the nationalists' feelings concerning the government and the Jews. Shortly after the Rathenau incident, Lenard began acquainting his students with the name and the beliefs of Adolf Hitler, whose fledgling Nazi Party was gaining new members rapidly in south Germany. The substantial support Hitler's movement received from students at German universities resulted in part from the championing of the Nazi cause by Lenard and other prominent academicians.

Lenard met Hitler in person in 1926, and a friendly relationship developed. According to Albert Speer's memoirs, Lenard became Hitler's personal expert in physics. In that capacity, he denigrated Einstein and "Jewish" nuclear physics, which he clearly separated from "German" nuclear physics in his four-volume *Deutsche Physik* (1936-1937). Lenard's advice to Hitler on those matters contributed to the expulsion of Jewish physicists from Germany and to the relative weakness of Hitler's scientists' efforts to develop a nuclear bomb during World War II.

During World War II, Lenard published three volumes of an intended four-volume recapitulation of his scientific work. It was the final act of a scientific career distinguished by discoveries which laid the foundations for modern nuclear physics and besmirched by association with a widely despised political and racial ideology.

## Bibliography

*Primary*

PHYSICS: *Über Kathodenstrahlen*, 1906; *Über Äther und Materie*, 1910; *England und Deutschland zur Zeit des grossen Krieges*, 1914; *Über Relativitätsprinzip, Äther, Gravitation*, 1918; *Über Äther und Uräther*, 1921; *Grosse Naturforscher: Eine Geschichte der Naturforschung in Lebensbeschreibungen*, 1929; *Deutsche Physik*, 1936-1937.

*Secondary*

Beyerchen, Alan D. *Scientists Under Hitler: Politics and the Physics Community in the Third Reich*. New Haven, Conn.: Yale University Press, 1977. This book virtually ignores Lenard's early contributions to science, concentrating instead on his support for Hitler and the Nazi movement and his attacks on "non-Aryan" physics. The account of Lenard's feud with Einstein, of his efforts to cleanse German physics of Jewish influence, and of the consequences of those efforts are the most complete available in English.

Cohen, I. Bernard. *Revolution in Science*. Cambridge, Mass.: Harvard University Press, 1985. Cohen's book is a literate and compelling history of science centered on the theme of scientific revolutions, which have often mirrored political and social revolutions. Cohen pays scant attention to Lenard's achievements, instead concentrating on his affiliations with Hitler and his opposition to Einstein.

Hartshorne, Edward Yarnall, Jr. *The German Universities and National Socialism.* London: Allen & Unwin, 1937. Hartshorne mentions Lenard only briefly, but he places him at the helm of the movement to expel Jews from academic and scientific life in Germany during the Nazi era. Hartshorne points out that Lenard's later writings, particularly *Deutsche Physik*, were ridiculed by Jewish scientists abroad even at the time they were published.

Heathcote, Niels Hugh de Vaudrey. *Nobel Prize Winners in Physics, 1901-1950.* New York: Henry Schuman, 1953. Heathcote does not mention Lenard's political peculiarities at all, concerning himself instead with Lenard's contributions to the field of physics, which were considerable. In addition to accurate descriptions of the experiments that won Lenard the Nobel Prize, there are accounts of several other major discoveries made by Lenard, including the photoelectric effect and the theory that the atom is composed mostly of empty space.

Schneer, Cecil J. *The Search for Order: The Development of the Major Ideas in the Physical Sciences from the Earliest Times to the Present.* New York: Harper & Row, 1960. This older work on the history of science contains several references to Lenard, primarily in the context of his resistance to relativity theory. Lenard's anti-Semitic actions are described as attempts to discredit relativity theory, which he saw as pure scientific sophistry.

*Paul Madden*

# 1906

## Physics
Sir Joseph John Thomson, Great Britain

## Chemistry
Henri Moissan, France

## Physiology or Medicine
Camillo Golgi, Italy
S. Ramón y Cajal, Spain

## Literature
Giosuè Carducci, Italy

## Peace
Theodore Roosevelt, United States

# SIR JOSEPH JOHN THOMSON
## 1906

*Born:* Cheetham Hill, near Manchester, England; December 18, 1856
*Died:* Cambridge, England; August 30, 1940
*Nationality:* British
*Area of concentration:* Particle physics

*Thomson opened up the field of subatomic particle physics with his work on the electron. Through his experiments, he showed that cathode rays were made up of particles and determined the mass of these particles. Thomson is usually acknowledged as the discoverer of the electron*

## The Award

*Presentation*

Professor J. P. Klason, President of the Royal Swedish Academy of Sciences, presented the Nobel Prize in Physics to Sir Joseph John Thomson in December, 1906, on behalf of the Academy and the King of Sweden. Klason noted that electricity had an increasing role in everyday life and reviewed the significant historic contributions to the understanding of electricity. He mentioned the fundamental work of Hans Christian Ørsted, who in 1820 discovered the influence of electric current on a magnetic needle; André-Marie Ampère's theory linking magnetism with electricity; and the investigations of James Clerk Maxwell, who in 1873 provided a theory of electromagnetic fields that unified all these phenomena.

To this illustrious group was added the name of Professor J. J. Thomson. Despite earlier advances in the field of electricity, said Klason, scientists still had not been able to determine the size of an atom's electrical charge, whether the charge was carried by a particle within the atom, and, if it was, the mass of that particle. In a series of experiments, Thomson had been able to determine the exact value of the electrical charge and that this negative charge was carried by a particle, the "electron." Further experiments had provided additional evidence for other properties of the electron, including its mass and velocity.

*Nobel lecture*

Thomson's lecture, titled "Carriers of Negative Electricity," was presented on December 11, 1906. It was an account of his investigations in determining the mass of the electron. (Thomson called electrons "corpuscles.") At the early stages of his investigations using the cathode-ray tube, a piece of equipment that could discharge electricity through a near-vacuum, there had been two prevailing points of view. English physicists thought that negatively charged electric particles were shot from the cathode; German physicists thought that the rays were vibrations, or waves. Jean-Baptiste Perrin had offered evidence that the rays were negatively charged, but

Heinrich Rudolf Hertz had demonstrated that the discharge would penetrate thin sheets of metal. The smallest known particle at the time was the hydrogen atom, and it was unlikely that such a large and slow-moving particle could penetrate thin metal plates.

Thomson's investigation took place in two stages. First, he determined the velocity of the discharge. Using a magnetic field of a known strength, he calculated the rays' velocity to be about 60,000 miles per second. Second, he determined the particles' mass. An electric discharge is like a bullet fired from a gun; it will eventually be pulled down by gravity to a place determined by its mass. Consequently, Thomson was able to show that the particles discharged by the cathode tube had a mass about seventeen hundred times less than that of the hydrogen atom. To complete this study, Thomson had to prove that the particles' ability to penetrate sheets of metal was a result of the smallness of their mass rather than the greatness of their charge. To do this, he made use of Charles Wilson's discovery that a sudden drop in temperature in a container will cause condensation of water from the air and that the water will form droplets around dust particles. Thomson devised an elegant experiment in which he condensed water vapors around each particle of the discharge and was thus able to compute the value of each charge.

Thomson concluded his lecture by demonstrating that the mass of the electron is significantly smaller than that of the hydrogen atom.

*Critical reception*

When the Nobel Prize in Physics was presented to Thomson in 1906, it was only the sixth time that the award had been given. Although all the recipients of the award up to that time had been leaders in and pioneers of physics, neither the scientific community nor the world press regarded receiving this award as the pinnacle of achievement in physics. *The Times* of London greeted the award with a few lines noting the "well-established" nature of the Cavendish Laboratory, which Thomson directed, and the fact that Thomson had "gathered together researchers from the whole world." On the day before Thomson was to receive his prize, *The Times* reported his intention to donate half the award monies to scientific research; the next day, it provided only a summary of all the recipients, including the winners in chemistry, physics, medicine, and literature. In a similar fashion, *The New York Times* recognized the award in a brief paragraph.

The assessment of Thomson's achievement from the scientific community would come in other ways. Thomson was recommended for knighthood by the prime minister of England in 1908. Curiously, he was somewhat reluctant to accept the honor, but he thought that it would contribute to the success of the British Association meeting, over which he was to preside. He received the Order of Merit in 1912 and became president of the Royal Society in 1915. Over the years, Thomson would also receive numerous awards from sectors of the scientific community: the Hodgkins Medal, from the Smithsonian Institution, in 1902; the Franklin Medal and the Scott Medal, in 1923; the Dalton Medal, in 1931; and the Faraday Medal, in 1938. He also held honorary doctorates from twenty-three of the leading universities in the world, including Princeton, Columbia, and Johns Hopkins. Thomson's final honor was his burial in Westminster Abbey, near the body of Sir Isaac Newton.

## Biography

Joseph John Thomson was born on December 18, 1856, in Cheetham Hill, near Manchester, England. He was the son of a bookseller and grew up in a city that was rapidly becoming an industrial and manufacturing center. His father favored an engineering career for his son, but the waiting list for apprentices was long, and young Thomson enrolled in Owens College (later Manchester University) in 1871 to gain a basic education in engineering. Thomson spent three years studying for a certificate in engineering and, at the age of seventeen, decided to remain for two more years to concentrate on mathematics and physics. He was particularly close to Thomas Barker, a professor of mathematics at Owens, and he was advised by Barker to compete for a mathematics scholarship at Trinity College, Cambridge. Unsuccessful at first, he competed for another mathematics scholarship and arrived in Cambridge in 1876.

For the next four years, Thomson devoted his attention to mathematics and had little time for physical experimentation. He was well liked as a student and was universally known, even to his son, as "J. J." He was graduated in 1880 and the next year was elected a fellow of Trinity; he was to remain there for the rest of his life. When Lord Rayleigh (John William Strutt) resigned his position as director of the Cavendish Laboratory at Cambridge in 1884, Thomson applied for the position. He remained director of the laboratory until 1918.

Thomson visited America twice, once in 1896 and again in 1904, to deliver a series of lectures. In addition to the Nobel Prize, Thomson held a long list of awards and honors and was knighted in 1908.

## Scientific Career

For half a century, Thomson's career as a physicist and the history of the Cavendish Laboratory were so closely linked that it would be difficult to separate one from the other. Even after Thomson resigned from the directorship of the Laboratory in 1918, his colleagues and students would continue either to lead that institution or to compete for the highest prizes in physics. These include seven Nobel Prize winners, twenty-seven Fellows of the Royal Society, and many professors of physics appointed throughout Great Britain and the British Commonwealth.

Thomson began his research in the area of electrical discharges through gases because the use of the cathode-ray discharge mechanism seemed to point to a promising exploration of matter. Earlier, James Maxwell had suggested this investigation, and Rayleigh had intended to begin such a study at the Cavendish Laboratory. Furthermore, science, particularly physics, was increasingly being used by governments to promote national pride. At the time, German physicists believed that cathode rays were made of waves, whereas British physicists were certain that these discharges consisted of particles. Thus, further research at the Cavendish Laboratory would promote both advances in physics and national interests.

Thomson was the ideal person to take up the study of gas discharge. He had more than enough ability to create the necessary models to explain experimental results, and although he was not an experimental genius, being clumsy with his hands, he could produce elegant experiments. Thomson began his investigations into electrical discharges by using a variety of media, such as benzene, paraffin, and oil, to find out if discharges obeyed Ohm's law. Between 1884 and 1894, he pursued a variety of experiments. During this period, he held to the theoretical notion that electrical discharge in gas is like the process of electrolysis in fluids; that is, he believed that an electric current disrupts a gas's chemical bonds. By 1889, he had discovered that heated gases conduct electricity more efficiently. This finding suggested that an electrical discharge would break gas molecules into "atoms" or "ions." Over the next two years, however, Thomson began to realize that while he had accumulated a large amount of information, he was no closer than before to a theoretical model that would explain these phenomena. He therefore changed his strategy and spent two years experimenting with discharges as if they were light waves, using a revolving mirror to measure their velocity. He found that discharges from a positive electrode traveled at about half the speed of light. Yet, even while he was using an experimental framework that treated electrical discharges as waves, he never gave up the notion that they consisted of particles.

During the early 1890's, when the Germans—under Heinrich Hertz and later under his student, Philipp Lenard—discovered that electrical discharges would penetrate metal foil, Thomson began to promote his particle theory more aggressively. Even though Thomson had shown that the velocity of the discharges was half that of light, and though other British physicists had demonstrated that the discharges would curve in a magnetic field like charged particles, a definitive proof of the particle theory was nevertheless necessary. Moreover, before Thomson could discover the electron, Wilhelm Röntgen discovered X rays and provided further ammunition for the German wave theory. Although Thomson acknowledged that X rays could explain the penetration of electrical discharges, he also recognized that when a discharge struck a metal film, other particles might be produced on the other side.

In 1895, Thomson began working with Ernest Rutherford, using X rays to cause gases to conduct electricity. Rutherford had come from New Zealand and was the first of a new group of Cambridge graduate students who had not done their undergraduate work there. Cambridge and the Cavendish Laboratory were becoming international research centers, and Thomson utilized the fresh sources of talent wherever he could. The X-ray experiments were fruitful, because the radiated gases retained their conductivity after the radiation had ceased. This retention could only be explained if either positive or negative charges were produced by radiation.

By now, Thomson was aware that the discharge particles had to be significantly smaller than the hydrogen atom. Before announcing his conclusion, however, he conducted an experiment using a thin stream of cathode rays. The rays were attracted to a positively charged plate in a target area which showed that the particles were negatively charged. He next found the mass of these particles. Finally, using a thin stream of rays in a magnetic field, Thomson was able to determine the ratio of the particles' charge to their mass. In a subsequent experiment, he compared this ratio to that of a charged hydrogen atom and came to the conclusion that the electrical discharge particle, which he called a "corpuscle," was smaller than the hydrogen atom by a factor of one thousand. In a lecture given at the Royal Institution on April 30, 1897, Thomson gave his first public account of his discoveries.

Thomson's conclusion about the mass of the electron was not regarded by the physics community as an entirely new discovery. Physicists were slow in recognizing the implications of Thomson's results; in addition, Emil Wiechert and Walter Kaufmann had independently inferred a similar conclusion from their earlier experiments. Nevertheless, neither Wiechert nor Kaufmann could be credited with the discovery of the electron, since they both had rejected the existence of such a charged particle. Within two years, Thomson would verify his findings in other experiments. He later measured the value of the electron's electrical charge by capturing each electrical charge in liquid droplets through condensation. Since he knew the size of the overall charge and the number of separate charges, he could now calculate the value of each electrical charge. A few gaps remained in the theory, however, and other physicists would provide the necessary links before Thomson could claim the discovery of the electron.

In 1899, Thomson published his view that the atom is surrounded by negatively charged particles on the outside. By 1904, he had developed this model of the atom further; it included electrons accelerating on concentric rings surrounding the atom, with the innermost ring containing the fewest number of electrons and the outer rings containing progressively more electrons. Particle and nuclear physics can be dated from this moment, and all work in the field has depended, to some extent, on Thomson's contributions.

After the discovery of the electron, Thomson devoted much of his remaining research years to determining the nature of "positive electricity." This phenomenon was identified by Wilhelm Wien, and by 1913 Thomson had developed an instrument sensitive enough to analyze the positive electron. It is through this work that Thomson became one of the first scientists to isolate isotopes of elements. During World War I, Thomson served on the Board of Inventions and Research, which reviewed the thousands of suggestions that came before it and their potential use in the British war effort. Thomson himself designed a mine that would explode without contact. At the end of the war, the position of Master of Trinity College became vacant, and at the age of sixty-one, Thomson was appointed to that post. He thus became the most eminent living British scientist. In 1919, he resigned his position at the Cavendish Laboratory and was replaced by Rutherford. Thomson served as the Master of Trinity for the rest of his life, guiding the affairs of the college until a few months before his death in 1940.

# Bibliography

*Primary*

PHYSICS: *A Treatise on the Motion of Vortex Rings: An Essay to Which the Adams Prize Was Adjudged in 1882, in the University of Cambridge*, 1883; *Elements of the Mathematical Theory of Electricity and Magnetism*, 1897; *The Discharge of Electricity Through Gases: Lectures Delivered on the Occasion of the Sesquicentennial Celebration of Princeton University*, 1898; *Conduction of Electricity Through Gases*, 1903; *Electricity and Matter*, 1904; *Rays of Positive Electricity and Their Application to Chemical Analyses*, 1913; *Beyond the Electron*, 1928.

OTHER NONFICTION: *Recollections and Reflections*, 1936.

*Secondary*

Crowther, J. G. *The Cavendish Laboratory, 1874-1974*. New York: Science History Publications, 1974. This work covers the history of the laboratory, and some seventy pages focus on the person who laid the facility's foundations and determined its research directions for the future. Various chapters cover Thomson's early years here, his initial work as the director, his assistants and students, his work on the electron, and the later period through the end of World War I—all the high points of Thomson's career. In addition, two early chapters discuss his predecessor John William Strutt, and eight subsequent chapters provide information on his successor Ernest Rutherford.

Segrè, Emilio. *From X-Rays to Quarks: Modern Physicists and Their Discoveries*. San Francisco: W. H. Freeman, 1980. Segrè was one of a handful of physicists who not only participated directly in nuclear physics (he received a Nobel Prize for his work) but also wrote a number of popular books on the history of physics. The earlier sections of this volume cover the discoveries and theories of those who produced a coherent picture of the atom. It allows the reader to appreciate the full significance of Thomson's contribution to the field of nuclear physics.

Strutt, Robert John, fourth Baron Rayleigh. *The Life of Sir J. J. Thomson, O.M., Sometime Master of Trinity College*. Cambridge, England: Cambridge University Press, 1942. Half of this work covers the same territory as the work by Crowther, although in greater detail; the remainder of the text covers Thomson's many other activities. These include the presidency of the Royal Society, the mastership of Trinity College, his views on education, and aspects of his personal life. An advantage of this work is that Rayleigh (the son of Thomson's predecessor at Cavendish Laboratory) was at Cambridge and a friend of Thomson and so can give a firsthand account of the events that took place.

Thomson, George Paget. *J. J. Thomson and the Cavendish Laboratory in His Day*. London: Thomas Nelson, 1964. This volume attempts to detail the work done by Thomson and those men who worked around him. Although the bulk of the information in this volume is also covered by Crowther and Rayleigh, its advantage lies in its detailed descriptions of the experiments, excellent drawings of the experimental equipment, and photographs of the experimental results. The illustrations provide an added dimension for readers who find it difficult to follow verbal descriptions of complicated equipment and experiments.

Thomson, J. J. *Recollections and Reflections*. London: G. Bell, 1936. Thomson's autobiography contains many surprises and important information on his life. Although the Nobel Prize goes virtually unmentioned, there is an entire chapter on "psychical research." There are several lengthy chapters on his visits to the United States and his abiding interest in that country. There are also extensive sections on his education and on persons who influenced his life and work.

*Victor W. Chen*

# 1907

## Physics
Albert Abraham Michelson, United States

## Chemistry
Eduard Buchner, Germany

## Physiology or Medicine
Alphonse Laveran, France

## Literature
Rudyard Kipling, Great Britain

## Peace
Ernesto Teodoro Moneta, Italy
Louis Renault, France

# ALBERT ABRAHAM MICHELSON
## 1907

*Born:* Strelno, Prussia; December 19, 1852
*Died:* Pasadena, California; May 9, 1931
*Nationality:* American
*Areas of concentration:* Optics, spectroscopy, and interferometry

*In 1887, at Case School of Applied Science in Cleveland, Ohio, Michelson and Edward Morley attempted to measure the effect of Earth's orbital motion on the speed of light. What they found in conducting the now-famous Michelson-Morley experiment revolutionized not only science but also the way people view the world*

## The Award
*Presentation*

Professor K. B. Hasselberg, a member of the Royal Swedish Academy of Sciences, presented the Nobel Prize in Physics to Albert Abraham Michelson in December of 1907. Because of the death of King Oscar II, the presentation ceremony was canceled and Hasselberg's speech was not delivered orally.

The award was granted for Michelson's development of optical precision instruments and his application of them to precise measurements in metrology (the determination of the standard meter) and spectroscopy (the study of the color composition of light sources). Hasselberg stressed the contributions of these instruments and measurements to the exact sciences of astronomy and physics. He outlined the high degree of accuracy that, with the new devices, could be obtained in studies of a variety of physical phenomena.

Hasselberg specifically mentioned the development of the Michelson interferometer, which makes use of the laws of light interference. The application of this device allowed measurements twenty to a hundred times more precise than those previously achievable with the best microscopes. Hasselberg explained at length that the interference phenomena of light, with Michelson's techniques, allowed the measurement of a "desired value—usually a length is measured—. . . in numbers of wavelengths of the type of light in use in the experiment." The number of wavelengths was determined by observing, in the interferometer, the changes in the image caused by interference. Such procedures allowed for an accuracy of one-fiftieth of a wavelength or one-hundred-thousandth of a millimeter. Hasselberg mentioned a number of important practical applications of the technique, such as measuring the heat expansion of solid bodies and the elastic behavior of various substances under stress. He also listed the scientific applications, such as measuring the gravitational constant (the force of gravity pulling together two masses of one kilogram each at a distance of one meter from each other) and the mass of Earth.

The presentation speech went on to outline the importance of Michelson's research in the field of astronomy. His techniques allowed scientists to measure the diameters of Jupiter's satellites and the distance between close binary stars. As a result, the measurement of stellar diameters, which had been considered an insoluble problem, became feasible. Hasselberg stated,

> Thus astronomy has once again received from physics in the interferometer—as earlier in the spectroscope—a new aid to research which seems particularly suited to tackling problems whose solution was formerly impossible, as there were no, or at the most inadequate, instruments available.

Professor the Count K. A. H. Mörner, President of the Royal Swedish Academy of Sciences, gave a short oral presentation during a private ceremony at the Academy, summing up Hasselberg's presentation speech and honoring Michelson.

## Nobel lecture

Michelson gave his Nobel lecture on December 12, 1907. Titled "Recent Advances in Spectroscopy," the lecture summarized the status of the science of spectroscopy and described how this field of physical optics could be improved by using the property of light known as interference.

The speech began with a summary of the work of Sir Isaac Newton and his famous discovery of the laws of gravitation as they apply to astronomy. Newton's work on the motion of bodies and its spectacular application to motions in the heavens is familiar even to nonscientists. Michelson pointed out that Newton also made great discoveries in optics, specifically in spectroscopy, which can be applied to astrophysics. Newton's invention of the spectroscope, a device that disperses light according to color, not only led to the study of the chemical composition and physical properties of various astronomical objects, but also opened up new fields of astrophysics and physics. The invention of the laser and of many types of advanced spectrometers can be identified as direct outgrowths of the basic work done by Newton around 1700.

Michelson traced the development of spectroscopy from Newton's time to the early twentieth century. He stressed the importance of using devices known as diffraction gratings rather than prisms to analyze the color distribution of light sources. He then discussed the resolution (the ability to detect fineness of detail) of telescopes versus that of spectrometers. The resolution of a spectrum is a measure of how much the spectrum can be spread out, or dispersed. Michelson showed, in technical detail, how his invention, the interferometer, could be used in conjunction with other instruments and devices to obtain better spectroscopic resolution. He went on to say that such techniques could even be applied to the establishment of a natural standard of length using the exact dimensions of light waves as the basic unit of length.

Curiously, as was the case for the next half century, Michelson never mentioned the ether drift experiments he had performed with Edward Morley.

*Critical reception*

There was great rejoicing in the United States as a result of Michelson's receiving the Nobel Prize. Most of the prominent newspapers featured a lengthy article on the front page. Many small-town newspapers did the same, and more articles followed within the next few days. The prize became a topic of conversation throughout the country, even though most people did not understand its scientific significance. Its political significance, however, was understood, at least to some degree, by almost everyone.

The University of Chicago gave a banquet to honor Michelson, and many more awards followed. The Copley Medal of the Royal Society of London specifically honored Michelson and Morley's ether drift experiment. Michelson, in his few public speeches and interviews, made a plea for more and quicker advancement in American science.

The long-term reaction of the scientific community was harder to gauge. It now appears that Albert Einstein was only lightly influenced by the Michelson-Morley experiment in his development of special relativity theory. Much has been written on how much Einstein really knew about the experiment. Yet, shortly after the publishing of the special and general theories of relativity in 1905 and 1916, Einstein and others noted the significance of what could be said to be the greatest "null result" experiment ever undertaken.

## Biography

Albert Abraham Michelson was born in Strelno, on the Polish-Prussian border, in 1852. He was the oldest child of Samuel and Rosalie Przylubska Michelson, who were Jewish store merchants. The family fled Europe for the United States during political upheaval and widespread persecution when Albert was only two years old. After a short stay in New York City, the Michelson family moved to California. During Albert's youth, the family lived in Murphy's Diggings, California, and Virginia City, Nevada, both of which were frontier towns whose economies were based on gold and silver mining. His parents nevertheless insisted on his maintaining studious habits and recognized his high mathematical abilities. During his early teens, he went to San Francisco to live with his aunt and uncle, where he attended San Francisco Boys' High School. At sixteen, after overcoming a series of political obstacles, he obtained a special appointment to the U.S. Naval Academy from President Ulysses S. Grant, partly because of his family's influence and his own persistence. In 1873, he was graduated ninth in a class of twenty-nine students. In spite of his high scholastic ranking, Mike, as he was called by his friends, ranked twenty-fifth in seamanship.

After his college graduation, Michelson performed his active duty and carried out optics research on the speed of light. In 1875, he became a physics instructor at the Naval Academy, and while there, he made the most precise determination of the speed of light that had ever been attained. Michelson was married to Margaret Heminway of New Rochelle, New York, in 1877. They had two sons and a daughter.

From 1873 to 1920, Michelson had appointments at four major universities in the United States: He went to the U.S. Naval Academy, Annapolis, Maryland, in 1873; Case School of Applied Science, Cleveland, Ohio, in 1883; Clark University in Worcester, Massachusetts, in 1890; and the University of Chicago, as head of the physics department, in 1892. The pressures and time-consuming nature of his work resulted in divorce from his first wife. Soon after, he was married to one of his former students, Edna Stanton of Lake Forest, Illinois. They had one son and three daughters.

From 1901 to 1903, Michelson was president of the American Physical Society, and in 1923, he became president of the National Academy of Sciences. During World War I, he served in the Naval Reserve in Washington, where he developed military applications of optical equipment. He retired from the University of Chicago in 1929 and moved to Pasadena, California, where he continued his velocity of light experiments at Mount Wilson until his death on May 9, 1931.

## Scientific Career

As an instructor at the Naval Academy, Michelson began his long love affair with light and its measurement. One of his first tasks was to demonstrate to his students Jean-Bernard-Léon Foucault's measurement of the speed of light. During this time, he redesigned the experiment and made his own measurements using the simple equipment available to him at the academy. Michelson set up his experiment by the Severn River at Annapolis along the old seawall. He used a baseline, between mirrors, of 605 meters. The experiment increased the precision of the measurement of the speed of light by a factor of almost two hundred. Michelson reported these results at a meeting of the American Association for the Advancement of Science in St. Louis, Missouri; he also published them in the *American Journal of Science*. The scientific community throughout the world became aware of Michelson's work.

Michelson's research attracted the attention of the great astronomer Simon Newcomb, the director of the Nautical Almanac Office of the U.S. Naval Observatory in Washington, D.C. Through Newcomb's influence, both with the Navy and as a scientist, Michelson ceased active duty and began to work with Newcomb on further measurements of the velocity of light.

In 1880, with Newcomb's help, Michelson traveled to Europe to study and do research at the University of Berlin, the University of Heidelberg, and the Collège de France. During this stay in Europe, he invented the interferometer, a device which made possible the splitting and recombining of a beam of light so that very fine measurements of the resulting interference patterns could be made. This device is generally acknowledged to be his most important contribution to instrumental physics and is still widely used. The money to build the first of these devices was donated by Alexander Graham Bell.

The interferometer permits light rays moving at right angles to each other to be recombined along the same direction using beam splitters and half-silvered mirrors.

The resulting combined beams either reinforce or cancel each other and create a characteristic pattern of "interference fringes," which are used to measure minute distances. Simply put, the combined beams can be placed out of phase with respect to one another by amounts equal to any number of wavelengths—for example, by one, two, or ten wavelengths. One wavelength of light is very tiny, and the disparity is the basis for measuring tiny distances.

While in Europe, Michelson was appointed to the newly founded Case School of Applied Science, in Cleveland, which later became Case Western Reserve University. In addition to teaching, he continued his research projects and made more improvements in the measurement of the speed of light. Michelson set up his first Cleveland experiment along the north side of the Nickel Plate Railroad tracks at the back of what was to become the campus of Case Institute of Technology. The outcome of this experiment was to increase the accuracy of the measured speed of light to a level unsurpassed for forty-five years. Michelson refined the measurement even further in the mid-1920's.

During October of 1884, Michelson attended the lectures of Sir William Thomson (later to become Lord Kelvin) at The Johns Hopkins University in Baltimore, Maryland. There he met the highly respected Edward Williams Morley, a professor of physical chemistry. Their friendship and resulting scientific collaboration led to their joint investigations of the velocity of light. Their research on the motion of light through water helped Albert Einstein in his development of certain aspects of the special theory of relativity. In 1887, they conducted the now-famous Michelson-Morley experiment, which was designed to measure the velocity of light through the luminiferous ether, the medium that had been assumed to exist throughout the universe and through which light waves were believed to travel. Ample evidence existed to support the theory that light consisted of waves, and it was necessary to postulate a medium through which the light waves could move, just as water transmits waves in the ocean or air transmits sound waves. Michelson reasoned that the ether should affect the speed of light, as measured by an observer on Earth moving in orbit around the Sun. For example, light should travel along the direction of Earth's orbital path more slowly than it would travel at a right angle to Earth's motion.

Michelson and Morley used the interferometer to split and recombine a beam of light waves and tried to observe changes in the pattern of interference fringes produced by the light traveling along two different paths, one at a right angle to Earth's motion and the other parallel to the motion. This setup was comparable to the motion of a boat taking a round trip up and down a river current equal in distance to a trip back and forth across the river. It was well-known that the boat's trip along the current would take longer than the trip across the current. A similar result was expected for the speed of the light parallel to Earth's motion versus its speed at right angles to Earth's motion.

The measurements involved were extremely delicate. Michelson and Morley decided on a rotating platform on a sturdy base that would stabilize their equipment and prevent erroneous experimental results. The platform used was a large sand-stone slab that measured five feet square and one foot thick. They mounted an interferometer on the slab. To minimize vibrations and possible jarring of the interferometer, the base floated in a circular pool of mercury.

The interferometer consisted of several mirrors to reflect the split beam of light back and forth from one to another until the path traveled by each beam measured about 32 meters. Such a long path length would allow for a high degree of accuracy. The apparatus was so well adjusted that the pressure of a finger could make it slowly rotate for hours, completing a revolution about every six minutes. Measurements were made at various stages marked off along the base. The light source was a lamp, and the beams were split at ninety-degree angles by passing them through half-silvered mirrors in the center of the interferometer. These mirrors split the initial beam and sent two beams reflecting back and forth between the mirrors on the rim of the slab. When the beams were reunited and observed through a telescope mounted on one corner of the stone, the interference fringes could be seen. By observing the change in the interference patterns as the apparatus rotated, the scientists could determine how much the speed of the light beams had changed.

When the last measurements of this experiment were taken, the results added up to precisely nothing. There was no denying the evidence: The supposed ether had had no effect whatsoever on the speed of the light. The "null result" that Michelson and Morley achieved in Cleveland during the summer of 1887 was to have a profound effect on man's understanding of nature. The experiment disproved the hypothesis that space was filled with ether, a medium through which light, an electromagnetic wave, could propagate. Although scientists were confused by the results of the experiment at the time, the findings eventually helped Einstein to develop the special theory of relativity and other physicists to construct the science of quantum mechanics.

In 1889, Michelson was appointed to the first Chair of Physics at the newly founded Clark University in Worcester, Massachusetts. At about the same time, John D. Rockefeller formed the University of Chicago, which hired Michelson. While at Chicago, he received many honors, including several honorary doctorates from several universities. Shortly after his appointment at Clark University he had standardized the international meter in terms of light waves by perfecting the methods he and Morley had used earlier. More than thirty years later, the International Committee on Weights and Measures adopted this standard meter. Michelson's precise measurements have been used to determine the standard length of a meter ever since.

In 1907, Michelson became the first U.S. citizen to receive the Nobel Prize. In his remaining years, he divided his time among a number of scientific activities. He remeasured the speed of light, while in Pasadena, California, after his retirement from the University of Chicago in 1929. He was also involved in using a specially designed version of his interferometer to measure the diameters of Jupiter's satellites and some of the brighter stars.

## Bibliography

*Primary*

PHYSICS: Among the more important of the many publications of Michelson are the following: "On a Method of Measuring the Velocity of Light," *American Journal of Science*, vol. 15, 1878; "Experimental Determination of the Velocity of Light," *Proceedings of the American Association for the Advancement of Science*, vol. 27, 1878; "The Relative Motion of the Earth and the Luminiferous Ether," *American Journal of Science*, vol. 22, 1881; "Influence of Motion of the Medium on the Velocity of Light," *American Journal of Science*, series 3, vol. 31, 1886 (with E. W. Morley); "On the Relative Motion of the Earth and the Luminiferous Ether," *American Journal of Science*, series 3, vol. 34, 1887 (with Morley); "On the Feasibility of Establishing a Light Wave as the Ultimate Standard of Length," *American Journal of Science*, series 3, vol. 38, 1889 (with Morley); "On the Application of Interference Methods to Astronomical Measurements," *Philosophical Magazine*, vol. 30, 1890; "Comparison of the International Meter with the Wave Length of the Light of Cadmium," *Astronomy and Astrophysics*, vol. 12, 1893; *Light Waves and Their Uses*, 1903; "The Echelon Spectroscope," *Astrophysics Journal*, vol. 8, 1921; "Measurement of the Diameter of Alpha Orionis with the Interferometer," *Astrophysics Journal*, vol. 53, 1921 (with F. G. Pease); *Studies in Optics*, 1927.

*Secondary*

Haugan, Mark P., and Clifford M. Will. "Modern Tests of Special Relativity." *Physics Today* 40 (May, 1987): 69-76. An article about plans for new experiments, particularly those based in space, for testing the special theory of relativity.

Jaffe, Bernard. *Michelson and the Speed of Light*. Garden City, N.Y.: Doubleday, 1960. This delightful book details Michelson's scientific career. Michelson's scientific accomplishments are discussed in chronological order. Stresses the importance of his experiments to the advancement of physics in the twentieth century. Suitable for general audiences.

Livingston, Dorothy Michelson. *The Master of Light*. New York: Charles Scribner's Sons, 1973. This lengthy book was written by one of Michelson's daughters from his second marriage. It details many of Michelson's personal and professional papers, including letters sent to and received from colleagues all over the world. Much of the information presented by the author was obtained in interviews with people who knew or worked with Michelson. In many ways, this book is the most complete assessment of the United States' first experimental master. Lengthy, but understandable to the general reader.

Moyer, Albert E. "Michelson in 1887." *Physics Today* 40 (May, 1987): 50-56. An article about Michelson as he was about the time of his famous experiment.

Swenson, Loyd S., Jr. "Michelson and Measurement." *Physics Today* 40 (May, 1987): 24-30. This article surveys Michelson's measurement experiments and his techniques. The text is straightforward and suitable for general audiences.

Wilson, John Henry. *Albert A. Michelson: America's First Nobel Prize Physicist.* New York: Julian Messner, 1958. This short account of Michelson's life is a standard biography. Although scientific accomplishments are mentioned and simply explained throughout the book, the emphasis is on Michelson's life and character. Suitable for the lay reader.

*James Charles LoPresto*

# 1908

### Physics
Gabriel Lippmann, France

### Chemistry
Lord Rutherford, Great Britain

### Physiology or Medicine
Paul Ehrlich, Germany
Ilya Mechnikov, Russia

### Literature
Rudolf Christoph Eucken, Germany

### Peace
Klas Pontus Arnoldson, Sweden
Fredrik Bajer, Denmark

# GABRIEL LIPPMANN
# 1908

*Born:* Hollerich, Luxembourg; August 16, 1845
*Died:* At sea, en route from Canada to France; July 13, 1921
*Nationality:* French
*Area of concentration:* Applied mathematical physics

*Lippmann recognized in the 1880's that interference phenomena could cause reflected light of different wavelengths to be recorded at different levels in a photographic film, which resulted in the invention of color photography*

## The Award

*Presentation*

King Gustav V of Sweden presented the Nobel Prize in Physics to Gabriel Lippmann on December 10, 1908. The presentation address was given the day before by Professor K. B. Hasselberg, President of the Royal Swedish Academy of Sciences, who mentioned the pioneers of photography—Joseph Niepce, Louis Daguerre, and others—and cited Alexandre-Edmond Becquerel's finding in 1849 that a silver chloride-on-silver plate exposed to colored light took on the color of the light. The image was impermanent, however, and no photographic technology was established. An explanation based on wave interference was advanced by Wilhelm Zenker and later by Lord Rayleigh. In 1890, Otto Wiener confirmed the production of colors in reflected light by wave interference, and color photographs based on this phenomenon became theoretically possible.

In 1891, Lippmann displayed his method to the Paris Academy of Sciences. A glass plate spread with a fine-grained emulsion of silver nitrate and potassium bromide in gelatin was backed with mercury metal, and the picture was taken *through* the glass plate, so that light reflected from the mercury. In this way, the half-wavelength layers of silver atoms were produced when the plate was exposed. When it was developed by normal means and illuminated by white light, the many layers of silver mirrors at any point reinforced one wavelength (color) of light while other colors traveled non-wavelength paths that destroyed them by interference.

Although three-color photography using pigmented layers existed at the turn of the century, Lippmann's method was the first that could produce color photographs on a single plate with a single exposure. For this reason, and for the grasp of both theoretical and applied physics that led him to his process, the Swedish Academy chose Gabriel Lippmann as the 1908 recipient of the Nobel Prize in Physics.

*Nobel lecture*

Lippmann's Nobel lecture, delivered on December 14, 1908, runs to fewer than one thousand words and takes perhaps six minutes to recite; even with one demonstration and a series of slides it could not have been more than twelve to fifteen minutes long. Nevertheless, as with Lippmann's many short papers, it covered the subject. He began with a review of the background of the problem recapitulating that given by Professor Hasselberg, differing only in pointing out that Becquerel's colored plates cannot be explained by interference, although the other observations can. His explanation of his method is essentially that given above, adding the comparison that selective color reflection in thin films is the same interference phenomenon seen in soap bubbles and mother of pearl. He then demonstrated the necessity for maintaining the spacing of the reflecting layers of silver atoms by projecting a photograph of a color spectrum onto the screen and wetting the projection plate. As the gelatin expanded the colors disappeared because the spacing was no longer correct; and as it dried they reappeared one by one, beginning at the red end of the spectrum.

After this demonstration Lippmann alluded to the problem of many colors being recorded at the same point on the plate, which one might suppose would give an infinity of planes of silver atoms amounting to a continuous block. He only hinted at the depth of theory underlying his method by stating that Fourier analysis had resolved this difficulty and had given a general statement of the conditions of interference and reinforcement of waves of varying length. He then discussed the technology of the process, mentioning his own success with albumen emulsions and the improvements of Vladimir Valenta and August and Louis Lumière (inventors of the cinematograph) with grainless gelatin plates. "Colour photography," he concluded, "has been perfected." He supported this claim by projecting a series of plates— paintings, flowers, landscapes—in color. All were taken using one-minute exposures, he explained, and most were developed "on the mantelpiece of a hotel room" in about a quarter of an hour. The exposure was still too long, although it was originally fifteen minutes. "Progress may continue. Life is short and progress is slow."

*Critical reception*

Because the popular and semipopular press had been reporting Lippmann's work in photography since 1892, reaction to his receipt of the Nobel Prize was reasonably knowledgeable and generally favorable. In its Sunday editions of May 24 and June 21, 1908, *The New York Times* discussed Lippmann's technique (later known as "integral photography"), which produced images with a three-dimensional aspect by use of a plate with thousands of tiny spheres of gelatin or glass, each of which took a separate picture. When the Nobel awards were reported on December 11, *The New York Times* followed up with an editorial stating that Lippmann's "attainments in [his] special field may be equaled by some others, but are probably not surpassed." The Parisian daily *Le Temps* was not so forthcoming, failing to report any Nobel Prizes except the peace award (although in earlier years it had run articles on the photographic methods). The French semipopular scientific journal *La Nature* reported on December 12 that "the Prize in physics is awarded to M. Gabriel Lippmann, whose notable discovery of color photography has popularized his name with the public, but who was already well-known among physicists for his work in electro-capillarity, polarization of batteries, electrical techniques, etc." The article also mentions the integral photography work. The British journal *Nature* also reported on December 17 that Lippmann had received the physics prize, but made no comment.

False rumors abounded in 1908. On November 12, *The New York Times* announced: "It is unofficially stated . . . that William [*sic*] Marconi . . . is to receive the next Nobel Prize in Physics." On December 3, *Nature* stated that "the Nobel prize for physics has been awarded to Prof. M. Planck," only to retract it a week later and give Lippmann's name. The week before the generous appraisal given above, *La Nature* announced that "the Nobel prize will be given this year . . . in physics to professor Max Plank [*sic*] of Berlin." No indication is given of the source of these incorrect reports.

## Biography

Gabriel Jonas Lippmann was born in Hollerich, Luxembourg, on August 16, 1845. His father, a tanner, came from Lorraine; his mother was Alsatian. He had two younger sisters. In 1848 the family moved to Paris, where he entered the Lycée Napoléon at age thirteen. An irregular student, he excelled in science and mathematics, French, English, and history, and he tried to avoid all else. At seventeen he chose physics as a vocation, but when he entered the École Normale at twenty-three, he failed the *agrégé* examination that would have made him a teacher. He came to the attention of Louis-Émile Bertin, the under-director at the École Normale, however, and of the Minister of Public Instruction, Jules Simon, who sent him to German universities for liaison and study. He earned the *Dr.phil.* at Heidelberg in 1874 and the *Dr.-ès-sc. phys.* a year later at Paris, on the strength of his researches.

In 1878, Lippmann joined the Faculty of Science at the University of Paris in the position of *maître de conférences*. In 1883 he became professor of mathematical physics; and three years later he was made professor of experimental physics, succeeding Jules Jamin. He also became director of the research laboratory, an installation later transferred to the Sorbonne. He held this position until his death.

Lippmann became a member of the Academy of Sciences (Paris) in 1883 and was president in 1912. He was a member of the Board of the Bureau of Longitudes, Paris. In 1908 he was elected a Foreign Member (Fellow) of the Royal Society, London. He wed the daughter of the writer Victor Cherbuliez in 1888. In the years following World War I, Lippmann studied the organization of research support in Great Britain and the United States, in relation to that in France. His involvement led him to accompany Marshal Fayolle on a mission to the United States and Canada in 1921. On his return from the latter country, he was struck by an infection that led to renal failure. He died on board the ship *La France* on July 13, 1921, and was buried five days later in the cemetery in Montparnasse, Paris.

## Scientific Career

Lippmann was fortunate during the years of his education to encounter people who recognized his abilities despite his determination not to conform to the rigid pattern of French instruction. These men acted as mentors and not infrequently gave him positions for which he was well fitted but not formally qualified. The first major influence was Charles d'Almeida, an eccentric scholar who had been imprisoned (falsely) as a spy in the American Civil War and who had founded the Société Française de Physique and the *Journal de physique*. Through d'Almeida, Lippmann chose physics when he was only seventeen, never wavering thereafter as he studied all the mathematics and physical science available to him. This single-mindedness could only hold him back in the French educational system. He came to the École Normale at the relatively late age of twenty-three and failed the *agrégé* examination at the end of the course. Fortunately, he became attached to the under-director, Bertin, who was an editor of the *Annales de chimie et de physique* and set Lippmann to analyzing and abstracting English and German articles for the journal. This excited his interest in contemporary (1860's) research in electricity, and his early efforts in this line brought him to the attention of the Minister of Public Instruction Jules Simon. Simon arranged for three consecutive missions to German universities, intended to promote cooperation with their laboratories but also to allow Lippmann to continue his studies. This he did, with Wilhelm Kühne and Gustav Kirchhoff in Heidelberg, and with Hermann von Helmholtz in Berlin, earning his doctorate as a research degree in March, 1874. His French doctorate in July, 1875, was also based on research rather than prescribed studies.

Lippmann's research began in the very active field of electrical phenomena, and his doctoral work at Heidelberg produced a device that was employed thereafter in laboratories throughout the world, the capillary electrometer. When Lippmann first went to Heidelberg, Kühne showed him a long-known phenomenon: When a bead of metallic mercury is covered with dilute sulfuric acid and touched with an iron wire, the mercury recoils almost as if alive. Reasoning that the surface tension of the mercury must be altered by electrolytic action between the two metals, Lippmann found that the effect could be increased or decreased when a potential was impressed on the metals, and that the potential-recoil relation could be quantified. Enclosing the mercury, the wire, and the acid solution in a slighty tilted glass tube produced the capillary electrometer, capable of measuring potential differences as small as a millivolt. The device could be calibrated and used for absolute measurements, but it was more commonly employed as a null indicator in potentiometer circuits and the like. Later Lippmann published the mathematical theory of the device, based on an electrical double layer at the interface between the metals; his work confirmed an independent treatment by Helmholtz. The original work was published in 1873 in Poggendorffs *Annalen der Physik*, at fourteen pages one of Lippmann's longest publications, and was judged good enough to serve as his thesis at Heidelberg, earning for him the doctorate summa cum laude. The thesis for the French doctorate in 1875 was an extension of the same work.

For the first decade of his career, Lippmann concentrated on electricity and turned out a body of work, headed by the ubiquitous capillary electrometer, that could by itself earn for him a place in the history of physics. The mercury capillary studies led him into investigation of surfaces of metals, water, and solutions: charged, polarized, modified by solutes, and showing altered optical properties. He demonstrated the equivalence and reversibility of motion and potential in the electrometer, and he even produced a motor based on the phenomenon. He established the principles of conservation of electricity and inertia of static electricity. He demonstrated the coulombic attraction of electrolyte solutions. He produced further instruments based on the mercury-surface effect: a galvanometer, an electrodynamometer, and a device for measuring quantity of electricity. Like the capillary electrometer, these instruments were not affected by magnetic fields (such as that of Earth)—an important attribute at a time when the principal alternative was the permanent-magnet galvanometer. Lippmann also built a "spherical" electrometer in which charge was measured by the physical force of repulsion between two metal hemispheres. He was much concerned with early precision measurements of the unit of electrical resistance, the ohm; this concern led him into other precision measurements: of time, temperature, and astronomical properties.

In the years after this first decade, Lippmann produced another galvanometer, this one astatic (without any tendency toward a rest position). He followed up on some early work in thermodynamics with a theoretical demonstration of the equivalence of heat and electrical energy, positing that absolute temperature and electrical potential are equivalent measures in the two systems. He also published theoretical studies of the properties of circuits with no electrical resistance that were later confirmed by work in superconductivity. He investigated the internal thermal osmosis of gases and liquids, and the effect of external forces on the vapor pressure of liquids.

Lippmann's interest in methods of measurement led him into astronomy and seismology and established his connection with the Bureau des Longitudes in Paris. He began with efforts to measure absolute time, independent of the diurnal motion of Earth, for which he devised electrical methods of measurement. He also developed stroboscopic methods for comparing the frequencies of pendulums or tuning forks, and he found that if the energy that keeps a pendulum swinging is applied exactly at the bottom of its arc (electrically), the period is not perturbed. Application of photography to astronomy led him to devise the coelostat, a device with a rotating mirror that held an entire portion of the sky motionless long enough for exposure of a photographic plate. This was a great improvement of the earlier siderostat, which held one star in place while other objects made circular tracks around it. Further applications of photography allowed measurements of coordinates for stars and the Sun, and of longitudinal differences on Earth's surface. In the course of these investigations, Lippmann published many papers describing improvements in scopes, collimators, and the like, and he devised a photographic method to eliminate the "personal equation" in measuring the times of astronomical events.

Optical methods also produced Lippmann's first seismograph, which fixed on the image of the Sun and measured the acceleration of tremors by the disturbance of the Sun's image. Later he suggested the use of the telegraph both for early warning and for measurement of velocity of propagation of earthquake waves. His final seismograph design used a liquid column to measure tremors. Lippmann's observation of earthquake waves and the difference of their velocities in crust and mantle led him to an early statement of what is now called the principle of isostasy: that since the crust is "floating" on the mantle, the high parts (mountains) must be balanced by correspondingly deep roots, while the low parts (coastal plains) will rest on a thin layer of crust.

Finally, the photographic investigations for which Lippmann received the Nobel Prize were published in more than two dozen papers during the decades from 1890 to 1910, and presented orally at conferences both in France and abroad. Lippmann also wrote three textbooks for his classes at the Sorbonne, on thermodynamics (three editions), absolute electrical units, and acoustics and optics. His lifetime output runs to more than two hundred papers of an elegant brevity that averaged about three and a half pages each but covered the material nevertheless.

## Bibliography

*Primary*

PHYSICS: "Relation entre les phénomènes électriques et capillaires," *Comptes rendus hebdomadaires des séances de l'Académie des sciences*, vol. 76, 1873; "Sur une propriété d'une surface d'eau électrisée," *Comptes rendus hebdomadaires des séances de l'Académie des sciences*, vol. 81, 1875; "Extension du principe de Carnot à la théorie des phénomènes électriques," *Comptes rendus hebdomadaires des séances de l'Académie des sciences*, vol. 82, 1876; *Cours de thermodynamique, professé pendant le premiere semestre 1885-1886*, 1886, revised 1889; *Leçons d'acoustique et d'optique*, 1889; "Photographies colorées du spectre, sur albumine et sur gélatine bichromatées," *Comptes rendus hebdomadaires des séances de l'Académie des sciences*, vol. 115, 1892; "Sur la théorie de la photographie des couleurs simples et composées par la méthode interférentielle," *Comptes rendus hebdomadaires des séances de l'Académie des sciences*, vol. 118, 1894; "Sur un coelostat," *Comptes rendus hebdomadaires des séances de l'Académie des sciences*, vol. 120, 1895; "Sur l'entretien du movement du pendule sans perturbations," *Comptes rendus hebdomadaires des séances de l'Académie des sciences*, vol. 122, 1896; "Méthodes pour comparer, à l'aide de l'étincelle électrique, les durées d'oscillation de deux pendules réglés sensiblement à la même période," *Comptes rendus hebdomadaires des séances de l'Académie des sciences*, vol. 124, 1897; *Unités électriques absolues: Leçons professées à la Sorbonne*, 1899; "Sur l'emploi d'un fil télégraphique pour l'inscription des tremblements de terre et la mesure de leur vitesse de propagation," *Comptes rendus hebdomadaires des séances de l'Académie des sciences*, vol. 136, 1903; "Appareil pour enregistrer l'accélération absolue des mouvements séismiques," *Comptes rendus hebdomadaires des séances de l'Académie des sciences*, vol. 148, 1909;

"Sur une méthode photographique direct pour la détermination des différences des longitudes," *Comptes rendus hebdomadaires des séances de l'Académie des sciences*, vol. 158, 1914; "Méthode pour le réglage d'une lunette en collimation," *Comptes rendus hebdomadaires des séances de l'Académie des sciences*, vol. 158, 1914.

*Secondary*

Appell, M. P. "Gabriel Lippmann." In *Annuaire publié par le Bureau des longitudes*. Paris: Bureau des Longitudes, 1923. Presents some material not found in other references, particularly quotations from contemporaries concerning Lippmann's character and personality.

Berthelot, Daniel. "La Vie d'un savant: Gabriel Lippmann." *Revue de deux mondes* 7, no. 10 (1922): 19-46. The most complete of several obituaries which appeared in various French journals, by the son of the eminent scientist Marcelin Berthelot. The scientific judgments are sound, and the piece contains interesting material about Lippmann's early scientific associations and about his knowledge and judgment in music and the other arts.

Lebon, Ernest. *Gabriel Lippmann: Biographie, bibliographie analytique écrits*. Paris: Gauthier-Villars, 1911. A short (seventy-page) but very thorough bibliography of Lippmann's works, preceded by a biographical note that treats both Lippmann's personal and his scientific life up to his sixty-fifth year, when all but a dozen or so of his publications had appeared. Some of the later obituary notices seem indebted to this volume in their choice of anecdotes and phrasing. The publications are arranged according to category of research and many of the entries have an analytical abstract. Better yet, nearly all the entries cite one or more analyses or reactions by other scientists in other journals. A four-page listing or degrees, positions, prizes, and decorations gives many more than the few listed in this article's text.

Picard, Émile. "La Vie et l'œuvre de Gabriel Lippmann." *Revue scientifique: Revue rose* 70 (1932): 131-141. A highly laudatory account in which anecdotes of Lippmann's personality and thinking are as important as accounts of his scientific achievements, which lack technical depth.

Schlessinger, Bernard S., and June H. Schlessinger, eds. *Who's Who of Nobel Prize Winners*. Phoenix, Ariz.: Oryx Press, 1986. The brief entry on Lippmann is one of the few accessible resources in English in addition to the present article.

Turner, H. H. "Some Notes on the Use and Adjustment of the Coelostat." *Monthly Notices of the Royal Astronomical Society* 56 (1896): 408. Another rare English resource, this one is on Lippmann's area of scientific research.

*Robert M. Hawthorne, Jr.*

# 1909

## Physics
Guglielmo Marconi, Italy
Karl Ferdinand Braun, Germany

## Chemistry
Wilhelm Ostwald, Germany

## Physiology or Medicine
Emil Kocher, Switzerland

## Literature
Selma Lagerlöf, Sweden

## Peace
Baron d'Estournelles de Constant, France
Auguste Beernaert, Belgium

# GUGLIELMO MARCONI
## 1909

*Born:* Bologna, Italy; April 25, 1874
*Died:* Rome, Italy; July 20, 1937
*Nationality:* Italian
*Area of concentration:* Radiotelegraphy

*Marconi's insight into the potential of using long electromagnetic waves for telegraphic communication led to the development of a wireless telegraphy system, by which transatlantic communication was made possible*

## The Award

*Presentation*

Hans Hildebrand, President of the Royal Swedish Academy of Sciences, presented the Nobel Prize in Physics to Guglielmo Marconi and Karl Braun, the cowinner, on December 10, 1909, on behalf of the Royal Swedish Academy of Sciences and King Gustav V, from whom Marconi accepted the prize. Hildebrand's presentation acknowledged some of the theoretical and experimental discoveries upon which Marconi's accomplishments were based: Michael Faraday (1791-1867) had believed that electricity and the behavior of light were connected; James Clerk Maxwell (1831-1879) had developed a mathematical description of this relationship; Heinrich Hertz (1857-1894) had demonstrated experimentally that electric currents can give rise to waves that propagate through space at the speed of light. Marconi was the first to realize the potential application of this knowledge, and although others attempted to send wireless communications over significant distances, it was Marconi who was the first to succeed. Beginning with his first effective trial at communicating via Hertzian waves in 1895, Marconi progressively developed a reliable means of transatlantic wireless communication, used also by shipping firms and navies. Marconi's original method of transmission suffered from a phenomenon called "damped oscillations," the result of which was that the signals were very weak at the receiving end, and therefore subject to interference from other transmissions. Professor Braun's contribution was a modification to the transmitter circuitry that reduced the damping in the waves, leading to stronger signals at the receiving station. The presentation ended with the recognition that it was now possible to communicate with distant places that were previously unreachable by telegraphy using wires.

*Nobel lecture*

Marconi's Nobel lecture, "Wireless Telegraphic Communication," is an account of his experimental research over the preceding fourteen years and reflects on the practical significance of some of the results. The lecture takes an empirical perspective, in keeping with Marconi's own research philosophy. Marconi was careful to cite the theoretical and experimental work of others which contributed to his efforts;

he began with acknowledgment of the connection between discoveries in the propagation of "electric waves" and advances in wireless telegraphy. Even without formal training in physics, Marconi became interested in the writings of Heinrich Hertz, Édouard Branly (1844-1940), and Augusto Righi (1850-1920). His own experiments in the applications of Hertzian waves for communications purposes began in 1895, with the realization soon thereafter that this means of transmitting signals held great potential advantages over other methods that depended upon clarity of the atmosphere.

Marconi's first important innovation was an improvement to the Branly coherer (a rudimentary device for detecting radio signals, which consisted of a glass tube containing iron filings, whose electrical resistance decreased when subjected to Hertzian waves); he increased its sensitivity by replacing the iron with silver and nickel filings. This allowed reception of signals at a distance of one-half mile, where previously only a few yards had been possible. Next, he made the coherer act as a trigger for a sensitive relay connected to a Morse telegraphic recording device.

Marconi's next contribution was the introduction of earth (ground) connections and high-elevation antennas for both the transmitting and receiving devices. This practice allowed transmissions between France and England by 1899.

The lecture then describes the use of "syntonized" (tuned) receivers, which allowed communications without interference to other wireless systems. Marconi explained how he and Braun had worked simultaneously to some extent (unbeknown to each other) on tuned, coupled oscillator-antenna systems, whose resonance achieved a highly efficient radiation of the electric waves.

In addressing the problem of communication via wireless telegraphy over great distances and geographic obstacles, Marconi cited Sir John Ambrose Fleming's book *The Principles of Electric Wave Telegraphy and Telephony* (1906) and its treatment of superior wave propagation over a conducting surface; the use of earth connections at the receiving and transmitting ends of a wireless system to enhance current flow between the stations is thus justified.

An extended discourse on transmissions over water followed, in which Marconi noted the poor propagation of signals during daylight hours and Fleming's analysis, which partially corroborates this phenomenon for long wavelengths. The Canadian government supported construction of a wireless station at Glace Bay, Nova Scotia, to further Marconi's efforts at transatlantic communication, which he achieved on December 16, 1902, between Glace Bay and Poldhu, in Cornwall, England. With the discovery that very long wavelengths (approximately 12,000 feet) allowed transatlantic communications even during the daylight hours, Marconi developed several more efficient antenna systems, which he described in some detail. Two other important inventions were a modified rotating spark gap, which created several hundred sparks per second, thus producing a musical note in the receiving apparatus (rather than a series of clicks), making the transmitted signal more easily distinguishable from atmospheric static and also resonating better in the tuned circuit; and the magnetic detector, which replaced the Branly coherer in most receivers.

The lecture concludes with pronouncements of the importance that wireless telegraphy has attained for commercial shipping, communication with isolated places, and transmission of messages between countries. This form of communication, Marconi noted, was now established and would continue to progress.

## Critical reception

By 1909, Marconi's identity was so well established that *The Times* of London announced the Nobel awards referring to him simply by surname. In her book *My Father, Marconi* (1962), Degna Marconi claims that the joint award to Marconi and Braun was "to the surprise of the whole world," with both men being equally puzzled about sharing the prize. Niels Hugh de Vaudrey Heathcote, in *Nobel Prize Winners in Physics, 1901-1950* (1953), notes that while Marconi's name was quite familiar to the public, and Braun's obscure, the contributions of the latter were considered no less worthy by the scientific community. *The New York Times* ran a short editorial on December 11, praising the selections of all the prizewinners in the sciences.

## Biography

Guglielmo Marconi was born in Bologna, Italy, on April 25, 1874, to Giuseppe and Annie (née Jameson) Marconi, who provided private tutoring for him until, at age twelve, he entered the Istituto di Cavallero Via delle Terme in Florence for a year, followed by enrollment at the technical institute at Leghorn. He went to England in February, 1896, to secure financial support for his experiments. In recognition of the importance of his work, the Italian government allowed him to fulfill his military obligation as naval attaché to the Italian Embassy in London, which afforded him time to conduct his experimental research. After amassing private support in England, in 1897 he formed the Wireless Telegraph and Signal Company, Ltd. (which in 1900 became Marconi's Wireless Telegraph Company, Ltd.).

Marconi wed Beatrice O'Brien on March 16, 1905, and had three children: Degna (born 1908), Giulio (1910), and Gioia (1916). An avid motorist, Marconi lost his right eye in an accident in 1912. During World War I, he served in the Italian army and navy. His first marriage was annulled in 1927; he was remarried to Countess Maria Cristina Bezzi-Scali the same year, and had another daughter, Elettra, in 1930.

Marconi received numerous honors: He was knighted in Italy in 1902; he was made a freeman of Rome in 1903; he received the Albert medal of the Royal Society of Arts and the Franklin and John Fritz medals in 1909; he was made an honorary Grand Cross of the Victorian Order in 1914; he served as plenipotentiary delegate to the peace conference in Paris in 1919, where he signed the peace treaties with Austria and Bulgaria; he was made a *marchese* and was nominated to the Italian senate in 1929; and he was elected president of the Royal Italian Academy in 1930. Marconi died in Rome on July 20, 1937, and is buried in Bologna.

## Scientific Career

It was an obituary of Heinrich Hertz describing his discovery of electric waves which catalyzed the idea for Marconi, at once both subtle and profound, of using Hertzian waves for communications across space. It is only the pervasiveness of this means of communication in modern times that makes the idea seemingly trivial in retrospect.

Although he never attended a university, Marconi was influenced by Professors Vincenzo Rosa of the Liceo Niccolini and Augusto Righi at the University of Bologna, who were themselves interested in the physics of Hertzian waves. Marconi's early experiments employed rather crude equipment: a spark gap (controlled by a Morse telegraph key), attached at either end to a horizontal rod with a metal plate at its endpoint, as the transmitter; and a Branly coherer on the receiving end, connected to a Morse telegraphic sounder, which emitted clicks corresponding to the opening and closing of the telegraph key. This system suffered two principal disadvantages: it was susceptible to interference from natural discharges of electric current (lightning) and was useful over only a few yards' distance. By attaching a vertical antenna to one end of the spark gap and grounding the other end, and by making the same arrangement with the coherer in the receiving apparatus, it was possible to send messages across a distance of one mile. Marconi would shortly receive the first patent ever in radiotelegraphy for this apparatus from the British.

Failing to secure financial support from the Italian government to construct more sophisticated and powerful transmitting equipment, Marconi went to Great Britain, where his efforts were advanced by Sir William Preece (1834-1913), Chief Engineer of the British Post Office. Preece gathered considerable public support and financial assistance through a series of lectures on Marconi's work. These funds were used to form what eventually became Marconi's Wireless Telegraph Company, Ltd., in 1900. The company, which held all Marconi's patents and financed his research and development, installed wireless systems in lightships and lighthouses along the British coast. Acknowledging Marconi's successes, the Italian government invited him to construct a station at Spezia, from which he communicated with Italian naval vessels twelve miles away. By March, 1899, transmissions across the English Channel to France, covering a distance of eighty-five miles, were possible.

In 1897, Sir Oliver Lodge (1851-1940) proposed using a receiver and transmitter tuned to the same frequency as a means of increasing the efficiency of power usage and reducing interference from other wireless systems using different frequencies. Lodge's suggestion was to adjust the resonant frequency in each device by means of a variable inductor. Marconi was the first actually to try this method, "syntonized wireless telegraphy," although he used a somewhat more sophisticated method involving both variable inductance and capacitance in the circuits. He filed a patent in 1900: No. 7777 Improvements for Apparatus in Wireless Telegraphy, which is generally cited as the most famous in the history of radiotelegraphy. Lodge also received a patent for his approach, which the Marconi company bought in 1911, in order to forestall potential legal conflicts.

Marconi's ambition was to achieve transatlantic communication by wireless, a goal that he approached systematically. By 1900, he had succeeded in transmitting messages over a distance of 150 miles, and in December, 1901, he achieved the first transatlantic communication (not documented by witnesses) between a temporary station at St. John's, Newfoundland (using an antenna attached to a kite), and Poldhu, Cornwall, a distance of 1,800 miles. The first documented success was in 1902, over a distance of 2,000 miles, between Glace Bay, Nova Scotia, and Poldhu. In London, *The Times* used this link in early 1903 to get reports from its New York correspondent.

During the course of these experiments, Marconi discovered the phenomenon of ionospheric refraction, in which radio waves of certain wavelengths are bent by the lower portions of the ionosphere (allowing propagation over great distances), while signals of other wavelengths are absorbed by the ionosphere; further, the absorption effect is more pronounced on the daylight side of Earth. It was correctly surmised by Marconi, Fleming, and others that this diurnal variation is caused by the flux of electrons from the Sun and the resultant increased conductivity in the ionosphere.

A dissatisfaction with the sensitivity of the Branly coherer as a detector led to the development and patenting of Marconi's magnetic detector (1902), which operated by moving a belt of iron wires through two coaxial coils of wire, one connected to the antenna and the other to a telephone receiver. The coils were subjected to a constant magnetic field from permanent magnets. An incoming signal generated a magnetic field in the first coil, thus changing the magnetization of the iron and resulting in a click in the telephone receiver. It would remain one of the standard detectors for three years, until Fleming invented the vacuum tube, which would ultimately lead to an amplifying receiver.

In his very first experiments, Marconi had attempted to direct the radiated signal, and thus strengthen it, by surrounding the transmitter with a hemispherical shell of copper. The shell was opened toward the receiver, whose antenna also had a copper dish to help concentrate the signal; this device was unsuccessful largely because the shells were too small relative to the dominant wavelengths being radiated. By 1905, however, Marconi had developed and patented the horizontal directional antenna, using only wire antenna elements, which worked well for long wavelengths (up to 30,000 feet). This antenna, which formed the basis for all modern radio communication, consisted of a horizontal antenna (the driven element), connected to the transmitter, and several additional wires of different lengths, all in the horizontal plane, lying parallel to the driven element. By adjusting the spacing between the elements, it was possible to induce them to reradiate the signal from the driven element in such a way that the signals added constructively in the desired direction but canceled one another to some extent in all other directions. It was this type of antenna (the multi-element beam system) that made communications between England and Australia possible in 1918.

Following World War I, Marconi revisited the idea of using reflectors around the antennas, only now with wavelengths on the order of 15 meters (shortwaves). Using a retired British navy yacht (purchased by his company and christened *Elettra*), Marconi was able to receive strong signals of the 15-meter wavelength at distances of 1,400 miles from Poldhu at a transmitting power of only 1 kilowatt. This corresponded to a hundredfold decrease in power from what was normally required, made possible through the use of the beam antenna system, as well as the increased ionospheric reflectivity at that wavelength. By 1924, long-distance communications were so successful that the Marconi company was contracted to establish a shortwave communication system which would link England with the rest of the British Empire.

Marconi continued to experiment with ever shorter wavelengths, down to 55 centimeters (microwaves). It was only in these tests, late in his career, that the initial idea of using metallic reflectors proved truly practical. Parabolic dish reflectors were found to give the best results for collimating the transmitted beam and for concentrating the received signal. Because of the strong directivity that could be achieved, and the attendant decrease in power required, this system made it possible to communicate with less chance of interception by other receiving equipment, a feature that found some military applications. In 1932, Marconi installed the first microwave radio-telephone system, for communication between Vatican City and the pope's summer palace at Castel Gandolfo. During that same period, he pioneered the development of radio navigation, making use of his improved microwave technology. While it was widely claimed that Marconi was developing a microwave weapon for use by Italy's Fascist regime (which he and his second wife, Cristina, openly supported), he denied such claims, always preferring to emphasize the lifesaving role that radio played.

## Bibliography

*Primary*

PHYSICS: "Wireless Telegraphy," *Proceedings of the Institution of Electrical Engineers*, vol. 28, 1899; "Recent Progress in Wireless Telegraphy," *London Electrician*, February 9, 1900; "A Note on the Effect of Daylight upon the Propagation of Electromagnetic Impulses Over Long Distances," *Proceedings of the Royal Society (London)*, June 12, 1902; "A Magnetic Detector of Electric Waves Which Can Be Employed as a Receiver for Space Telegraphy," *London Electrician*, July 18, 1902; "The Practicability of Wireless Telegraphy," *Scientific American Supplement*, June 28, 1902; "The Progress of Space Telegraphy," *Scientific American Supplement*, July 26, 1902; "On Methods Whereby the Radiation of Electric Waves May Be Mainly Confined to Certain Directions and Whereby the Receptivity of a Receiver May Be Restricted to Electric Waves Emanating from Certain Directions," *London Electrician*, May 4, 1906; "Radio-Telegraphy," *Nature*, June 29, 1911; "Radio Telegraphy," *American Institute of Electrical Engineers Journal*, vol. 4, no. 8, 1922; "Results Obtained Over Very Long Distances by Short Wave Directional Wireless Telegraphy, More Generally Referred to as the Beam System," *Royal Society of Arts Journal*, July 25, 1924; "Radio Communication," *Proceedings of the Institute of Radio Engineers*, January, 1928; "Radiotelephony with Ultra-Short Waves," *Engineering*, December 30, 1932; "Radiocomunicazioni con onde cortissime," *Alta frequenza*, March, 1933.

*Secondary*

Coe, Douglas. *Marconi, Pioneer of Radio*. New York: Julian Messner, 1943. This book, intended for young audiences, takes a simple approach to Marconi's life and includes a large number of fictitious dialogues involving his family and associates. It contains excellent descriptions of the wireless devices and their theory of operation for the nontechnically oriented.

Collins, A. Frederick. *Wireless Telegraphy: Its History, Theory and Practice*. New York: McGraw Publishing Co., 1905. A rigorous scientific treatment of the subject, this book contains plentiful diagrams and photographs of the apparatus in use during Marconi's early work. The detailed physical explanations of the equipment reveal a fascinating cleverness and pure simplicity in the designs of that era.

Dunlap, Orrin E., Jr. *Marconi: The Man and His Wireless*. New York: Macmillan, 1937. Written by a former wireless operator in the Marconi company, this book is a serious study of Marconi's life, with extensive quotations from newspaper accounts of his progress and qualitative descriptions of his accomplishments. The perspective is more personal than technical.

Heathcote, Niels Hugh de Vaudrey. *Nobel Prize Winners in Physics, 1901-1950*. New York: Henry Schuman, 1953. This book contains extensive quotations from the Nobel lectures, along with biographies of the laureates and descriptions of their scientific work. In the case of Marconi and Braun's prize, the author asserts that their respective contributions, practical implementation, and rigorous scientific investigation were decisive complements in the advance of radiotelegraphy.

Marconi, Degna. *My Father, Marconi*. New York: McGraw-Hill, 1962. A fond biography of her father, Degna Marconi's biography is one of the more complete treatments of his life, replete with unusual anecdotes, letters, and messages from Marconi to his oldest daughter. She believes that he was a "political innocent," unable to apprehend the ramifications of Fascism.

*Robert G. Melton*

# 1909

### Physics
Guglielmo Marconi, Italy
Karl Ferdinand Braun, Germany

### Chemistry
Wilhelm Ostwald, Germany

### Physiology or Medicine
Emil Kocher, Switzerland

### Literature
Selma Lagerlöf, Sweden

### Peace
Baron d'Estournelles de Constant, France
Auguste Beernaert, Belgium

# KARL FERDINAND BRAUN
## 1909

*Born:* Fulda, Hesse-Kassel, Germany; June 6, 1850
*Died:* Brooklyn, New York; April 20, 1918
*Nationality:* German
*Area of concentration:* Wireless telegraphy

*Braun made modifications in both the transmitting circuit and the receiving system developed by Guglielmo Marconi, thereby improving wireless telegraphy*

## The Award

*Presentation*

Hans Hildebrand, President of the Royal Swedish Academy of Sciences, presented the Nobel Prize in Physics to Karl Ferdinand Braun and Guglielmo Marconi on December 10, 1909. Their work in the practical application of electrical theories to the development of wireless telegraphy was responsible for the honor bestowed on them. Hildebrand cited theoretical and experimental physicists who had paved the way for Braun and Marconi's discoveries, including Michael Faraday (1791-1867), the British physicist who investigated the relationship between light and electricity, and James Clerk Maxwell (1831-1879), who developed the electromagnetic theory of light. Maxwell's famous mathematical equations led the way for the work of German scientist Heinrich Rudolph Hertz (1857-1894), who proved the existence of electromagnetic waves. His discovery, made in 1888, formed the basis for modern telegraphy development. Guglielmo Marconi (1874-1937), who harnessed electromagnetic waves for use in telegraphy, was responsible for the practical application of the theoretical advances made by these earlier physicists.

Hildebrand discussed Marconi's experimental progress, beginning with his first experiment in 1895. He noted that in 1897, telegraphic apparatus could function over a distance of only 20 kilometers. The waves generated from the transmitting station would very quickly lose power, resulting in poor and confused reception at receiving stations. Hildebrand stated, "It is due above all to the inspired work of Professor Ferdinand Braun that this unsatisfactory state of affairs was overcome." He then went on to describe briefly the basic improvements by which Braun had solved the problems. Braun had made a modification in the circuitry of the transmitter which resulted in an intense, sustainable wave, produced by means of resonance. Braun's work was credited with linking all parts of the world, freeing communications from spatial constraints.

*Nobel lecture*

Braun introduced his lecture topic with the comment that he would speak not on telegraphy in general but on his contributions to its development. The paper was titled "Electrical Oscillations and Wireless Telegraphy."

Experimentation with wireless telegraphy between 1895 and 1897, performed chiefly by Marconi, resulted in only limited transmission distances. In 1898, Braun's attention was drawn to the problem, and he resolved to strengthen the electromagnetic waves produced by the transmitter, thereby increasing the transmission distance. In his lecture, Braun described the theories and ideas which were prevalent at the time. Hertzian waves, it was known, were very sensitive to the quality of the spark with which they were generated, and that same spark, if the spark gap were lengthened, would lose power. Obviously, the solution lay in a different wave generation system. Braun's thoughts turned to a closed "Leyden-jar" circuit of a large capacity. If the average value of oscillations created by a sparkless antenna were to equal the initial spark value in the transmitter devised by Marconi, transmission would be more effective.

Braun worked with three types of circuits: direct, inductive, and a combination of the two. The direct circuit was grounded; the inductive had a "symmetry wire" running parallel to the ground. The compound circuit configuration consisted of several circuits wired together. Braun calculated that these circuits had to discharge within one-tenth of a millionth of a second of each other to be effective. He spent considerable time and thought on the problem and eventually developed the "energy coupling," which placed the circuits in a circle.

In the spring of 1899, experiments performed at Cuxhaven, on the northern coast of Germany, solved many problems. Experiments dealing with interference with the receiving station and theoretical work with the coherer (a kind of detector used before the vacuum tube) were some of the many studies conducted by Braun's two assistants. In November, 1900, Braun gave his first public lecture on telegraphy in Strasbourg, to the Natural Sciences Society. Two more lectures followed closely, demonstrating his advances, particularly in his work on the receiver. Braun believed the capacitor circuit, which was coupled directly to the antenna, to be a vital part of the receiver.

In his lecture, Braun went on to explain in detail the concept of resonance, using two examples: first, Anton Oberbeck's coupled pendulums, and then tuning forks. He then discussed his tuning of the resonator to one of the two oscillations transmitted to the antenna. This procedure resolved the difficulty that had been encountered when the earlier receiver could not distinguish any one signal. Experimentation in Strasbourg in 1902 was to strengthen the receiver system. By taking the signal from the antenna coil and transferring the oscillations to a second coil, which was removed a certain distance from the first, Braun intensified and strengthened the signal. These experiments also resulted in the invention of a measuring device for wireless engineering. This was a major breakthrough for scientific investigations with oscillation.

Braun mentioned the cathode-ray tube, which he had used to investigate the behavior of closed and open circuits. He also discussed earlier work, to which he had returned to solve telegraphy problems. Certain materials, such as galena and pyrite, he said, acted as a type of "valve" for closing and opening circuits, because of their resistance. This resistance seemed to be related to the direction and intensity of the flow of electrons. Braun also described his studies with "sputtering," which involved passing a strong pulse through a thin metal wire on a glass plate. These experiments had again driven his thinking back to the Leyden-jar circuit. He deduced that if the circuit could be switched out from the oscillating system as soon as it had given up its energy, the oscillations could occur in the transmitter at their natural, stronger frequency.

Braun concluded with the following:

> Sometimes, wireless telegraphy has been described as spark telegraphy, and so far a spark in one place or another has been unavoidable. Here, however, it has been made as harmless as possible. This is *important*. For the spark which produces the waves also destroys them again as Saturn destroyed his own children. What was pursued here could be truthfully described as *sparkless telegraphy*.

## Critical reception

The Nobel awards of 1909 were generally accepted as well deserved, according to *The Times* of London of December 11, 1909. According to *The Times*, the award given to Marconi and Braun would "satisfy the whole world. The eminence of these men, and the value of their services in their respective fields of science, are not disputed."

Degna Marconi, however, in her biography of her father, describes an amusing cartoon which appeared in a Swedish paper. In the cartoon, Marconi and Braun were meeting for the first time, and the cartoonist had indicated that someone of Marconi's stature should not have had to share the award with a little-known scientist who had merely extended Marconi's work. Braun himself did not seem to think of his wireless telegraphy developments as part of his major field of expertise. Degna Marconi also comments that Braun himself had told Marconi that he believed the Nobel Prize should have been Marconi's alone.

The nature of the period probably accounts for the paucity of written commentary on the prizes. Although World War I would not erupt until five years later, events leading to the war were already in progress. The Triple Alliance, in which Germany was involved, and the Triple Entente were developing. Military and economic power were being actively pursued by many nations, and immense unrest was apparent in international relations. The Nobel awards were probably considered a minor event in comparison with the major, nation-threatening issues of the day. Nevertheless, one can assume that there was general public approval of Braun's award, since the benefits of wireless telegraphy were obvious. Not only was communication now possible over huge distances and without wires, but radio programming was to remain a primary source of entertainment until the advent of television.

## Biography

Karl Ferdinand Braun was born on June 6, 1850, in the small town of Fulda, Hesse-Kassel, Germany. His parents were Konrad and Franziska (Gohring) Braun.

He went to elementary school in that village before attending both the University of Marburg and the University of Berlin. He received his doctorate from Berlin in 1872. He later worked at four different educational institutions: Würzburg University, the St. Thomas Gymnasium in Leipzig, the University of Marburg, and Strasbourg University. After another teaching post at the Technische Hochschule in Karlsruhe, he went in 1885 to the University of Tubingen. He was also married in 1885, to Amelia Buhler, with whom he had two sons and two daughters. Finally, ten years later, he returned to Strasbourg, taking the post of principal of the Physics Institute, where he remained.

In spite of his brilliant work in various areas, Braun was not extremely well-known. His travels were limited to Germany and neighboring countries. When he received his Nobel Prize, he and Guglielmo Marconi met for the first time. Braun always maintained an active professional teaching life, which meant that he had to allow some research to be carried out by his assistants. Moreover, since his antennae and transmitters required a considerable amount of uncluttered space, the experiments had to be performed in exasperatingly remote areas.

Braun's career came to an end when he was called to testify at a patent claims trial in New York, shortly after the beginning of World War I. He was detained at the conclusion of the trial as a citizen of a country with which the United States was at war. He was never able to return to his country. He died in Brooklyn, New York, on April 20, 1918.

## Scientific Career

Karl Braun began his scientific career when he earned his doctorate from the University of Berlin with a doctoral thesis on the oscillations of elastic strings. He took a post as an assistant to Professor Quincke at Würzburg University for two years and then went to the St. Thomas Gymnasium in Leipzig to teach. While at Leipzig, Braun became intrigued by the flow of electric currents through certain crystals, such as galena, pyrite, tetrahedrite, and pyrolusite. These crystals, he found, did not conform to Ohm's law; their resistance to the flow of electrons was not what was expected. After experimentation, Braun was able to use these crystals as a sort of valve with which to open and close a small inductor. Although he could not find an explanation for their properties, the unusual behavior of the crystals remained in his mind and was to prove useful at a later date. After another two years, he was appointed to the University of Marburg, where he had once studied as an undergraduate. There he filled the post of Extraordinary Professor of Theoretical Physics. After four years at Marburg, he took up the same post, but at the University of Strasbourg. Three years later, he moved to Karlsruhe, where he was a professor of physics. At Tubingen, where he moved in 1885, he created a new physics institute. During this period, he worked more with oscillation, adding more rigid structures, such as plastic rods, to his experiments. He also experimented with thermodynamics and the effects of heat on solubility and on inductance. Ten years later, in 1895, he moved back to Strasbourg to become principal of the Physics

Institute. He subsequently received an invitation to fill the post that had been vacated by G. Wiedemann at Leipzig University, but he chose to remain permanently at Strasbourg.

In 1895, several important events took place. Anton Oberbeck managed to mathematically calculate the oscillation of a coupled circuit; Marconi began his experimentation with telegraphy; and Braun made his first attempt to transmit signals with Hertzian waves. By 1897, however, only a distance of 21 kilometers had been achieved in telegraphic signal transmission. In 1898, Braun was working on the transmission of signals using Morse code, but through the medium of water. By autumn of 1898, he had decided to extend the transmission distance in air by increasing the voltage used in transmission.

Earlier, in 1897, Braun had modified a cathode-ray tube to create the cathode-ray oscillograph. In basic terms, he set up an electromagnetic field which diverted the electrons in the tube from their path, thereby bending the tube's green fluorescent light. With this oscillograph, variations in an electric current could be detected and studied. This invention was actually a very early step in the development of television.

Braun took into consideration the conclusions of Heinrich Hertz regarding the damping of sparks and their tendency to consume their own power when the spark gap is increased. Braun assumed that the larger the voltage, the greater would be this energy consumption; therefore, he turned to capacitors to achieve a voltage increase without the power drain which had plagued the earlier sparked antennae. Braun believed that if he could design a capacitor whose average oscillation value equaled that of the original Marconi spark, he would have a steady source of power and a more effective transmitter. Three circuit designs arose from his calculations: one inductively excited the transmitter, one directly excited it, and one was a mixture of the two.

In an effort to avoid any possible problems with spark resistance, Braun began working with "energy coupling," connecting several capacitors to increase voltage. One of his designs involved three circuits, linked in a circular arrangement. The main difficulty he encountered was the necessity that the capacitors fire within one-tenth of a millionth of a second of each other. The circular formation seemed to solve the simultaneous discharge problem best.

In the experiments which began in the spring of 1899 at Cuxhaven, Germany, a broad range of problems was explored. Braun needed to determine how the coherer functioned and whether there was a better and more scientifically useful replacement. Interference with the receiving antenna resulting from ground clutter was also investigated. Unfortunately, Braun's teaching duties prevented his performing the experimentation in person until the autumn of 1900.

It was not until November of 1900 that Braun, now fifty, gave his first public address on his findings. The first lecture in a series of three was delivered in Strasbourg; Braun explained his circuitry and its advantages for tuned telegraphy. The next February, in 1901, he again spoke to the Natural Sciences Society in

Strasbourg, this time on his methods of tuning the receiver. In the autumn of the same year, he spoke in Hamburg on much the same topic, but he also discussed research gleaned from additional work at Helgoland. Also in 1901, his combined papers were published under the title *Drahtlose Telegraphie durch Wasser und Luft* (wireless telegraphy through water and air).

In 1902, Braun erected antennae on two forts in Strasbourg to determine the best system for the receiver. He used a coupled circuit tuned to vibrate at its natural frequency. The receiver was tuned to find this frequency. The receiver antenna coil then inductively set a second coil in action. To his surprise, Braun discovered that when the two coils were separated, both the intensity and quality of the signal were increased. The same was not true of the transmitter, in which the coil separation produced a weaker signal.

This set of experiments had two important results: The receiver could be tuned to focus on one signal, and an important measuring instrument, the electrometer, was created. With this device, which Braun had invented to help with his experimentation, a wide range of wavelengths could be measured. The electrometer replaced more cumbersome equipment and became a valuable telegraphy engineering tool. Additionally, Braun established that an antenna inclined 10 degrees made a directional receiver. These results were published in March, 1903. He also worked with three antennae and calculated the angles required to create a directional transmitter.

Braun later studied the Hertzian grid experiments, conducted by Leopold Ambronn in 1896, in which a vaporization effect occurred. He hoped to use this vaporization in the primary circuit of the transmitter, causing that circuit to cut off and allow the primary energy to oscillate at its own natural frequency, unhindered by the original spark. Other scientists, including Max Wien, advanced this concept further.

Braun's development of wireless telegraphy opened the door for radar and television. The measuring devices which evolved from his experimentation also led to further scientific achievement. The crystals that he implemented as valves in his circuitry were soon to be replaced by the vacuum tube, but the crystals resurfaced fifty years later when solid-state systems came into use. Braun's studies with oscillation led to increased understanding of the characteristics of electricity, which changed the standard of living for most of the world's population. Indeed, Karl Ferdinand Braun, in the words of Alfred Nobel, "conferred the greatest benefit on mankind."

## Bibliography

*Primary*

PHYSICS: *Über den Einfluss von Steifigkeit, Befestigung und Amplitude auf die Schwingungen von Saiten,* 1872; *Über Enblocreposition, mit Beschreibung eines durch Operation geheilten Falles,* 1888; *Über elektrische Kraftübertragung Insbesondere über Drehstrom,* 1892; *Über die Leitung elektrisirter Luft,* 1896; "Über der Verfahren zur Demonstration und zum Studium des zeitlichen Verlaufes variabler Strome," *Annalen der Physik und Chemie*, vol. 60, 1897; *Über physikalische forschungsart*, 1899; *Drahtlose Telegraphie durch Wasser und Luft*, 1901; *Über die Erregung stehender elektrischer Drahtwellen durch Entladung von Condensatoren*, 1902; *Télégraphie sans fil*, 1903; *Methods for Increasing the Transmitter Energy of Wireless Telegraph Systems*, 1904; *Einrichtung, um in vakuum entfernungen andern zu konnen*, 1904; *Über drahtlose telegraphie und neuere physikalische forschungen*, 1905; *On Directed Wireless Telegraphy*, 1906; *Phase-Shifted High-Frequency Oscillations*, 1906; *Briefe an die Redaktion (vom Jahrbuch der drahtlosen Telegraphie und Telephonie*, 1914 (with Jonathan A. Zenneck); *Was misst man mit Unipolardetektor und Parallelohmmethode?*, 1914; *Zur Berechnung von Antennen*, 1914; *Physik*, 1915; *Zum 100. Geburtstag vom Ferdinand Braun*, 1918 (with Zenneck).

CHILDREN'S NONFICTION: *Der junge Mathematiker und Naturforscher*, 1876.

*Secondary*

Asimov, Isaac. *Asimov's Biographical Encyclopedia of Science and Technology.* Garden City, N.Y.: Doubleday, 1964. This encyclopedia contains an excellent entry on Braun and is a good overall source for the younger student or the researcher who is unversed in technological terminology. The entry provides basic information and highlights major aspects of Braun's work, although it contains little detail.

Heathcote, Niels Hugh de Vaudrey. *Nobel Prize Winners in Physics, 1901-1950.* New York: Henry Schuman, 1953. This study contains a brief biographical sketch of each laureate and a short description of the work he or she performed. Since parts of the actual award papers are quoted, a certain level of scientific knowledge is helpful for comprehension. Not all the relevant research or experimentation of each winner is mentioned. An excellent source of basic information.

Marconi, Degna. *My Father, Marconi.* New York: McGraw-Hill, 1962. This is a very easy to read biography for the general public, containing reminiscences of the famous scientist's daughter. Only a very small segment deals with Braun, but it includes interesting personal insights.

Nobelstiftelsen. *Physics.* Vol. 1. New York: Elsevier, 1964-1967. This source gives the complete text of each award presentation along with a brief biography of the laureate. The terminology and descriptions presuppose at least a university-level knowledge of physics. References to other scientists and scholarly works are common. An excellent primary research text.

Sharlin, Harold I. "Ferdinand Braun." In *Dictionary of Scientific Biography*, edited by Charles Coulston Gillespie, vol. 2. New York: Charles Scribner's Sons, 1970. This entry consists mainly of a brief biography of Braun, with a partial listing of his primary works. There is also a secondary bibliography. The description of his scientific work is generally easy to read; the younger student should begin here.

*Ellen F. Mitchum*

# 1910

## Physics
Johannes Diderik van der Waals, Netherlands

## Chemistry
Otto Wallach, Germany

## Physiology or Medicine
Albrecht Kossel, Germany

## Literature
Paul Heyse, Germany

## Peace
International Peace Bureau

# JOHANNES DIDERIK VAN DER WAALS
## 1910

*Born:* Leiden, Netherlands; November 23, 1837
*Died:* Amsterdam, Netherlands; March 8, 1923
*Nationality:* Dutch
*Area of concentration:* Equation of state theory

*Van der Waals' discovery of the law of corresponding states of liquids and gases explained apparent anomalies in the behavior of gases subjected to fairly high pressures. The gas laws of Robert Boyle and J.-A.-C. Charles seemed not to apply to gases at high pressures, but van der Waals showed that even at pressures sufficient to transform gases into liquids, no essential change in the nature of the substances occurred; instead, a more complicated equation and the postulation of a new force of attraction were needed to explain the discrepancies with the older laws*

## The Award

*Presentation*

At the Nobel ceremonies in December, 1906, Professor O. Montelius, President of the Royal Swedish Academy of Sciences, made the presentation speech for the award of the Nobel Prize in Physics to Johannes Diderik van der Waals. Montelius' presentation detailed the significant achievement made by van der Waals in identifying the nature of molecules as the same in both gaseous and liquid states, thereby accounting for the failure of gases under fairly high pressure to comport themselves according to the previously accepted simple gas laws. The Dutchman had demonstrated that there is a continuum of behavior when substances convert from gases to liquids and that there is no need for new considerations and calculations to explain molecular behavior after a shift to a different state.

When molecules become crowded together in a liquid form, Montelius explained, the mutual attraction of the molecules creates a high internal pressure of cohesion which tends to maintain the substance as a liquid until a certain "critical temperature" is reached. When that temperature is achieved, the liquid will volatilize. If, however, the liquid is prevented from volatilizing after the temperature has been raised beyond the critical point, the liquid and gaseous states become impossible to distinguish from one another. Further, the ascertaining of the critical temperature for a substance allows the physicist to predict its state at any given temperature and pressure, once a table of behavior has been established for the substance.

Montelius praised van der Waals' famous "equation of state," which explains the behavior of both gases and liquids at varying temperatures and pressures, noting that van der Waals' work had been of great significance not merely in the research laboratory but also in the commercial field of refrigeration technology. Van der Waals' studies had thus been of signal importance to agriculture and industry.

*Nobel lecture*

Van der Waals' Nobel lecture, delivered in German on December 12, 1906, and titled "The Equation of State for Gases and Liquids," was a concise summary of his life's work. It focused on one comparatively simple equation, an equation then and later of great significance to physics. Rudolf Clausius (1822-1888), an early molecular theorist, had published a treatise in 1857 on the nature of motion generated by heat, a publication which the young van der Waals was to find seminal to his career—indeed, a "revelation." Van der Waals explained how his line of thinking had continued after he had read Clausius' paper. If molecules can be regarded as mere points, mere moving particles, then even liquids must be composed of such particles, and, in fact, liquids can "only be regarded as compressed gases at low temperature." Thus the idea came to him that there is no essential difference between gases and liquids.

Next, van der Waals told how he had introduced the factor $b$, representing the total real volume of the moving points, into his equation, and he explained how he had conceived of his other constant, $a$, representing the mutual attraction of the molecules. Both $a$ and $b$ have different values for different gases. Van der Waals then presented his famous "equation of state," which includes $a$ and $b$, while humbly admitting his doubt about "whether there is a better way" of expressing the relationships. He maintained that a lingering doubt about his equation continually obsessed him, saying, "I can never free myself from it."

Continuing in the same vein, van der Waals spoke of how he had never regarded his equation as anything more than a qualitative expression of the relationships contained within it. He never expected it "to give results numerically in agreement with experiment," but, he said, "people almost always act as though that were my opinion." He reported that he had discovered to his "great joy" and "not without astonishment" that his two equations used to determine $a$ and $b$ from experimental data had been recently proved accurate. This corroboration came from the "admirable experiments" of Sydney Young (1857-1937) on the volumes of coexisting gases and liquids and on Young's work with establishing saturation-level pressures at different temperatures.

The laureate went on to detail his most recent work, which he termed "pseudo association" (the "van der Waals force") to distinguish it from chemical bonding. The only way to achieve agreement between the equation of state and laboratory data, he maintained, was to postulate the existence of large complexes of molecules, especially in liquids. He recalled concluding in his dissertation, completed in 1873, that intermolecular attraction decreases rapidly with distance, "indeed that the attraction only has an appreciable value at distances close to the size of the molecules." Considering that recent work by Ludwig Boltzmann (1844-1906) and Peter J. W. Debye (1884-1966) had predicted the existence of such molecule complexes, van der Waals felt justified in his postulation of pseudo association. He noted the differences between true chemical bonding and pseudo association, and he went on to mention that as early as 1890 he had published an article treating binary mixtures, mixtures some of whose molecules are formed into complexes by pseudo association and some of whose molecules are free.

In the conclusion to his address, van der Waals said, "In all my studies I was quite convinced of the real existence of molecules . . . I never regarded them as a figment of my imagination, nor even as mere centers of force effects." He noted that "the real existence of molecules is universally assumed by physicists" and that his theory "may have been a contributory factor."

*Critical reception*

Van der Waals' receipt of the Nobel Prize occasioned little comment in the popular press. *The Times* of London made two brief mentions of the prize; *The New York Times* ignored the Nobel science awards altogether. The prestigious German journal *Annalen der Physik* (annals of physics), familiar with van der Waals' work, was not in the habit of running news items and so took no notice of the prize. Meanwhile, the major British scientific journal *Nature* noted only that van der Waals was present in Stockholm to receive his award and deliver his lecture.

Van der Waals' Nobel lecture was reviewed by the Cornell University-based *Journal of Physical Chemistry* (December 10, 1910) in a piece by Wilder D. Bancroft which stated, "This is the address delivered on receiving the Nobel prize. The author sketches the development of his well-known equation of state. Very interesting is the statement that apparently no equation of state is possible unless one postulates an association of molecules to form complexes."

This relative lack of evaluative response can perhaps be attributed to two factors: First, in 1910, when the Academy gave the prize to van der Waals, the award was still relatively young, having been first bestowed only a decade earlier. Second, van der Waals was apolitical, and his work itself was noncontroversial among both the public and the scientific community. The Dutchman had been a pioneer in the once-contentious area of investigation into the existence of molecules, but by 1910 van der Waals' work was well accepted by the profession.

## Biography

Johannes Diderik van der Waals was born in Leiden in the province of South Holland in the Netherlands on November 23, 1837, the son of Jacobus van der Waals, a carpenter, and Elisabeth van den Burg. After completing secondary school in his hometown, van der Waals taught in a local elementary school. The young man was fortunate to live at the seat of the Netherlands' finest university, and, seeking to improve himself, he studied at Leiden University from 1862 to 1865 while supporting himself with his teaching. He obtained high school teaching certificates in physics and mathematics.

In 1864 he received a better job, teaching physics at a secondary school in Deventer, and so could afford to wed Anna Magdalena Smit in that year. They were to have four children, three daughters and a son, before Anna came to an early demise. In 1866, van der Waals moved his growing family to The Hague, where he found employment first teaching and then serving as principal of a secondary school.

The Hague, unlike farther-removed Deventer, was within easy railroad-commuting distance of Leiden, and he resumed his studies part-time at his old university. Not having been in the pre-graduate school program in secondary school, van der Waals had not studied classical languages, then a requirement for doctoral work, but that handicap was removed from him by a law introduced in the late 1860's which exempted science students seeking a Ph.D. from examinations in those languages. In 1873 he obtained his doctorate with a sensational dissertation that launched the former elementary school teacher into the ranks of internationally known scientists and, in 1877, won for him a professorship at the new University of Amsterdam.

His son, Johannes Diderik, Jr., taught physics at the University of Groningen from 1903 to 1908 and then succeeded to his father's physics chair at Amsterdam. One of the daughters, Anne Madelaine, ran the house for her father; Jacqueline Elisabeth taught history and became well-known for her poetry, and Johanna Diderica taught English. Their father retired from teaching in 1907, continued active research and publication until about 1913, and died on March 8, 1923.

## Scientific Career

Van der Waals' scientific career began very suddenly in 1873 with the publication of his doctoral dissertation *Over de continuiteit van den gas- en vloeistoftoestand* (1873; *On the Continuity of the Gaseous and Liquid States*, 1888). A partial translation into English appeared in *Nature* in 1874, and the full translated text was published in 1888 and again in 1890. Translations were also made into German (1881) and into French (1894).

Thus, he came to the attention of the scientific world, and in 1877 he was appointed to the physics chair at the University of Amsterdam, a position he would hold for the rest of his career. James Clerk Maxwell (1831-1879), a renowned British physicist, declared that the dissertation put the name van der Waals "at once . . . among the foremost in molecular science." In fact, the dissertation set the stage for van der Waals' entire subsequent career—all his investigations into the nature of the molecules in gases and liquids and the forces that attract those molecules to one another.

The newly famous van der Waals was elected to the Royal Netherlands Academy of Science and Letters in 1875 and in his maturity served as the academy's secretary from 1896 to 1912. The organization's *Proceedings* was the medium for the initial publication of much of his research. He also accepted an invitation to join the French Academy of Sciences, although he did not write in French.

The anomalous nature of gases under pressure had intrigued van der Waals from his earliest laboratory studies. According to Robert Boyle (1627-1691) and Jacques-Alexandre-César Charles (1746-1823), gases behaved regularly, and the volume of a gas varied inversely with increases in pressure and directly with increases in absolute temperature. A third law can be deduced from the foregoing, stating that for the volume to remain the same, pressure and absolute temperature must vary proportionately and directly.

Those laws were for an "ideal" gas, but van der Waals discovered that gases under high pressures behaved in a manner far from the ideal. Even later work on the kinetic theory of gases by Maxwell and Boltzmann, which refined Boyle's and Charles's laws, only worked if individual gas molecules were assumed not to attract one another and assumed to be of zero volume. Reflecting on possible reasons for the inconsistent performance of real gases and their conversion into liquids led van der Waals to consider the very nature of matter itself. What *was* a liquid? How did the constituent particles of a liquid or gas behave? Was matter in different states composed of different particles?

Scientists had already conceived of the atom, the smallest particle of a given element, but van der Waals became convinced that in the real world one confronted not the elemental atom but a larger aggregation: the molecule. In the 1870's, the existence of molecules was not universally accepted by physicists, but van der Waals believed that he had to postulate molecular existence and intermolecular attraction to explain the behavior of gases and liquids. Even in a pure gas of elemental hydrogen, oxygen, or nitrogen, he thought, the atoms link together into molecules. Further, those molecules do not change their basic structure when a gas is placed under such high pressure that it becomes a liquid. A liquid, he concluded, is merely a highly compressed gas at low temperature.

To account for irregularities of behavior in compressed gases, van der Waals was compelled to conclude that molecules attract one another by some force other than chemical bonding. Chemical bonding, he knew, forms actual compounds, but he believed another force to be operating as well, one far weaker than chemical bonding but stronger than gravitation. (Gravitational attraction among the comparatively few molecules in a gas is negligible.) Van der Waals called his new force "pseudo association," but it came to be known in physics as the "van der Waals force." He represented it by the letter *a* in his new equation of state, which linked matter in the gaseous and liquid states.

Van der Waals also considered that gases have a real volume apart from the spaces between their molecules. That constant he represented in his formula with the letter *b*. Both *a* and *b* varied for different gases. Thus modified, the old gas laws of Boyle and Charles worked, at least qualitatively, for gases under all conditions. Having discovered new, unsuspected phenomena, van der Waals had proceeded to account for them mathematically. After further investigation, he refined his equation in 1880 into the law of corresponding states, which permitted greater congruence with experimental data.

Much work in cryogenics was made possible by van der Waals, who was continually conducting experiments at Amsterdam. As he labored on supercooled gases, he discovered the existence of "binary solutions," a phenomenon which he brought to the profession's attention only in 1890 after he overcame his doubt about the universality of his equation of state. Appearing in *Archives néerlandaises* (Netherlands archives), *Nature*, and elsewhere, van der Waals' article stunned his colleagues by maintaining that gases cooled to the critical temperature do not merely shift from one state to another but exist in both states at once. Such a binary solution results from some of the molecules being linked by the van der Waals force into larger liquid aggregates, while some of the molecules remain independent in the rarer distribution of a gas. Van der Waals calculated the critical temperature below which a given gas must be cooled in order to be liquefied. He compiled a table of such temperatures, enabling physicists to enter into the equation of state the particular temperature of a gas under investigation and then to predict the behavior of the gas at various temperatures and pressures.

When the gas's critical pressure and the critical volume coincide with the critical temperature, the "critical point" is reached. At this point, a gas or a liquid will exhibit strange behavior. Carbon dioxide has a critical temperature that is fairly high and therefore easily obtained (31 degrees Celsius); when carbon dioxide is compressed into a liquid and cooled to 31 degrees, the molecules seem to be in both a gaseous and a liquid state simultaneously.

Hydrogen, however, has a critical temperature so much lower that it was not until 1898 that Sir James Dewar (1842-1923), in England, succeeded in liquefying it. Helium has the lowest critical temperature of all: -269 degrees Celsius, or four degrees above absolute zero. Helium was finally liquefied in 1908, by van der Waals' younger colleague and friend Heike Kamerlingh Onnes (1853-1926) in his marvelously equipped laboratory at Leiden University. These studies of temperatures approaching absolute zero were based on van der Waals' work.

Van der Waals' fame continued to increase as the turn of the century approached. A review of his articles on binary solutions appeared in the French *Journal de physique* in 1897. The review was favorable, but it referred to van der Waals merely as "l'auteur" (the author) of the articles. By 1908, however, the same journal, in a review of two of van der Waals' articles, dubbed him "l'illustre professeur d'Amsterdam" (the illustrious professor from Amsterdam). The following year he was called "l'illustre savant" (the illustrious scholar).

Meanwhile, the savant, with some assistance from P. Kohnstamm, published a full book in German: *Lehrbuch der Thermodynamik* (1908; textbook on thermodynamics), the first part of a projected two-volume set. It was reviewed in Leipzig's *Physikalische Zeitschrift* (physics magazine), which, while noting that the work reflected "the methods of the Dutch school," praised the book as coming "von der Hand eines Meisters" (from the hand of a master). In 1912, the Dutch master completed his magnum opus by adding a hefty second volume to the slimmer first volume of the thermodynamics text. It received an excellent review by American Wilder D. Bancroft in the *Journal of Physical Chemistry*, in which Bancroft "found it delightful to note the calm way in which van der Waals straightens out" certain squabbles. He concluded by remarking that the book's "most striking characteristic . . . is its calm sanity." Coming at the end of a long career, the massive thermodynamics text represented van der Waals' life's work.

In his later researches, van der Waals delved into the force of pseudo association, or the van der Waals force, which not only causes gases to behave strangely but which accounts for surface tension, capillarity, and other phenomena. Later scientists subdivided the attractive-repulsive forces into several subforces, and some confusion still exists as to their nomenclature.

The van der Waals force is caused by a permanent or momentary dipole charge in a molecule or molecule complex, which is to say that not all molecules are electrically neutral all the time. Around the atoms of a molecule are clouds of electrons, and those electrons might at a given moment be concentrated on one side of the molecule. As electrons are negative, that side of the molecule becomes negatively charged, leaving the other side positively charged, and a dipole is formed. The dipolar molecule then either is attracted to a preexisting neighboring dipole or induces a previously neutral molecule to become a dipole. When they get too close to each other, however, the van der Waals dispersion force is activated when the mutual repulsion of the electron clouds takes over. The molecules then are held at a certain distance from each other in a weakly bonded crystal formation. The forces are discussed in every modern textbook of chemistry or physics. Especially important studies of them were done by Peter Debye, a Dutch scientist who studied under van der Waals and worked under Kamerlingh Onnes. Debye credited van der Waals' theory of "universal molecular attraction" with destroying the model of molecules as "rigid electrical structures." Linus Pauling, who won both the Nobel Prize in Chemistry, in 1954, and the Nobel Peace Prize, in 1962, did much work on chemical bonding, and in his widely used text on the subject, he employed the term "van der Waals radius" to express half the distance between molecules held together by the van der Waals force. As recently as 1980, Ad van der Avoird used "van der Waals forces" to mean "all the attractive and repulsive interactions between chemically nonbinding molecules."

The work of van der Waals and his successors in cryogenics has enabled engineers to make great advances in refrigeration in the twentieth century, and studies of van der Waals forces have led to greater understanding of such disparate topics as the mechanics of water passing through soils and the mechanism by which anesthetics function. Other studies have involved the mechanics of viral self-assembly and the biochemistry of muscle-cell action. Dieter Langbein, in *Theory of Van der Waals Attraction* (1974), explains not only that van der Waals forces affect biological functions, but that an understanding of the forces is necessary in the field of adhesion, including "washing, dyeing, pouring and sliding, wetting, lubrication, powder compaction and pulverizing, and cold welding." He also notes that it is "a basic requirement of detergents that their dielectric properties diminish van der Waals attraction between clothing and dirt."

Van der Waals, because of the equation of state which he formulated and because of the forces he discovered, was lionized in his lifetime. His name still appears regularly in physics and chemistry texts. His studies of the behavior of matter paved the way for considerable later work in physics, chemistry, and engineering. In fact, van der Waals did much to help make the modern scientific and technological world possible.

## Bibliography

*Primary*

PHYSICS: *Over de continuiteit van den gas- en vloeistoftoestand*, 1873 (*On the Continuity of the Liquid and Gaseous States*, 1890); *Nature*, 1874-1875, 1890 (articles); *Extraits des Archives néerlandaises*, 1890-1913 (articles); *Lehrbuch der Thermodynamik in iher Anwendung auf das Gleichgewicht von Systemen mit gasförmigflüssigen Phasen*, 1908-1912.

*Secondary*

Boschke, F. L., ed. *Van der Waals Systems*. Vol. 93 in *Topics in Current Chemistry*. New York: Springer-Verlag, 1980. This book contains three lengthy treatises on different aspects of the van der Waals force.

Chu, Benjamin. *Molecular Forces: Based on the Baker Lectures of Peter J. W. Debye*. New York: Interscience, 1967. This volume has an introduction by Debye, a physicist who studied under van der Waals at the University of Amsterdam. The content is presented simply and is all based on Debye's own material.

Companion, Audrey L. *Chemical Bonding*. New York: McGraw-Hill, 1964. A standard text on the nature of chemical bonding, this book devotes a large section to van der Waals forces.

Heathcote, Niels Hugh de Vaudrey. *Nobel Prize Winners in Physics, 1901-1950*. New York: Henry Schuman, 1953. The seven-page section on van der Waals provides an excellent synopsis on his work. Although not overly technical, the piece might be difficult for the lay reader.

Langbein, Dieter. *Theory of van der Waals Attraction*. Vol. 72 in *Springer Tracts in Modern Physics*. New York: Springer-Verlag, 1974. This book provides an excellent treatment of the highly technical aspects of the van der Waals force, and it also details any practical applications of van der Waals' theories.

Pauling, Linus C. *The Nature of the Chemical Bond and the Structure of Molecules and Crystals: An Introduction to Modern Structural Chemistry*. 3d ed. Ithaca, N.Y.: Cornell University Press, 1960. A classic treatment of chemical bonding, this book by Nobel chemistry laureate Pauling gives full credit to van der Waals for his pioneering work.

Sebera, Donald K. *Electronic Structure and Chemical Bonding*. Waltham, Mass.: Blaisdell, 1964. This text contains a section which provides a good description of the various types of van der Waals bonding.

*Allan D. Charles*

# 1911

### Physics
Wilhelm Wien, Germany

### Chemistry
Marie Curie, France

### Physiology or Medicine
Alvar Gullstrand, Sweden

### Literature
Maurice Maeterlinck, Belgium

### Peace
Tobias Asser, Netherlands
Alfred Fried, Austria

# WILHELM WIEN
# 1911

*Born:* Gaffken, near Fischhausen, East Prussia; January 13, 1864
*Died:* Munich, Germany; August 30, 1928
*Nationality:* German
*Area of concentration:* Thermal radiation

*Wien postulated two laws governing the distribution of thermal radiation in the spectrum and the effects of temperature variation on that distribution. The first of these two laws, Wien's displacement law, has been fully confirmed by experiment. The second, Wien's distribution law, was proved incorrect by Max Planck, in research that led him directly to the formulation of the quantum theory of radiation*

## The Award

*Presentation*

Dr. E. W. Dahlgren, Librarian of the Swedish National Library and President of the Royal Swedish Academy of Sciences, presented Wilhelm Wien with the Nobel Prize in Physics for 1911 at the award ceremonies in December of that year. Dahlgren began his presentation by briefly recounting the genesis of research into thermal radiation. He pointed out the importance of such research in the development of modern physics and gave credit to several of the pioneers in the field for their contributions to the search for valid laws governing thermal radiation.

Dahlgren then explained the theoretical and experimental research that had won for Wien the Nobel Prize. Wien and an associate had formulated a method in 1895 whereby a "black body" (a body which neither reflects light nor allows any light to pass) could be constructed. Other physicists, using the black body device, had been able to solve a major problem in radiation theory, but others remained. Dahlgren pointed out that one of the most perplexing of those remaining problems had been addressed by Wien in a paper published in 1893. In this paper, Wien had proposed his displacement law, which provided a theoretical explanation for the connection between the radiation wavelength and the temperature of a radiating black body. Other physicists, Dahlgren went on, had shown that Wien's displacement law was valid for the radiation of bodies other than black bodies, and they subsequently were able to ascertain the temperature of the fixed stars and of the Sun.

Wien's distribution law, proposed in 1894, did not succeed in solving the remaining problems of thermal radiation. Nevertheless, it did lead to the solution of those problems. With only a slight alteration of Wien's original formula, Max Planck was able to establish the elusive link between radiation energy, wavelength, and black body temperatures, thereby solving one of the major problems which had confronted physicists in the quest to understand and explain the cosmos. In his presentation speech, Dahlgren concluded that Wien had made the "greatest and most significant" contributions to the solution of this important question and therefore was a most worthy recipient of the Nobel Prize.

*Nobel lecture*

Wien delivered his Nobel lecture, titled "On the Laws of Thermal Radiation," on December 11, 1911. He began with an explanation and justification of "mental experiments," which may fruitfully be performed when practical experiments are not possible. Showing that mental experiments had often been instrumental in explaining natural processes in many disciplines, Wien paid particular attention to Gustav Kirchhoff's development of the theory of heat radiation and absorption through the mental experiment of postulating a completely black, or nonreflecting, body.

Wien then explained at some length the reasoning behind his own mental experiment which led him to postulate his famous law of thermal displacement. He explained each step in his reasoning carefully, giving full credit to those theories and experiments of other physicists that had guided and inspired him. He then explained how his displacement law could be used to ascertain the temperatures of celestial objects, using the Sun as an example. He also discussed the use of the displacement law in calculating the wavelength of X rays. Wien argued that the law had exhausted the information to be gleaned from thermodynamics with regard to radiation theory and that the law had been fully confirmed by experience and by other experiments.

Thermodynamics and the displacement law cannot, Wien continued, determine the intensity of radiation in the various wavelengths. This determination necessitated another mental experiment, which Wien described; this experiment had yielded the distribution law. His first attempt had resulted in a formula which agreed well with observed radiation phenomena in which the product of temperature and wavelength was moderate but which deviated widely from observations in which that product was large.

Wien then discussed attempts by other physicists to modify his distribution law by mental experiments of their own, paying particular attention to the efforts of Lord Rayleigh and Max Planck. Rayleigh's calculations, though seemingly sound, had led to a radiation theory which contradicted experience and demonstrated the inadequacies of then-current electromagnetic theory. Planck had introduced a slight modification of Wien's original distribution law that explained the deviation from expected results at high temperatures and wavelengths. Nevertheless, Wien expressed reservations as to whether Planck's formula would prove completely satisfactory.

The rest of Wien's lecture concerned the remaining barriers to arriving at a general radiation theory which would explain observed phenomena. He argued that only through mental experiments—that is to say, through theoretical physics—could the problems be solved. Wien concluded his lecture by expressing hope that a complete solution would be found to the problem of thermal radiation. He speculated that "profound insight" would result from knowledge of the fundamental processes that occur within the atom.

## Critical reception

The awarding of the Nobel Prize to Wien passed virtually unnoticed in the American press. *The New York Times*, in a very brief story on page 10 in its November 8, 1911, edition, noted that Wien had won the prize despite the expectation in the United States that Thomas Edison would be the recipient. On December 11, the date of Wien's Nobel lecture, *The New York Times* ran another, longer, story concerning all the Nobel laureates. Most of the piece was devoted to a long and complimentary account of Marie Curie and her work. Wien was accorded one brief paragraph. This seeming denigration of Wien's work by the American press may have been a result of its theoretical nature; it was so abstract as to be incomprehensible even to most of the intellectuals of the day. The lack of attention may also have reflected the growing sympathy in the American press for the Triple Entente powers: England, France, and Russia. Germany, Wien's homeland, was a member of the Triple Alliance, the European power block increasingly seen as hostile toward the Triple Entente. Wien's prize received equally brief mention in *The Times* of London and the *Paris le temps*.

Wien fared much better in German newspapers. The *Berliner Tageblatt* ran a multicolumn account of Wien's work on November 8 and a follow-up on December 12, with excerpts from his lecture and complimentary comments by other physicists, all of whom expressed the opinion that he was deserving of the award.

## Biography

Carl Wien and Caroline Gertz Wien gave their only child the formidable name Wilhelm Carl Werner Otto Fritz Franz Wien when he was born on January 13, 1864, at their farm home at Gaffken, near Fischhausen, East Prussia (now Primorsk in the Soviet Union). His parents were both descendants of the Prussian landowning aristocracy. In 1866 his parents moved to a smaller farm in the Rastenburg district of East Prussia, where Wien spent the remainder of his youth.

At age eleven, he enrolled at the secondary school at Rastenburg, but he showed little aptitude for or interest in formal academic study. He left the school in 1880, without having received a degree, and returned to the family farm to learn agriculture. His parents retained a private tutor for him who continued his instruction in academic subjects as he was learning to farm. In 1881, at the urging of his mother, Wien enrolled at the Altstädtisches Gymnasium in Königsberg, East Prussia, from which he was graduated in 1882. In the summer of that year, he enrolled at the University of Göttingen to study mathematics and natural science. He stayed there for only one semester, then returned home with the renewed intention of taking over the management of the family farm. Again, rural living apparently palled on him, and he enrolled the following year at the Free University of Berlin to study mathematics and physics with Hermann von Helmholtz; there, he found his life's work.

Still troubled by the responsibility he felt for the management of his family's estate, he was relieved when in 1890 a drought forced his parents to sell it. They subsequently moved to Berlin to be near their only child, who had received his doctorate in 1886 and accepted a post as assistant to Helmholtz at his newly established laboratory in the Charlottenburg district of Berlin.

In 1896 he accepted an offer from the technical high school at Aachen to succeed Philipp Lenard in its physics department. During his stay in Aachen, he wed Luise Mahler, with whom he would have four children. In 1899, the University of Giessen chose Wien to be a professor of physics, a post he left after only six months to accept a similar position at the University of Würzburg. Wien remained at Würzburg for twenty years, during which time he acquired an international reputation as a leader in both theoretical and experimental physics. His leadership was recognized in 1911 when he won the Nobel Prize in Physics. He traveled extensively throughout Europe lecturing on his research, and in 1913 he delivered lectures at Columbia University in New York.

Wien was deeply distressed by the outcome of World War I, especially by what he perceived as the triumph of socialism and the injustices of the Treaty of Versailles. In 1920, he accepted an appointment at the University of Munich, which offered to build for him a new physics institute. Despite his conservative political views, he never became closely involved with the growing Nazi Party, which shared many of his convictions. He fell ill in 1926 and resigned his post as rector of the Physics Institute. Wien died in Munich on August 30, 1928.

## Scientific Career

Wien's first published scientific work, which appeared in 1885, was derived from his dissertation research. Titled "Über den Einfluss der ponderablen Theile auf das gebeugte Licht," it examined the diffraction of light when it strikes a metallic surface. Over the next few years, he demonstrated that then-extant theories failed to explain observable light diffraction on various surfaces.

When he became Helmholtz's assistant in 1890, Wien turned his attention to the measurement of thermal radiation. He and a coworker, Ludwig Holborn, in 1892 developed a thermoelectric temperature scale expressed as a function of temperature to the third power. While at the Charlottenburg laboratory, Wien continued his earlier research on refraction and extended it into a search for explanations of the energy of thermal radiation. This research allowed him to establish that the energy of electrodynamic radiation is in perpetual motion. His findings allowed him to propose his displacement law of radiation the next year. The law has become one of the foundations of modern nuclear physics. Using brilliantly designed experiments, Wien verified several of the phenomena suggested by the displacement law and also noted its shortcomings. Working from the premises discovered through his experiments, Wien then used theoretical methods to arrive at his famous distribution law, published in 1896. Although at first greeted with hostility and skepticism by other physicists, Wien's distribution law, with modifications, was later verified through experiment and, like its predecessor, became a mainstay of modern physics.

At his new post in the technical high school at Aachen and using the equipment left by Johannes Stark, another German physicist, Wien in 1897 turned his attention to cathode rays. He established that they are high-velocity particles of negatively charged electricity. During the same series of experiments, he investigated positive rays, determining their corpuscular nature and their velocity. Most of the experimental results of this stage of Wien's research were published after he became a professor of physics at the University of Würzburg in 1900. During his twenty-year tenure at Würzburg, Wien continued his research into the actions of various forms of radiation in a vacuum. He was able to demonstrate in 1905 that the lower boundary of the mass of positive electrons (then called *Kanalstrahlen* in Germany) was the hydrogen atom.

In 1907, in an attempt to measure the lengths of Röntgen waves by measuring their impulse width, he correctly concluded that the waves themselves arise through the slowing of electrons in an electromagnetic field. He subsequently anticipated Max von Laue by five years in predicting that Röntgen waves could be accurately measured through the use of a crystal lattice. He turned his attention in 1908 to the subject that occupied much of his time for the rest of his life: the mechanism by which electrons radiate light and the measurement of the decay time for those electrons. During World War I, in 1916, Wien constructed an important proof of relativity theory.

In 1919, Wien devised a method whereby electrons could be observed in a vacuum tube without the necessity of causing electron collisions, by separating the area in which the positive rays are produced from the area in which they are observed. Using ten diffusion air pumps to empty a vacuum tube, Wien allowed the positive rays to enter the tube through a narrow slit while maintaining a constant pressure in the space in which the rays were produced. Wien's device later became instrumental in the development of modern particle accelerators.

In 1920, Wien accepted a post at the University of Munich, perhaps drawn there by a political atmosphere more congenial to his own increasingly conservative views. The attempt of Kurt Eisner to establish a Marxist republic in Bavaria had just been resoundingly defeated by patriotic political groups which had great support in Munich, the birthplace of German National Socialism. When Wien arrived in Munich, Adolf Hitler was beginning to attract a sizable following in that city by preaching a curious mixture of anti-Marxism, judeophobia, and chauvinistic nationalism.

Despite the affinities of some of their political and social views, Wien never joined Hitler's movement; he was certainly aware of it, since he was in Munich when the Nazis staged their abortive Beer Hall Putsch in an effort to overthrow the Bavarian state government preparatory to a march on Berlin. Unlike some of his colleagues, most notably his fellow Nobel laureates Johannes Stark and Philipp Lenard, Wien neither endorsed Hitler's movement from his classroom podium nor sympathized with a feature of Hitler's ideology that cast a shadow of ignominy over

Stark's and Lenard's careers: anti-Semitism. Instead, Wien continued his research and in 1922 successfully separated arc lines from spark lines for the first time. (Arc lines are light emitted by uncharged atoms; spark lines are light from atoms whose positive or negative charges can be demonstrated by electrostatic deflection.) This success proved to be Wien's last. He fell ill in 1926 and died two years later. His autobiography, published posthumously in 1930, contained nothing that had not previously been revealed in his numerous books and articles in scholarly journals.

Wien has never received the credit that is his due for the groundbreaking work he did in both experimental and theoretical physics, the Nobel Prize notwithstanding. Many of his discoveries were essential to the development of modern nuclear physics. The greatest tragedy of his untimely death is that had he lived, he might well have mitigated the circumstances of the Jewish scientific community during the years of Nazi ascendancy in Germany. Although he shared many of the conservative political ideas of Hitler's "tame" physicists, Stark and Lenard, he did not share their animosity toward the Jews. Stark and Lenard attacked Jews in the German academic community and especially in German physics as the formulators of a type of theoretical physics which they denounced as unscientific and un-German. Wien, with his unquestionable Prussian ancestry, could not possibly have been dismissed by anti-Semitic members of the scientific community.

Having mastered both theoretical and experimental physics and having played a major role in the development of the supposedly "Jewish" science of nuclear physics, Wien would, by his very presence, have refuted many of the charges leveled by Lenard and Stark. Indeed, Wien's reconciliation of theoretical and experimental physics must rank as one of his most important accomplishments. On the eve of the Great War, in 1914, Wien published a memorable article in a scientific journal in which he clearly demonstrated the mutual dependence of mental experiments and practical experiments in the quest of modern physics to understand the cosmos. A careful reading of Wien's article reduces the charges of Stark and Lenard against theoretical physics to absurdities.

## Bibliography

*Primary*

PHYSICS: A complete listing of Wien's voluminous works can be found in his memoirs, *Aus dem Leben und Wirken eines Physikers*, 1930. Among the more important are the following: "Über den Einfluss der ponderablen Theile auf das gebeugte Licht," *Sitzungensberichte der Königlich Preussischen Akademie der Wissenschaften zu Berlin*, vol. 2, 1885; "Über die Messung hoher Temperaturen," *Zeitschrift für Instrumentenkunde*, vol. 12, 1892 (with Ludwig Holborn); "Über die Energievertheilung im Emissionsspectrum eines schwarzen Körpers," *Annalen der Physik*, vol. 294, 1896 ("On the Division of Energy in the Emission-Spectrum of a Black Body," 1897); "Untersuchungen über die elektrische Entladung in verdünnten Gasen," *Annalen der Physik*, vol. 301, 1898; "Zur Theorie der Strahlung schwarzer Körper: Kritisches," *Annalen der Physik*, vol. 308, 1900;

"Über die Möglichkeit einer elektromagnetischen Begründung der Mechanik," *Archives néerlandaises des sciences exactes et naturelles*, vol. 5, 1900; "Über die Natur der positiven Elektronen," *Annalen der Physik*, vol. 314, 1902; *Vorlesungen über neuere Probleme der Theoretischen Physik, gehalten an der Columbia-Universität in New York im April 1913*, 1913; *Ziele und Methoden der theoretischen Physik*, 1914; "Über Messungen der Leuchtdauer der Atome und die Dämpfung der Spektrallinien," *Annalen der Physik*, vol. 365, 1919.

*Secondary*

Cohen, I. Bernard. *Revolution in Science.* Cambridge, Mass.: Harvard University Press, 1985. Cohen pays close attention to the development of modern relativity theory and nuclear physics, but he barely mentions Wien, an early champion of Einstein's theories. This omission is curious, considering the pivotal role played by Wien in the development of the new physics.

Heathcote, Niels Hugh de Vaudrey. *Nobel Prize Winners in Physics, 1901-1950.* New York: Henry Schuman, 1953. Heathcote presents a fair assessment of the importance of Wien's work and a brief but informative account of his life.

Miller, Arthur I. *Albert Einstein's Special Theory of Relativity: Emergence (1905) and Early Interpretation (1905-1911).* Reading, Mass.: Addison-Wesley, 1981. Although Miller concentrates on Einstein and his famous theory, he also recounts many of the discoveries made by other physicists that made Einstein's work possible. He does not give Wien as much credit as he might, but he acknowledges his contributions to modern physics.

Pais, Abraham. *"Subtle Is the Lord . . .": The Science and the Life of Albert Einstein.* New York: Oxford University Press, 1982. This biography of Albert Einstein contains much information about the great man's contemporaries in physics, including Wien. In Pais's account, however, Wien's work is represented as little more than a sidelight to the work of the real genius behind the revolution in physics, Albert Einstein.

Pledge, Humphrey T. *Science Since 1500: A Short History of Mathematics, Physics, Chemistry, Biology.* New York: Philosophical Library, 1947. This older history of science contains numerous references to Wien's work and comes close to according him his rightful place in the front ranks of twentieth century physicists. It supplies virtually no details of Wien's life but does justice to his work.

*Paul Madden*

# 1912

### Physics
Nils Gustaf Dalén, Sweden

### Chemistry
Victor Grignard, France
Paul Sabatier, France

### Physiology or Medicine
Alexis Carrel, France

### Literature
Gerhart Hauptmann, Germany

### Peace
Elihu Root, United States

# NILS GUSTAF DALÉN
## 1912

*Born:* Stenstorp, Sweden; November 30, 1869
*Died:* Lidingö, Sweden; December 9, 1937
*Nationality:* Swedish
*Area of concentration:* Engineering

*Dalén's invention of a fuel-saving and reliable acetylene gas lighting system, which was installed in lighthouses and lightbuoys around the world, benefited mankind by saving numerous lives as well as money*

## The Award

*Presentation*

Being seriously injured, Nils Gustaf Dalén was unable to attend the Nobel ceremony in person. Instead, the prize medal and diploma were handed over to his brother, Professor Albin Dalén, by King Gustav V on December 10, 1912.

The presentation speech was given by Professor H. G. Söderbaum, the President of the Royal Swedish Academy of Sciences. After discussing earlier problems connected with acetylene gas lighting, Söderbaum explained the three main features of Dalén's revolutionary lighting system. By developing a porous mass, which could safely contain large amounts of acetylene, Dalén had made it possible to handle this substance without any risk of explosion. Through two other inventions, Dalén had also managed to reduce acetylene consumption greatly, thus creating a lighting system that needed recharging only once a year on average. First, with an automatically working flashlight mechanism it was no longer necessary to have beacons shine all the time. Instead, Dalén's system used short flashes, without reducing navigation safety. Second, a "solar valve" made sure that the light was turned on each evening and went out each morning.

In addition to these technicalities, Söderbaum focused on the economic and human advantages of Dalén's work. Since his beacons required comparatively little supervision, maintenance costs had decreased substantially, and it was now possible to erect lighthouses even at distant locations that were hard to reach. This meant that navigation had become much easier and that the number of calamities at sea had been greatly reduced.

At the end of his presentation, Söderbaum noted that Dalén was indeed a true hero in Alfred Nobel's spirit. During one of his experiments—carried out in the service of mankind—Dalén had lost his eyesight after a terrible explosion.

*Nobel lecture*

As a result of the accident that had occurred two months earlier, Dalén had not been able to write a Nobel lecture. Nevertheless, it is easy to reconstruct from existing biographies those events that led him to the three revolutionary inventions.

As a consulting engineer to the Gasaccumulator Company, Dalén had spent numerous evenings trying to improve acetylene lighting. Most of these experiments had been carried out in Dalén's own apartment in Stockholm. There, his flashlight apparatus had been tested for several months before it was released onto the market in 1906. With this device, acetylene consumption decreased by 90 percent, promising the company a bright future. The handling of acetylene gas was still dangerous, however, and Dalén set out to solve this problem together with Harry Sköldberg, a chemical engineer at Gasaccumulator. It was already well-known that the risk of explosion was diminished if acetylene, dissolved in acetone, was stored in a porous mass—acting similar to a sponge. The problem was that existing substances tended to collapse during transportation, and Dalén and Sköldberg now developed a stable mass. It contained primarily asbestos and charcoal and was named *aga* mass, after the Swedish name of the company, Svenska Aktiebolaget Gasaccumulator.

Dalén was still not satisfied. He found it uneconomical to have lighthouses and lightbuoys flash all day and developed a very sensitive device in 1907, a sun valve. This device operated on the principle that a black piece of metal expands more than a glossy piece, if light intensity increases. After Dalén had tested the device on the windowsill of his apartment, the company could go on to manufacture this apparatus, using it to activate and deactivate lighthouse lamps automatically. This reduced acetylene consumption by another 30 to 40 percent. It had taken Dalén and his colleagues less than two years to develop these central parts of the system.

*Critical reception*

Dalén was not a typical Nobel laureate. He was an engineer and inventor, not a scientist. Through his work he had advanced the frontier of technology, not of science. When E. J. Ljungberg, managing director of the Great Copper Mine Company, suggested that Dalén be considered for the physics prize, he was met with a mixed response. Among the men in the Royal Swedish Academy of Sciences the engineers were in a minority, but that year they won—as they had done in 1909, when Guglielmo Marconi had been honored. Dalén's backers emphasized, in particular, the passage in Alfred Nobel's will which stipulated that the prize be awarded to those who "have conferred the greatest benefit on mankind." Undoubtedly, the recent accident that had made Dalén blind also contributed to the Academy's final decision on November 12, 1912.

In Sweden, the news was generally met with happiness and pride. *Stockholms Dagblad*, a daily paper, stated the feelings of most Swedes: "Dalén receives the Nobel Prize as a reward for both his inventions and his sacrifice," referring to the accident that had blinded him. Swedish papers and engineering journals described Dalén's system in enthusiastic terms. In interviews, the blind hero was depicted in the most poignant terms. Another Stockholm daily, *Dagens Nyheter*, said that Dalén, one day after he had received the news, was "calm, unaffected, and amiable." Despite the recent accident, his mind was "triumphant and unwavering."

The same enthusiasm could be found among professional societies in Sweden. On December 9, 1912, the Swedish Engineering Society held a meeting in Dalén's honor. Its chairman called Dalén one of the true heroes of our time. These positive responses reveal the ideals of the age: The early twentieth century was a time of great feats in engineering, and the engineer was idolized as a self-sacrificing, lonely figure working toward the technological betterment of mankind.

There were one or two hesitant commentators, as well. *Göteborgs Aftonblad* wondered why the prize had not been given to Gustaf de Laval, "the grand old man" of Swedish engineering and a prolific inventor. The paper claimed that Laval's contributions, among them a cream separator, had benefited mankind just as much as Dalén's lighthouse devices. *Svenska Dagbladet* raised the fundamental question of whether it had really been Nobel's intention to reward commercially successful engineers. Rather, the paper claimed, the prize ought to be restricted to scientists, whose economic situations are usually much more precarious.

Internationally, the announcement was met with silence. *The Times* of London was typical in that it ran only a very short notice, in which Dalén was mistakenly said to be a Swiss, not a Swedish, engineer. Clearly, news about the Nobel Prize was not always seriously treated at the beginning of the century; both Dalén's own name and that of his company are misspelled in the paper. Most technical and scientific journals were also quiet. *Engineering*, a London periodical, was unusual in that it contained a brief article describing Dalén's work and approving of the Academy's decision to give the prize to an engineer. In short, Dalén's prize was an "in-house," Swedish affair.

## Biography

Nils Gustaf Dalén was born in the village of Stenstorp in southwest Sweden on November 30, 1869. The son of a farmer, Gustaf was expected to tread in his father's footsteps, and so he did—but only initially. Growing increasingly interested in the technical aspects of agriculture, Dalén decided in 1892 to give up farming for engineering. Four years later, he was graduated from Chalmers' technical institute in Gothenburg, Sweden, and went on to study for one and a half years at the famous Polytechnische Hochschule in Zurich, Switzerland. Hence, he was comparatively old when he finally began to work as an engineer. On the other hand, his background was versatile, enabling him to attack problems both theoretically and practically.

During the first ten years of his engineering career, Dalén worked simultaneously on several projects for a number of firms. When Dalén was made director of Svenska Aktiebolaget Gasaccumulator in 1909, he became increasingly involved with business activities. He would remain so until his death, on December 9, 1937. Apart from his main work at Aktiebolaget Gasaccumulator, Dalén was a member of several boards of directors. He also participated in the activities of a number of professional societies, the Royal Swedish Academy of Sciences among them. In 1918, Lund University gave Dalén an honorary doctorate. Politically, he was actively working with the Conservative Party. Dalén was married to Elma Persson in 1901, and they had five children, one of whom died very young. During the first decade of marriage, they lived in an apartment in Stockholm, but as business improved, they were able to move into a large house in Lidingö, east of Stockholm.

## Scientific Career

Having begun as a farmer, it is no wonder that Dalén's first inventions were in the service of agriculture. As he owned a small dairy, he sensed a need for an apparatus which could measure the fat content of milk. After having designed such a device in the early 1890's, he approached the famous Gustaf de Laval with it, only to find that Laval had recently filed a patent application for a similar instrument. Still, Laval was impressed by Dalén's ingenuity and suggested that he complement his practical abilities with more theoretical studies. Despite the setback, Dalén continued experimenting in the agricultural area. After the turn of the century he developed a milking machine, called *Alfa*. It was exploited by one of Laval's firms and was quite popular for a time. Like many other of Dalén's inventions, this one was developed in order to save labor.

When Dalén returned home from his studies in Zurich, he turned his attention to turbines: rotating machines, similar to waterwheels, which are usually driven by steam or gas. In the 1880's steam-driven turbines had come into use, and Dalén attempted to design an automobile propelled by steam. The obstacles to a steam-driven automobile soon proved insurmountable, however, and Dalén and his collaborator, Artur Hultqvist, decided to design an engine driven by a gas turbine instead. Its principle of operation was rather simple: A fuel was ignited, and expanding hot air was made to drive the turbine. In practice, the principle encountered several problems: One problem was that friction losses turned out to be much larger than Dalén had calculated. Furthermore, it was difficult to find an alloy that could stand the high speeds and temperatures of the turbine. Although Dalén and Hultqvist received substantial financial support, first from Hultqvist's father and later from Laval's Steam Turbine Company, the engine never operated at the desired degree of efficiency. When Laval's Stockholm-based firm became responsible for the experiments, Dalén moved to the Swedish capital. There, his mind soon turned to new, more promising areas. Acetylene lighting was one of them.

In those days, at the turn of the century, electricity had not yet come to dominate the lighting business. Acetylene seemed to be a good choice, where very bright light was needed far away from electricity-producing stations. At sea and along railroad lines, but also in streets and in headlights, acetylene might become a serious alternative. Once more, Dalén began to cooperate with a young engineer whose father was wealthy enough to pay the initial costs. The engineer's name was Henrik von Celsing, and together he and Dalén founded the Dalén and Celsing Company. They patented an acetylene burner and began to cooperate with an existing firm, the Swedish Carbide and Acetylene Company. Business went well: Several Swedish cities decided to install acetylene gasworks, despite the potential hazards of explosion.

Still, Dalén was not satisfied with all the technical features of the acetylene system. In order to make the gas burn more evenly and brighter, he developed an incandescent mantle—a metal net covering the flame. In order to prevent explosions, the Carbide and Acetylene Company adopted a French "dissous" method, whereby the flasks used to transport acetylene were filled with a spongelike mass. Dalén and his collaborators also tried to find new areas where acetylene could be applied. An acetylene/oxygen welding apparatus was designed, but it did not catch on until several decades later. Another area of expansion would prove to be very successful much sooner: lighthouses and lightbuoys at sea.

Dalén and the others at Carbide and Acetylene, renamed Svenska Aktiebolaget Gasaccumulator in 1904 and usually called AGA from then on, realized that technology for lighthouses had requirements that differed from that used for streetlights or railroad lanterns. In particular, beacons at sea ought to work automatically as long as possible, without the need for maintenance or recharging, as they were often situated at remote locations. They also required very high-intensity light beams to be perceived at great distances. Dalén and AGA now set out to develop a system that could attract investors in this area.

Dalén's first move was to design a flashlight apparatus, each flash lasting approximately three-tenths of a second. Between flashes, acetylene was only needed to feed a very small eternally burning flame, and hence large amounts of gas were saved. If, for example, 2.7 seconds elapsed between flashes, almost 90 percent of the acetylene was saved. Of course, each beacon could be given its own intervals. Compared to flashlight apparatuses already on the market, Dalén's could produce many more flashes for a certain amount of gas. In other words, Dalén's was not the first device of its kind, but it was far superior to its counterparts. In Dalén's design, the gas was allowed to pass through the burner intermittently by means of a diaphragm which oscillated to and fro. No engine was required, as the mechanism was driven by the pressure of the expanding acetylene gas. Magnets were used to bring the diaphragm back to its original position.

When a lighthouse beacon needed recharging, high-pressure acetylene had to be transported to the lighthouse in large metal flasks at high pressure. The above-mentioned French "dissous" method was not safe enough, Dalén thought. Recurring explosions threatened the reputation of the whole acetylene industry, and something had to be done. The answer was to fill the flasks with a mass which did not pack during transportation. The *aga* mixture was found to meet the requirements. Thereafter, acetylene could be transported quite safely.

Dalén returned to the question of gas consumption. If lighthouses could be turned off in the daytime, acetylene was saved, and recharging need not be done as often. The thought led him to his sun valve, consisting of one black and three gilded metal rods. It initially met with doubt; Thomas Alva Edison is reported to have said that it would never work. When Dalén's proved effective, it gained wide acclaim. When the sun valve was exposed to light, the black piece of metal expanded more than the other three. Even though the relative movement was very slight, it could be transferred by a lever and gear mechanism to the burner, turning it off.

There remained one problem for Dalén: how to increase light intensity. It goes without saying that safety would be enhanced if beacons could be seen from a greater distance—especially as airplane navigation was expected to become more important in the future. Dalén and AGA solved the problem of light intensity in four ways. The first and most straightforward measure was to install an optical lens system, which increased the focus of the light beam. Dalén and his coworkers developed a very elaborate system, consisting of several lenses rotating around the burner. No engine was needed here either, even though the lens system was quite heavy. Second, by introducing the so-called Dalén mixer, the optimal ratio between air and acetylene gas was reached. It was known that an acetylene flame is most intense when the ratio of air mixed with acetylene is nine to one. Dalén managed to reach this optimum by a complicated but reliable system of ducts, diaphragms, valves, springs, and filters. The third measure was to introduce the incandescent mantle in lighthouses and lightbuoys. This had not been done earlier, because mantles had a limited life span. Since the overall goal was as self-regulating a system as possible, in order to avoid having to remount mantles on beacons at distant locations, the company decided that it had to develop a device that changed mantles automatically. The solution to the last problem was suggested by Dalén himself in 1917, five years after he had lost his eyesight and received the Nobel Prize. When a mantle broke, it was automatically replaced by a new one by means of an elevator mechanism. Hence, it was not necessary to visit beacons only to change mantles.

Dalén contributed far less to engineering after 1912. Instead, he became increasingly involved in business and politics. Most of the commercial projects, ranging from automobiles to airplanes, proved to be rather unsuccessful—with one important exception, the *aga* cooker. Launched in 1929 after five years of experimental work, this apparatus, intended for individual households and larger kitchens, combined high fuel efficiency with a minimum of supervision and maintenance. Loaded with coke once or twice a day, the apparatus could be used not only for cooking but also for heating dishwater and the kitchen area. Because the fire was on all the time, hot plates and ovens were always ready to use—an important advantage over other stoves. Even though it was expensive to buy, Dalén's cooker was extremely popular, particularly in Sweden and England.

The cooker was Dalén's last original invention. Clearly, he had "conferred benefit on mankind" in many ways during his lifetime, but it is not at all clear that this work was as original as his receiving the Nobel Prize indicates. Nowadays, not many young people in Sweden know who he was, and elsewhere his name is even less familiar. His lighting apparatuses sold well around the world, but he never received international fame. The fact that Dalén's name is very hard to find in histories of technology, in the engineering literature, and even in trade journals from his own time suggests that his inventions did not break revolutionary new ground. Nevertheless, Dalén contributed substantially to the advancement of technologies that were essential, both in his time and in the coming age of air navigation.

## Bibliography

*Primary*
Dalén was a designer of technical artifacts; he did not publish any of his writings.

*Secondary*
Aktiebolaget Gasaccumulator. *AGA and Its Products*. Stockholm: Author, 1946. This is one of several brochures describing the works of Dalén and his company. Like *AGA's Contribution to Engineering and Science* (1951) and similar booklets produced by AGA, this brochure is well illustrated and provides a good sense of the company's products, including historical surveys. Available through larger university libraries and business history archives.
Jolley, Leonard B. W., John M. Waldram, and George H. Wilson. *The Theory and Design of Illuminating Engineering Equipment*. London: Chapman and Hall, 1930. Though his book does not directly discuss Dalén's work, it offers a complete overview of lighting technology in the early twentieth century. One chapter is devoted to beacons and other signaling devices, including lighthouses.
Nylander, Erik, ed. *Modern Sweden*. Stockholm: General Export Association of Sweden, 1937. After a one-hundred-page introduction, which outlines the general features of Sweden's industry, commerce, and agriculture, this volume describes roughly 120 Swedish companies. Eight pages are devoted to Aktiebolaget Gasaccumulator, focusing on the company's technological achievements.
Strandh, Sigvard. *A History of the Machine*. New York: A and W Publishers, 1979. This large volume, richly illustrated, explains the history and functioning of a large number of machines. Among them is the gas turbine, the discussion of which stresses Dalén's contributions. Highly recommended for the layperson.
Wästberg, Erik. *Gustaf Dalén: En stor svensk*. Stockholm: L. Hökerberg, 1938. Although in Swedish, this is the most comprehensive biography of Dalén. Filled with photographs, it may also be of value to those who do not read Swedish. The author, writing soon after Dalén's death, is unable to distance himself from his subject, making the tone of the writing emotional. Nevertheless, the most complete source on Dalén.
──────────. "Sweden's Gustaf Dalén: Bringer of Light." *Reader's Digest*, February, 1944. This brief, easy-to-read article outlines Dalén's life and his most important inventions. Although plagued by the emotionalism of the author's above-listed biography, it is still one of the more accessible sources in English.
Williams, Trevor I., ed. *A History of Technology*. Vol. 7. Oxford: Clarendon Press, 1978. This is one volume of an eight-volume standard work which presents the historical development of most technologies, sometimes relating it to economic

and social changes. Although his work on beacons is not mentioned, Dalén's *aga* cooker is depicted and described at some length. Richly illustrated and generally accessible.

*Mikael Hard*

# 1913

## Physics
Heike Kamerlingh Onnes, Netherlands

## Chemistry
Alfred Werner, Switzerland

## Physiology or Medicine
Charles Richet, France

## Literature
Rabindranath Tagore, India

## Peace
Henri Lafontaine, Belgium

# HEIKE KAMERLINGH ONNES
## 1913

*Born:* Groningen, Netherlands; September 21, 1853
*Died:* Leiden, Netherlands; February 21, 1926
*Nationality:* Dutch
*Area of concentration:* Low temperature physics

*By testing extensively Johannes Diderik van der Waals' equation of state, which determined the relationship between pressure, volume, and temperature for various substances and at different temperatures, Kamerlingh Onnes was able to liquefy helium*

## The Award

*Presentation*

Th. Nordström, President of the Royal Swedish Academy of Sciences, presented the Nobel Prize in Physics to Heike Kamerlingh Onnes on December 11, 1913. Nordström stated that the study of the behavior of gases at different temperatures and pressures had long occupied physicists and that such studies were crucial in the development of thermodynamics.

Kamerlingh Onnes embarked on the experimental study of the theory of Johannes Diderik van der Waals (1837-1923) concerning the behavior of gases and especially the "law of corresponding states," according to which all gases behave in exactly the same way and obey the same equation of state (an equation expressing the relationship between the volume, pressure, and temperature of a gas) when the units in which pressure, volume, and temperature are measured are adapted to the specific gas under consideration. The theory involved assumptions that did not take into consideration all the particularities of the different gases. Hence, when various gases were subjected to examination there were necessarily deviations from the predictions of the theory.

The most systematic study of these deviations and of their dependence on temperature and molecular structure was undertaken by Kamerlingh Onnes in his laboratory at the University of Leiden from 1882 onward. In the process of testing van der Waals' theory, Kamerlingh Onnes was able to establish the first laboratory where work could be performed along several programs in low temperature physics. His continuous improvements of the apparatus led to the attainment of ever lower temperatures. Michael Faraday (1791-1867) by the mid-1820's was able to liquefy nearly all the then-known gases. Among the gases he could not liquefy were oxygen, nitrogen, and hydrogen. Raoul-Pierre Pictet (1846-1929) and Louis-Paul Cailletet (1832-1913) first obtained small droplets of oxygen and nitrogen in 1877. Zygmunt Florenty von Wróblewski (1845-1888) and Karl Stanislav Olzewski (1846-1915) liquefied oxygen in appreciable quantities in 1883. Karl Paul Gottfried von Linde (1842-1934) and William Hampson (1854-1926) made significant improvements to the apparatus for reaching low temperatures. Hydrogen was liquefied in

1898 by James Dewar (1842-1923) at −252 degrees Centigrade, and at that temperature all known gases became liquid—except helium, which was discovered in
Earth's atmosphere in 1895. Though many people, notably Dewar, tried to liquefy
helium, it was Kamerlingh Onnes who in 1908 prepared liquid helium for the first
time.

Kamerlingh Onnes was able not only to produce very low temperatures but also
to sustain them for a relatively long time so that the values of various physical
parameters could be measured in these low temperatures. This was extremely
important, since at low temperatures both the properties of matter and the course
followed by the physical phenomena are, in general, quite different from those at
normal or higher temperatures. One such phenomenon was the observation by
Kamerlingh Onnes that resistance to electrical conduction at helium temperatures
was totally different from that at higher temperatures. Because electricity was
conducted by the electrons, the new developments warranted a change in the theory
of electrons. That theory would not be completed until 1957.

*Nobel lecture*

Kamerlingh Onnes started his Nobel speech by recalling his intention, after his
appointment as professor of experimental physics at the University of Leiden, to
make Leiden a laboratory devoted to work in low temperature physics. Though the
aim of most of the people working in the field was the liquefaction of gases, there
was no systematic examination of a host of phenomena at low temperatures, where
new effects might surface that could not otherwise be observed because they would
be dominated by thermal motions.

Van der Waals' theory, especially the law of corresponding states, became the
main guiding force of Kamerlingh Onnes' research. In order to measure the deviations from the predictions of this law for substances of simple molecular structure,
it was necessary to improve existing instrumentation so that more precise measurements could be made while constant temperatures could be maintained for a long
time. Using the law of corresponding states and its reformulation by Kamerlingh
Onnes based on the principle of mechanical similarity, it was conceivable that
starting from a given temperature of a liquefied gas, one could reach lower temperatures and thus liquefy gases with a lower critical temperature. Thus starting from
the temperature of liquid oxygen, one could liquefy hydrogen. Nevertheless, long
before Kamerlingh Onnes had the opportunity to use this method, Dewar liquefied
hydrogen in 1898. Dewar invented the vacuum flask that bears his name, which
consists of two flasks, one inside the other, where the space between the outer walls
of the inner flask and the inner walls of the larger flask is a vacuum minimizing the
flow of heat from the environment to the liquid gas stored inside the inner flask.
Such vessels, among other things, were used to transport liquid gases from the
liquefying apparatus to the experimental setups where measurements of various
physical parameters were to be made. Many other people collaborated in the research concerning van der Waals' equation of state, especially Willem Hendrik

Keesom (1876-1956), who dealt extensively with a large number of theoretical problems connected with the equation of state.

One of the most crucial undertakings at Leiden was the measurement of the helium isotherms that contributed decisively in the liquefaction of this gas that was discovered in the atmosphere by Sir William Ramsay (1852-1916) in 1895. Information from the isotherms of a substance indicates whether the behavior of that particular substance follows the law of corresponding states. If it does, then it is possible to have an approximate estimate of its critical point.

Kamerlingh Onnes then related in a detailed manner the events of the day when helium was first liquefied. The experiment started at 5:30 A.M and continued until 9:30 P.M. Liquid helium was formed around 6:30 P.M. and could not be seen while it was flowing into the container because of its extreme transparency. Its presence was confirmed only when it filled the vessel; its surface "stood sharply against the vessel like the edge of a knife." Helium was found to have its boiling point at 4.25 degrees above absolute zero, and a critical temperature of about 5 degrees. Absolute zero is at about −273 degrees Celsius (or Centigrade); it is not possible to reach lower temperatures, not because of technical difficulties but for theoretical reasons. It did not become possible to solidify helium by further lowering the temperature, and in fact its solidification was achieved only in 1926 by decreasing the temperature as well as increasing the pressure.

Liquid helium displayed an unusual property. Its density at first dropped with the lowering of temperature; then it increased, reaching a maximum at 2.2 degrees above absolute zero; then it started dropping again as the temperature decreased. This behavior was not expected based on the law of corresponding states, and the insight to be gained from the deviations from that law for liquid helium appeared very promising to Kamerlingh Onnes.

In the final section of his talk, Kamerlingh Onnes described some of the experiments that had led to his 1911 discovery of superconductivity, the complete absence of resistance to the electrical current passing through a conductor. Experiments carried down to the freezing temperatures of hydrogen had indicated the likelihood of the resistance becoming zero at helium temperatures, provided one had very pure samples of platinum. By measuring the resistance of platinum at the temperatures of liquid helium, it was found that it decreased with decreasing temperature, becoming constant after a certain point. Thinking that this was caused by slight impurities in the samples, which would be present even in gold, Kamerlingh Onnes decided to repeat the experiment with samples of mercury that could be prepared to be in an extremely pure state. It was found that while the resistance was decreasing with decreasing temperature, at 4.2 degrees above absolute zero it abruptly became zero. This was considered to be a new state for mercury (in addition to the solid, liquid, and gaseous states), and it was termed the state of superconductivity. It was then found that both tin and lead were found to be superconductive as well. Nevertheless, the superconducting state could not be maintained when the applied currents were above a certain value, this value being higher the lower the temperature. When currents above this threshold value were passed through the superconductor, the initial resistance was restored. Kamerlingh Onnes proposed that the resistance was restored because of the heat produced in the wire with the increase of the current density. He was, however, fully aware that the explanation may lie in quantum theory, but instead of trying to provide such an explanation, he planned to concentrate on further experimental work. The absence of resistance at low temperatures implied very long free paths (the distance traveled between two consecutive encounters with other bodies) for the electrons when compared with the situation in normal conductors.

*Critical reception*

Kamerlingh Onnes, in his inaugural lecture after his appointment at the University of Leiden, emphasized the principle of "knowledge through measurement," and in that respect he was very influential in establishing a particular style of scientific research that became characteristic of Leiden and that contributed appreciably to the numerous experimental discoveries at his laboratory.

Though Kamerlingh Onnes has been universally regarded as the founder of low temperature physics, this recognition did not come until after he had received the Nobel Prize. His numerous achievements were well-known among his colleagues in various countries, but hardly anyone knew of his work outside this relatively small group of people. The first article for a wider audience was written in the *Scientific American* in 1914, after the announcement that he had received the Nobel Prize.

## Biography

Heike Kamerlingh Onnes was born in Groningen, in the Netherlands, on September 21, 1853. He was the son of Harm Kamerlingh Onnes, the owner of a brickworks, and Anna Gerdina Coers. He completed his secondary education at the Hoogere Burgerschool in his native town and in 1870 entered the University of Groningen. In the following year he obtained what roughly corresponds to the bachelor's degree, and from October of 1871 to April of 1873 he was at Heidelberg. He won the gold medal for a competition sponsored by the Natural Sciences Faculty of the University of Utrecht and the silver medal for a similar competition at the University of Groningen. Both of the essays that he submitted for the competitions were about methods for the study of chemical reactions. In Heidelberg he studied first with Robert Wilhelm Bunsen (1811-1899) and then with Gustav Robert Kirchhoff (1824-1887). He was also able to win the Seminarpreis and become one of the two assistants of Kirchhoff. He returned to Groningen, where in 1879 he obtained his doctoral degree with a thesis titled *Nieuwe bewijzen voor de aswenteling der aarde* (new proofs of the rotation of Earth). Kamerlingh Onnes showed that an experiment conducted by Jean-Bernard-Léon Foucault (1819-1868), who had used a pendulum to demonstrate the rotation of Earth around its own axis, could be regarded as a special case of a larger set of phenomena that could, equally convincingly, show the rotation of Earth.

By 1878, Kamerlingh Onnes had become an assistant to Johannes Bosscha (1831-1911), delivering lectures in his place during 1881 and 1882. In 1881, he published his *Algemeene theorie der vloeistoffen* (general theory of liquids). This work marks the beginning of the kind of research Kamerlingh Onnes would pursue to the end of his life. His most outstanding contribution was to reformulate van der Waals' law of corresponding states in terms of mechanical parameters: the mass of the molecules, their size, the strength of the intermolecular forces, and the like. In 1882, Kamerlingh Onnes was appointed professor of experimental physics and meteorology at the University of Leiden. He initiated a major reorganization of the university's laboratory, aiming at the establishment of a facility where low temperature phenomena could be studied rather than one devoted exclusively to the liquefaction of gases. An important factor in the success of this undertaking was his founding, in 1901, of a training school for instrument makers and glass blowers.

Kamerlingh Onnes was a member of numerous scientific societies in many countries (Germany, Norway, England, Poland, the United States, Denmark, Sweden, France, Italy, Spain, and Austria) and received a large number of awards. He was one of the founding members of the Association (later Institut) Internationale du Froid and was president of its scientific committee for many years. On February 21, 1926, after a short illness, he died in Leiden. He was survived by his wife, Maria Adriana Wilhelmina Elisabeth Bijleveld, and his son Albert, who was a high-ranking civil servant at The Hague.

## Scientific Career

The only work that Heike Kamerlingh Onnes produced before his appointment in Leiden was a theoretical treatise on the various problems of fluids, which he completed while he was at Delft in 1880. He began at the University of Leiden in 1881 and remained there until his retirement in 1923.

Before Kamerlingh Onnes' appointment at Leiden, two Dutch physicists, who were to make fundamental contributions to physics, had already received their doctorates from Leiden. Johannes Diderik van der Waals in 1873 completed his dissertation on the continuity of the gaseous and liquid states, and in 1875 Hendrik Antoon Lorentz completed his dissertation on the reflection and refraction of light, making extensive use of James Clerk Maxwell's equations. Kamerlingh Onnes' work in molecular physics, as well as on the magnetic, electric, and optical properties of the various substances, was an outgrowth of the work of these two physicists. Their remarkable theoretical contributions inspired a program in experimental physics whose realization in such a relatively short time remains unique.

A year before he was appointed professor of experimental physics and meteorology at the University of Leiden, Kamerlingh Onnes published his paper on the general theory of liquids. In this work, van der Waals' influence is evident. In 1873, van der Waals had proposed an equation that determined the relationship between pressure, volume, and temperature. He was able to derive his equation by assuming that molecules in gases have a spherical shape and that there are two kinds of forces that determine their movements. These were the attractive forces, with long range, and the repulsive forces, with short range. Van der Waals, using his equation, was able to derive the available experimental results and prove that the transition from the gaseous state to the liquid state, as temperature is lowered, is a continuous process. This fact had first been hypothesized by Thomas Andrews (1813-1885) in 1869, who observed that carbon dioxide could not be liquefied by an increase in pressure unless it was below a certain temperature: the critical temperature. In 1880 van der Waals reformulated his equation by expressing pressure, volume, and temperature in terms of their critical values, and he found that the resultant equation could be valid independent of the nature of the particular substance. This he called "the law of corresponding states."

Kamerlingh Onnes was able to reformulate the law of corresponding states in terms of mechanical rather than thermodynamic parameters. Like every equation based on hypotheses that idealize physical entities and do not take into consideration all the possible factors that affect the behavior of matter, van der Waals' equation of state did not always predict experimental results perfectly. Kamerlingh Onnes became convinced that the investigation of the law of corresponding states for a particular substance would give results suggestive of the behavior of a "similar" substance. Thus he started measuring the isotherms of many gases in temperatures that ranged from about −260 to +100 degrees Centigrade. As a result of the information he was gathering and the constant improvements to the cryogenic (low temperature) apparatus, he liquefied hydrogen in 1906. Though Dewar had liquefied hydrogen for the first time in 1898, he had never published detailed diagrams of his apparatus. Hence, the liquefaction of hydrogen by Kamerlingh Onnes was a very important step, since it showed that his particular method could indeed be successful.

Knowing that the parameters used by van der Waals to express the strength of the attractive and repulsive forces between molecules could not be independent of temperature and pressure, Kamerlingh Onnes expressed the original equation of state in series. It was expressed as the sum of terms that contained twenty-five parameters in all. Extensive measurements were made to determine the values of certain of these parameters and to understand the reasons for the deviations from the predicted "ideal" values. The exhaustive and systematic measurements of the isotherms of monatomic and diatomic gases became one of the main preoccupations of Kamerlingh Onnes for the duration of his tenure at Leiden. Part of this research was aimed at determining the critical values of the thermodynamic parameters for helium, which eventually led to its liquefaction. The apparatus used by Kamerlingh Onnes to liquefy helium was an improved version of the apparatus used by Pictet to liquefy oxygen and by Linde to liquefy air. They, in turn, had developed their liquefaction techniques based on principles discovered by James Prescott Joule (1818-1889) and Lord Kelvin (William Thomson, 1824-1907), who had found that the temperature of a gas drops when it is made to expand very quickly. Gases could be liquefied by increasing the pressure while at constant volume, provided the critical temperature was reached.

Another aspect of Kamerlingh Onnes' research program was the study of the electrical properties of various substances at low temperatures. Dewar had made extensive measurements of the variation of electrical resistance at low temperatures, even before he liquefied hydrogen. He had found that for gold and platinum the resistance decreased as the temperature dropped; he thought that the resistance would vanish at absolute zero. When he measured the resistance for the same substances at liquid hydrogen temperatures, he found that its value became practically a constant and was not particularly responsive to the lowering of temperature. In 1911, Kamerlingh Onnes conducted the first measurements of electrical resistance at liquid helium temperatures. The same trends as in the temperature range of liquid hydrogen were manifested at these temperatures.

Thinking that impurities might contribute to such behavior, Kamerlingh Onnes planned to measure the electrical resistance of a substance that could be prepared in an extremely pure state. Mercury was such a substance, and when its resistance was measured, it was observed that it became zero at 4.2 degrees above absolute zero. What was unexpected was that the resistance fell *abruptly* to zero, at a temperature well above absolute zero. The experiments were repeated in 1913 and new properties of superconductivity were discovered. It was found that superconductivity was a property not only of pure samples, but of particular substances as well. For example, gold and platinum, even in a state of very high purity, were not superconductors. A current would circulate in a superconducting loop for a very long time after its source had been shut off, but there was an upper limit to the intensity of such a "persistent" current. Superconductivity was destroyed when the current had an intensity higher than a certain value. The same was true of magnetic fields: When superconducting samples were placed in a magnetic field, superconductivity could not be maintained when the value of the magnetic field was above a particular value—different for each substance.

The magnetic properties of a large number of substances were also studied at low temperatures. The study of the magnetization of liquid and solid oxygen and its compounds was the focus of Kamerlingh Onnes' research on magnetism. These magnetic researches had started very early in Leiden and had continuously added important contributions to low temperature physics, in fact dominating the activities of the work in Leiden after Kamerlingh Onnes' death in 1926.

In 1885, Kamerlingh Onnes founded the *Communications from the Physical Laboratory at the University of Leiden*, where all papers with results from experiments performed in the laboratory were published in English, a few in French or German. Theoretical papers were published in the *Supplement to the Communications*. The great majority of papers had originally been published in Dutch in the *Proceedings of the Royal Academy at Amsterdam*. Kamerlingh Onnes was the author or coauthor of more than four hundred papers. *Communications* remains a remarkable chronicle of the work done in the Leiden laboratory and of the development of low temperature physics up to about the end of the 1920's.

# Bibliography

*Primary*

PHYSICS: *Nieuwe bewijzen voor de aswenteling der aarde*, 1879; *Algemeene theorie der vloeistoffen*, 1881; *Methods and Apparatus Used in the Cryogenic Laboratory*, 1899-1900?; *On Measurement of Very Low Temperatures*, 1900?; *Over het bereiken van temperaturen, belangrijk beneden het kookpunt van helium*, 1910; *Experiments at the Cryogenic Laboratory at Leyden*, 1910-1911; *Notes on the Work of the Section for Physics, Chemistry, and Thermometry of the First International Commission of the Association Internationale du Froid*, 1913; *Selected Papers of Heike Kamerlingh Onnes, 1853-1926*, 1989.


*Secondary*

Brush, Stephen G. *Statistical Physics and the Atomic Theory of Matter, from Boyle and Newton to Landau and Onsager.* Princeton, N.J.: Princeton University Press, 1983. The first half of this book provides a wealth of information about the developments that preceded the formulation of van der Waals' theory, which in turn was so decisive for Kamerlingh Onnes' research.

Casimir, Hendrik Brugt Gerhard. *Haphazard Reality: Half a Century of Science.* New York: Harper & Row, 1983. Written by one of the protagonists in the development of low temperature physics who completed his doctorate at the University of Leiden right after Kamerlingh Onnes' death, this book describes life and work at the physics laboratory at Leiden and includes many reminiscences of Kamerlingh Onnes and his successors.

Cohen, Ernst. "Kamerlingh Onnes, Memorial Lecture." *Journal of the Chemical Society*, 1927: 1193-1209. This is the text of a lecture delivered after Kamerlingh Onnes' death by one of the best-known physical chemists in the Netherlands. It contains much information on Kamerlingh Onnes' life and work prior to his appointment to the University of Leiden.

Dahl, P. G. "Kamerlingh Onnes and the Discovery of Superconductivity: The Leyden Years, 1911-1914." *Historical Studies in the Physical Sciences* 15 (1984): 1-37. This article traces in a very detailed manner all the work by Kamerlingh Onnes that led to the discovery of superconductivity, as well as the experiments he did right after its discovery in order to study its various characteristics. Includes an almost complete list of all the works by Kamerlingh Onnes and his collaborators that relate to the discovery of superconductivity.

De Bruyn Ouboter, Rudolf. "Superconductivity: Discoveries During the Early Years of Low Temperature Research at Leiden, 1908-1914." *IEEE Transactions on Magnetics* MAG-23 (1987): 355-370. This article examines the innovations and improvements in the apparatus for low temperature physics that preceded the liquefaction of helium. It includes a comprehensive account of the helium liquefier originally used by Kamerlingh Onnes.

Gavroglu, Kostas, and Goudaroulis Yorgos. "Heike Kamerlingh Onnes's Researches at Leiden and Their Methodological Implications." *Studies in the His-*

*tory and Philosophy of Science* 19 (1988): 243-274. This article articulates the "physics culture" as developed at Leiden during Kamerlingh Onnes' tenure there. Three research programs are exhaustively studied: those on the equation of state, the electrical research, and the magnetic research.

—————————. *Methodological Aspects in the Development of Low Temperature Physics, 1881-1956: Concepts Out of Context(s)*. Dordrecht: Kluwer, 1988. The purpose of this book is to investigate a series of methodological issues that appear to be particular to the development of low temperature physics, especially those associated with the manifestation of quantum mechanics on a macroscopic scale. There is a detailed discussion of the study of the properties of liquid helium that eventually led to the discovery of superfluidity. Includes an exhaustive bibliography.

Mendelssohn, Kurt. *The Quest of Absolute Zero: The Meaning of Low Temperature Physics*. 2d ed. London: Taylor and Francis, 1977. This book, written for a wider audience, traces developments in the history of low temperature physics, especially the liquefaction of the gases, during the nineteenth century. The author has made important discoveries concerning the phenomenon of superfluidity, so naturally there is emphasis on the activities surrounding this subject.

*Kostas Gavroglu*

# 1914

### Physics
Max von Laue, Germany

### Chemistry
no award

### Physiology or Medicine
Robert Bárány, Austria

### Literature
no award

### Peace
no award

# MAX VON LAUE
## 1914

*Born:* Pfaffendorf, near Koblenz, Germany; October 9, 1879
*Died:* Berlin, Germany; April 23, 1960
*Nationality:* German
*Area of concentration:* X-ray optics

*Laue provided the theoretical support for the discovery that X rays can be diffracted by a crystal. This discovery led to the formation of two new branches of science: X-ray crystallography and X-ray spectroscopy*

## The Award

*Presentation*

In the summer of 1914, even before the outbreak of World War I, the Swedish Academy of Sciences had decided to postpone the 1914 Nobel Prize ceremonies until 1915. Academy members were afraid of further inflaming already agitated nationalistic feelings. When the war did come, its brutality seemed to some to justify the Academy's action, but others accused the Academy of caving in to barbarism instead of maintaining the high ideals of Alfred Nobel. During the early months of 1915, uncertainty continued about whether the Academy would defer all awards until peace returned to Europe, but in the fall, the committee responsible for selecting the prizewinner in physics decided to announce the 1914 and 1915 awards within a few days of each other.

In the second week of November, 1915, the Swedish Academy disclosed that the Nobel Prize in Physics for 1914 would be given to Max von Laue for his discovery of the diffraction of X rays by crystals. Shortly thereafter, the Academy announced that the Nobel Prize in Physics for 1915 would be awarded to Sir William Henry Bragg and Sir Lawrence Bragg for their work in the analysis of crystal structures by means of X rays. This dual announcement of prizewinning work by a German scientist and two British scientists, whose countries were then at war, was not accidental. Amid the hostilities, the Academy wished to spotlight the international cooperation that had led to these closely interconnected and beautiful discoveries.

Because of the war, Laue was unable to travel to Stockholm to give his Nobel lecture until June 3, 1920, when the presentation speech of Professor G. Granqvist, Chairman of the Nobel Committee for Physics, was also delivered. In his talk, Granqvist explored the historical roots of Laue's discovery of X-ray diffraction. After X rays had been discovered by Wilhelm Röntgen in 1895, a controversy had developed about their nature: Were these rays particles or waves? Röntgen believed that X rays might be light waves of very short wavelength, but he could find no evidence to prove his contention. By 1911, however, some good evidence had been found to suggest that X rays consisted of electromagnetic waves. That was the situation when Laue reasoned that X radiation penetrating a crystal should be diffracted as light is by a diffraction grating (a glass plate etched by a large number of closely spaced, equidistant grooves, which break incident light into various colors). Walter Friedrich and Paul Knipping did the experimental work that confirmed Laue's idea.

The discovery of X-ray diffraction proved that X rays had the same wave nature as light, with a wavelength ten thousand times shorter than that of visible light. The discovery also had important implications for crystallography, for it made possible the precise determination of atomic positions in crystals. Granqvist concluded that these important consequences of Laue's discovery, obvious so soon after it had been made, showed that his award coincided with Alfred Nobel's intentions more closely than any other Nobel Prize ever had or perhaps ever would.

*Nobel lecture*

Like Granqvist's presentation, Laue's lecture, "Concerning the Detection of X-ray Interferences," was a historical survey of the discoveries in physics leading up to the famous discovery of X-ray diffraction. Laue modestly noted that, throughout his early life as a physicist, he had never believed that it would be his good fortune to solve the problem of whether X rays were wave phenomena or the trajectories of tiny particles. In the decade after Röntgen's discovery, the hypothesis that X rays are very short electromagnetic waves came to be viewed as plausible, and the problem was to reveal X rays' wave nature by devising some way of manifesting their interference. Finding the evidence proved difficult, because interference between waves can occur only if the dimensions of the sources of the interference— for example, particles or apertures—are not very much greater than the lengths of the waves themselves. Unfortunately, a diffraction grating proved much too coarse for X rays, whose waves, if they existed, would have to be extremely short.

After detailing the history of research into X rays and wave interference, Laue told how he became involved in the study of X-ray interference. From his childhood, he had been interested in optics and the wave theory of light. Through his studies, he had cultivated what he called "a special feeling or intuition for wave processes." His doctoral dissertation dealt with this topic, as did the paper that qualified him for his lectureship at the University of Berlin. When, in 1909, he went to Munich, he found himself at the same university as Röntgen, with the natural result that to his interest in optics he added an interest in X rays. At Munich, too, was Arnold Sommerfeld, who, to judge by his many distinguished students, may have been the greatest teacher of theoretical physics who ever lived. It was through Sommerfeld that Laue undertook a mathematical investigation of the theory of cross-gratings (diffraction gratings with two sets of lines, one at a right angle to the other).

Munich was also the university home of Paul von Groth, a professor of mineralogy who championed the theory that crystals are lattices, or three-dimensional arrays of atoms. This theory was first put forward by Auguste Bravais in 1848 and further developed by Leonard Sohncke in 1879 and by Evgraf Federov and Artur

Schoenflies in 1891. Paul P. Ewald, one of Sommerfeld's students, had been assigned the task of creating a mathematical treatment of the behavior of light waves in a lattice, but he had encountered difficulties. Early in February, 1912, he discussed his problem with Laue. During the conversation, Laue had the idea that someone should irradiate crystals with X rays, for, if the atoms of the crystal truly formed a lattice, this process should produce interference similar to the light interference in optical gratings.

Soon, Walter Friedrich, one of Sommerfeld's assistants, heard of Laue's idea and wanted to test it experimentally, but Sommerfeld and other physicists expressed serious doubts. As Laue tactfully said in his lecture, "a certain amount of diplomacy was necessary before Friedrich and Knipping were finally permitted to carry out the experiment according to my plan." When the experiment was finally performed, around Easter, the photograph of the X rays transmitted through a crystal of copper sulfate showed, besides the incident X rays, a circle of spots diffracted by the lattice. This and further experiments conclusively demonstrated that X rays were a form of wave motion and that crystals had repetitive structures in three dimensions. Laue's conclusion had also been reached by another physicist. The Englishman Sir Lawrence Bragg visualized X-ray diffraction as a reflection of the incident beam from the internal planes of atoms in the crystal. Bragg's idea, along with his father's invention of the X-ray spectrometer, helped them to unravel the structures of many important crystals.

Laue concluded his lecture by expressing hope that X-ray analysis would provide the answer to the question of mixed crystals. At the time, scientists agreed that mixed crystals formed space lattices in the same manner as ordinary crystals, but they disagreed about how the atoms of the two compounds were distributed. Some said that the distribution was completely arbitrary, while others maintained that it occurred systematically. Laue thought that random distribution was more probable, although he admitted that recent experiments had suggested otherwise. X-ray crystallography, which had already solved so many structural problems, would eventually solve this one.

*Critical reception*

If, as the great mathematician Jules-Henri Poincaré once said, the value of a discovery must be measured by the fruitfulness of its consequences, then Laue's discovery of X-ray diffraction must rank among the most important findings of modern physics. This discovery was as important as the original discovery of X rays themselves, and physicists around the world were quick to recognize this. So obvious was the value of Laue's discovery for elucidating the nature of both X rays and crystals that his Nobel Prize followed his work by only three years, a surprisingly prompt recognition by a traditionally conservative Academy.

The reaction to Laue's award among physicists in both of the warring nations was overwhelmingly favorable. For example, Albert Einstein called Laue's discovery one of the most beautiful in physics, and the Braggs ranked X-ray diffraction as one of the epoch-making discoveries in the history of physics. World War I, however, considerably diminished the popular reaction to Laue's prize. If the award had been given in peacetime, there may have been extensive analyses in the popular press, but war news pushed articles about the prize to the back pages. German newspapers did express strong approval of the Swedish Academy's choice, but reaction in the popular press of the Allies was more muted. *The Times* of London, for example, had only a very small note at the bottom of one of its back pages on November 13, 1915. Similarly, *The New York Times* on the same day did little more than state that the Nobel Prize had been given to Laue. American newspapers were much more enthusiastic about the Nobel Prize in Chemistry for 1914, which had been awarded to Theodore William Richards, the first laureate in chemistry from the United States.

Before the war, knowledge of X-ray diffraction had spread to France, Holland, Russia, Japan, and the United States. After the war, Laue's discovery exerted an even greater influence. It opened up new fields of research, and with each new field a flood of light was shed on the behavior and properties of matter. It extended scientists' ability to observe minute structures ten thousand times beyond the power of the microscope. Physics, chemistry, biochemistry, metallurgy, mineralogy, and other sciences were transformed by this new way of looking at matter. Since then, the story of X-ray analysis has been one of its application to ever more complex structures. The stature of Laue's discovery grew, and its anniversaries were celebrated with an increasing awareness of how richly deserved his Nobel Prize was. Many other honors followed the award: the Max Planck Medal of the German Physical Society, honorary degrees from Manchester and Chicago, and membership in American and French physical societies. Laue's discovery is so much a part of modern science that it is easy to forget the revolutionary role that X-ray analysis played in transforming scientists' ideas about the structure of matter.

## Biography

Max Theodor Felix von Laue was born in the small village of Pfaffendorf, near Koblenz, Germany, on October 9, 1879. His father, an important military court official, moved frequently, so Max spent his childhood in Brandenburg, Altona, Posen, Berlin, and Strasbourg. In the last three places he attended the *Gymnasium*, the classical German secondary school, where he studied nine years of Latin and six years of Greek. His interest in science was sparked by an excellent teacher in Strasbourg. He lost his mother, to whom he was greatly devoted, at an early age, and this loss may have contributed to the great reserve that characterized his personality.

After he was graduated from the Strasbourg *Gymnasium* in 1898, Laue studied science and mathematics at the University of Strasbourg while simultaneously fulfilling a year of compulsory military service. He then transferred to the University of Göttingen, where Woldemar Voigt's lectures on theoretical physics so impressed him that he decided to dedicate his life to it. After a semester at the University of Munich, he spent three semesters at the University of Berlin studying under Max

Planck, who became his mentor and friend. Laue obtained his doctorate at Berlin in 1903; he then went back to Göttingen as a postdoctoral student before returning to Berlin in 1905 as Planck's assistant.

In 1909, Laue became an unsalaried lecturer at Munich, and a year later he married Magdalena Degen, with whom he had a son and a daughter. At Munich, he lectured in optics and thermodynamics, published a comprehensive monograph on Einstein's theory of relativity, and did the work on the interference of X rays for which he received the Nobel Prize. In 1912 he was appointed associate professor in theoretical physics at the Univeristy of Zürich, a position he held until 1914, when he was named full professor at the University of Frankfurt am Main. During World War I, he worked with Wilhelm Wien at the University of Würzburg on improving military communications equipment. Laue fully supported Germany's position in the war, and in later years he continued to think of Germany as the injured party.

Desiring to be near Planck, Laue arranged in 1919 an exchange of teaching posts with Max Born: Born left Berlin to go to Frankfurt, and Laue returned to Berlin. In the 1920's, Laue, with Planck and Einstein, made the University of Berlin into a world center for theoretical physics. This situation changed abruptly when the Nazis came to power in 1933. Laue protested vigorously against Einstein's dismissal as head of the Kaiser Wilhelm Institute for Physics. In 1937 he sent his son to the United States to escape conscription by the Nazis, but he decided to remain in Germany to mitigate in whatever way he could the negative effects of Nazism on German science. He helped colleagues who were dismissed to get positions in other countries, and during the war he took the risk of concealing people whose lives were endangered. After his retirement from Berlin in 1943, Laue moved to Württemberg, where the Kaiser Wilhelm Institute had relocated. Although he did not participate in the German uranium project, he was sent to England after the war for questioning about Germany's wartime scientific programs. He returned to Germany in 1946, when he became director of the Max Planck Institute and professor of physics at the University of Göttingen. He played a major role in refounding German physical societies and research associations and in rebuilding German science. In 1951, at the age of seventy-one, he took over the directorship of the Fritz Haber Institute in Berlin-Dahlem. He retired from this position seven years later.

His death was unexpected. While on his way to a committee meeting, his car collided with a motorcyclist and overturned. He suffered a concussion, and after seeming to improve in a Berlin hospital, he died on April 23, 1960.

## Scientific Career

Max von Laue was one of a handful of great physicists who helped bridge the transitional period from classical to quantum physics. Although he made contributions to nearly all branches of physics, he devoted most of his creative efforts to optics, relativity theory, thermodynamics, and superconductivity. Best known for his discovery of X-ray diffraction, he took only a cursory interest in the later developments of crystal-structure analysis; he maintained an avid interest in X-ray optics, however, until the end of his life.

Laue himself traced the origin of his scientific career to a chance remark by a Berlin *Gymnasium* teacher on the deposition of copper from a copper sulfate solution by an electric current. This first contact with physics so impressed the twelve-year-old boy that he wandered around his home for several days lost in thought. When his mother discovered the cause of his behavior, she encouraged his interest in science by taking him to the Urania, a Berlin museum with displays of workable scientific apparatus. He also began to read Hermann von Helmholtz's books on science. At the University of Strasbourg, Ferdinand Braun's introductory physics course increased Laue's enthusiasm still further.

Max Planck, the founder of quantum theory, was the greatest influence on Laue's scientific career. With Planck as his guide, Laue wrote his dissertation on the theory of interference in plane parallel plates. Interference is the interaction between intersecting light waves, which tend to weaken or reinforce each other depending on their phases. In July, 1903, Laue passed his doctoral examination magna cum laude, with mathematics and philosophy as minor subjects. His interest in philosophy was genuine, and he later spent much time studying Immanuel Kant's writings.

During the early years of his scientific career at Göttingen and Berlin, Laue's research centered on the thermodynamic analysis of the coherence of light waves (Light waves are coherent if a fixed relationship exists between their phases.) In thermodynamics, scientists are concerned with the relative effects of energy and probability on the systems that they study. They use the term "entropy" to represent the probability that a substance is in a certain state. Laue was concerned with the system in which a light beam is separated into a reflected and a refracted ray. He showed that the entropy of the two beams resulting from reflection and refraction is exactly equal to that of the entering beam. In other words, he proved that this process is reversible: The two coherent rays, by appropriate reflection or refraction, can be reunited into a single ray.

The next important direction of Laue's research derived from a meeting of the Berlin Physics Colloquium in which Planck reported on a 1905 paper by Albert Einstein on the electrodynamics of moving bodies. Laue was fascinated with this paper, and although Einstein's new ideas of space and time raised many objections in his mind, Laue overcame them and became an early, enthusiastic defender of the theory of relativity. Indeed, Laue helped to furnish this controversial theory with experimental confirmation. In 1851, Armand Fizeau, a French physicist, had discovered a formula to express the results of his experiments on the speed of light in flowing water, and in 1907 Laue showed that the Einstein theorem for the addition of velocities yielded Fizeau's equation. Laue wrote a book on relativity theory in 1911 that contributed to the early acceptance of the theory. Einstein called it a masterpiece.

In 1909, Laue moved to the University of Munich, where Arnold Sommerfeld was building up a strong school of theoretical physics. At first Laue continued to work on relativity, but he returned to his interest in optics when Sommerfeld asked him to write an article on wave optics for the *Encyclopedia of the Mathematical Sciences*. This project required Laue to express mathematically the action of a diffraction grating on light waves. This work helped him to see that the passage of X-ray waves through a periodic crystalline arrangement of particles might give rise to inter-ference, or diffraction.

After Friedrich and Knipping confirmed Laue's idea of X-ray diffraction, he began to develop a theory of the crystal grating. He pictured the crystal as a symmetric arrangement of atoms that is repeated over and over again, like a pattern on wallpaper. He assumed that these atoms in the crystal are set vibrating by incident X rays and that these oscillating atoms in turn emit waves in various directions. He was able to account for some of the spots on the diffraction photo-graph by calculating the total effect of all these waves at certain points.

Sir Lawrence Bragg's treatment of the diffraction of X rays by crystals was much simpler than Laue's. For Bragg, when an X-ray wave falls on a plane, it is reflected; if it falls on a number of atoms in a plane, they act as centers of disturbance, so that the secondary waves from the atoms build up a wave front. The intensity of the reflected wave depends on the number of atoms present in the crystal plane, the intensity increasing as the density of atoms in the plane is increased.

During the 1930's, Laue became interested in superconductivity. This phenome-non had been discovered in 1911 by Heike Kamerlingh Onnes, a Dutch physicist who first liquefied helium. He observed that mercury and other metals suddenly lose all electrical resistance as soon as the temperature reaches a certain critical point characteristic of the metal. He later found that it was possible to annul superconductivity by a magnetic field. Laue became interested in this problem when he became a consultant in Berlin-Charlottenburg. He began to participate in discussions of Walther Meissner's work on superconductivity. Meissner was trying to understand why the magnetic-field strength required to destroy superconductivity depended on the orientation of the axis of the wire superconductor. It occurred to Laue that the superconducting wire itself distorts the field in such a way that the field is actually strengthened at certain points on the wire surface, leading to a failure in superconductivity. Laue wrote many papers on various aspects of super-conductivity, and in 1947 he incorporated his ideas into an influential treatise on the subject.

When Laue began his work, the nature of X rays was still disputed. His discovery of X-ray diffraction helped to establish the wave nature of X rays and two new branches of science, X-ray crystallography and X-ray spectroscopy. He also did elegant theoretical work in relativity and superconductivity. For many physicists, however, Laue's accomplishments as a human being were more important than his scientific achievements. During a most difficult time in German history, Laue courageously maintained his integrity. According to Max Planck, Laue kept alive the tradition of theoretical physics during the Nazi regime. After World War II,

Laue was at the center of the effort to rebuild German science. All this did not come easily to him, for he was subject to severe depressions and feelings of persecution. Though not outwardly religious, he had a rich interior life, and he asked that his tombstone carry the words that he died firmly trusting in God's mercy.

## Bibliography

*Primary*

PHYSICS: *Über einen Versuch zur Optik der bewegten Körper*, 1911; *Das Relativitätsprinzip*, 1911; *Über die Auffindung der Röntgenstrahl-interferenzen*, 1920; *Die Relativitätstheorie*, 1921; *Das physikalische Weltbild*, 1921; *Korpuskular- und Wellentheorie*, 1933; *Die Interferenzen von Röntgen- und Elektronenstrahlen*, 1935; *Röntgen-strahl-interferenzen*, 1941; *Materiewellen und ihre Interferenzen*, 1944; *Geschichte der Physik*, 1946 (*History of Physics*, 1950); *Theorie der Supraleitung*, 1947 (*Theory of Superconductivity*, 1952); *Gesammelte Schriften und Vorträge*, 1961.

EDITED TEXTS: *Vorlesungen über Elektrodynamik und Theorie des Magnetismus*, 1907; *Stereoskopbilder von Kristallgittern*, 1926 (with Richard von Mises); *Das Wiensche Verschiebungsgesetz*, 1929; *Vorlesungen über Thermodynamik*, 1954; *Physikalische Abhandlungen und Vorträge*, 1958.


*Secondary*

Bacon, George E., ed. *X-Ray and Neutron Diffraction*. Oxford: Pergamon Press, 1966. Students have traditionally learned physics from textbooks rather than from original scientific papers. This book, part of a series, attempts to remedy this situation by showing how modern studies of the physics and chemistry of solids rest on the work of earlier scientists. The book is written at the level of the undergraduate science student and, besides the author's text, contains reprints in English of many of the classical papers on the subject of X-ray diffraction.

Ewald, Peter Paul. "Max von Laue, 1879-1960." *Biographical Memoirs of Fellows of the Royal Society* 6 (1960): 135-156. Ewald, who narrowly missed making the discovery of X-ray diffraction himself, presents a sympathetic account of Laue's career and a good general analysis of his scientific accomplishments. The article also contains a section on Laue's personality and a complete bibliography of his articles and books.

_____, ed. *Fifty Years of X-Ray Diffraction*. Utrecht: A. Oosthoek's Uitgeversmij, 1962. The articles in this book were written to celebrate the fiftieth anniversary of Max von Laue's discovery of the diffraction of X rays by crystals. The book contains much material on the background and consequences of this famous discovery. Particularly noteworthy is Max von Laue's "Autobiography" and the section titled "Laue's Discovery of X-ray Diffraction by Crystals." Many of the articles are accessible to the general reader, but some require an understanding of advanced mathematics and physics for their full comprehension.

Forman, Paul. "The Discovery of the Diffraction of X-Rays by Crystals: A Critique of Myths." *Archive for the History of Exact Science* 6, no. 1 (1969): 38-71. This article is the most extensive historical analysis of the discovery of X-ray diffraction to date, but it should be read together with the article by P. P. Ewald that immediately follows it: "The Myth of Myths: Comments on P. Forman's paper on 'The Discovery of the Diffraction of X-Rays Crystals.' "

Lipson, Henry S. *Crystals and X-Rays*. London: Wykeham, 1970. Lipson's book, part of the Wykeham Science Series, aims to broaden the outlook of the advanced high school student and introduce the college undergraduate to the present state of X-ray crystallography. Lipson provides an explanation of X-ray diffraction in elementary physical terms, and he tries to encourage younger readers to discover for themselves the fascination of X-ray crystallography. The book is profusely illustrated with photographs and diagrams.

Segrè, Emilio. *From X-Rays to Quarks: Modern Physicists and Their Discoveries*. San Francisco: W. H. Freeman, 1980. This book is based on a series of lectures delivered by the author at the University of California, Berkeley, at the University of Chicago, and at the Accademia Nazionale dei Lincei in Rome. The lectures were addressed to a general audience, and the book takes the same approach. Laue's work is briefly discussed in terms of the evolution of twentieth century physics.

*Robert J. Paradowski*

# 1915

## Physics
Sir William Henry Bragg, Great Britain
Sir Lawrence Bragg, Great Britain

## Chemistry
Richard Willstätter, Germany

## Physiology or Medicine
no award

## Literature
Romain Rolland, France

## Peace
no award

**SIR WILLIAM HENRY BRAGG**

**SIR LAWRENCE BRAGG**

# SIR WILLIAM HENRY BRAGG and
# SIR LAWRENCE BRAGG
# 1915

## Sir William Henry Bragg

*Born:* Westward, near Wigton, Cumberland, England; July 2, 1862
*Died:* London, England; March 12, 1942
*Nationality:* British
*Areas of concentration:* Radioactivity, X-ray spectroscopy, and X-ray crystallography

## Sir Lawrence Bragg

*Born:* Adelaide, South Australia, Australia; March 31, 1890
*Died:* Ipswich, Suffolk, England; July 1, 1971
*Nationality:* British
*Area of concentration:* X-ray crystallography

*William Henry Bragg and his son Lawrence founded X-ray crystallography. The elder Bragg built the first X-ray spectrometer and created the field of X-ray spectroscopy. His son provided the theoretical basis for crystal-structure analysis and made many important crystal-structure determinations*

## The Award

*Presentation*

World War I confronted the Swedish Academy of Sciences with the problem of whether the Nobel Prizes should be awarded during the conflict. Even before the war's outbreak, the Academy had decided to postpone the 1914 awards until 1915. Academy members became still more cautious when they saw the brutality of the war, some even wanting to defer all awards until peace returned. This wary approach brought much criticism, and some accused the Swedish Academy of capitulating to the war's barbarity instead of remaining a needed symbol of civility. These critics viewed the bestowal of the Nobel Prizes in wartime as very much in the spirit of Alfred Nobel's idealism.

In the early months of 1915, reports appeared in the newspapers that, as in 1914, distribution of the Nobel Prizes would probably be suspended because of the war. By the summer, however, sentiment was growing among Academy members that the prizes should no longer be withheld. In the fall, the committee responsible for selecting the prizewinner in physics reported that a prominent English scientist under consideration as a candidate had fallen in battle. This scientist was most likely Henry Moseley, who had used X rays to determine the atomic numbers of the elements. His work on X-ray spectra was much admired, but he was killed in August at Gallipoli in Turkey. Moseley's work grew out of the X-ray studies of the

Braggs, and so it was natural for the committee to turn to his compatriots when they learned of Moseley's death.

On November 6, 1915, a prominent article on the front page of *The New York Times* reported that the Swedish government had decided to award the Nobel Prize in Physics to Thomas Alva Edison and Nikola Tesla. The announcement was both premature and erroneous. It was also indicative of the rumors running rampant because of the disruptions caused by the war. A week later, the Swedish Academy announced that the physics prize for 1914 would be awarded to Max von Laue for his discovery of the diffraction of X rays by crystals. A few days after that, the Academy announced that the physics prize for 1915 would be awarded to William Henry Bragg and Lawrence Bragg for their work in the analysis of crystal structures by means of X rays. The elder Bragg was then fifty-three and his son twenty-five.

Because of the war, 'no Nobel Prize ceremonies were held in 1915. Even if the ceremonies had not been canceled, it is doubtful that either Bragg could have attended. Lawrence Bragg was serving with the British army on the Belgian front, and his father was deeply involved in testing optical glass for the British government. Moreover, neither Bragg would have been in the mood to celebrate, for they had recently learned of the death of Robert Bragg, William's younger son, at Gallipoli.

After the war, the Swedish Academy arranged a presentation ceremony for the 1915 awards, but neither Bragg was able to attend. In remarks written for the occasion, G. Granqvist of the Royal Swedish Academy of Sciences reviewed how the Braggs had used Laue's discovery of X-ray diffraction to determine the actual positions of atoms in crystals. Granqvist pointed out that Lawrence Bragg should be given credit for showing how X rays modified by an encounter with a crystal could be analyzed to give the distance between atom-rich planes in the crystal. William Henry Bragg's great contribution was the X-ray spectrometer, which measures the strength of an X-ray beam reflected from a crystal face. With the father's spectrometer and the son's mathematical analysis, the Braggs had been able to determine the structures of such crystals as zinc blende, diamond, and sodium chloride. Because of the work of the Braggs, Granqvist concluded, a completely new world had already been explored with marvelous precision.

### Nobel lecture

Because no Nobel ceremonies were held in 1915, no Nobel lectures were given. Even after the war, the Braggs encountered difficulties in finding time to make the trip to Stockholm. Indeed, William Henry Bragg never gave a Nobel lecture. His son, after being unable to accept the Swedish Academy's first invitation, was finally able to come to Sweden in 1922. On September 6, in the hall of the Technical University of Stockholm, Lawrence Bragg gave a lecture titled "The Diffraction of X Rays by Crystals." The lecture broke no new ground; it was essentially a summary of the work for which he and his father had been awarded the Nobel Prize.

The work of the Braggs was deeply indebted to Max von Laue's discovery that crystals could diffract X rays. Although Lawrence Bragg was technically correct in his lecture in stating that his own study of diffraction involved no new principle that was not already implicit in Laue's mathematical treatment, his modesty obscures the great contribution he made in interpreting diffracted spots as caused by the reflection of X rays from the sheets of atoms in a crystal. Bragg had certainly made an important conceptual breakthrough, for now X rays could be used to discover previously hidden arrangements of atoms in crystals.

The first person stimulated by Lawrence Bragg's work had been his father, who in 1913 had made sure that the reflected X rays could be detected in an ionization chamber. This led him to construct the X-ray spectrometer, which for decades was the principal tool for crystal-structure analysis in England. Laue's discovery of X-ray diffraction, then, led to two important branches of research: X-ray spectroscopy and crystal-structure analysis.

Before 1912, scientists had little genuine knowledge of the solid state of matter. Crystallography was largely a geometric science. Crystallographers believed that the regularities they studied indicated that something in the crystal must be systematically arranged in space, but they did not know whether the repetitive unit was an atom, a molecule, part of a molecule, or several molecules. X-ray crystallography gave scientists a way of actually looking into the interior of a crystal, and this examination allowed them to gain insights into the many ways in which atoms are arrayed in solids.

Bragg devoted a significant portion of his 1922 Nobel lecture to an explanation of the method of X-ray crystallography. He showed how X-ray reflections from a crystal can be used to determine the spacing of the planes of atoms and the dimensions of the unit cell (the basic repeating structure). By using the crystal's density, crystallographers can calculate the number of atoms or molecules contained in the unit cell. The second step in crystal analysis consists in discovering the way in which atoms are grouped together to form the unit cell. This more difficult step is done by analyzing the strength of various X-ray reflections. In some directions, the atoms conspire to give a strongly reflected beam, whereas in other directions, the beams coming from the atoms cancel each other by interference. The X-ray crystallographer deduces the exact arrangement of the atoms in the crystal by comparing the strengths of the reflections from different faces.

Bragg's lecture was not restricted to an analysis of his own work. He also discussed other methods of X-ray analysis of crystals, such as the powder method developed by Peter Debye and Paul Scherrer in Switzerland and by A. W. Hull in the United States. In this method, X rays are passed through a thin layer of powdered metal. Certain fragments will be oriented in such a way as to guarantee reflection, and so the crystalline powder gives a series of diffracted halos which can be recorded on a photographic film. An analysis of this series of rings allows the crystallographer to determine the structure of the atoms in the metal.

The conclusion of Bragg's lecture is an encomium to X-ray analysis. So powerful is this method that it can be used to determine the structure of the atom itself. Since the wavelength of X rays is less than the size of an atom, and since the rays are diffracted by the electrons of the atom, scientists can use X-ray analysis to obtain an understanding of the distribution of these electrons. The greatest strength of X-ray analysis, however, is its revelation of the exact arrangement of atoms in solids. At the time Bragg delivered this lecture, many crystals' structures had not yet been determined, and so the future of the field was full of challenges. Lawrence Bragg lived to see his method applied to the very complex molecules that make up living things.

*Critical reception*

World War I considerably dampened reactions to the award of the Nobel Prize in Physics to the Braggs. Had the prize been awarded in peacetime, there might have been extensive critical commentaries about the award in the popular and scientific press, but the confusion in the announcement of the awards, the lack of ceremonies, and the delayed presentation all contributed to a reception that was similarly extended and attenuated. The award, however, was in no way controversial; in fact, most physicists expressed strong approval of the Swedish Academy's choice. In the major news media, the response was conventional and subdued. For example, *The Times* of London simply noted the "great distinction" conferred on William Henry Bragg and his son. On November 13, 1915, *The New York Times* did little more than state that the Nobel Prize had been awarded to the Braggs. The American newspapers were more concerned about the award of the Nobel Prize in Chemistry for 1914 to Theodore William Richards for his accurate determinations of the atomic weight of a large number of chemical elements. Richards was the first American Nobel laureate in chemistry.

Before World War I began, knowledge of the Braggs' technique had spread to France, the Netherlands, Germany, Russia, Japan, and the United States. The war brought not only a disruption of international relations but also a crippling of X-ray diffraction studies. Nevertheless, some development took place. For example, Arthur A. Noyes, a physical chemist associated with the Massachusetts Institute of Technology and with what would become the California Institute of Technology, was deeply impressed by the Braggs' methods. It was largely because of his encouragement that C. Lalor Burdick and James H. Ellis made the first crystal structure determination in the United States in 1917. It is noteworthy that chemists were more responsive to the Braggs' work in the United States. In Europe, their work received a more favorable critical reception from physicists.

After the war, it became increasingly clear that the reaction to the Braggs' Nobel Prize was overwhelmingly favorable. Scientists throughout the world recognized that the Braggs had created an entirely new field of science with deep implications for physics, chemistry, and mineralogy. As more and more complex crystals had their structures determined in the 1920's and 1930's, it became obvious to everyone that the Swedish Academy had chosen wisely in honoring the Braggs. William Henry Bragg was knighted in 1920 and his son in 1941. This delayed recognition was gratifying and in a sense more in keeping with the personalities of both Braggs, who constantly stressed in their writings that scientists should work not for awards but for the joy of discovering the hidden truths of nature.

## Biographies

William Henry Bragg was born on his father's farm in the north of England in 1862. He was the eldest of the three sons of Robert John Bragg, a former officer in the merchant navy, and Mary Wood, the daughter of a vicar. His mother died when he was seven, and for six years he lived with his uncle, a pharmacist in Market Harborough in Leicestershire. In 1875, when he was thirteen, he went to King William College on the Isle of Man, where he eventually distinguished himself academically in what was at first a strange and hostile environment. In 1881 he began his studies at Trinity College, Cambridge. He was especially good in mathematics and finished third in his class. He also studied physics under Sir Joseph John Thomson, who helped him to get his first professional appointment as Professor of Mathematics and Physics at the University of Adelaide in South Australia. He remained in this position for twenty-four years, from 1885 to 1909. In 1889, he married Gwendoline Todd, the daughter of the postmaster general and government astronomer of South Australia. William Lawrence was born in 1890, followed by Robert and Gwendolen.

When he was forty-two, Bragg became interested in radioactivity and began a series of researches that brought him international recognition. Lawrence Bragg absorbed some of his father's interests, and he studied mathematics and physics at the University of Adelaide. William Henry Bragg was offered the Cavendish Professorship of Physics at the University of Leeds in 1908, and the following year, the family returned to England. Lawrence Bragg entered Trinity College, Cambridge, intending to become a mathematician, but during his second year he switched to physics. He earned his degree with first-class honors in 1912, just in time to participate, with his father, in extending Max von Laue's discovery of X-ray diffraction to the study of crystal structures.

In 1914, Lawrence Bragg was elected fellow and lecturer at Trinity College, and in 1915 his father accepted the Quain Professorship at University College, London. Both father and son participated in war work during World War I. After the war, William Henry Bragg assembled a large research group to work on the X-ray analysis of organic crystals. Lawrence Bragg, in 1919, succeeded Ernest Rutherford as Langworthy Professor of Physics at Manchester University, where he remained until 1937. During this time, he devoted himself to elucidating the structures of the silicate minerals.

In 1923, William Henry Bragg became director of the Royal Institution in London. He continued to do scientific work, but largely by directing others. He began to spend more of his time in general lecturing and on scientific advisory committees. He continued to lecture and write about X-ray crystallography until shortly before his death in 1942.

Meanwhile, Lawrence Bragg was encountering difficulties in Manchester. World War I had caused great dislocations of personnel and programs, and Lawrence Bragg had no previous administrative experience. He also had the cares of a new family. He had married Alice Hopkinson in December, 1921, and they had had four children, two boys and two girls, all of whom had been born during his Manchester tenure. In 1937, Bragg became director of the National Physical Laboratory, and the following year he accepted a concurrent appointment as Cavendish Professor of Physics at Cambridge, a position he held until 1953. From 1954 until his retirement in 1966, Bragg was director of the Royal Institution in London, a post held earlier by his father. He, too, became a popular general lecturer and sought-after science adviser. After his retirement, he continued to lecture and write on scientific topics, completing a history of X-ray crystallography shortly before his death in 1971.

### Scientific Careers

Throughout the first four decades of his life, William Henry Bragg gave little indication that he would become a distinguished scientist. At Cambridge he published nothing, and in his first eighteen years at Adelaide he wrote only three minor papers on electromagnetism. Impressed by Wilhelm Conrad Röntgen's discovery of X rays, Bragg set up Adelaide's first X-ray apparatus, and when Lawrence Bragg shattered his left elbow in a tricycle accident, his father used X-ray photographs to reveal the details of his boy's injuries. This was the first recorded medical use of the Röntgen ray in Australia. These experiences with X rays, however, did not stimulate Bragg to begin to do research.

A turning point occurred in 1904, when he was called on to deliver a presidential address to a section of the Australian Association for the Advancement of Science. His lecture, "On Some Recent Advances in the Theory of the Ionization of Gases," reviewed the work of Antoine-Henri Becquerel, Marie Curie, Sir Joseph John Thomson, and Ernest Rutherford on radioactivity. After the discovery of radioactivity, scientists had conducted extensive experiments to determine the nature of the radiation streaming from certain kinds of matter. One of their chief techniques was to study how these emissions were absorbed by gases and solids. For X rays, the absorption was exponential, as it was for beta rays (electrons). Scientists had assumed that the absorption of alpha particles (the nuclei of helium atoms) was also exponential, but Bragg believed that an alpha particle, because of its mass, should pass through most matter practically undeviated. Consequently, the exponential law of absorption, which held for a beam of electrons, should not apply to a beam of alpha particles. To test his idea, he began research on the range of alpha particles and their ability to produce ionization in gases. His experiments showed that the alpha particles emitted by radium bromide form well-defined groups, with each group's particles traveling the same distance before being absorbed by a blocking substance. Each group, he found, corresponds to a different radioactive source, so measurement of alpha-particle ranges is a valuable tool in identifying the type of nucleus from which the particles come.

These fundamental researches carried out in Adelaide between 1904 and 1908 quickly established Bragg's reputation among physicists throughout the world. He was elected a Fellow of the Royal Society in 1907, and in 1908 he received the offer of the Cavendish Professorship of Physics at Leeds. As Cavendish Professor, he developed and refined his view that X rays and gamma rays are corpuscular in nature. During the late nineteenth and early twentieth centuries, physicists were uncertain about whether X rays and gamma rays were particles or waves (pulses of energy). Bragg's previous work on the ionization of gas by X rays convinced him that the rays were particulate. X rays are not deflected in a magnetic or electric field, however, and to explain this, Bragg hypothesized that the rays were actually neutral pairs of material particles which, on breaking up, released a positive particle and a negative electron. This "doublet" theory successfully explained the conversion of cathode rays into X rays and the release of electrons by X and gamma rays. Under criticism from other physicists, Bragg backed off somewhat from his concrete model of the X ray and gamma ray, emphasizing their corpuscular rather than their material nature, but he did not abandon his idea of the X ray as an electron with its charge neutralized until after the discovery of X-ray diffraction in 1912.

During the summer and fall of 1912, Max von Laue's discovery that X rays could be diffracted by crystals caused much excitement among physicists. Bragg, who realized that this discovery challenged his view on the corpuscular nature of X rays, was fascinated, and he discussed the interference patterns produced by the diffracted rays with his son. Lawrence Bragg became convinced that Laue's wave picture of X rays was correct, but he believed that Laue's explanation of X-ray diffraction, involving interfering wavelets in three-dimensional space, was needlessly complicated. He discovered a much simpler explanation: X-ray diffraction by a crystal could be interpreted as a result of the reflection of the X rays by planes of atoms in the crystal. In other words, the waves are not merely diffracted in certain directions, as Laue had assumed, but reflected by certain layers of atoms, which behave like mirrors.

In a crystal, atoms are arranged regularly in space, so that if a plane is passed through one set of atoms—for example, a crystal face—then a parallel plane may be passed through the next set of atoms lying underneath the first layer. The waves reflected from the atoms in the lower plane may or may not be in phase with the waves reflected from the top layer. Whether they are depends on the perpendicular distance between the planes, the wavelength of the incoming X rays, and the angle of incidence between the ray and the surface of the plane. The mathematical relationship between these variables was derived by Lawrence Bragg and is now known as Bragg's law.

While his son was working on the theoretical aspects of X-ray diffraction, William Henry Bragg was inventing an instrument for detecting and measuring the diffracted X rays. In January, 1913, he succeeded in detecting the reflected rays with an ionization chamber, and by March, he had constructed the first X-ray spectrometer. In this instrument, an X-ray beam reflected from a crystal face is intercepted by an ionization chamber, and the current in the chamber measures the intensity of the reflected X rays. In the spring of 1913, father and son began to collaborate by using their experimental and theoretical techniques to determine the structures of crystals. In their early work, they established that there are no actual molecules in crystals such as sodium chloride, only sodium ions and chloride ions arranged in geometric regularity. This conclusion disturbed chemists, because for years they had assumed that salt crystals were composed of molecules. The Braggs published a paper in July, 1913, showing the carbon atoms in diamond to be arranged tetrahedrally, a result immediately acceptable to both chemists and physicists. By the end of 1913, the Braggs had standardized the X-ray analysis of crystals.

World War I brought this period of intense research to an end. During the war, William Henry Bragg worked for the antisubmarine division of the Admiralty. He and his team developed the hydrophone, or underwater receiver, which proved to be very useful in battles against German submarines. In his war work, Lawrence Bragg developed a theory of sound-ranging that allowed soldiers to locate enemy guns from the sound of their firing. After World War I, Lawrence Bragg became much more intensively involved in X-ray crystallography than his father, whose position at the Royal Institution increasingly drew him into more general concerns. During his time at Manchester, Lawrence Bragg improved X-ray methods for crystal structure determination. For example, he tried to establish a reliable set of atomic sizes; he sought to make measurements of the absolute intensities of X-ray reflections, which would show directly the effective number of electrons contributing to each reflection; and he tried to determine the structures of ever more complex crystals. In 1925, he began an intensive program of research on the silicate minerals. He first described the structure of the olivines, then made an analysis of beryl. Linus Pauling, working at the California Institute of Technology, was also interested in the silicates, and he and his coworkers determined the structures of many; unlike Bragg, who was reluctant to recognize the importance of silicon's tetrahedral units surrounded by four oxygen atoms, Pauling made these units a central element in his successful coordination theory of crystal structures.

In his later years, Lawrence Bragg, like his father, became more involved with administration and less concerned with the details of scientific work. Nevertheless, he continued to take a deep interest in the development of X-ray crystallography. For example, he encouraged Max Perutz in his attempt to use X-ray techniques to study globular proteins. Despite great difficulties, Perutz and others like him pressed on and eventually achieved important successes in determining the structures of gigantic molecules. In this way, Lawrence Bragg was an important part of the entire history of X-ray crystallography.

## Bibliography

*Primary*
*Sir William Henry Bragg*
PHYSICS: *Studies in Radioactivity*, 1912; *Electrons and Their Waves*, 1921; *Crafts-*

*manship and Science*, 1928; *An Introduction to Crystal Analysis*, 1928; *The Story of Electromagnetism*, 1941.

OTHER NONFICTION: *Science and Faith*, 1941.

CHILDREN'S LITERATURE: *The World of Sound*, 1920; *Concerning the Nature of Things*, 1924; *The Universe of Light*, 1933.

*Sir Lawrence Bragg*

PHYSICS: *The Structure of Silicates*, 1930; *The Crystalline State*, 1933-1965; *Electricity*, 1936; *Atomic Structure of Minerals*, 1937; *The Atomic Structure of Alloys*, 1938; *The History of X-Ray Analysis*, 1943; *Crystal Structure of Minerals*, 1965 (with Gordon F. Claringbull); *The Start of X-Ray Analysis*, 1967; *Ideas and Discoveries in Physics*, 1970; *The Development of X-Ray Analysis*, 1975.

*Sir William Henry Bragg and Sir Lawrence Bragg*

PHYSICS: *X Rays and Crystal Structure*, 1915.


*Secondary*

Andrade, Edward Neville da Costa. "William Henry Bragg, 1862-1942." *Obituary Notices of Fellows of the Royal Society of London* 4 (1943): 277-300. Andrade, an English physicist, was a good friend of Bragg, and this obituary essay gives an excellent survey of his life and work. The article also contains a complete chronological bibliography of Bragg's writings.

Bragg, Lawrence, and Gwendolen Bragg Caroe. "Sir William Bragg, F.R.S. (1862-1942)." *Notes and Records of the Royal Society of London* 16 (1961): 169-182. This eulogistic article written by Bragg's son and daughter reveals both the family man and the scientist. It quotes liberally from a biographical memoir that Bragg was working on before his death. The emphasis is on the early part of Bragg's life and career.

Caroe, G. M. *William Henry Bragg, 1862-1942: Man and Scientist*. Cambridge, England: Cambridge University Press, 1978. This biography of William Henry Bragg was written by his daughter for the general reader. Caroe has adeptly used quotations from her father's notes about his early life and from his correspondence with Ernest Rutherford to describe how Bragg became first a scientist and then a spokesman for science during the second and third decades of the twentieth century.

Ewald, Peter Paul, ed. *Fifty Years of X-Ray Diffraction*. Utrecht: A. Oosthoek's Uitgeversmij, 1962. The articles in this book were written to celebrate the fiftieth anniversary of Max von Laue's discovery of the diffraction of X rays by crystals. William Lawrence Bragg contributed an article on "The Growing Power of X-Ray Analysis," and the work of the Braggs is extensively discussed by many of the contributors. Several of the articles are historical and accessible to the general reader, but other articles require an understanding of advanced mathematics and physics for full comprehension.

Forman, Paul. "The Discovery of the Diffraction of X-Rays by Crystals: A Critique of Myths." *Archive for the History of Exact Science* 6, no. 1 (1969): 38-71. This article is the most extensive historical analysis of the famous discovery of X-ray diffraction to date, but it should be read together with the article by P. P. Ewald that immediately follows it: "The Myth of Myths: Comments on P. Forman's paper on 'The Discovery of the Diffraction of X-Rays in Crystals.'"

Lipson, Henry S., et al. "Dedicated to Sir Lawrence Bragg on His Eightieth Birthday." *Acta Crystallographica* A26 (March 31, 1970): 171-188. This special issue of *Acta Crystallographica* contains, in addition to two articles of reminiscences by Bragg, homages and memoirs by several of his students and colleagues.

Phillips, David. "William Lawrence Bragg, 31 March 1890-1 July 1971." *Biographical Memoirs of Fellows of the Royal Society* 25 (1975): 75-143. The most extensive biographical article on Lawrence Bragg yet written. It gives a good presentation of the life and work of the scientist, a complete bibliography of his papers and books, and some good general references. It was written with the cooperation of Lady Bragg and Stephen Bragg, and the author made use of material in the Bragg Archives of the Royal Institution.

*Robert J. Paradowski*

# 1917

## Physics
Charles Glover Barkla, Great Britain

## Chemistry
no award

## Physiology or Medicine
no award

## Literature
Karl Adolph Gjellerup, Denmark
Henrik Pontoppidan, Denmark

## Peace
International Red Cross Committee

# CHARLES GLOVER BARKLA
## 1917

*Born:* Widnes, Lancashire, England; June 7, 1877
*Died:* Edinburgh, Scotland; October 23, 1944
*Nationality:* British
*Areas of concentration:* X-radiation and secondary radiation

*Barkla's research into secondary X rays proved that each element produces a characteristic spectrum. He also proved that an element's electrical charge determines its place in the periodic system. His work helped physicists to deduce much about the structure of atoms*

## The Award

*Presentation*

The Nobel Prize in Physics was presented to Charles Glover Barkla in 1918 by Professor G. Granqvist, Chairman of the Nobel Committee for Physics of the Royal Swedish Academy of Sciences. The presentation emphasized Barkla's discovery of secondary X rays, which are emitted when a sample of a chemical element is placed in the path of X rays. This secondary radiation consists of two types. The first type has absorption coefficients that are the same as those of the incident X rays; as a result, these rays have the same penetrability as the primary rays. They also have so many qualities in common with the primary X rays that they must be regarded as diffused primary radiation. The first type of secondary radiation is wholly independent of the primary radiation. Its absorption coefficient is determined by the irradiated substance, not by the incident radiation. Thus, Barkla proved that every chemical element emits a characteristic secondary radiation, which he named the "characteristic X-radiation." The emission of this radiation involves the element's absorption of X rays. The qualities of the atoms alone determine the amount of absorption; such factors as density, temperature, state of aggregation, and chemical composition are irrelevant.

Every chemical element emits two types of rays of different penetrability when irradiated by X rays. Barkla named the two types the "K-series" and the "L series." K-series rays have greater penetrability. Barkla proved that every chemical element possesses a characteristic X-ray spectrum by showing that the absorption for rays belonging to the same series can be expressed in terms of the atomic weight of the element emitting the radiation.

Granqvist's presentation stressed the importance of Barkla's findings for physical investigation by briefly exploring the far-reaching effects that they had had on subsequent research on the inner structure of atoms. Later investigations had revealed that the electrical charge of the nucleus of an atom determines its place in the periodic system, and not its atomic weight as had previously been thought. The presentation ended with the assertion that Barkla had made the most important discovery in the field of spectroscopy since the discovery of the discontinuous spectra from flames and electric sparks.

It is important to note that the presentation did not discuss Barkla's investigation of the "J series" of extremely penetrating rays, which he believed existed. Since the results of these studies could not be confirmed by other workers, the existence of the J series was not and still is not part of accepted scientific theory. Barkla was ostracized by the rest of the scientific community because of his adherence to his theory of the J phenomenon.

## Nobel lecture

Because of war conditions, Charles Barkla could not attend the presentation ceremony for his award. He delivered his Nobel lecture, titled "Characteristic Röntgen Radiation," on June 3, 1920. Barkla introduced his lecture by explaining why he had decided to discuss only the quantum theory of radiation and the evidence for a J series of characteristic radiation: His previous work was so "old" and so familiar to his audience, he said, that an account of his current research would be much more interesting to them.

Barkla began his lecture on the quantum theory by explaining what he meant by the "scattering of X rays." He said that when X rays travel through an element, this element emits a type of radiation similar in character to that of the primary radiation falling upon it. This scattered radiation results from the agitation of electrons while the element is under the influence of the electrostatic field in the primary radiation. According to the quantum theory, radiation consists of definite, indivisible bundles, or quanta. According to Barkla's theory, however, the scattered radiation can occur in any quantity; in other words, scattered radiation is not confined to quanta.

Barkla divided secondary radiation into three categories—the K, L, and M series—all of which are uncontrolled by the primary radiation which produces them. The absorption of these series takes place in quantities that are very small in comparison with a quantum. Barkla said his research had suggested that a quantum of radiation does not exist.

In the next section of his lecture, Barkla elaborated on a new series of radiation which he had introduced in the previous section. J radiation is distinguished from the other series by its higher frequency. Although Barkla admitted that he and other researchers, such as the American physicist William Duane, had been unable to prove the existence of the J series, he explained its elusiveness by suggesting that J radiation was either weaker than the other series, and therefore harder to detect, or impossible to excite. At the end of his lecture, Barkla accounted for Niels Bohr's inability to accept the existence of the J series by proposing that J radiation may be emitted by an unknown type of electron, a type which would not fit into Bohr's theories.

## Critical reception

Most researchers agree that Barkla's receipt of the Nobel Prize was justified by his discoveries' impact on subsequent investigations into the nature of the atom. Although G. Sagnac and Pierre Curie discovered in 1902 that radiation consisted in part of negatively charged electrons, Barkla was the first physicist to examine secondary radiation in detail. His discovery of the two types of secondary radiation, the K series and the L series, was the first step toward understanding the distribution of electrons within the atom, a subject on which Karl Manne Siegbahn and Niels Bohr would elaborate much later. Siegbahn, in collaboration with Henry Moseley, took up where Barkla had left off by developing the powerful method of X-ray spectroscopic analysis and applying it more precisely to the relations implied by Barkla's research. Barkla's work on secondary radiation paved the way for other researchers, who found that characteristic X rays were also emitted when an element was used as the anticathode in an X-ray tube and was exposed to cathode rays. Barkla's study of X-ray scattering, which occurs when X rays pass through a material and are deflected by the atomic electrons, was very useful to the study of atomic particles. Barkla also contributed to the evolution of the concept of atomic number by showing that an element's amount of charge, not its atomic mass, determines that element's place in the periodic table.

Even though Barkla had achieved an international reputation as the leading physicist in his field for the work that he had done between 1902 and 1912, by 1916, he had acquired a reputation for eccentricity. In his Bakerian lecture of 1916, which he repeated almost verbatim in his Nobel lecture of 1920, he expressed views on the absence of quantum effects in the scattering of X rays which were not supported by subsequent research, most notably that of Arthur Holly Compton in 1927.

## Biography

Charles Glover Barkla was born on June 7, 1877, in Widnes, Lancashire, England, to John Martin, secretary of the Atlas Chemical Company, and Sarah Glover, a member of a local family of watch manufacturers. After studying at the Liverpool Institute, he went in 1895 to University College, Liverpool, with scholarships. He concentrated primarily on mathematics and physics and was allowed to study experimental physics under Oliver Lodge after taking honors in mathematics. After obtaining his bachelor's degree in 1898 and his master's degree in 1899, he entered Trinity College at Cambridge, again with a scholarship. While there, he studied under another famous scientist, Sir Joseph John Thomson, at the Cavendish Laboratory. As a result of his work with Thomson, he received the Cambridge bachelor of arts degree. Because of his desire to sing in the choir, he transferred in 1901 to King's College, Cambridge, after eighteen months at Trinity, but he refused the offer of a choral scholarship, which would have enabled him to remain at Cambridge. Thus, in 1902, he returned to University College, Liverpool, as Oliver Lodge Fellow.

In 1904, he was awarded a doctorate. Between 1905 and 1909, he was a demonstrator, an assistant lecturer, and a special lecturer. By this time, he had published twenty-six papers. Barkla became Wheatstone Professor of Physics at King's College, London, in 1909. He accepted the Chair of Natural Philosophy in the University of Edinburgh in 1913, only ten years after the publication of his first paper on X rays. He held this position until his death. Barkla became a Fellow of the Royal Society in 1912 and was appointed Bakerian lecturer for 1916. In November, 1918, Barkla was awarded the Nobel Prize in Physics for 1917 for his discovery that each element emits a characteristic spectrum of X rays.

Although Barkla became recognized worldwide as an authority on secondary X rays in 1911, his reputation later suffered because of his pursuit of a scientific will-o'-the-wisp which he called "J radiation." His gradual isolation from the scientific community was caused in large part by his inability to believe in the value of the work and experimental results of others; he seemed to believe that only his research was important and that only his theories were true.

Barkla married Mary Esther Cowell, the elder daughter of the receiver-general of the Isle of Man, in 1907. They had one daughter and two sons; the younger son, Michael, was killed in action in 1943. The loss of his son was largely responsible for Barkla's decline in health. Barkla was especially fond of golf and singing. He was a very religious man who faithfully attended the local Methodist church. He died at his home in Edinburgh on October 23, 1944.

### Scientific Career

Charles Glover Barkla was one of the pioneers of X-ray research. Among his most important contributions were those showing that when X rays are scattered by light atoms, the secondary radiation is of the same wavelength as the primary X-ray beam, and when X rays are incident on heavy atoms, these atoms emit characteristic radiation of a longer wavelength than the primary beam. He called the two types of characteristic secondary radiation the "K series" and the "L series."

Barkla carried out his first major piece of research while he was still a student at the Cavendish Laboratory. This research involved measuring the speed at which electromagnetic waves travel along wires of different thickness and composition, a phenomenon which Sir Joseph John Thomson and Arnold Sommerfeld, among others, had studied only theoretically. During his third year at Cambridge, he began investigating secondary X rays emitted by substances in the path of a beam of X-radiation, a subject to which he devoted most of his subsequent career. In the first paper that he published on this phenomenon, he showed that for gases of elements with a low atomic mass, the secondary scattered radiation is of the same average wavelength as that of the primary X-ray beam to which the gas is subjected. He also found that the extent of such scattering is proportional to the atomic mass of the gas concerned. He knew the scattering was caused by charged particles, so he was able to deduce that the more massive an atom is, the more charged particles it contains. Barkla furthered the evolution of the concept of atomic number by demonstrating the importance of an atom's amount of charge to an element's position in the periodic table.

Barkla next turned his attention to the polarization of X rays. By 1904, Barkla found that the heavy elements produced secondary radiation of a longer wavelength than that of the primary X-ray beam. In his polarization measurements, he found that the polarization of the secondary radiation tended to disappear as the atomic weight of the scatterer increased, which led him to acknowledge the existence of "softened" secondary radiation emitted by the heavier elements. He went on to produce a polarized beam of X rays by a secondary radiator, thus proving that X rays are a form of transverse electromagnetic radiation, like visible light, and not longitudinal waves, like those of sound, as Wilhelm Röntgen had thought.

Barkla began his most important work in 1907. With the assistance of two students, A. L. Hughes and C. A. Sadler, Barkla undertook a series of experiments in which the absorption of the characteristic radiations from different metal radiators was measured in copper, zinc, iron, and the like. Their first results, which were published that September, demonstrated that the secondary radiation was "homogeneous." Over the next four years, they added to this fundamental discovery by proving that the radiation from the heavier elements is of two characteristic types: A and B. They also showed that the characteristic radiation is emitted only after a heavy element is exposed to X-radiation "harder" (more penetrating, because of a shorter wavelength) than its own characteristic emissions. This finding was the first indication that X rays are monochromatic.

By 1911, Barkla had decided to change the names for the types of characteristic radiation from A and B to K (for the more penetrating emissions) and L (for the less penetrating emissions). Certain that other series of emissions with different penetrances might also exist, Barkla devoted much of his research after 1916 to investigating a hypothetical J series of extremely penetrating radiations. Barkla's first publication on the J series was included in his Bakerian lecture to the Royal Society, given in 1916. In a paper published in 1917, Barkla and M. P. White argued for the existence of a type of extremely penetrating emissions, the J series.

In 1924, Barkla's research in J radiation was called into question by Arthur Holly Compton, whose quantum theory of X-ray scattering dismissed the existence of J radiation. Barkla and his students continued their experiments on J radiation, however, by filtering a heterogeneous beam of X rays with aluminum. Barkla published ten papers on the J phenomenon from 1925 to 1933, in which he reported that the J phenomenon had proved elusive. After Barkla's Nobel lecture of 1920, other physicists started to look for J radiation, but they too were unsuccessful and were forced to conclude that it simply did not exist. Barkla stated his disagreement with this conclusion in a letter that he wrote to *Nature* in 1933. He published no more scientific papers after 1933, although he continued to do research.

## Bibliography

*Primary*
PHYSICS: "Secondary Röntgen Radiation," *Philosophical Magazine*, 6th series, vol. 11, 1906; "Spectra of Fluorescent Röntgen Radiation," *Philosophical Magazine*, vol. 22, 1911; *Radiation and Matter*, 1920.

*Secondary*

Abbot, David, ed. *Biographical Dictionary of Scientists: Physicists*. New York: Peter Bedrick Books, 1984. This reference work is important because it not only provides a brief biography and history of Barkla's career but also explains how subsequent research benefited from Barkla's contributions. Unlike most sources, it touches upon Barkla's standing in the scientific community after 1916.

Allen, H. S. "Charles Glover Barkla, 1877-1944." *Obituary Notices of Fellows of the Royal Society of London* 5 (1947): 341-366. Written by a colleague of Barkla in the physics department of King's College, this indispensable biography combines a lucid description of Barkla's experiment with a personalized account of Barkla's private life. Potentially beneficial for the scientist and nonspecialist alike.

Asimov, Isaac. *Asimov's Biographical Encyclopedia of Science and Technology*. Garden City, N.Y.: Doubleday, 1964. Contains a capsulized history of the highlights of Barkla's life and career. The entry is a solid introduction to Barkla.

Forman, Paul. "Charles Glover Barkla." In *Dictionary of Scientific Biography*. New York: Charles Scribner's Sons, 1970. This article is strongly recommended for students interested in Barkla's life as well as for students interested primarily in Barkla's scientific accomplishments. Although the article is frequently technical, it is valuable to the nonspecialist because of the portrait it paints of the physicist's steadily deteriorating mental state after 1916.

Heathcote, Niels Hugh de Vaudrey. *Nobel Prize Winners in Physics, 1901-1950*. New York: Henry Schuman, 1953. This source contains an excellent article on Barkla. The entry is divided into three sections: "Biographical Sketch," "Description of the Prize-Winning Work," and "Consequences in Theory and Practice." The "Description" section is technical enough to be of interest to a student with a physics background; the last section places Barkla's work in the context of the history of physics research.

Schlessinger, Bernard S., and June H. Schlessinger, eds. *Who's Who of Nobel Prize Winners*. Phoenix, Ariz.: Oryx Press, 1986. This reference book contains a very brief description of Barkla's life and publications. The entry is valuable because it lists works relating to Barkla. The "Commentary" section discusses the nature of Barkla's research and explains why Barkla won the Nobel Prize.

Stephenson, Reginald J. "The Scientific Career of Charles Glover Barkla." *American Journal of Physics* 35 (February, 1967): 141-152. This article is indispensable for science students who are interested primarily in the technical details of Barkla's research. The chronological study is useful in that it covers Barkla's work both before and after 1916. This work also features a detailed explanation of Barkla's conflict with Arthur Holly Compton in the 1920's.

*Alan Brown*

# 1918

### Physics
Max Planck, Germany

### Chemistry
no award

### Physiology or Medicine
no award

### Literature
no award

### Peace
no award

# MAX PLANCK
## 1918

*Born:* Kiel, Schleswig; April 23, 1858
*Died:* Göttingen, West Germany; October 3, 1947
*Nationality:* German
*Area of concentration:* Quantum physics

*The Nobel Prize was awarded to Planck for pioneer investigations that challenged the classical law of conservation of energy. Planck posited that when energy is emitted by atoms, such emissions occur in discrete "bundles," or quanta. The Planck constant, when applied to different atomic substances, made it possible to approach this phenomenon mathematically*

## The Award

*Presentation*

The Nobel Prize in Physics for 1918 was presented to Max Planck by Dr. Å. G. Ekstrand, President of the Royal Swedish Academy of Sciences. Dr. Ekstrand indicated that Planck's predecessors in the field of radiation theory had accepted the Kirchhoff principle: that the intensity of radiation depends only on the wavelength of the radiation and the temperature of the radiating body. By the end of the nineteenth century, however, scientists were aware that this was not in accord with observable conditions. To proceed, a mathematical formula for a general radiation law was needed. Planck's first major contribution occurred in 1900. In addition to elaborating the major radiation formula incorporating the now-famous Planck constant, Planck discovered a second figure, the Avogadro constant, which made it possible to determine the number of molecules in a gram molecule of matter. Planck's Nobel award, however, came as a result of the obvious importance of his mathematical work as the basis of the emerging field of quantum theory.

*Nobel lecture*

Planck's Nobel lecture, "The Genesis and Present State of Development of the Quantum Theory," was delivered on June 2, 1920. The title of his lecture suggests that he was conscious of the effects of his discoveries on different fields. Initial concerns with "the problem of the distribution of energy in the normal spectrum of radiating heat" stemmed from Planck's dissatisfaction with Gustav Kirchhoff's mid-nineteenth century proposition that levels of heat radiation depend only on temperature and wavelength and have no connection with the physical properties of the radiating substance. To investigate this claim, Planck used a device incorporating Hertzian linear oscillators surrounded by a sphere of reflecting walls, creating the "black body" radiation phenomenon which would make him famous.

Planck's early testing enabled him to elaborate on his first general laws of emission and absorption of radiated energy. First he studied mathematical connections between the "energy" of a resonator and both the period of vibration and the amount of electromagnetic energy radiation in its surrounding field. He found that this mathematical relationship was not dependent on the nature of the resonator. He welcomed this discovery because it meant that, instead of concentrating on the energy of radiation itself (the focus of Kirchhoff's analysis), he could direct his attention toward finding the energy "key" of the resonator being tested.

Planck's early contentions were contested by his colleague Ludwig Boltzmann. Boltzmann held that, until an "important connecting element or term" could be found to substantiate Planck's theory, the laws of classical dynamics—which, according to the law of conservation of energy as it was then understood, maintained that radiating energy "bounces back" if reflected and is reabsorbed for re-emission—best explained the source of the energy Planck observed in his surrounding radiation field.

To respond to Boltzmann, Planck turned in 1899 to the second law of heat theory. He concentrated not on temperature but on the question of entropy in resonators. (The study of entropy involves consideration of thermal energy which becomes unavailable for work, a stumbling block in the application of the classical conservation of energy law to electromagnetics.) Planck was convinced that the "energy loss" reflected in entropy could be expressed more accurately as a quantitative, perhaps absolute, value. His work challenged Hannover researcher Friedrich Paschen's use of Wilhelm Wien's energy distribution law to establish a theory of dependence between radiation intensity and temperature. Wien's law would have connected these two factors by an exponential function. Planck went well beyond Wien when he used his law to calculate the connection between the entropy and the energy of a resonator. He found that the reciprocal value of the differential coefficient, which he called $R$, was directly proportional to the energy. Planck then posited that the quantity of $R$ should become the basis for an entirely new energy distribution law. The way thus seemed prepared for finding the missing "important connecting element" to which Boltzmann had referred and assigning a mathematical value to it. Planck would refer to this quantity as the "second universal constant of the radiation law."

Planck's idea of an "elementary quantum of action" was to be taken up within a few years by Albert Einstein. Einstein saw that the energy quanta theory could be relevant, in dealing with the action of light, to the study of electron emission and gas ionization. Essential to Einstein's approach was the assumption of a "single natural vibration" for each specific "type" of atom.

Einstein's "natural vibration" would ultimately become an essential component of Planck's quantum theory, which stated that the "size" of a quantum (that is, its "vibration") relating to any phenomenon of electromagnetic radiation was in direct proportion to its frequency. The ratio established between quantum size and frequency could, it appeared, be an absolute constant, which Planck formulated mathematically as $h$. Indeed, once Planck's second universal constant of the radiation law was adopted more widely, what Einstein called the "vibration" (the "quantum of action," in Planck's terminology) occurring as electrons "jump" from one state to another in atomic patterns became basic to understanding not only radiation but also a series of energy transfer phenomena. The so-called Nernst chemical constant, developed by O. Sackur, applied to the absolute value of the entropy of a gas. Working in another field in which entropy was also an important factor, James Franck and Gustav Hertz used quantum theory to study the critical velocity an electron must possess to emit a light quantum, or photon, upon impact with a neutral atom. Planck recognized his "greatest support," however, in Niels Bohr's work combining atom theory and spectrum analysis.

All these researchers, approaching quantum theory from different experimental perspectives involving entropy, contributed the corroborative mathematical results that enabled Planck to calculate the precise and universal magnitude of the quantum of action ($h$), which has become known as the "Planck constant."

*Critical reception*

The fact that Max Planck, a German, received the Nobel Prize in Physics immediately after World War I brought on certain political repercussions. Even several years before the outbreak of the war, there were signs of potential controversy in the Nobel Committee. Hints of concern over the accomplishments of the Second Reich were particularly visible in 1905, when three out of five Nobel awards went to Germans. Criticisms of nationalistic indiscretion were aroused by German journalists' use of implicitly anti-French slogans while covering the Nobel awards. The world would also be surprised that the German press, possibly as a form of nationalistic recognition of German scientists' impressive record of Nobel awards, introduced the now-traditional practice of calculating the cumulative percentages of laureates by nationality.

Unfortunately, in 1918, after four years of war in Europe, public reaction to the award of three Nobel Prizes to Germans in one year still bore the mark of political suspicion. The single mention in *The New York Times* of Max Planck's award, published on November 15, 1919, for example, did not even take the form of a descriptive article. It merely announced, "Three Awards for Science go to German Professors." Accounts elsewhere of the 1918 chemistry prize won by Planck's colleague at Berlin, Fritz Haber (for research that had in fact contributed to the development of poisonous gases), were even less complimentary. (See "The Dubious Nobel Award," in *The Literary Digest* of March 13, 1920.) Thus, the resumption of Nobel competition in 1919 occurred in a very atypical climate of public opinion.

Reaction to Planck's award came mostly from his scientific colleagues. For several years, between 1900 and about 1908, Planck's work had interested only a relatively small circle of specialists in radiation theory. As noted above, Einstein's publication in 1905 of his own "light quantum" thesis had the effect of widening the circle of scientific interest in quantum theory, but until the 1920's, Einstein's theory proved to be even less acceptable to defenders of classical physics than Planck's idea of the quantum of action. When Planck received a single nomination for the Nobel Prize in 1908 and near-unanimous support from the Nobel Committee for Physics, the Royal Swedish Academy of Sciences chose not to follow the recommendation; scientific consensus still favored Wilhelm Wien's 1896 radiation law. Nevertheless, Planck was nominated for the prize every year between 1909 and 1919. He did not, however, receive the physics committee's support again until the year in which he won.

Two developments which occurred before 1919 probably helped to change this climate. First, Wien won the Nobel Prize in 1911, specifically for his work with heat radiation. Second and more important, Niels Bohr effectively combined quantum theory and Ernest Rutherford's model of the atom in 1913. Despite the wariness surrounding the concept of the quantum, Bohr's work extended its usefulness to the sphere of spectroscopic analysis. Thus, one of Planck's five nominators in 1913 was able to cite four areas of physics that had begun to use the $h$ constant: radiant heat energy, photoelectric radiation, X-radiation, and specific heats at low temperatures.

In 1919 (when Plank's six nominators included Einstein, himself one of those nominated), Nobel Committee for Physics member Svante August Arrhenius' report called for acceptance of the importance of Planck's quantization of energy concept. Yet, despite its recognition of areas in which quantum analysis was actively being applied in experimental physics, the special committee report still reserved judgment. The Planck constant, it stated, "corresponds to some reality in the constitution of matter, and . . . gives the measure of an atomistic property, albeit of yet unknown nature."

Although numerous researchers throughout the world had already incorporated the hypothetical model of the quantum of action into their research programs, signs of restraint continued into the 1920's. Even critics of quantum theory at the time of Planck's Nobel Prize, however, came to recognize that others, especially Einstein, were going on to prove that "the energy exchange between matter and ether must take place in such a way that an atom [always] emits or absorbs a quantum of energy $hv$ where $v$ is the frequency." Planck's constant, they finally concluded, had entered Einstein's necessary mathematical vocabulary, and, through him, the accepted scientific building material of the twentieth century.

## Biography

Max Karl Ernst Ludwig Planck was born in Kiel, Schleswig, in 1858. His family, which had produced a long line of professional jurists, was originally from south Germany. Most of Planck's youth, including his initial university years between 1875 and 1877, was spent in Bavaria. Despite an early interest in music and the humanities, Planck was attracted most to the fields of mathematics and theoretical physics. Hoping to develop his knowledge through direct contact with Germany's most notable leaders in these fields, he went to Berlin in 1878 to study with professors Hermann von Helmholtz and Gustav Kirchhoff. It was his work in thermodynamics, however, that gained for him a doctoral degree at the University of Munich in 1879.

Planck's early career as a teacher included a five-year inaugural post in Munich, followed by an appointment in his native town of Kiel. In 1889, he moved to the University of Berlin, where he would remain until 1928. It was here, in the prestigious Physikalisch Technische Reichsanstalt, headed by his former professor Helmholtz, that Planck conducted the important research that led to his elaboration of the quantum theory.

Although opposed to the dictatorial principles of Adolf Hitler's regime, which came to power during his 1930-1935 tenure as president of the Kaiser Wilhelm Society, Planck did not, as many famous scientists did, leave Germany during the height of the Nazi period. His active public career, however, seems to have been suspended. After fleeing the bombings of Berlin, and under psychological stress following the tragic political execution in 1945 of his second son, Ernst, Planck died two years after World War II in Göttingen, West Germany.

## Scientific Career

Planck's first scientific papers attempted to apply the concept of entropy (the measurement of the "unavailable" energy in a system) to thermodynamics. Because his approach went against classical conceptions of the conservation, or predictable exchange, of energy, however, it was initially not very well received. It was during his early years at the University of Kiel that Planck published his first book, *Das Princip der Erhaltung der Energie* (1887; the principle of the conservation of energy) which was honored by an award from the Academy of Göttingen. This award helped him to gain an appointment at the University of Berlin in 1889. During his first years in Berlin, Planck began to explore the theoretical thermodynamics of temperature radiation. By 1892 he had become a full professor alongside his former teacher Hermann von Helmholtz, whose work on the principle of the preservation of energy was widely recognized. It was in Berlin that Planck wrote his widely recognized textbook on thermodynamics, which continued to be used in German universities throughout the first half of the twentieth century. There is no doubt, however, that it was his theoretical exploration of radiation and of the possibility of applying the quantum concept to analysis of energy transfers within the microscopic universe of the atom that established his world reputation.

Any summary of the state of theoretical physics around 1900 must refer to the Dutch physicist Hendrik Antoon Lorentz's and other scientists' attempts to "unify" general fields of knowledge about physical phenomena, particularly electromagnetism and radiation. Such references help the modern reader to evaluate the initial impact and significance of Max Planck's propositions concerning quanta, which were still, even at the time of his Nobel award, enigmatic "bundles" of energy. Planck's work would pose theoretical problems for defenders of the classical principle of the conservation of energy, which had stood since the mid-nineteenth century. According to the then-standard views on the conservation of energy in mechanical processes, the amount of energy which a moving force puts into the body moved is matched by a loss of potential energy on the part of the acting force. Planck's theories required scientists to expand their perceptions of the law of conservation of energy to encompass energy transfers that were not simply mechanical, in the Newtonian sense of the term. By the turn of the century, as Planck himself stated in his essay "The New Science," researchers were experiencing a "movement away from dealing with differentials of energy [easily understood in terms of Newtonian mechanical principles] toward dealing with [energy in terms of] absolute values."

In 1892, Lorentz had proposed an "electromagnetic world picture" which held the promise of reducing all of physics to the consequences of a "primary source" of energy which affects a variety of observable phenomena. For Lorentz, the sources of the electromagnetic field were oscillating electrons "moving in an all-pervasive and absolutely resting ether." Fourteen years after positing this view, but without reference to Max Planck's work with the quantum of energy concept, Lorentz developed the idea of a "deformable electron" (the charge of which contracts as the mass of the electron is displaced in movement) to replace classical physics' "mechanical worldview" explanations of interactions between matter and space. The refinement of Lorentz's electromagnetic theory aimed, among other things, at dealing with the theoretical problem of dependency between mass and velocity at the microatomic level, something that would attract the attention of both Max Planck and Albert Einstein. The former developed an approach that eventually overthrew both the mechanical and the electromagnetic worldviews as keys for unifying the physics of minuscule particles and very high speeds. This approach began with an examination of energy transmission in the experimental framework of "cavity," or "black body," radiation.

It was in the Physikalisch Technische Reichsanstalt in Berlin that experimental use of black body radiation for measuring illumination intensity had been pioneered. Working there with linear oscillators surrounded by reflecting walls, Planck sought to disprove the Kirchhoffian premise that the intensity of heat radiation depended only on temperature and wavelength. His major discovery posited a link between atomic structure, specifically the "jumping" actions of electrons moving from one "allowed" level of bonding or unbonding to another, and the emission of energy. As his new radiation law gradually unlocked the formula of the Planck constant, as described above, he established the idea that energy is emitted and absorbed in tiny, discrete amounts, or quanta, which are measurable as multiples of a basic minimum value which depends on the inherent internal structure of the particular matter in question.

Planck's "quantum of action" was bound to attract the attention of others who were uncomfortable both with the classical law of the conservation of energy—which depended on a predictable continuity, or flow, of energy, not discontinuous quantum jumps—and with Lorentz's electromagnetic alternative. It was only after Ernest Rutherford's major discoveries in 1911 concerning the nuclear structure of the atom, however, that Planck and other physicists were able to identify (theoretically, at least) the quantum of action and its vehicle, the electrons surrounding the nuclei of atoms, as the "main actors" not only in radiation but in energy transmission and entropy generally. This step helped to complete Planck's theory that energy values are determined by the nature of the energy-emitting substance and brought quantum theory to the center of the emerging field of nuclear physics. Continued study corroborated the supposition that the electrons of each separate atomic material can have only specifically allowed energy values. On one level, therefore, the use of Planck's constant gradually enabled experimenters not only to pinpoint actual amounts of energy involved in normal chemical reactions as electrons "jump" from one atomic arrangement or level of orbit to another, but, in Planck's lifetime, to consider the magnitude of energy transfers occurring in what was to become the universe of atomic fission.

Any summary of Max Planck's scientific career should include mention of the writings he published in the field that might be called "scientific humanism." The Nobel laureate's *Scientific Autobiography and Other Papers* (1947), published in Germany after his death, and two other full-length books dealing with philosophical approaches to science reveal aspects of Planck's work that are quite accessible to the nonspecialist. It is significant that the first English edition of his book *The Philosophy of Physics* was published in 1936, just as the Hitler regime was consolidating its control over Germany. Its focal subjects, including general essays on "Causality in Nature" and "Science and Faith," may have allowed Planck a means, not to rationalize the regime which was striving to bring science—by force, if necessary—into its service, but to emphasize universally relevant themes implied by his work with the microcosm of the atom. Writings such as these have definitely outlived the years of Planck's scientific career, and, like the quantum theory he pioneered, they ask as many new or timeless questions as they try to answer.

While at the height of his career, Max Planck held a number of prestigious scientific positions. From 1930 to 1935, after four decades of teaching at the University of Berlin, he served as president of the Kaiser Wilhelm Society for the Advancement of Science, later reconstituted as part of the famous Max Planck Institute. He also became editor of the German journal *Annalen der Physik* (annals of physics) and a member of the Royal Society in London, England.

## Bibliography

*Primary*

PHYSICS: *Das Princip der Erhaltung der Energie*, 1887; *Vorlesungen über Thermodynamik*, 1897; *Acht Vorlesungen über theoretische Physik*, 1910; *Einführung in die allgemeine Mechanik*, 1916; *Das Wesen des Lichts*, 1920; *The Origin and Development of the Quantum Theory*, 1920; *Theory of Light*, 1932.

OTHER NONFICTION: *Kausalgesetz und Willensfreiheit*, 1923; *Das Weltbild der neuen Physik*, 1929; *Die Physik im Kampf um die Weltanschauung*, 1935; *The Philosophy of Physics*, 1936; *Scientific Autobiography and Other Papers*, 1947.

EDITED TEXT: *Abhandlungen über Mechanische Wärmetheorie*, 1898 (by Gustav R. Kirchhoff).

*Secondary*

Arons, Arnold B. *Development of Concepts of Physics*. Reading, Mass.: Addison-Wesley, 1965. Although a general college-level text, this book is very useful for its multiple references to Planck's contributions to physics. Its primary advantage is that, because its chapters deal with different physical phenomena, it allows the student to see how quantum theory affected diverse fields, such as study of the motion of particles, quantitative relations between work and heat, and wave-particle duality.

Darrow, Karl K. "The Quantum Theory: The Early Years." *Scientific American* 186 (March, 1952): 47-54. This article, much like Planck's Nobel award speech, surveys ways in which his initial quantum theory was taken up by other physicists who either extended it into other theoretical domains or devised experimental approaches to prove or disprove its hypotheses.

Franck, James. "Max Planck, 1858-1947." *Science* 107 (May 21, 1948): 534-537. This obituary was originally presented in the form of a memorial lecture at the 1948 meeting of the American Physical Society. Its principal value is in its description of Planck's personal attributes, his methods of work, his interactions with other scientists, and his place as a representative of the twentieth century's most important transitional generation of scientists.

Klein, M. J. "Max Planck and the Beginnings of Quantum Theory." *Archives for the History of Exact Sciences* 1 (1962): 459-479. Of the several brief articles on quantum theory cited here, this is perhaps the most concise in technical analytical content.

Partington, J. R. "Prof. Max Planck, For Mem. R.S." *Nature* 161 (January 10, 1948): 47-48. This obituary account of Planck's career was written by an English physicist who studied under the Nobel laureate at the University of Berlin. Instead of surveying the vast domains of science affected by quantum theory, Partington recalls features of Planck's personality as a teacher and emphasizes his concern for the philosophical implications of new directions in the technical field in which he taught.

Rosenthal-Schneider, Ilse. *Reality and Scientific Truth: Discussions with Einstein, von Laue, and Planck*. Detroit: Wayne State University Press, 1980. This book is made up of a combination of firsthand discussions and correspondence with three eminent scientists: Albert Einstein, Max von Laue, and Max Planck. Topics covered comparatively include "The Universal Constants of Nature," "Concepts of Substance and Conservation," and "The Smallest Length."

*Byron D. Cannon*

# 1919

### Physics
Johannes Stark, Germany

### Chemistry
no award

### Physiology or Medicine
Jules Bordet, Belgium

### Literature
Carl Spitteler, Switzerland

### Peace
Woodrow Wilson, United States

# JOHANNES STARK
## 1919

*Born:* Schickenhof, Bavaria, Germany; April 15, 1874
*Died:* Traunstein, Bavaria, West Germany; June 21, 1957
*Nationality:* German
*Area of concentration:* Electrical conduction in gases

*Stark's detection of the Doppler effect in a terrestrially generated light source led to his discovery that a strong electrical field will split the spectral lines of chemical elements*

## The Award

*Presentation*

Dr. Å. G. Ekstrand, President of the Royal Swedish Academy of Sciences, presented the Nobel Prize in Physics for 1919 to Johannes Stark on behalf of the Swedish royal family. Because of the unexpected death of the royal princess shortly before the ceremony, no member of the royal family was present. In his presentation, Ekstrand briefly summarized Stark's experiments and the experiments of other scientists which had helped to lead Stark to his discovery.

Ekstrand credited Johann Hittorf's experiments with cathode rays in 1869, Wilhem Röntgen's discovery of X rays, the identification of the nature of X rays by Max von Laue, Charles Glover Barkla's demonstration of the X-ray spectrum of chemical elements, and the identification of the nature of canal rays by Wilhelm Wien and Sir Joseph John Thomson with pointing the way for Stark's discoveries. Ekstrand lauded Stark for predicting in 1902 that the Doppler effect would be detected in canal rays (streams of positively charged ions) and for devising an experiment in 1905 that proved his prediction correct. In subsequent experiments that extended through 1913, Ekstrand continued, Stark and his students had shown that a strong electric field will split the spectrum of hydrogen gas, a discovery that complemented Pieter Zeeman's discovery that serial lines can be split by a magnetic field. Stark subsequently had found that the effects of electrical fields on the line spectra of a number of substances are very different from the effects of magnetic fields. Ekstrand concluded his remarks by underlining the "extraordinarily significant" nature of Stark's work in the evolving field of atomic physics.

*Nobel lecture*

Stark's Nobel lecture was titled "Structural and Spectral Changes of Chemical Atoms" and was delivered on June 3, 1920. In it, he made only brief reference to the nineteenth century discoveries in physics on which his own discoveries were based. Instead, Stark concentrated on the experiments which had led to his discovery of the "Stark effect," how and why those experiments were designed, and how they complemented concurrent work by other physicists. In the second paragraph of the lecture, Stark obliquely introduced the issue which had cast a cloud over his entire career and which has sullied his reputation with contemporary physicists: judeophobia.

The lecture began with a brief denigration of the "mind" of the ancient Greeks, who evolved the concept of the atom through philosophical speculation but were unable to bring the concept to productivity through experimental research. That was only accomplished, according to Stark's lecture, through the "mind" of the "Germanic peoples." A very brief account of the atomic discoveries made during the nineteenth and early twentieth centuries followed; Stark omitted the names of the physicists involved. He then gave a succinct account of the reasoning that had led to his own experiments and the theories of his colleagues that had inspired those experiments. Notably absent from the list of physicists whom Stark credited were the many Jewish physicists active at the time. Stark next gave a brilliant and exciting account of the experiments that had led, finally, to the discovery of the Stark effect—the splitting of spectral lines observed when radiating atoms, ions, or molecules are subjected to a strong electrical field.

Stark's lecture ended with a few brief speculations on the future of research into the nature of the atom. He voiced confidence that eventually the structure of the atom would become as well-known as that of the solar system as a result of "Germanic research." Stark's comments in the lecture clearly displayed the attitudes that brought him national prominence in Germany during the Third Reich and resulted in a four-year prison sentence imposed by a de-Nazification court in 1947.

*Critical reception*

The press and the international scientific community virtually ignored the awarding of the 1919 Nobel Prize in Physics to Stark. The strange silence of the media and of his peers was almost certainly related to his notorious views concerning what he considered the degenerative and disruptive influence of Jews on society in general and on physics in particular.

*The New York Times* recognized Stark's achievement with a five-line story on November 15, 1919, buried on page 11. The story gave no details of the work for which Stark had received the prize; it did not even give his first name. *The Times* of London gave little more information in a story a day later, and even the *Berliner Tageblatt* made only a passing reference to Stark's achievement in an article concerning all the prizewinners for 1919 which appeared on November 10. American scientific journals merely noted, without comment, that Stark had won the award. Only the journal founded by Stark, *Jahrbuch der Radioaktivität und Elektronik*, gave substantial details about the work for which he had been honored. Of all the recipients of the Nobel Prize in Physics, Stark was undoubtedly the most ignored.

## Biography

Johannes Stark was born in Schickenhof, Bavaria, on April 15, 1874, to peasant parents. He studied at the secondary schools of Beyreuth and Regensburg before enrolling at the University of Bavaria in 1894. After studying chemistry, crystallography, mathematics, and physics for three years, he received his doctorate for a dissertation titled "Untersuchungen über Russ" (investigations into lampblack). After successfully completing the state examinations required for teaching higher mathematics, he assumed the post of assistant to Eugen Lommel of the Physical Institute at the University of Munich in October, 1897. Shortly thereafter, he wed Luise Uepler, with whom he had five children.

In 1900 he became a *Privatdozent* (lecturer) at the University of Göttingen. In 1904, he founded the *Jahrbuch der Radioaktivität und Elektronik*, which he edited until 1913. In 1907, he became the first editor of a scientific journal to request an article from Albert Einstein concerning his theory of relativity. Stark received an appointment in 1906 as a professor extraordinary at the technical high school in Hannover, where he incurred the enmity of his superior, Julens Precht. Precht eventually managed to have Stark transferred to similar posts in Greifswald, in 1907, and Aachen, in 1909. In 1910, the Vienna Academy of Science awarded Stark the Baumgartner Prize, and in 1914 he won both the Vahlbruch Prize of the Göttingen Academy of Sciences and the Matteucci Medal of the Rome Academy. During his stay at Aachen, he performed the experiments that won for him the Nobel Prize in Physics for 1919. In 1917, Stark accepted the post of professor at the University of Greifswald, and he took a similar post at the University of Würzburg in 1920.

Despite the international recognition accorded his work in physics, Stark's enemies forced him to resign from the two most important science foundations in Germany because of his outspoken judeophobia. In 1922, he resigned his university post in disgust at what he perceived to be the growing "Jewish dominance" in German academic life and retired to the area where he was born to pursue private research. When Adolf Hitler and the Nazi Party came to power in Germany in 1933, Stark came out of retirement to lead the fight against "Jewish influence" in German intellectual life. The Nazi Party arranged his appointment as president of two powerful scientific organizations in 1933 and 1934, from which he conducted a campaign to expunge the "Einsteinian spirit" from German physics. Several influential German physicists opposed Stark's efforts in this direction, and he was obliged to retire again from public life in 1939.

In 1947, Stark stood trial before a de-Nazification court for his activities on behalf of the Third Reich and his attacks on Jews. The court sentenced him to four years in a labor camp, which he was forced to serve despite his advanced years. He died at his home in Traunstein, Bavaria, on June 21, 1957.

## Scientific Career

Stark's productive career spanned approximately the years from 1902 to 1928. After 1920, he became increasingly involved in what might be called the racial politics of German science. Stark's most important work involved electrical conduction in gases, which was the subject of his first published book. His discoveries were based on the "Doppler effect." Christian Johann Doppler had predicted as early as 1842 that a luminous object moving toward a stationary observer would appear to be a color different from the color it would appear to be if it were moving away from the observer. Doppler theorized that all stars emit neutral or white light and that the colors perceived by an earthly observer are caused by the stars' relative velocities toward or away from Earth. Doppler's theory was modified in 1845 and again in 1848 by other physicists and finally confirmed in 1870, thanks to advances in spectroscopy.

It was not possible to detect the Doppler effect with any source of light generated on Earth until the twentieth century, because no terrestrial light source could attain sufficient velocity. In his 1902 book, Stark correctly predicted that the Doppler effect might be observed in canal rays (streams of positively charged ions which occur in discharge tubes). Eugen Goldstein had discovered in 1896 that if the cathode in a cathode-ray tube is placed in such a way that it divides the tube into two equal parts and the cathode is pierced with a number of holes, many brightly colored rays will be observed entering the space behind the cathode through the holes and traveling in straight lines. Goldstein named these rays *Kanalstrahlen* (canal rays).

A number of physicists subjected these canal rays to intense investigation in the early part of the twentieth century, but it fell to Stark to demonstrate the Doppler effect in canal rays in an ingenious experiment which revealed it in the hydrogen lines. Stark immediately proposed his experiment as a proof of Einstein's special theory of relativity and, a year later, as evidence supporting quantum theory; these contentions put him in the forefront of what he later contemptuously dismissed as "Jewish physics," and he remained a champion of the new hypotheses until 1913. In that year, his animosity toward Jews increased to grotesque proportions, partly because of personal rivalries and professional jealousy.

From 1913 until his death, Stark opposed what he perceived to be the pernicious Jewish influence in science which perverted the discoveries and debilitated the course of "Germanic" science. After 1913, he virulently denounced quantum theory, the special theory of relativity, and the Jewish champions of those theories from every forum to which he had access. His reactionary position regarding the "new physics" and his open judeophobia combined to make him many enemies in German academia and ultimately led to his being denied membership in the two most prestigious scientific organizations in Germany and finally to his first retirement in 1922. His last important scientific work, *Atomstruktur und Atombindung* (atomic structure and atomic attraction), appeared in 1928. The book reiterated the judeophobic views that had made him unpopular with many of his colleagues and had forced his retirement. Stark would almost certainly have remained in an obscure retirement and would have had no more impact on German science after 1922 had circumstances not brought Adolf Hitler to power in 1933.

A combination of factors resulted in the triumph of a political regime in Germany that shared Stark's animosity toward Jews and his determination to eliminate the so-called destructive influence of Jews from "Germanic" physics. These factors included the economic dislocations caused by recurrent economic crises in postwar Germany, which had culminated in a great depression; disappointment and bitterness in many segments of German society concerning the lost war of 1914-1918 and the universally despised Treaty of Versailles that had ended it; and Hitler's own mesmeric oratorical abilities.

The Nazi Party brought Stark out of retirement and appointed him president of the Physikalisch Technische Reichsanwalt on April 1, 1933. This position gave him considerable influence over appointments to academic positions in German universities and the allocation of research funds. His enemies within the academy nevertheless prevented his election as president of the German Physics Association that year and barred him from the prestigious Prussian Academy the next. In June, 1934, however, the Nazis appointed Stark president of the German Research Association. His two presidencies and the concurrent passage of the so-called Nuremberg Laws allowed Stark to exercise enormous influence on the course of physics research and teaching in Germany. The Nuremberg Laws established that only "Aryans" were citizens of the Reich and that noncitizens could not hold government posts. Since professors were government employees, the laws gave Stark legal authority to purge the German universities of most Jewish professors. A few "non-Aryans" were able to keep their jobs because of stipulations in the laws that noncitizen government employees who had served honorably on the front lines during the Great War or whose fathers had died in the war could retain their posts.

After the outbreak of widespread anti-Jewish violence in Germany on the so-called *Kristallnacht* in 1938, Stark was able to "retire" the remaining Jewish professors "for their own protection," but still he was not satisfied. In 1938 and 1939, he waged a heated campaign against the "viceroys of the Einsteinian spirit," the "white Jews of science," and their continued championing of the "new physics." Stark characterized Jewish physics as having an "un-German" predilection for theory over experiment. He was never able to remove all of his opponents from their positions, but he did much to retard the acceptance of theories which contained within them the seeds of the atom bomb. He was also largely responsible for the exodus of the German physicists, both Gentile and Jewish, who enabled the Allies to develop the first atom bomb in 1945.

Stark's formidable accomplishments in science have been greatly overshadowed by the ignominy attached to his name by his affiliations with the Nazis. He exerted a considerable positive influence on physics during his early years but an even greater negative influence later in his life. He will be remembered as the discoverer of the Stark effect (considered by many physicists today to be of comparatively little practical value in the analysis of complex spectra and atomic structure) and as the Nazis' "tame physicist."

## Bibliography

*Primary*

PHYSICS: Stark's publications are voluminous, comprising more than three hundred titles; all are in German, except for *Effect of H-Beta and H-Epsilon Wave Length*, 1928. Some of the more important are *Die Elektrizität in Gasen*, 1902; "Der Doppler-Effekt bei den Kanalstrahlen und die Spektra der positiven Atomionen," *Physikalische Zeitschrift*, vol. 6, 1905; "Über die Lichtemission der Kanalstrahlen in Wasserstoff," *Annalen der Physik*, 4th series, vol. 21, 1906; "Elementarquantum der Energie, Modell der negativen und positiven Elektrizität," *Physikalische Zeitschrift*, vol. 8, 1907; "Beziehung des Doppler-Effekts bei Kanal strahlen zur Planckschen Strahlungstheorie," *Physikalische Zeitschrift*, vol. 8, 1907; "Neue Beobachtungen zu Kanalstrahlen in Beziehung zur Lichtquantenhypothese," *Physikalische Zeitschrift*, vol. 9, 1908; *Prinzipien der Atomdynamik*, 1910-1915; "Beobachtungen über den Effekt des elektrischen Feldes auf Spektrallinien, I-VI," *Annalen der Physik*, 4th series, vol. 43, 1914; *Die elektrischen Quanten*, 1922; *Die gegenwärtige Krisis in der deutschen Physik*, 1922; *Die Axialität der Lichtemission und Atomstruktur*, 1927; *Atomstruktur und Atombindung*, 1928; *Adolf Hitler und die deutsche Forschung*, 1935; *Jüdische und deutsche Physik*, 1941 (with Wilhelm Muller).

*Secondary*

Cohen, I. Bernard. *Revolution in Science*. Cambridge, Mass.: Harvard University Press, 1985. Cohen's book is a literate and compelling history of science centered on the theme of scientific revolutions, which have often mirrored political and social revolutions. Cohen evaluates Stark's contribution to modern physics and places him squarely in the camp of scientific reactionaries. Unlike most other works that deal with Stark, Cohen does not omit references to Stark's Nazi associations, but he explains them in terms of resistance to change rather than as manifestations of pathological racism. He points out that Stark was neither the first nor the last scientist to attempt to make the laws of science conform to his own political views.

Hartshorne, Edward Yarnall, Jr. *The German Universities and National Socialism*. London: Allen & Unwin, 1937. This book, written during the period when Stark was attempting to purge German physics of Jewish influence, is of interest because it contains an English translation of parts of an address delivered by Stark at the University of Heidelberg in 1935. The address includes an attack on the Jewish "Einsteinian" influence in German physics, which was still being championed by some German scientists, notably Max von Laue, Max Planck, and Werner Heisenberg, all Nobel laureates and old enemies of Stark.

Heathcote, Niels Hugh de Vaudrey. *Nobel Prize Winners in Physics, 1901-1950*. New York: Henry Schuman, 1953. Heathcote accords Stark only seven pages in his account of the first fifty Nobel laureates in physics; it is one of the shortest entries. In the biographical sketch that introduces each laureate, there is no mention of Stark's Nazi affiliations, nor is there any reference to the books Stark wrote defining and contrasting German and Jewish physics. The description of the work that earned the Nobel Prize for Stark consists exclusively of quotations from Stark's Nobel lecture, but the references therein to "Germanic" physics are not included.

Hermann, Armin. "Johannes Stark." In *Dictionary of Scientific Biography*, edited by Charles Coulston Gillespie, vol. 2. New York: Charles Scribner's Sons, 1975. Hermann's brief sketch of Stark's career includes a considerable amount of information concerning the many feuds between Stark and his contemporaries in the scientific community, both in Germany and around the world. He explains Stark's complete reversal of position concerning the theory of relativity not as a result of his judeophobia but rather as a result of his compulsion always to oppose the accepted point of view.

MacDonald, James Keene Lorne. *Stark-Effect in Molecular Hydrogen in the Range of 4100-4700 A*. Montreal: McGill University Publications, 1931. Although Mac-Donald's discussion of the Stark effect is technical, it does contain some biographical details about Stark and the research that led to his discovery of the Stark effect, which won for him the Nobel Prize in 1919.

*Paul Madden*

# 1920

## Physics
Charles-Édouard Guillaume, Switzerland

## Chemistry
Walther Nernst, Germany

## Physiology or Medicine
August Krogh, Denmark

## Literature
Knut Hamsun, Norway

## Peace
León Bourgeois, France

# CHARLES-ÉDOUARD GUILLAUME
## 1920

*Born:* Fleurier, Switzerland; February 15, 1861
*Died:* Sèvres, France; June 13, 1938
*Nationality:* Swiss
*Areas of concentration:* Metallurgy and metrology

*Observing that nickel-iron alloys show anomalies in thermal expansion and magnetic properties, Guillaume commenced a long-term and extraordinarily thorough investigation of alloys containing varying percentages of nickel. The results were of major importance to metrologists and makers of chronometers: the alloys invar and elinvar, with, respectively, near-zero thermal expansivity, and zero or negative change in elasticity with temperature*

## The Award

*Presentation*

Gustav V, King of Sweden, presented the Nobel Prize in Physics for 1920 to Charles-Édouard Guillaume at the award ceremonies held in December of that year. The presentation address was made by Dr. Å. G. Ekstrand, President of the Royal Swedish Academy of Sciences. He began by citing the Greek view that numbers are the reality behind appearances, and related this to the concern of the physical sciences for precise and accurate standards of measurement. Reviewing the establishment of the metric system in 1793 and the founding of the International Bureau of Weights and Measures in 1869, he arrived at Guillaume, since 1915 director of the bureau. Guillaume was occupied with the bureau's ongoing task of distributing copies of metric primary standards to the nations of the world. In this work he was necessarily concerned with the effect of temperature changes on the materials of which the standards were constructed. Temperature fluctuation can create errors by changing volumes and lengths of standards. In measuring thermal expansivity of many materials, Guillaume tested samples of nickel steel, some of which had a lower expansivity than the platinum alloy used for metric standards. This suggested that an alloy might be found that did not change length at all with changes in temperature, and he investigated the full range of nickel-iron alloys, with and without other elements, testing expansivity, elasticity, hardness, and resistance to change in aging. The result was invar, whose coefficient of thermal expansivity is very close to zero. Invar was used for precision instruments, particularly in geodesy, the measurement of land areas; it also replaced platinum in the bases of incandescent lamps. The constant-elasticity form of the alloy, elinvar, was used in chronometers of improved precision and in low-cost, accurate watches. Guillaume's studies also had theoretical importance, confirming Henry Louis Le Châtelier's hypotheses on binary and ternary alloys. In presenting Guillaume to King Gustav, Dr. Ekstrand cited his early work in thermometry but reemphasized that the Royal

Academy was recognizing the nickel steel investigations and the discovery of invar in choosing Guillaume for the Nobel Prize.

*Nobel lecture*

Guillaume delivered his Nobel lecture, "Invar and Elinvar," on December 11, 1920. In it, he presented his work in developing these alloys and discussed their applications. The General Conference on Weights and Measures in 1889 decided that "prototype" standards of mass and length should be distributed to those nations of the world that subscribed to the metric system. The platinum-iridium alloy of the original standards proved too expensive for general use, and by 1891 Guillaume had hit upon pure nickel as a metal for standards. For manufacturing reasons, however, nickel could not be used for the 4-meter measuring rods of geodesic survey.

In 1895-1896, Guillaume found that nickel-iron alloys showed interesting anomalies in magnetic behavior in the range 20 to 50 percent nickel and that some of these alloys showed a thermal expansivity about one-third that of platinum. Reasoning that as both properties arise from crystal structure, they would probably show similar patterns of anomaly with increasing nickel content, he tackled the simpler investigation of magnetic susceptibility first (asking the simple question, Is a particular sample magnetic at a given composition and temperature?). He found that nickel steels up to about 25 percent nickel become magnetic when cooled to relatively low temperatures (below 300 degrees Celsius, in the critical region 20 to 25 percent nickel) and when reheated retain their magnetism up to temperatures in excess of 600 degrees Celsius. Above 25 percent composition, the transition from magnetic to nonmagnetic and back takes place at a single temperature.

This defined the range for the more difficult measurements of expansivity: 25 percent nickel and above. Guillaume found that thermal expansivity falls sharply in this range, to a minimum at 35.8 percent nickel of about one-tenth the expansivity of iron or nickel alone. Further treatment in finishing the metal (forging, controlled-temperature cooling) could reduce this effectively to zero. The nickel steel of this composition was named invar, because of the invariability of its expansion with temperature.

Investigation of this range of composition also revealed a minimum of variation of elasticity with temperature and produced a new alloy, elinvar, which could actually be made with a negative temperature coefficient of elasticity. Here the investigation was more complex, as the best alloys were ternary, with 10 to 12 percent chromium added to the iron-nickel mixture. Finally, investigations of alloy compositions and metal-finishing protocols showed how to make invar that did not change length with many years' aging.

Applications of invar and elinvar were many, both scientific and commercial. The property of appearance and disappearance of magnetism at a definite temperature led to thermostats based on a magnetic coil. The ability to make alloys with variable thermal expansivity led to compositions with the same expansion as glass; these replaced the much more expensive platinum leads in the glass bases of the light bulbs of the time. In measurement, perhaps the most spectacular success was in geodesy, the measurement of baselines and angles of large areas of land. Baselines were measured with a 4-meter rod aligned at each end by microscopes and protected against temperature variation by movable huts. As a baseline was commonly up to 10 kilometers long, this procedure could take days and required a team of about sixty skilled workers. At the request of E. Jäderin, leader of the Spitzbergen (surveying) Expedition of 1899-1900, Guillaume produced a 24-meter invar wire that could be coiled for carrying and used without the elaborate precautions, including the microscopes, previously required. Jäderin reported measurement of a baseline more than 10 kilometers long with an error of only 19 millimeters.

Invar was quickly applied in mechanically operated railroad switches and signals, with cables extending many hundreds of meters from station to signal; low temperatures could contract a steel cable and trip the signal, while high temperatures could make the cable so slack as to be inoperable. Finally, both invar and elinvar improved precision chronometry in many ways. Invar pendulum arms did away with the necessity of compensating for change of length with temperature. Elinvar and invar applied in various ways in the balance wheel mechanisms of chronometers replaced a number of devices, some very complicated, that used pairs of metals (usually steel and brass) whose temperature errors more or less canceled each other.

In concluding, Guillaume characterized his research as broadening from an initial search for an inexpensive metal for metrological standards into an investigation that had major consequences in both laboratory science and industrial applications.

## Critical reception

Reaction to Guillaume's receipt of the 1920 Nobel Prize is notable principally for its absence. The Parisian daily *Le Temps* merely mentioned Guillaume as the winner in physics, in a longer article about all the prizes that appeared on December 13, 1920. *L'Humanité* failed to mention him at all. *The New York Times* covered Guillaume in a six-line squib on November 13 (datelined November 11), describing his title and the area of his research correctly but giving his name as Charles Édouard Guillaume Breteuil. (The Breteuil "Pavilion" is one of the laboratory buildings of the International Bureau of Weights and Measures in Sèvres, where Guillaume worked.) In a long story on December 11 about the ceremonies held in Christiana, Norway, on the tenth, *The New York Times* did not mention Guillaume at all. The semipopular scientific journals also failed to comment; the British *Nature* and the French *La Nature* merely noted the award. In its February, 1921, issue *Scientific American Monthly* carried an article by the journalist Jacques Boyer on Guillaume as head of the bureau, which described the equipment and techniques of measurement and mentioned Guillaume's Nobel Prize but gave no critical commentary or assessment of its importance. The *Proceedings of the Physical Society* (London), which produced a handsome obituary on Guillaume's death, had nothing to say in 1920 about his receipt of the Nobel Prize.

This lack of popular and professional acclaim appears to have had three roots. First, metrology is inherently undramatic and not likely to produce well-known figures such as the earlier Nobel laureates Wilhelm Conrad Röntgen and the Curies; moreover, professional scientists are all too likely to regard precision measurement as necessary spadework for more valuable investigations. Second, the Nobel Prizes for both 1919 and 1920 were awarded in the latter year, which automatically halves the attention given to any single figure. Third, the peace prizes were really the story of the year, going to Woodrow Wilson (1919) and Léon Bourgeois (1920) for their work in establishing the League of Nations. This may be the most telling fact, as the newspapers generally dwelt on these prizes and gave the names of other winners almost as an afterthought.

## Biography

Charles-Édouard Guillaume was born on February 15, 1861, in Fleurier, Neuchâtel Canton, in western Switzerland, about 85 kilometers from Geneva. His father and grandfather were clock- and watchmakers. Guillaume attended local schools, then the *Gymnasium* in Neuchâtel, and entered the technical university in Zurich at the age of seventeen. He received his doctorate five years later, in 1883, with a thesis on electrolytic capacitors. After a few months as an artillery officer, he joined the International Bureau of Weights and Measures in Sèvres, France, where he spent the rest of his professional career. He did all of his important research work at the bureau, becoming its assistant director in 1902 and its director in 1915. He held this post until his retirement in 1936, when he became the bureau's honorary director.

Guillaume was married to A. M. Taufflieb in 1888; they had three children. Many honors came to Guillaume during his lifetime, including membership in the French Legion of Honor, the Physical Society's Duddell Medal, presidency of the French Society of Physics, and honorary doctorates from Geneva, Neuchâtel, and Paris. He died in Sèvres on June 13, 1938.

## Scientific Career

The nickel steel work that Guillaume described in his Nobel lecture was the largest of his investigations but by no means the only one. He worked in precision thermometry and in the mass-volume relation of water, the original mass standard of the metric system. He published regular reports, and occasional longer volumes, on the state of international metric measurement and the activities of the International Bureau of Weights and Measures. In addition, he wrote from time to time on physics outside his immediate sphere of interest: the nature of matter; radiation, particularly X rays; and mechanics, in a text that went through many editions and translations. Several of his publications in research journals were of such value that they were later issued as books or pamphlets.

The first task that the bureau gave Guillaume in 1883 was to study the mercury-in-glass thermometer, its calibration and its stem corrections (the corrections necessary when the thermometer is only partially immersed in the medium measured).

This resulted in the *Études thermométriques* (1886; studies in thermometry), published originally in *Travaux et mémoires du Bureau des poids et mesures*, volume 5, then as a separate volume. By 1889, this was expanded as *Traité pratique de la thermométrie de précision* (practical manual of precision thermometry), a 336-page volume that became the standard text in the field. Guillaume's second major metrological study overlaps the nickel steel investigations and appeared in 1907. This is the determination that a kilogram of water at 4 degrees Celsius, its temperature of greatest density, does not occupy the cubic decimeter (1,000 cubic centimeters) of the metric definition, but in fact has a volume of 1,000.028 cubic centimeters. This result was published first in the bureau's *Travaux et mémoires*, volume 14, then separately as *Détermination du volume du kilogramme d'eau* (determination of the volume of the kilogram of water). This led three generations of chemists to make the careful distinction of measuring in milliliters, leaving the inaccurate cubic centimeters to their medical colleagues. In 1964 the units were declared equal, but the distinction persists.

Of the major research work, this leaves the nickel steel investigations. Begun in 1895, they continued well past the time of the Nobel award, with the last summation in 1927: *Recherches métrologiques sur les aciers au nickel* (metrological studies on nickel steels), a 321-page publication that originally appeared in the bureau's *Travaux et mémoires*, volume 17, in the same year. The thoroughness of these investigations cannot be overemphasized. The alloy rods and bars tested numbered in the thousands. In addition to the properties outlined in the summary of Guillaume's Nobel address, others were investigated, such as the change of composition with the temperature of application; for example, a metal that is to be used at 300 degrees Celsius has its minimum of expansibility at about 41 percent nickel instead of the 35.8 percent of standard invar. The effect of alloying elements on finish and corrosion resistance was evaluated. In addition to the elements iron, nickel, and chromium already described, carbon, manganese, tungsten, copper, and silicon were tested in carefully controlled quantities. Carbon, for example, was found to be detrimental to long-term stability of length, which is unacceptable in standards of length. As this element is ubiquitous in steels because of carbon smelting methods, it was necessary to find the correct percentage of tungsten, which has an affinity for carbon, to offset the effects of carbon. Careful temperature programs in the annealing process, including holding at 100 degrees Celsius for up to one hundred hours, also improved stability.

These and still other findings testify to the scope and thoroughness of Guillaume's work on the alloys themselves. To this must be added his concern for the applications of the alloys, which found its expression in a series of publications beginning in 1904 with *Les Applications des aciers au nickel avec un appendice sur la théorie des aciers au nickel* (applications of nickel steels, with an appendix on the theory of nickel steels). In the next year, *Les Nouveaux Appareils pour la mesure rapide des bases géodésique* (new apparatus for rapid measurement of geodesic baselines) appeared, written by Guillaume's colleague at the bureau, Jean-René

Benoît, with Guillaume's collaboration. This became a standard in the field and went through many editions. Later publications dealt with applications of invar and elinvar in horology and chronometry, including a section in the *Horlogerie théoretique* (1908-1912; theoretical horology) of J. Grossmann, and a separate text on the nickel steel pendulum, *Le Pendule en acier au nickel* (1908; the nickel steel pendulum).

Guillaume's tireless search for applications of invar in metrology is what raises his work to Nobel status. Taken by itself, the nickel steel work is no more than a very competent empirical investigation with occasional theoretical overtones. In the hands of a man who knew exactly what he wanted the alloys for, however, its findings revolutionized standards and methods of measurement at a time when standards were necessarily physical and material, not the electronically measured wavelengths of light that are used as standards today. This is the true importance of Guillaume's work, and it is why Dr. Ekstrand, speaking for the Royal Swedish Academy at the Nobel ceremonies, was at some pains to point out that it was not Guillaume's other excellent work, but specifically the nickel steel research, that was being honored with the award.

Guillaume's writings for the International Bureau of Weights and Measures might of themselves be considered the solid career output of an able scientist and administrator. They begin with *Unités et étalons* (1893; units and measures), continue in the year of his appointment as assistant director with *La Convention du mètre et le Bureau international des poids et mesures* (1902; metric standards and the International Bureau of Weights and Measures), and are rounded out as he approached retirement by *La Création du Bureau international des poids et mesures et son œuvre* (1927; establishment of the International Bureau of Weights and Measures and its work). In addition to these books, he produced biennial reports, *Les Récents Progrès du système métrique* (recent advances in the metric system, 1907 through 1933), ranging in length from twenty to more than one hundred pages. Published initially in the bureau's *Travaux et mémoires*, many of the reports (1907, 1909, 1911, 1913, 1921, 1933) were later issued in book form.

Finally, in the years before bureau affairs demanded much of his administrative attention, Guillaume interested himself in more general topics in physics. In 1896 he published *Les Radiations nouvelles: Les Rayons X et la photographie à travers les corps opaques* (the new rays: X rays and photography through opaque bodies); a second edition appeared in the following year. (It should be remembered that Röntgen had announced his discovery of X rays only in 1895.) Guillaume's interest in the nature of matter produced *La Vie de la matière* (1899; the life of matter) and *Des états de la matière* (1907; on the states of matter). Two years later, the first edition of his textbook *Initiation à la mécanique* (1909; *Mechanics*, 1914) was published; it went through five French editions over the following decade and appeared in English translation.

Guillaume continued his work as director of the bureau through his seventy-fifth year, retiring in 1936 to become honorary director. Two years later, he died.

## Bibliography

*Primary*

PHYSICS: *Über electrolytische Condensatoren*, 1883; *Études thermométriques*, 1886; *Traité pratique de la thermométrie de précision*, 1889; *Unités et étalons*, 1893; *Les Radiations nouvelles: Les Rayons X et la photographie à travers les corps opaques*, 1896; *Recherches sur les aciers au nickel*, 1897; *Recherches sur le nickel et ses alliages*, 1898; *La Vie de la matière*, 1899; *Les Aciers au nickel*, 1900; *La Convention du mètre et le Bureau international des poids et mesures*, 1902; *Les Applications des aciers au nickel avec un appendice sur la théorie des aciers au nickel*, 1904; *Les Nouveaux Appareils pour la mesure rapide des bases géodésique*, 1905 (with Jean-René Benoît); *Des états de la matière*, 1907; *Détermination du volume du kilogramme d'eau*, 1907; *Le Pendule en acier au nickel*, 1908; "Les Aciers au nickel et leurs applications à l'horlogerie," in Jules Grossmann, *Horlogerie théoretique*, 1908-1912; *Les Aciers au nickel et leurs applications à l'horlogerie*, 1912; *Initiation à la mécanique*, 1909 (*Mechanics*, 1914); *Recherches métrologiques sur les aciers au nickel*, 1927; *La Création du Bureau international des poids et mesures et son œuvres*, 1927.

*Secondary*

Chaudron, Georges. "Charles Édouard Guillaume," in *Dictionary of Scientific Biography*. Vol. 5. New York: Charles Scribner's Sons, 1981. One of the few biographical treatments of Guillaume, including a bibliography of his works.

*Nature*. "Dr. C.-E. Guillaume." CXLII (August 20, 1938): 322-323. This obituary gives a brief account of the laureate's life.

Schlessinger, Bernard S., and June H. Schlessinger, eds. *Who's Who of Nobel Prize Winners*. Phoenix, Ariz.: Oryx Press, 1986. The entry on Guillaume lists vital data, selected publications, and a brief commentary.

*Robert M. Hawthorne, Jr.*

# 1921

### Physics
Albert Einstein, Germany, Switzerland, and United States

### Chemistry
Frederick Soddy, Great Britain

### Physiology or Medicine
no award

### Literature
Anatole France, France

### Peace
Karl Branting, Sweden
Christian Lous Lange, Norway

# ALBERT EINSTEIN
# 1921

*Born:* Ulm, Württemberg, Germany; March 14, 1879
*Died:* Princeton, New Jersey; April 18, 1955
*Nationality:* German/Swiss; after 1940, American
*Area of concentration:* Theoretical physics

*Einstein received the Nobel Prize for his work with the light quantum and photoelectric effect, in which he broached questions of the reality of molecules and the molecular underpinnings of modern physics. His most celebrated work was in the areas of relativity, special and general, and of Brownian motion*

## The Award

*Presentation*

Presenting Albert Einstein for the Nobel Prize in Physics for 1921, Svante August Arrhenius (the 1903 Nobel laureate in chemistry) compared Einstein's discovery of the law of photoelectric effect to Michael Faraday's discovery of the laws of electromagnetic induction and electrolysis not quite a century earlier. Arrhenius contended that as Faraday had established the basis for electrochemistry, Einstein had established the basis for photochemistry.

Although the award was not made for Einstein's work in relativity, Arrhenius acknowledged the centrality of relativity theory to any discussion of Einstein. He referred to the sustained debate that relativity had generated in philosophical circles since Einstein had first articulated his special theory of relativity in 1905. Arrhenius alluded to Einstein's early work in kinetic theory, in which Einstein identified the major properties of liquid suspensions.

The Swedish Academy, however, was granting the award to Einstein for his work, predicated on Max Planck's quantum theory of 1900, stipulating that radiant energy consists of *quanta*: minute, individual light particles comparable to atoms. Arrhenius noted that impediments in Planck's work had inhibited further research until Einstein's work on specific heat and the photoelectric effect was published in 1905, demonstrating that when an electrical spark passes between two spheres, its progress is enhanced if its path is illuminated by another electrical discharge, whose velocity depends on its frequency, not on the intensity of the light that illuminates the path. Einstein's work demonstrated that a light quantum can yield only the whole of its energy.

Arrhenius noted that Einstein had established that no matter how high a light's intensity, the photoelectric effect can be brought about only by light that has a frequency higher than a certain stipulated limit. Experimental research by Robert Andrews Millikan (1868-1953) and his students verified Einstein's theory long after Einstein expounded it.

*Nobel lecture*

Because unique circumstances surrounded Einstein's receiving the Nobel Prize, the recipient gave no acceptance speech as such. Rather, on July 11, 1923, three months after Sweden's ambassador to Germany had delivered the award insignia to its recipient, Einstein delivered a lecture entitled "Fundamental Ideas and Problems in the Theory of Relativity" to a meeting of the Nordic Assembly of Naturalists in Göteborg, Sweden. This lecture, attended by Sweden's king, is generally viewed as Einstein's acceptance speech, although it occurred months after the official presentation of the award and did not focus on the subject for which it was made. Svante Arrhenius suggested the subject of the lecture to Einstein, who agreed, even though he would have preferred to lecture on unified field theory, on which he later produced four papers, building on the theoretical base constructed by Arthur Stanley Eddington (1882-1944). Arrhenius, both in his presentation speech and in his suggestion of a topic for Einstein's paper, obviously considered Einstein's work in relativity of more universal importance than his work on the photoelectric effect.

Einstein asserted in his lecture that motion is not an absolute but must be thought of relatively, only as it relates to the system of coordinates implied when motion is considered. To Einstein, motion is relative, time absolute. He noted that in physics, the coordinate system is usually considered a practically rigid body. Einstein had great difficulty with this notion, because he knew the rigid body can be achieved only approximately in nature. He therefore necessarily rejected the idea of basing all physical consideration on the notion of the rigid body, which is itself reconstructed atomically by using elementary laws of physics arrived at by employing a rigid measuring body. Einstein realized the circularity of this approach, which, until his time, most physicists had accepted.

Einstein recognized in his speech that the law of inertia, a problem since the time of Sir Isaac Newton (1642-1727), remained problematical because it did not explain what causes the special physical positions of the states of motion of inertial forms relative to all other states of motion. Einstein sought an explanation in his general theory of relativity, which does not make a distinction between inertial and gravitational effects. He also sought to establish an identity between gravitational and electromagnetic fields, and doing so, he questioned the validity of much Euclidian and Riemannian geometry. He showed that in situations involving two infinitely adjacent points of a distance in which the coordinate of differentials plays a crucial role, Euclidian geometry is valid only in any infinitely small region. The Riemannian means of measuring it creates a correlation that, based upon the rigid body concept, Einstein rejected.

Einstein closed his speech by expressing the hope that, by tracking the simplest differential equations that can conform to an affine correlation, physicists would be able to reach generalizations about gravity that could lead to the formation of the laws of the electromagnetic field. He acknowledged the inadequacies of relativity theories to address some of the most significant physical problems of his day, but speculated that his theories would retain their importance, possibly as limiting laws to future physicists—a modest expectation in the light of subsequent physical research that made indispensable use of Einstein's theories of relativity.

## Critical reception

Albert Einstein was first nominated for the Nobel Prize in 1910, five years after his four most significant papers were published in 1905 and three years after he had articulated his renowned formula, $E = mc^2$ (the energy of an object at rest equals the mass of the object times the speed of light squared). He was nominated in every year after 1910 except for 1911 and 1915. Confident that he would eventually receive the prize, when he divorced his wife, Mileva, in 1919, he agreed that she should receive the prize payment, a sum paid to her in 1923.

The public had become increasingly familiar with Einstein, who quickly developed into the most celebrated physicist in the world. Large segments of this public were dismayed each year when the Nobel Prize was awarded to someone lacking Einstein's celebrity. Nevertheless, the Swedish Academy adhered strictly to the stipulations of Alfred Nobel's bequest, providing that the prize in physics be bestowed upon the scientist considered to have produced original work that was of the greatest possible benefit to humankind. Questions were raised about whether Einstein's highly theoretical work was truly original or whether both relativity theories were instead a brilliant elucidation of basic work done by earlier scientists. When Einstein was nominated for the prize in fields outside relativity—theoretical physics, molecular physics, quantum physics, and mathematical physics—something had always stood in the way of his being honored.

In 1921, Max Planck again nominated Einstein, writing a forceful, spirited letter. More than ten other impressive and detailed nominations arrived from outstanding scientists around the world, all nominating Einstein in areas other than that in which he finally received the prize, photoelectric effect. For this work, however, Professor Carl Wilhelm Oseen of the University of Uppsala nominated Einstein in 1921. Meanwhile, the Nobel Committee asked Professor Allvar Gullstrand to prepare a critical paper on Einstein's work in relativity. Gullstrand concluded that the results that could be measured physically were so small that they could not yield valid experimental verification. It was now too late for Einstein to receive the award at the ceremonies on December 10, 1921.

During the next year, letters came from throughout a scientific community that clearly considered Einstein long overdue for the prize. Planck proposed that the 1921 Nobel Prize in Physics, which had been awarded to no one in the designated year, be awarded retroactively to Einstein, whom Oseen renominated for his work in photoelectric effect. The Swedish Academy agreed, and Einstein, then sailing for Japan, received a cable informing him that he had won the award.

Germany was in turmoil at this time. Anti-Semitism was rife, and Fascism was developing rapidly. Einstein had been accused, along with Walther Rathenau (1867-1922), a physicist who became foreign minister of the Weimar Republic, of being a member of a Jewish-Bolshevik conspiracy. Rathenau was assassinated in 1922. On his return from Japan, Einstein received threats that he would meet the same fate. The German press, as soon as it learned that the award would soon be announced, began to denounce Einstein. The *Deutsche Allgemeine Zeitung* of September 15, 1922, announced that Einstein was going to Russia to speak about relativity. On October 6, the *Berliner Tageblatt* announced that Einstein had left for Moscow, and on October 27, the *Berliner Borsenzeitung* reported that he would arrive in Petersburg the next day. The *Kieler Zeitung* of November 2 confirmed his arrival in Petersburg. This hysterical reporting is revealing in view of the fact that Einstein never visited Russia.

While Germany was castigating Einstein as a Bolshevik, Russia reacted to his receiving the Nobel Prize by calling his theories dangerous and bourgeois, as reported on the front page of *The New York Times* on November 16, 1922. Although reaction was not widely reported, most comments on his receiving the award were favorable. Many, like those in *Illustrated World* of January, 1923, and *Forum* of June, 1924, expressed dismay that the Nobel Committee had waited so long to honor Einstein.

Einstein's former friend and admirer, Nobel laureate Philipp Lenard (1862-1947), later a rabid Nazi, denounced Einstein's work when the Nobel Prize in Physics for 1921 was announced, but he did so strictly as a demonstration of his anti-Semitism. His early fondness for Einstein had deteriorated into hatred engendered by racial intolerance in a Germany going berserk. A number of eminent scientists who became German Fascists tried to use Einstein as their whipping boy and to discredit his theories on the basis of his Jewishness.

## Biography

Albert Einstein was the first of Hermann and Pauline (Koch) Einstein's two children; Maria (Maja) was the second. The Einsteins moved to Munich when Albert was one. Despite his innate curiosity, Einstein was a marginal student who disliked school. When his parents moved to Milan, Italy, in his fifteenth year, leaving him in Munich to finish school, Albert quit and joined his parents. He spent a sybaritic year in northern Italy, then finished his secondary education at the *Gymnasium* in Aarau, Switzerland. He continued his studies in mathematics and physical science at the renowned Eidenössische Technische Hochschule in Zürich, whose entrance examination he initially failed.

In 1902, the year after he took Swiss citizenship, he became technical expert third class in the patent office in Bern, where he remained for more than seven years, the happiest of his life. Early in 1903, he married Mileva Marič, who became the mother of his two sons, Hans Albert, born in 1904, and Éduard, born in 1910. During this period, Einstein regularly produced important scientific papers, including his initial papers on relativity, molecular dimensions, photoelectric effect, and Brownian motion—all completed in 1905, when Einstein's job allowed him only evenings and Sundays to write. By 1909, Einstein, now a professor at the University of Zürich, had received from the University of Geneva the first of his nearly two dozen honorary doctorates. After teaching briefly at the Karl-Ferdinand University in Prague and the Eidenössische Technische Hochschule in Bern, Einstein in 1914 became a professor without teaching obligations at the University of Berlin, where he was director of the embryonic Kaiser Wilhelm Institute for Physics under the auspices of the Prussian Academy of Sciences.

Divorcing Mileva in 1919, Einstein married his cousin, Elsa Lowenthal. Both were active in Zionist affairs and in 1923 visited Palestine. Two years earlier, Einstein had visited the United States with Chaim Weizmann, the future president of Israel, to raise funds for the establishment of Hebrew University in Jerusalem, to which Einstein later bequeathed his papers. Now, encroaching Nazism made significant inroads on Einstein's personal and professional life. In 1932, he became professor at Princeton's Institute for Advanced Studies, planning originally to divide his time between Princeton and Berlin. Unable to remain in Germany after Adolf Hitler became Führer in 1933, Einstein renounced his German citizenship and moved permanently to Princeton, New Jersey. He never left: When Chaim Weizmann died in 1952, Einstein, offered the presidency of Israel, declined the offer. He died in Princeton of a ruptured aortic aneurysm on April 18, 1955.

## Scientific Career

Playing with a small compass at age four completely intrigued Einstein. When the boy was thirteen, a friend introduced him to Aaron Bernstein's *Naturwissenschaftliche volksbücher* (1867-1869; *Popular Books on Natural Science*, 1869), Ludwig Büchner's *Kraft und Stoff* (1855; *Force and Matter*, 1864), and Immanual Kant's *Kritik der reinen Vernunft* (1781; *The Critique of Pure Reason*, 1838). Einstein began to blossom into a deep and original thinker. By the time he was nineteen, he had produced an essay on the state of the ether in the magnetic field and was showing signs of the unique brilliance that marked his career.

Having finished his formal education at the Eidenössische Technische Hochschule in 1900, Einstein, though unemployed, plunged into theoretical physics, a pursuit that his subsequent employment in the patent office permitted him to undertake without money worries. In 1903, he presented his "Theory of Electromagnetic Waves" to Bern's Naturforschende Gesellschaft. The paper was somewhat deficient because Einstein had little access to the scientific literature of his day, but it suggested a quantum theory of light that negated the widely accepted wave theory.

By 1905, Einstein was approaching topics that would dominate his thinking for the rest of his life. He produced his first paper on the light-quantum hypothesis (which led him to the work for which his Nobel Prize was awarded), his paper on Brownian motion, and two papers on the special relativity theory, which, as Max Planck realized, identified for the first time the principles underlying special relativity. Einstein's Ph.D. dissertation, "Eine neue Bestimmung der Molekuldimensionen" ("On a New Determination of Molecular Dimensions"), was also published, and Einstein was gaining respect among major scientists throughout Europe and beyond.

Einstein's conception of space-time relationships changed forever the way science would view them. Einstein suggested a new dimension, proposed a way of thinking that would ultimately pervade not only physics but all areas of the intellect as well. Einstein's relativity theories, more than any of his other work, were classically scientific, in essence broadly philosophical.

In 1906, Einstein wrote the first paper on the quantum theory of solids, and the next year he went on to discover the principle of equivalence for uniformly accelerated mechanical systems. He applied this important work to his investigation of electromagnetic fields in an effort to explain the redshift, ultimately theorizing that light can bend when it passes a huge body; the hypothesis was verified during the total solar eclipse of May 29, 1919. Einstein moved next to considering black body radiation, collaborating now with Johann Jakob Laub (1872-1962) on work that he would report in October, 1909, at the first physics conference that he ever attended, in Salzburg, Austria.

At the same time, Einstein was searching for a unified underlying theory of physics necessary to his radiation research. Although he did not discover a unified theory, he did come to the important conclusion that radiated light is composed of independent particles of energy, *quanta*. He used this theory to explain many of the perplexing properties of photoionization and fluorescence, and this work led him directly to his seminal findings about the photoelectric effect. Einstein's research of this period also led him to discover that the specific heats of all solids approach zero as the absolute temperature does, a conclusion fundamental to later research in superconductivity. His quantum theory of specific heats helped established the third law of thermodynamics, verified by the experiments of Walther Nernst (1864-1941).

Although his work moved in several directions simultaneously, Einstein doggedly quested after a single unified field theory, a quest that was to engage him for the rest of his life. His theories of light quanta did not have early support from some of the giants in the field, particularly Niels Bohr (1885-1962). Einstein persisted, however, and in time he was proved correct in his predictions. An Indian physicist, Satyendra N. Bose (1894-1974), sent Einstein a paper that he had written postulating the theory that radiation is a gas produced by light quanta. Bose, remarkably, had developed and employed a unique statistical system to count the states of gas, and had arrived at a distribution of equilibrium that supported Max Planck's radiation law, which Einstein considered to be complementary to his own work. Einstein used Bose's method to develop a theory that projected an ideal gas of material particles. This method revealed that below a given temperature an inordinately high number of the particles reach their point of lowest energy.

Generally contrary to what Einstein believed was the quantum mechanics developed in 1927, based in part on an earlier statistical interpretation by Max Born (1882-1970) of Erwin Schrödinger's wave function theory. Although Einstein had been uneasy about Born's research and had said so, a majority of his most renowned colleagues in physics embraced the new quantum mechanics, which, among other things, denied causality. For the rest of his life, Einstein wrestled with the problems posed by the new quantum mechanics, and his thoughts about the field often became more metaphysical than scientifically detached, as did his whole quest for a unified field theory.

Einstein's work brought the scientific community to the point that it could implement nuclear fission. As society moved into the age of nuclear energy, Einstein wrote a highly influential letter to President Franklin D. Roosevelt apprising him of the potential of nuclear power and of the danger posed by Germany's progress toward its development. After the Japanese capitulated in 1945, Einstein turned much of his energy to encouraging world peace and understanding. At the same time, he continued his search for an underlying theory that would explain the physical universe.

## Bibliography

*Primary*

PHYSICS: *Die Grundlage der allgemeinen Relativitätstheorie*, 1916; *Über die spezielle und die allgemeine Relativitätstheorie, Gemeinverständlich*, 1917 (*Relativity, the Special and General Theory: A Popular Exposition*, 1920, new edition 1954); *The Principle of Relativity*, 1920; *The Meaning of Relativity*, 1921; *Sidelights on Relativity*, 1922; *Untersuchungen über die Theorie der "Brownschen Bewegung,"* 1922 (*Investigations on the Theory of the Brownian Movement*, 1926); *Theory of Relativity: Its Formal Content and Present Problems*, 1931; *On the Method of Theoretical Physics*, 1933; *The Origins of the General Theory of Relativity*, 1933; *Essays in Science*, 1934; *The Evolution of Physics: The Growth of Ideas from Early Concepts to Relativity and Quanta*, 1938 (with Leopold Infeld).

LETTERS: *Warum Krieg? Ein Briefwechsel, Albert Einstein und Sigmund Freud*, 1933 (*Why War? "Open Letters" Between Einstein and Freud*, 1933); *Lettres à Maurice Solovine*, 1956; *Briefwechsel*, 1968 (with Arnold Sommerfeld); *Letters on Wave Mechanics*, 1968; *Briefwechsel 1916-1955*, 1969 (with Hedwig Born and Max Born; *The Born-Einstein Letters: Correspondence Between Albert Einstein and Max and Hedwig Born from 1916-1955*, 1971).

OTHER NONFICTION: *About Zionism: Speeches and Letters*, 1930; *Cosmic Religion, with Other Opinions and Aphorisms*, 1931; *Mein Weltbild*, 1934 (*The World as I See It*, 1934); *Out of My Later Years*, 1950; *Ideas and Opinions*, 1954.

*Secondary*

Bernstein, Jeremy. *Einstein*. New York: Viking Press, 1973. A book designed for the uninitiated reader. Its bibliography is brief but intelligently selective, listing both primary and secondary sources. The basic theories are explained in the clearest terms that Bernstein can contrive, although the complexity of some of Einstein's theorizing defies simple explanation.

Born, Max. *Einstein's Theory of Relativity*. New York: E. P. Dutton, 1924. An intelligent theoretical approach to Einstein's best-known theory that may, because of its technical nature, be daunting to readers unversed in physics. This splendid book is not for the beginner.

Frank, Philipp. *Einstein: His Life and Times*. New York: Alfred A. Knopf, 1947. The fullest, most comprehensive biographical treatment of Einstein to 1947. This frequently reprinted book is dated and has been replaced by Pais' biography but is nevertheless serviceable. Frank had a close forty-year association with Einstein, still alive when this book appeared; he wrote in Einstein's shadow. Well illustrated with photographs of Einstein. Full index; no bibliography.

Hoffman, Banesh, and Helen Dukas. *Albert Einstein: Creator and Rebel*. New York: Viking Press, 1972. Essentially a memoir of Albert Einstein coauthored by his secretary of twenty-seven years and a longtime colleague at the Institute for Advanced Study at Princeton, this illustrated book can be easily understood by lay readers. The documentation is internal. No bibliography, although there is an exhaustive index.

Holton, Gerald. "Influences on Einstein's Early Work in Relativity Theory." *American Scholar* 37 (Winter, 1968): 59-79. A well-written article, accessible to nonspecialists. It traces the beginnings of the theory of relativity, demonstrating how Einstein built on the work of Wilhelm Wien, Hendrik Lorentz, Albert Michelson, Edward W. Morley, George Francis FitzGerald, and others to construct his own elegantly designed theories.

Infeld, Leopold. *Albert Einstein: His Work and Its Influence on Our World*. New York: Charles Scribner's Sons, 1950. Leopold Infeld, coauthor with Einstein of *The Evolution of Physics*, writes about Einstein and his theories in the simplest possible terms in this brief book directed solely at the layperson. A scientist would consider the book simplistic, although the general reader will appreciate Infeld's approach. Limited bibliography of Einstein's writing.

Moszkoswki, Alexander. *Conversations with Einstein*. New York: Horizon Press, 1970. These conversations reported by Einstein's Boswell reveal fascinating personal insights, although its admiring author, who interviewed Einstein extensively, lacked the scientific background to ask the most penetrating and fruitful questions. Despite this limitation, the book makes a valuable, if general, contribution to Einstein scholarship.

Pais, Abraham. *"Subtle Is the Lord . . ."*: *The Science and Life of Albert Einstein*. New York: Oxford University Press, 1982. Highly readable, this book will appeal to the layperson as well as the specialist. It can be understood well even if the mathematical formulas occasionally baffle nonscientific readers. The illustrations are well chosen, the dual index helpful. Lacks a bibliography, although it is well documented and some sources can be traced through the copious endnotes.

*R. Baird Shuman*

# 1922

### Physics
Niels Bohr, Denmark

### Chemistry
Francis Aston, Great Britain

### Physiology or Medicine
Archibald Hill, Great Britain
Otto Meyerhof, Germany

### Literature
Jacinto Benavente y Martínez, Spain

### Peace
Fridtjof Nansen, Norway

# NIELS BOHR
## 1922

*Born:* Copenhagen, Denmark; October 7, 1885
*Died:* Copenhagen, Denmark; November 18, 1962
*Nationality:* Danish
*Areas of concentration:* Atomic structure and quantum theory

*Bohr was awarded the Nobel Prize in Physics for his investigation into the structure of atoms, the basic atomic components, their interaction, and the radiation that emanates from them*

## The Award

*Presentation*

Niels Henrik David Bohr was presented the Nobel Prize in Physics at the Royal Swedish Academy of Sciences in December of 1922. The presentation was made by the Chairman of the Nobel Committee for Physics at the Academy, Professor Svante August Arrhenius.

Arrhenius began his presentation with a review of the groundwork laid for Bohr from the earliest days of spectral analysis (1860) to the advances in that discipline that had enabled Bohr to conduct his inquiry into the atomic structure. Before the work of Bohr, the accepted theory had been advanced by Ernest Rutherford (1871-1937); it asserted the elegant and simple notion that electrons were negatively charged particles that orbited atomic nuclei like a planet orbits a star. James Clerk Maxwell (1831-1879) observed that an electron changed its orbit by a gradual declination toward the nucleus and in doing so emitted energy from the system in the form of light. He proved this by observing the spectra of solids and liquids. The spectra of a glowing gas did not, however, precisely fit this theory.

Through this single contradiction in theoretical atomic structural analysis, Bohr deduced that the electron did not simply orbit about the nucleus of the atom and, upon losing orbital position gradually, emit light. Bohr contended, as had Max Planck (1858-1947), that electrons emitted energy in bundles called "quanta" and that such emissions took place as an electron jumped discontinuously from one orbit to another.

Bohr's elegant theory revealed that an electron is not simply free to move to any orbit and that a certain number of transitions may *not* be achieved. He confined this idea in his "principle of correspondence." It stated that there are two kinds of electron-orbit configurations, specifically regarding the positions of the outermost electron tracks, and it is on these configurations that the chemical properties of all atoms depend. It is these limits that, in fact, define the nature of all matter, and since an electron cannot collapse inward beyond its innermost orbital extremity, each atomic structure is thus precisely and strictly delimited. Such definition prescribes matter itself, as Bohr was able to demonstrate.

*Nobel lecture*

Bohr's Nobel lecture, titled "The Structure of the Atom," related his work framed in a historical context. Bohr was perhaps overly optimistic in opening his lecture with the statement, "The present state of atomic theory is characterized by the fact that we not only believe the existence of atoms to be proved beyond a doubt, but also we even believe that we have an intimate knowledge of the constituents of the individual atoms." Bohr, perhaps, would have been astounded to know that more than half a century later that question was still being hotly debated, though he later acknowledged that the inner structure of the nucleus itself was "but little understood."

Nevertheless, he continued by giving a recollection of the research into atomic structure from the late nineteenth century to the work of Maxwell. Bohr went on to give the classic first college chemistry discourse on the atomic structure as characterized by electrons in orbit about the atomic nucleus. He then provided a few hints regarding his own conclusions with a discussion of the early recognition by Dmitri Mendeleev and Julius Lothar Meyer that when the elements are placed in order of their atomic weights, a certain periodicity emerges. Bohr then forthrightly stated that when one scrutinizes the relationship between specific periodicity and atomic placement in the periodic table, one encounters "profound difficulties, in that the essential differences between an atom and a planetary system show themselves. . . ."

Bohr stated that reliance on mechanical laws alone in order to deduce atomic structure is inadequate. He then admitted that reliance on the only other measurement tool available, the classical electrodynamic laws developed by Maxwell, was also inadequate to explain all the observed phenomena of atomic structure as revealed by spectral analysis. Bohr turned to the origins of his own unique approach in adoption of Planck's quantum theory and Albert Einstein's subsequent amplifications to assess his own observed contradictions. He related the then-recent work in X-ray diffraction spectrometry that had led to his theory of the correspondence principle.

Bohr pointed out that one appproach to the idea is that "the occurrence of transitions between the stationary states [of atomic systems] accompanied by radiation is traced back to the harmonic components into which the motion of the atom may be resolved. . . ." He was referring to spectral transitions which were not continuous but which showed abrupt transitions between energy levels, an event not allowed for under classical theory. He noted that this theory accounted for the resolution of an effect, called the "Zeeman effect," hitherto unexplained by either classical or quantum theory alone. In the Zeeman effect, the spectral lines of hydrogen are split in a specific, discontinous, but harmonic fashion.

Bohr noted that X-ray diffraction as a tool for atomic structure evaluation gives evidence of the atomic system by revealing atomic reorganization after a disturbance. From this evidence, it is possible to deduce the details of the atom's structure itself, which ultimately led to his own discoveries.

*Critical reception*

The early twentieth century was a time of unprecedented discovery, when Ernest Rutherford, Albert Einstein, Bohr, and others developed their monumental discoveries within short years of one another. These giants of science were publicly held in the highest esteem. At the time of his award, Bohr was the director of the Institute of Theoretical Physics at the University of Copenhagen. He had been the first to bring to bear the infant science of spectroscopic analysis to discover the internal structure of the atom. He combined the findings of Rutherford, Maxwell, and Planck, well-known physicists, to achieve his own discoveries. Consequently, few were surprised when he won the Nobel Prize; the honor had been foreshadowed by his winning the Royal Society's highest accolade, the Hughes Medal, in November, 1921. Soon thereafter, he had also been made an honorary member of the Royal Institution.

In the United States, *The Scientific Monthly* (February, 1923) summarized the response of both peers and public: "Bohr . . . is awarded the prize for the greatest discovery in physics. He is only thirty-seven now and he was only twenty-eight when he startled the world by his bold conception. . . ." Other reactions were equally enthusiastic and typical of the age: Fascism had yet to gain a significant foothold in Europe, and the great scientists were still free to pursue their philosophy. Ultimately, Albert Einstein would comment, "What is so marvelously attractive about Bohr as a scientific thinker is his intuitive grasp of hidden things combined with such a strong critical sense."

## Biography

Niels Henrik David Bohr was born into an academic family on October 7, 1885. He was the son of a professor of physiology at Copenhagen University, Christian Bohr. His mother, Ellen (née Adler), also had an academic background, ensuring that Bohr and his brother Harald would embark on academic careers (Harald became a professor of mathematics).

Bohr matriculated at the University of Copenhagen in 1903 under the tutelage of physicist C. Christiansen. While still a student at the university, he formulated a solution to a scientific problem advertised by the Academy of Sciences in Copenhagen, and his work was subsequently published in the *Transactions of the Royal Society* (1908). He earned his master of science degree in 1909 and his doctorate in 1911. He then left for England, where he worked with Sir Joseph John Thomson at the Cavendish Laboratory and Ernest Rutherford at his laboratory in Manchester. In 1912, Bohr was married to Margarethe Nørlund; together they would have six sons. One of them, Aage Bohr, would become a corecipient of the 1975 Nobel Prize in Physics.

After holding lectureships at Copenhagen University (1913-1914) and Victory University (1914-1916), intermittently continuing his work in Manchester, Bohr returned in 1916 to Copenhagen University to take a position as a professor of theoretical physics. In 1920, the Institute for Theoretical Physics (later to be called

the Niels Bohr Institute) was established for him by the university, and he would be
its director until his death in 1962.

## Scientific Career

Niels Bohr arrived at Cambridge in the autumn of 1911 for postgraduate study. By
the spring of the following year, he had moved to Rutherford's side at the University
of Manchester. Bohr was fascinated by Rutherford's contention that he understood
the structure of the atom. Even though Rutherford had won the Nobel Prize in
Chemistry in 1908 for his work in describing radioactive decay, by late 1911 he had
deduced the atomic structure itself. Rutherford was quick to pass on to his peers the
idea that the atom was made up of a dense central point (nucleus) surrounded by an
oppositely charged electron cloud, but they quickly saw that the concept was flawed
and rejected it outright. Under the laws of classical physics, the Rutherford atom
would be unstable and fall apart. Rutherford, meanwhile, insisted that the experimental evidence demanded that such a structure exist and held firm to his idea.

Bohr was at Manchester for only a few months before he recognized that the
wholly disparate fields of quantum mechanics and classical physics, when brought
together, would solve the dilemma of Rutherford's unstable atomic model.

In 1911, quantum mechanics was still in its infancy. It would ultimately describe
in pure mathematical terms the unseen particles of the atom, describing statistically
predictions of the position and speed of a given atomic particle. But in 1911-1912,
quantum mechanics dealt with the most bizarre speculations and fitting of observed
data of light frequencies to empirically developed and not wholly understood equations. The only noted physicist of the day to link it with any physical concept was
Albert Einstein, who matched quantum concepts to light particles (photons or light
quanta).

By the end of July, 1912, Bohr had returned to Copenhagen to marry, but was
caught up in an affair with his ideas. He persuaded his bride that no honeymoon
was necessary and rushed back to England to sell his abstractions to Rutherford.
Bohr then linked the quantum idea that energy is emitted only in well-defined
energy levels (frequencies) with his belief that these emissions related to electrons
falling or rising into stable orbits around the nucleus. This concept ensured that the
atom was always stable and that the atom only emitted or absorbed energy (light or
photons) when the electrons changed from one stable level to another. By linking
up an experimentally derived but invariant number from quantum mechanics,
Planck's constant, Bohr was able to derive the calculations that precisely described
the transitions of electrons from one orbit to another. More important, in this
brilliant postulation, Bohr defined the very nature of the atom itself. He published
these findings in 1913, for which he would win the Nobel Prize nine years later.

Ultimately, the correspondence principle was derived from these findings. Simply
stated, it meant that the model of the atom derived from quantum mechanics must
join smoothly with classical physics when the dimensions become large. This principle would vindicate Rutherford's insistence that physical (classical) evidence

proved his model was correct, even though he had no mathematical model to corroborate it. It would also absolve the ideas of quantum mechanics that had fallen on hard times. Now it, too, had a champion of irrefutable evidence on which to cling. The correspondence principle became the first tenacious link between the physical world of the classical physicists and the surreal world of the quantum.

In 1916, Bohr moved back to Copenhagen, now a celebrated physicist. By this time he had expanded his view of electron shells and the associated quantum descriptions to link it to an explanation of the periodic table of the elements. Bohr explained that the active properties (degree of stability) and ultimate character of matter itself were largely dependent on the arrangement of the electron shells of the elements.

In 1920, Bohr was named the director of the Institute for Theoretical Physics at Copenhagen. While he was creating the world's center of theoretical physics, he and his contemporaries were uncovering more evidence that the quantum world had a greater influence on the realities of physics than anyone had ever imagined. Yet the radical new concepts had created a rift in physics. The correspondence principle notwithstanding, science was in desperate need to define the clear line of demarcation between the quantum and the physical. Einstein had publicly balked at the emerging dominance of quantum theory, calling it "a stinking mess."

By this time, experiments had been conducted which proved that the nature of the electron was particulate, but another set of experiments conclusively proved it was a wave form. For Bohr, the whole controversy finally precipitated itself into a matter of physical philosophy. After all, science itself was a manifestation of philosophy, the ultimate edifice upon which Sir Isaac Newton had built all of classical physics. Bohr called his answer to the dilemma the "principle of complementarity."

Classical and quantum reality had given their own final interpretations of what was going on inside the atom, and each answer was finally and conclusively different. Bohr chose to answer in terms of pure philosophy, with an example provided by Sophocles' *Antigone*. Here was depicted the conflict of *social duty* and *commitment to family* which were mutually exclusive traits yet complementary nonetheless. Said Bohr, such were the ways of the atom. One observational technique necessarily and by definition excluded viewing results that only the other could obtain, but one did not disprove the other. The very act of observation changes the state of the electron itself. Taken together, the concepts were complementary proofs of the same manifestation.

So profound was the impact of this single observation of complementarity that on the strength of it alone, the centuries-old dominance of classical physics was ended. With it, the new and extraordinary insight of the quantum microcosm took resolute hold on the community of science and modern physics was engendered.

Inevitably, Bohr's work on the nature of atomic structure brought him into the emerging science of nuclear energy. When in 1939 the first evidence was presented that the nucleus of an atom could be split in a process that became known as nuclear fission, Bohr increased his work on nuclear interactions. He described the atomic nucleus in fission as behaving like a deformable droplet of liquid, providing a basis for quantitatively predicting such interactions. It was Bohr who predicted that fission occurred in the isotope uranium 235 more than in any other.

Political realities forced Bohr to escape Nazi occupation in 1943 by fleeing to Sweden, then Great Britain, and ultimately the United States. While a guest of the United States, Bohr and his son Aage assisted those at Los Alamos who were engaged in the production of the first atomic weapon.

Bohr returned to his native Copenhagen immediately following the war in 1945. There he became the chairman of the Danish Atomic Energy Commission. Concerned with the peaceful use of atomic energy, Bohr eventually chaired the first Atoms for Peace Conference held in Geneva in 1955. At the time of his death, Bohr had shown a keen interest in genetics and molecular biology. His last paper, unfinished, was concerned with this issue.

Bohr's ability to link concepts of classical physics with the newly emerging quantum mechanics was his most important single contribution. Bohr related the new science of quantum, subatomic physics to the macro-atomic world for the first time in a practically applied sense. In most college-level physics courses today, experiments demonstrating his principle of complementarity are performed alongside classical experiments. Einstein had some difficulty accepting all the notions of "randomness" associated with the new quantum philosophy. Indeed, Einstein stated that he did not believe that "God plays dice with the universe," in reference to quantum theory's event interdependent probabilities. Bohr apparently had little difficulty with such vagaries, indeed linking both as invariably interconnected and ultimately predictable.

With Bohr's approach to physics, he was able to visualize both the classical "macro-universe" and the quantum "micro-universe" of the atomic nucleus, where energy and particles are demonstrably complementary and interchangeable. It was just such notions that would change the world with the unleashing of atomic energy.

## Bibliography

*Primary*
PHYSICS: *The Theory of Spectra and Atomic Constitution*, 1922; *Atomic Theory and the Description of Nature*, 1934; "Neutron Capture and Nuclear Constitution," *Nature*, vol. 136, 1936; *Open Letter to the United Nations, June 9, 1950*, 1950; *Atomic Physics and Human Knowledge*, 1958; *Essays, 1958-1962, On Atomic Physics and Human Knowledge*, 1963.
MOLECULAR BIOLOGY: "Light and Life Revisited," in *Essays, 1958-1962*, 1963.
OTHER NONFICTION: *Open Letter to the United Nations*, June 9, 1950.

*Secondary*
Asimov, Isaac. *Understanding Physics*. Vol. 2, *Light, Magnetism and Electricity*. New York: Walker and Co., 1966. Written by one of twentieth century's most adept communicators of the sciences, this work is directed toward the general

reader. Its purpose is to explain the historical-chronological events of modern physics. The work includes Bohr's concept of complementarity and a look beyond Bohr's work to later twentieth century physics. Writing in a clear, historically relevant style accessible to readers with a high school knowledge of science, Asimov provides a superior look at Bohr's specific point of reference in modern physics, framed by the events before and after.

Folse, Henry J. *The Philosophy of Niels Bohr: The Framework of Complementarity.* New York: North-Holland, 1985. Folse demonstrates Bohr's concept of complementarity in a primarily philosophical orientation. He analyzes the concept in its broadest views and applications, encompassing not only the subatomic stratagem but nature itself in a broad, almost epistemological panorama of complementarity. Folse outlines the concepts of quantum mechanics in an absorbing and unique way that seeks to bridge surreal quantum "logic" with "real world" views, which tend to be constrained by empirical observation. The book is written for college-level readers with some foreknowledge of the philosophy of scientific thought and a rudimentary grounding in the approaches of modern physics.

French, Anthony, and P. J. Kennedy, eds. *Niels Bohr: A Centenary Volume.* Cambridge, Mass.: Harvard University Press, 1985. Although these essays vary widely in approach, appeal, and depth, they allow for wide and divergent insights into Bohr and his science; several were written by those who knew him. Recommended for readers at all levels.

Lamont, Lansing. *Day of Trinity.* New York: Atheneum, 1965. This work provides an important reference in understanding the world in which Bohr imposed his considerable influence. It pictures a world at war, a despotic dictator (Adolf Hitler), and a team of government scientists who sought to devise the "ultimate weapon" (the nuclear bomb) to stop him. It pictures the escape of Bohr from his occupied homeland in 1943 and his integration into the Manhattan Project. In this capacity, Bohr (code-named "Nicholas Baker"), Albert Einstein, Enrico Fermi, Richard Feynman, and others helped develop the bomb. A thrilling account throughout, discussing even the concern by some U.S. government officials that Bohr would leak the bomb's secrets to Joseph Stalin in his zeal to share the secrets of atomic power with the world.

Moore, Ruth. *Niels Bohr: The Man, His Science, and the World They Changed.* New York: Alfred A. Knopf, 1966. This biography stands as the definitive English-language sketch of Niels Bohr. It details for readers of all backgrounds the life of the great physicist from childhood, through academia and the days leading up to his acceptance of the Nobel Prize, to his final days as a champion of the peaceful use of atomic power.

*Dennis Chamberland*

# 1923

### Physics
Robert Andrews Millikan, United States

### Chemistry
Fritz Pregl, Austria

### Physiology or Medicine
Sir F. G. Banting, Canada
J. J. R. Macleod, Great Britain

### Literature
William Butler Yeats, Ireland

### Peace
no award

# ROBERT ANDREWS MILLIKAN
## 1923

*Born:* Morrison, Illinois; March 22, 1868
*Died:* San Marino, California; December 19, 1953
*Nationality:* American
*Areas of concentration:* The electronic charge and the photoelectric effect

*Millikan's experiments demonstrated the unit charge of the electron and confirmed the accuracy of Albert Einstein's equation for the photoelectric effect*

## The Award

*Presentation*

Professor A. Gullstrand, Chairman of the Nobel Committee for Physics of the Royal Swedish Academy of Sciences, presented the 1923 Nobel Prize in Physics to Robert W. Bliss, the American Minister to Sweden, in December of 1923. Bliss accepted the prize on behalf of Robert Andrews Millikan. Although the prize was given for experimental work on both the charge on the electron and the photoelectric effect, Gullstrand all but ignored the latter contributions in his presentation. Only in the last paragraph did he even mention the investigations of the photoelectric effect, crediting Millikan's experiments with giving value to Albert Einstein's law and support to Niels Bohr's theory. The rest of the presentation focused on the attempts to discover the elementary charge on the electron. Gullstrand briefly reviewed the laws of electrolysis and the early attempts to approximate the value of the unit of electrical charge. Millikan's objective was not only to determine the unit of charge but also to demonstrate that there was some physical reality corresponding to that charge. The unit charge could not simply be a statistical mean, but a specific charge, identical for each and every electron. Gullstrand then summarized the procedures and outcomes of Millikan's oil-drop experiments.

*Nobel lecture*

Millikan's Nobel lecture, titled "The Electron and the Light-Quant from the Experimental Point of View," was presented on May 23, 1924. It concisely recapitulated his experiments and the context in which they were conducted. Describing himself as "the mere experimentalist" who designed crucial experiments to test the theoretical ideas of other scientists, Millikan credited his success in the oil-drop experiment to his apparatus.

Millikan prefaced his description of the oil-drop experiment by claiming that experimentalists are empiricists, concerned with facts. They know nothing about the ultimate nature of electricity; they are concerned only with the physical manifestations of electrical charge. The definitions developed by experimentalists are only descriptions of the experiments and depend on no hypotheses. In performing his own experiments, Millikan was testing the theory of Benjamin Franklin that electricity existed in particles, or atoms.

He went on to give a more detailed description of his oil-drop experiment, replete with a drawing of the apparatus and a table of data, than that provided by Gullstrand. Millikan also gave a full account of his experiments on the photoelectric effect. His description of the measurement of the charge of the electron reiterated the two fundamental conclusions of his work: first, that the charge on the electron was always a definite integral multiple of the basic charge, never a fraction; and second, that observers of this experiment literally saw the electron. In his summary of the photoelectric experiments, Millikan again emphasized the empirical nature of his work. His concluding discussion concerned the physical validity of Einstein's concept of photons. In a statement he would conveniently forget in his later years, Millikan withheld his full agreement with what he called the "localized light-quanta."

*Critical reception*

The American public was informed of Millikan's selection on November 14, 1923. Reaction was relatively subdued. Despite the fact that Millikan was the first native-born American to win the Nobel Prize in Physics (Albert Abraham Michelson, the winner in 1907, had been born in Poland), with roots going back to colonial New England, and only the second American winner in physics, American newspapers generally did not indulge in a frenzy of nationalism. Many did not go beyond the printing of a brief announcement of the selection, identifying Millikan as the first scientist "to isolate and measure the electron." Even *The New York Times*, which provided comparatively extensive coverage, relegated the story to the middle or rear pages of the paper.

*The New York Times* ran five short articles on Millikan, some extremely brief. On November 14, it announced his selection, adding to the usual credits mentioned in newspaper accounts his role as preparer of a declaration that there was "no antagonism between science and religion." Discussion of Millikan was continued on the following day. In that article, all the American Nobel Prize winners to date were mentioned, and the failure of any American to have been selected for the literature prize was noted. An analogy was then drawn between Millikan's work and "idealistic literature." On December 2, there was an extended discussion of Millikan's scientific work, in which he was dubbed the "atom man." On December 12, there was a brief report on the ceremonies, and on May 26, 1924, an announcement of his arrival in Stockholm appeared at the rear of the paper.

Scientists viewed the award as the final acknowledgment of Millikan's victory over Felix Ehrenhaft in the controversy surrounding the electron's charge and nature. Millikan had demonstrated his ability to provide experimental underpinning for some of the major theoretical issues facing physics.

## Biography
Robert Andrews Millikan was born in Morrison, Illinois, on March 22, 1868, the

son of Silas Franklin Millikan, a Congregational minister, and Mary Jane Andrews, the former dean of women at Olivet College in Michigan. The second of six children, Robert was seven when the family moved to Maquoketa, Iowa, where he received his elementary and secondary education and helped work the family land. In 1886, he enrolled at Oberlin College in Ohio, the alma mater of both his parents. He spent seven years at Oberlin, receiving his bachelor's degree in 1891 and his master's degree two years later. He obtained a doctorate from Columbia University in 1895. At the suggestion of his Columbia mentor, Michael Pupin, Millikan spent the 1895-1896 academic year in Germany. In 1896, he faced a choice between two positions: an instructorship at Oberlin and an assistantship at the University of Chicago, where he had spent the summer of 1894. He chose the latter.

Millikan remained at the University of Chicago, with time out for service during World War I, until 1921. In 1902 he was married to Greta Irvin Blanchard; they would have three sons. During the war he was commissioned a lieutenant colonel in the Army Signal Corps. In 1921, he became director of the Norman Bridge Laboratory of the California Institute of Technology and chairman of that institution's executive council (in effect, president of the college), posts he held until his retirement in 1946. Millikan died in San Marino, California, on December 19, 1953.

## Scientific Career

Millikan spent his first years on the University of Chicago faculty concentrating on pedagogical activities. Responding to the priorities of the University, he authored or coauthored a number of textbooks and laboratory manuals. Among those which became standards in the field were *Mechanics, Molecular Physics, and Heat: A Twelve Weeks' College Course* (1902), *A Laboratory Course in Physics for Secondary Schools* (1906; with Henry Gordon Gale), and *A First Course in Physics* (1906; with Gale).

In the middle of the first decade of the twentieth century, Millikan decided to turn his energies from pedagogy to research. His first major effort was a series of measurements made with George Winchester, one of his graduate students, which led to the conclusion that the photoelectric effect (the emission of electrons from the surfaces of certain metals when struck by light waves) was independent of temperature. There was, however, little interest in Millikan's experiments, which were conducted in complete ignorance of Albert Einstein's theory of the photoelectric effect.

Frustrated, Millikan turned to the determination of the electronic charge. Examining a technique developed by Harold Albert Wilson, a student of Sir Joseph John Thomson (1856-1940), in which a charged cloud of water vapor fell under the influence of an electric charge, Millikan found inconsistencies in the measurements and unacceptable experimental uncertainties. He first modified the experiment by using individual drops rather than a cloud. His most significant change was the replacement of water, which was subject to evaporation, by oil. Able to measure the changes in the velocity of drops of oil for hours at a time, Millikan confirmed that the charges on the drops were integral-multiples; there was a unit charge for the electron. When Felix Ehrenhaft claimed that Millikan's data showed a variability which supported Ehrenhaft's theory of subelectrons, Millikan published additional experiments reconfirming the integral-multiple nature of the charge. In 1913, he established the value for the charge of the electron, which would stand for a generation.

By that time, he had returned with renewed energy to the problem of the photoelectric effect. He spent the summer of 1912 in Germany, lecturing on his oil-drop experiment, attending Max Planck's lectures on heat radiation, and interacting with the members of the German Physical Society. Now cognizant of Einstein's photoelectric equation, on his return to the United States he initiated a program to test its validity experimentally. He successfully completed that program by 1916. This success in confirming Einstein's equation did not, however, change Millikan's opinion that Einstein's hypothesis of the photon was just that—a hypothesis, not a description of physical reality. Millikan found the wave theory of light too compelling to acknowledge that his work confirmed the existence of the photon.

Millikan's successes in the laboratory were leading to honors and recognition from his colleagues. He was elected to the American Philosophical Society and the American Academy of Arts and Sciences in 1914, the National Academy of Sciences in 1915, and the presidency of the American Physical Society in 1916. He served as an associate editor of *Physical Review* from 1903 to 1916. In the latter year, he was named an editor of the *Proceedings of the National Academy of Sciences*. Just before his entrance into the army in 1917, he was selected as a vice-chairman and director of research for the National Research Council. Another sign of his increasing significance was an offer in 1913 from the American Telephone and Telegraph Company of a $500 annual consultant's retainer. Millikan remained a consultant to AT&T until 1931.

Millikan's major research interest in the years immediately after moving to the California Institute of Technology was in cosmic rays. There had been considerable debate during the second decade of the twentieth century over the cause and characteristics of radiation which had been discovered high in the atmosphere. Was it the result of radioactive decay in Earth's crust, or did the radiation originate from outside the atmosphere? Millikan began his research program by collecting data from balloons and mountain peaks, with inconclusive results. Once again, as with the photoelectric effect, his experiments were slow to bear fruit. In 1925, however, data collected from two high-altitude lakes led Millikan to the conclusion that the radiation was extraterrestrial in origin. Although *The New York Times* dubbed the radiation "Millikan rays," Millikan humbly suggested the name "cosmic rays." Subsequently, he would argue that cosmic rays were the result of nuclear transformations, photons created when hydrogen atoms fused together to form helium, oxygen, or silicon. Public attention was drawn to the theory by Millikan's description of cosmic rays as the "birth-cries" of neonate atoms. His theoretical explanation would undergo severe attack in the 1930's, however, as evidence mounted that cosmic rays were charged particles, not photons. By 1935, Millikan had revised his position; he admitted that at least some cosmic rays consisted of charged particles. Atoms were not, after all, being born.

This reversal, however, was still in the future. The announcement of the identification of cosmic rays, made in an address to the National Academy of Sciences on November 9, 1925, following so closely on the heels of the Nobel Prize, made Millikan a celebrity. He became the personification of the American scientist, at least to the media. An outspoken individual and popular lecturer, Millikan increasingly became recognized as a spokesman for American science between the world wars. Second perhaps only to Einstein in instant recognition and visibility, Millikan was homegrown, from the rural Midwest, exuding the appearance of a successful businessman and not the exotic personality that Einstein projected. He was in demand for appearances behind the lectern, on the radio, and in the popular press. *Time* magazine chose him for the cover of the April 25, 1927, issue, with the caption "detected the cosmic pulse."

Millikan frequently took public stands on issues concerning the public perception and support of science and on political and social issues. The reconciliation of religion and science was especially important to him. Unhappy with the fundamentalist approach to Christianity and the Bible typified by the Scopes trial of 1925, Millikan argued that the theory of evolution was not antireligious. He linked the scientific method to moral development. According to Millikan, there was room for both the practice of science and the teachings of Jesus in modern Protestantism.

Another issue which attracted his attention was economic recovery from the Great Depression. He was a conservative Republican, opposed to economic intervention on the part of government in general and the New Deal in particular. He feared big government, especially government patronage, which he felt would inevitably become corrupt. He defended Herbert Hoover's policies and campaigned against Franklin D. Roosevelt in 1940. His own solution to the Depression was more private investment in science; he contended that more science would result in new technologies, industries, and jobs. Consistent with his attitudes toward the public purse, Millikan was a strong opponent of the post-World War II efforts to establish the National Science Foundation. He argued that funding of science by the federal government was legitimate only if the ultimate purpose was national defense. Any other purpose would politicize the funding process, leading to patronage, pork barrel grants, and government control over scientific activities. Millikan's views placed him in the minority among scientists in the years just after the war.

During the last two decades of Millikan's life, his views on social issues and policies regarding the patronage of scientific research became increasingly unpopular. He was symbolic of a bygone era in American society and science. His revised theories regarding the nature of the cosmic rays had been rejected. Nevertheless, he remained an honored member of the American scientific community, respected for his Nobel Prize-winning research and his contributions to the development of American physics during the first third of the twentieth century.

Sadly, a new image of Millikan arose in the 1970's and early 1980's. His name was linked to fraud with respect to the very experiments that had led to his Nobel Prize. He was accused of ignoring the ethics of science to further his career. Claims were made that personal ambition, not the search for truth, was Millikan's driving force. When confronted with Ehrenhaft's counterinterpretation of his data, Millikan had published another series of experiments which confirmed the unit charge of the electron. What made these results so convincing was Millikan's claim that he was providing the data from "all the drops experimented upon during 60 consecutive days." The consistency of the data was overwhelming. In contrast, Ehrenhaft's repetition of Millikan's experiments showed scattered data. Prevailing theory supported Millikan's work, and the Nobel Prize was the public acknowledgment of that support. Millikan, however, had lied. Not all the data from the sixty-day period were included in his published paper. Reexamination of his laboratory notebooks reveals that he had published only some of the experiments, choosing only those raw observations which confirmed his position. Data not in agreement were rejected, with such explanations as "very low, something wrong."

It may be overly critical to label Millikan's actions fraudulous; it is perhaps more accurate to say that Millikan was a skilled self-deceiver. His *Autobiography* (1950) is filled with omissions, revisions of historical events, and errors. Perhaps his flaw was the inability to admit to a scientific mistake.

## Bibliography

*Primary*
PHYSICS: *Mechanics, Molecular Physics, and Heat: A Twelve Weeks' College Course*, 1902; *A First Course in Physics*, 1906 (with Henry Gordon Gale); *A Laboratory Course in Physics for Secondary Schools*, 1906 (with Gale); *A Short University Course in Electricity, Sound and Light*, 1908 (with John Mills); *Practical Lessons in Electricity*, 1914 (with Francis Bacon Crocker and Mills); *Elements of Electricity*, 1917 (with Edwin Sherwood Bishop); *The Electron, Its Isolation and Measurement and the Determination of Some of Its Properties*, 1917; *Electrons (+ and −), Protons, Photons, Neutrons and Cosmic Rays*, 1935; *Cosmic Rays: Three Lectures*, 1939.
OTHER NONFICTION: *Science and Life*, 1924; *Evolution in Science and Religion*, 1927; *Science and the New Civilization*, 1930; *Time, Matter, and Values*, 1932; *Autobiography*, 1950.

*Secondary*
Broad, William, and Nicholas Wade. *Betrayers of the Truth: Fraud and Deceit in the Halls of Science*. New York: Simon & Schuster, 1982. Millikan appears briefly as an example of a scientist misrepresenting and misreporting his results in order to vanquish a scientific competitor and obtain personal glory. He is the only Nobel Prize winner accused of fraud. The authors depend on the publications of Franklin and Holton (see below) for their information.

Du Bridge, Lee A., and Paul S. Epstein. "Robert Andrews Millikan." *Biographical Memoirs. National Academy of Sciences* 33 (1959): 241-282. The biographical information is borrowed from Millikan's *Autobiography*, but there is a valuable appreciation of Millikan's scientific endeavors by Epstein and a fairly extensive bibliography of Millikan's scientific publications and his textbooks and monographs. Not included in the bibliography are Millikan's popular magazine articles.

Franklin, Allan D. "Millikan's Published and Unpublished Data on Oil Drops." *Historical Studies in the Physical Sciences* 11 (1981): 185-201. The article was written after Holton's article (see below) raised the possibility that Millikan had manipulated his data to support his theoretical presuppositions. Franklin recomputes Millikan's data and determines what the results would have been if all the oil drops had indeed been included.

Holton, Gerald. "Subelectrons, Presuppositions, and the Millikan-Ehrenhaft Dispute." *Historical Studies in the Physical Sciences* 9 (1978): 161-224. The article that revealed that Millikan was not forthright in his treatment of his data. It provides a detailed analysis of the context of Millikan's and Ehrenhaft's experiments.

Kargon, Robert H. *The Rise of Robert Millikan: Portrait of a Life in American Science*. Ithaca, N.Y.: Cornell University Press, 1982. This source is not a biography but a highly selective portrait of major themes in Millikan's life. Kargon views Millikan as a conservative scientist caught up in revolutionary times and provides an excellent description of Millikan as an institution builder.

Kevles, Daniel J. "Millikan: Spokesman for Science in the Twenties." *Engineering and Science* 33 (April, 1969): 17-22. A study of Millikan's efforts to raise funds for scientific research from members of the business community.

——————. *The Physicists: The History of a Scientific Community in Modern America*. New York: Alfred A. Knopf, 1977. This book, a standard history of American physics, focuses on issues of patronage and the distribution of research funds and provides a clear picture of Millikan's status, power, and position. It contains a very useful bibliography.

*Marc Rothenberg*

# 1924

### Physics
Karl Manne Georg Siegbahn, Sweden

### Chemistry
no award

### Physiology or Medicine
Willem Einthoven, Netherlands

### Literature
Władysław Reymont, Poland

### Peace
no award

# KARL MANNE GEORG SIEGBAHN
## 1924

*Born:* Örebro, Sweden; December 3, 1886
*Died:* Stockholm, Sweden; September 26, 1978
*Nationality:* Swedish
*Area of concentration:* X-ray spectroscopy

*Siegbahn's investigation of the manner in which X rays are reflected and dif-fracted from crystals, and his development of extremely sensitive and precise in-struments and methods for pursuing these studies, led to the discovery of the M and N series of X rays and the consequent elucidation of the inner energy-level structure of atoms*

## The Award

*Presentation*

Professor A. Gullstrand, Chairman of the Nobel Committee for Physics, pre-sented the Nobel Prize in Physics for 1924 to Karl Manne Georg Siegbahn on De-cember 10, 1925, on behalf of the Royal Swedish Academy of Sciences and King Gustav V, from whom Siegbahn accepted the prize. Gullstrand's presentation speech, delivered in Swedish, reviewed the manner in which X-ray spectroscopy had been developed by Siegbahn's predecessors and then advanced to new heights by Siegbahn and his coworkers. Gullstrand said that even though X rays had been distinguishable only by their penetrating power, Charles Glover Barkla had been able to discover the K and L series of X rays by observing that heavier elements produce X rays of more penetrating power than lighter ones but that at a certain point in the periodic table, less penetrating rays are produced which again become more penetrating as heavier elements are tested.

Real progress in understanding X rays, however, awaited the revelations of Max von Laue, William Henry Bragg, and William Lawrence Bragg, who demonstrated X rays' wave nature by passing them through crystals and observing the resultant reflection and diffraction patterns. With this new tool of X-ray spectroscopy, Henry Moseley proceeded to relate the X rays produced by each different element to its atomic number, or its position in the periodic table, thereby suggesting that X-ray spectroscopy would be a powerful tool in the determination of atomic structure.

It was at this point that Siegbahn began his series of remarkably sensitive and accurate measurements of the characteristic X-ray spectra of numerous elements. These new data, coupled with the theoretical concepts of atomic structure proposed by Ernest Rutherford and Niels Bohr, provided the key to early attempts to under-stand the structure of the atom, one of mankind's oldest puzzles.

*Nobel lecture*

Siegbahn's Nobel lecture, entitled "The X-Ray Spectra and the Structure of the

Atoms," was devoted primarily to an elucidation of the way in which X rays had been used to determine the internal structure of atoms. Although Siegbahn made references to the many applications of X rays in medicine and other fields of science, he focused almost exclusively on the value of X rays as exploratory tools in the ongoing study of atomic structure. Pursuant to this goal, he noted that—unlike optical spectra, whose complexity of pattern is often completely overwhelming—X-ray spectra are generally simple enough and similar enough that quite clear inferences can be drawn from them.

Before outlining his results, however, Siegbahn reviewed the concepts and terminology used by workers in the field. Using Albert Einstein and Niels Bohr's formula, he showed how the atomic energy levels are related to the X-ray frequencies, which, in turn, are determined by the X-ray wavelengths. Thus, by measuring the observed wavelengths, one can establish a pattern of energy levels which gives an idea of how the electrons are arranged in the atom. This procedure, he pointed out, was common to both optical and X-ray investigations.

Siegbahn noted that, although both optical and X-ray spectra point to several distinct series of energy levels, the X-ray spectra show a common pattern for all the elements, whereas the optical spectra show these regularities for the alkaline elements only. With this observation as a guide, he said, he had drawn the inference that the inner regions of all atoms, which give rise to X rays, must be structurally similar to the outer regions of the alkaline elements. (Atoms' outer regions give rise to optical spectra.) The picture that fitted best, which was based on the model suggested by Niels Bohr for hydrogen, was one of electrons in "shells" of specified energy surrounding a central nucleus. The number of electrons, Siegbahn had found, increased from two in the first (complete) shell, to eight in the second (complete) shell, to eighteen in the third, and so on. Since the absolute energy values could be determined for some of the levels, it was possible to obtain a virtually complete picture of the energy states of the majority of the elements. The results from X-ray spectroscopy had been found to be in good agreement with the results from other fields of investigation.

In closing, Siegbahn pointed out that the work of X-ray spectroscopy was far from over. After referring briefly to some projected studies on how the phenomenon of X radiation is affected by the chemical properties of atoms, he gave a report on the investigations that he and his colleagues had been making in trying to understand certain discrepancies in the Bragg law for X-ray reflection. Noting that he and several others had obtained results indicating that X rays undergo refraction when they pass through various crystals, he suggested that the anomalies obtained in these studies should be pursued with great vigor, for it was in the study of similar phenomena in the field of ordinary optics that much light had been shed on the mechanism of radiation itself.

*Critical reception*

Siegbahn was awarded the 1924 Nobel Prize in Physics in 1925. The statutes of the Nobel Institute provide that, if there is no occasion to award a particular prize in any given year, the prize shall be reserved for award in the following year. This aspect of the 1924 award seems to have been of more interest to the press than Siegbahn's qualifications to receive it.

*The Times* of London for November 14, 1925, devoted almost its entire article to a discussion of the various provisions that control the awarding and nonawarding of the prizes. It pointed out that the 1925 awards for both chemistry and physics had been reserved for the following year and that the 1924 chemistry prize was being assigned to the Nobel Institute's reserve fund rather than being awarded to anyone. It did applaud Siegbahn's "remarkable work in spectrum analysis."

The British journal *Nature*, in its issue of November 21, echoed *The Times'* coverage, but it did add a rather extensive discussion of Siegbahn's accomplishments in X-ray spectroscopy. Noting that Alfred Nobel's primary intent had been to reward outstanding experimental work in science, it stressed that aspect of Siegbahn's work, pointing particularly to the six-significant-figure accuracy of Siegbahn's measurements, his investigations of the long-wavelength radiation in the region between normal X rays and ultraviolet rays, and his identification of three new elements. The article did not, however, ignore the theoretical value of Siegbahn's studies; it stressed theory's importance in determining the energy levels and electronic structure of atoms and molecules.

*Science* (November 27) devoted its entire coverage of the Nobel Prizes to a discussion of the reserved prizes. It stressed that the board of directors had made an unprecedented decision to withhold all five prizes for 1925, partly because of the lack of qualified candidates and partly because of the need for funds for the Nobel Library and the Physical and Chemical Institute. It went on to say that the heavy tax burden in Sweden was threatening the very existence of the Nobel Prizes and that efforts were under way to have the Nobel Foundation exempt from taxation. Almost as an afterthought, the article mentioned that Siegbahn had been awarded the 1924 physics prize for his "important discoveries in the X-ray spectra of the elementary substances."

*The New York Times* devoted several articles to the Nobel Prizes. Its coverage in the issues of November 3, 13, 18, and 19 concentrated on the nonawarding of the prizes and included a discussion of the controversy it had raised in the Swedish press; one writer had called the situation a "scandal and unworthy of the culture of such a nation as Sweden." The newspaper did mention, in a three-line article in its November 13 issue, that the 1924 physics prize had been awarded to Siegbahn, but it mistakenly labeled him a professor of physics at Lund University. (Siegbahn was a professor at the University of Uppsala.) A correction appeared in the November 18 issue.

*Time* magazine, on November 30, gave the most extensive coverage in the popular press. Its article dealt with Alfred Nobel himself, the Nobel family, the regulations surrounding the awarding of the prizes, notable past winners of the prizes, and the dissatisfaction of the Swedish press regarding the reservation of the prizes for 1925.

The one thing the article did not mention was that Siegbahn had been awarded the physics prize for 1924.

Probably the most informative coverage of the topic was provided by *Scientific Monthly* is its issue of January, 1926. Including a full-page picture of Siegbahn in his laboratory at Uppsala, it discussed the technical merit of Siegbahn's work and its place in the history of spectroscopy and the determination of atomic structure. It also reviewed Nobel's work, the establishment of his prizes, and the nonawarding of the prizes for 1925.

### Biography

Karl Manne Georg Siegbahn was born in Örebro, Sweden, on December 3, 1886, the son of Nils Reinhold Georg Siegbahn, a stationmaster of the State Railways, and Emma Sofia Mathilda Zetterberg. In 1906 he matriculated at the University of Lund, where he immediately began the study of physics, serving as clerk in the physics institute there. In 1908 he received his bachelor's degree, and in 1910 he was appointed as an assistant at the physics institute and received his master's degree. In 1911 he completed his thesis on magnetic field measurements and received his doctor's degree; he was then appointed as a lecturer in physics under Janne Rydberg. In 1915, Siegbahn became a deputy professor of physics under Rydberg, and he became a professor on Rydberg's death in 1920.

Although all of his degrees came from the University of Lund, Siegbahn had studied abroad during several summers: at the University of Göttingen in 1908, at the University of Munich in 1909, and in Paris and Berlin in 1911. In 1914 he wed Karin Hogbom; they had two sons, one of whom, Kai, eventually came to hold the same professorship that his father was to hold at the University of Uppsala and to win a Nobel Prize in Physics in 1981, raising to six the number of children to follow a parent in winning a Nobel Prize.

Although Siegbahn was well established and had developed an international reputation at Lund, the advantages of a superior laboratory and enhanced research opportunities lured him to the University of Uppsala in 1923, where he remained as a professor of physics until 1937. In 1924-1925, Siegbahn made an extensive tour of the United States and Canada, where he lectured and exchanged ideas with colleagues at such universities as Columbia, Yale, Harvard, Cornell, Chicago, the University of California at Berkeley, and the California Institute of Technology in Pasadena. In 1937 the Nobel laureate was offered an appointment to a position newly created by the Nobel Institute and the Swedish government: Research Professor of Experimental Physics at the Royal Swedish Academy of Sciences. In the same year, he became the first director of the physics department of the Nobel Institute, retiring in 1964. From 1937 to 1956, he was a member of the International Commission on Weights and Measures. He was president of the International Union of Pure and Applied Physics from 1938 to 1947.

Besides the Nobel Prize, Siegbahn received the Hughes Medal (1934) and the Rumford Medal (1940) from the Royal Society of London; was made a member of the Royal Society of London, the Royal Society of Edinburgh, the Académie des Sciences, Paris, and the Soviet Academy of Sciences; and received numerous honorary degrees.

## Scientific Career

Although Siegbahn's career was long and varied, his primary contributions can be grouped under two main headings: advances in X-ray spectroscopy and the development of world-class research institutions in Sweden. He was both a master experimenter and a master organizer of cooperative experimental efforts. He was a brilliant designer, builder, and interpreter of intricate, subtle, and important experiments, and he was able to transmit this ability to the many people who gathered around him. His productive career spanned almost seven decades, from his earliest publication in 1908 until his last efforts in the 1970's.

Siegbahn's earliest work, performed while he was still a student at the University of Lund, was in the area of electricity and magnetism, where he concentrated on instruments useful in the study of variable currents and magnetic fields. His doctoral thesis, completed in 1911, was on the subject of magnetic field measurements. For the next three years, he continued to focus on electrical measurements and associated instruments, publishing more than a dozen papers in this area. In 1914 he published his first paper on X-ray spectroscopy, the topic which was to dominate his work for the next three decades and beyond.

The field of X-ray spectroscopy was very young when Siegbahn became involved in it. Although Wilhelm Conrad Röntgen had discovered X rays in 1895, it was not until 1912 that Walter Friedrich, Paul Knipping, and Max von Laue showed, by means of diffraction in a crystal, that X rays are electromagnetic rays, similar to light rays but of a shorter wavelength. Later that same year, William Henry Bragg and William Lawrence Bragg, father and son, showed that the angles at which X rays are reflected from the surfaces of crystals are directly related to the X-ray wavelengths by a very simple formula, thereby making possible the use of crystals for measuring X-ray wavelengths (as in the X-ray spectrometer). It was this development that provided the direction for the remainder of Siegbahn's career.

Siegbahn, however, was not the first to investigate the possibilities of X-ray spectroscopy. A young Englishman, Henry Moseley, preceded him; in fact, the work that Moseley produced in the years 1912-1914, before his untimely death on the battlefield in World War I, was in a sense a model for what Siegbahn was to accomplish later with much greater precision and a much broader scope. It seems certain that, had Moseley lived, he would also have been recognized with a Nobel Prize for his work in X-ray spectroscopy.

The scheme behind X-ray spectroscopy is as follows. A beam of X rays is created when electrons are accelerated by a high voltage across a vacuum tube and come crashing into a metal target called the "anticathode." The X rays produced, which are characteristic of the metal target, are then directed onto a crystal surface, where they are reflected at particular angles according to the Bragg relationship. The angles at which the X rays emerge are determined by the interatomic spacing of the crystal; they are measured by the direction from which the X rays strike the detector, usually a photographic plate. The wavelengths are then determined from the Bragg relationship. The accurate determination of these angles constitutes the principal challenge of spectrometry.

Moseley, during his brief career, had startled the scientific community by showing that the X-ray wavelengths obtained from the various chemical elements could be neatly arranged in certain patterns which, he argued, could be related in a very direct manner to the atomic number (the numbered space on the periodic table) of each of the elements. Discussing this information with Niels Bohr—who had just proposed his "planetary" model of the atom, in which electrons are seen as circling around a central, massive, and highly charged nucleus—Moseley came to the conclusion that the atomic number of each element was not only its place-number on the periodic table but also the number of positive charges on its central nucleus. This idea gave new significance to the arrangement of the elements in the periodic table and suggested that X-ray spectroscopy could help to unlock the secrets of atomic structure.

Siegbahn took over where Moseley had left off. Involving his students at Lund, he designed and produced X-ray tubes, crystal spectrographs, and high-vacuum systems which enabled him to improve the precision of X-ray spectroscopy a thousandfold. With this new instruments and techniques, Siegbahn not only extended Moseley's results to nearly all the chemical elements but also found new phenomena. Moseley had investigated only two series of characteristic X rays, the K and L series; Siegbahn found two more, labeling them "M" and "N." He found that, while the K series consists of a single wavelength for each element, the L series consists of three, and the M series five, closely spaced wavelengths. This detailed knowledge of the X-ray wavelengths, translated into energy levels for the appropriate electron shells, was instrumental in clarifying the ideas that later became basic to the emerging quantum mechanics of Werner Heisenberg, Erwin Schrödinger, and Paul Adrien Maurice Dirac.

On Janne Rydberg's death in 1920, Siegbahn was appointed as a professor of physics at Lund; the promotion, however, did not change the nature of his work. He and his students continued to improve and extend their X-ray investigations, establishing new standards of precision and accuracy. Siegbahn also visited laboratories in other countries, sharing his results and learning from other investigators. In 1921, he participated in the Solvay Congress in Brussels, where fundamental questions of the nature of radiation and atomic structure were discussed by leading members of the physics community from all over the world.

In 1923, Siegbahn left Lund for the University of Uppsala, where a new and modern physics institute promised even more successful research. Further improvements to his spectrometers enabled him to increase the intensity and precision of the X rays produced, resulting in the discovery of additional detail in the X-ray spectra and the extension of his investigations to other materials. In 1924, he and his coworkers were able to demonstrate a long-sought phenomenon: the refraction of X rays. That was the last major hurdle in showing that X rays do indeed exhibit all the properties of light and other electromagnetic radiations. The extreme precision of this work revealed that slight modifications of the Bragg equation were required under certain conditions; these adjustments showed that there is an anomalous dispersion for X rays, just as there is for ordinary light.

Another area of investigation involved the use of ruled gratings rather than the interatomic spacing of crystals to produce X-ray spectra. Once again Siegbahn's skill in designing and producing equipment was evident, for his ruling engine (the device used to produce the gratings) was unusually accurate. Since ruled gratings do not depend on any unknown distances, such as interatomic spacings, the absolute determinations of wavelength that were obtained led to a modification of several fundamental physical constants, such as the charge on the electron. In addition, the use of gratings made it possible to extend the X-ray investigations into the extremely long wavelength region, thus providing an overlap with the heretofore separate region of ultraviolet radiation. With the same equipment, yet another series of X-ray wavelengths, the O series (beyond the M and N series) was found.

When, in 1936, the Nobel Foundation decided to fund a research institute for experimental physics, to be created in Stockholm by the Swedish Academy of Sciences, Siegbahn was named its first director, taking office in 1937. His final year at Uppsala was thus crowded with his ongoing investigations in X-ray spectroscopy at Uppsala and planning for the new institute in Stockholm. Although Siegbahn made plans to continue with his first love, X-ray spectroscopy, at the new institute, he realized that other areas of research had to be included as well if Sweden were to keep abreast of current developments in physics. Nuclear physics, beta-ray spectroscopy, and electron microscopy were only a few of the areas to be developed, and Siegbahn was actively involved in providing for their inclusion. Later, he also saw the need to include theoretical physicists, engineers, radiation physicists, radiation biologists, and others to complete the institute's research programs.

Although many of Siegbahn's accomplishments were results of his own genius and effort, much of his work was done in collaboration with others. He attracted many promising students to both Lund and Uppsala and seasoned colleagues to the Nobel Institute. Not only did he make numerous trips abroad to share his results with, and to learn from, others, but he received many visitors from abroad as well. Before and during World War II, he welcomed numerous refugee scientists who had fled from persecution in Europe, providing at the same time a means of keeping the research at his Institute fully activated. After the war, Siegbahn continued to provide active leadership in the many areas of physics he had initiated, working closely with the various specialists who had been assembled at the Institute. Although he officially relinquished his directorship in 1964 at the age of seventy-eight, he continued to maintain close ties with both the people and the projects long afterward.

Siegbahn's publications are numerous, reflecting both the intensity and range of his interests and the length of his career. Although most of his more than one hundred journal articles deal with his particular speciality, X-ray spectroscopy, he published some twenty papers on other topics, including electrical and magnetic measurements and measuring devices, ruling engines, vacuum pumps, and the lives of other physicists. Probably his most influential work, *Spektroskopie der Röntgenstrahlen* (1924) was a detailed exposition of all facets of the science of X-ray spectroscopy; it was translated into English (as *The Spectroscopy of X Rays*) in 1925, and it appeared in a second, updated and enlarged edition in 1931. Another influential, and less technical, publication was his article on X-ray spectroscopy for the 1929 *Encyclopædia Britannica*, which appeared in that and all subsequent editions up to 1973.

## Bibliography

*Primary*

PHYSICS: *Spektroskopie der Röntgenstrahlen*, 1924 (*The Spectroscopy of X-Rays*, 1925); "Spectroscopy, X-Ray," in *Encyclopædia Britannica*, 14th ed., 1929; "Messung langer Röntgenstrahlen mit optischen Gittern," in F. Hund and F. Trendelenburg, eds., *Ergebnisse der exakten Naturwissenschaften*, vol. 16, 1937.

EDITED TEXT: *Untersuchungen über die Beschaffenheit der Emissionsspektren der chemischen Elemente*, 1922.

*Secondary*

Edlén, Bengt. "Manne Siegbahn, 1886-1978." *Nature* 277 (January 25, 1979): 333. This obituary notice, by one of Siegbahn's colleagues, is a brief but comprehensive overview of Seigbahn's entire career. As such, it reviews both his work in X-ray spectroscopy and his later involvement in nuclear physics at the Nobel Institute, pointing out the role this latter work played in bringing Swedish science up to date in post-World War II research. It contains a photograph of Siegbahn in middle age.

Heathcote, Niels Hugh de Vaudrey. *Nobel Prize Winners in Physics, 1901-1950*. New York: Henry Schuman, 1953. Reprint. Freeport, N.Y.: Books for Libraries Press, 1971. This work includes a concise biographical sketch of each of the prizewinners, a description of the prizewinning work in both the author's words and the words of the prizewinner himself, and an evaluation of the work in terms of its consequences in theory and practice. It contains pictures of the laureates and some diagrams.

Herzberg, Gerhard. "Manne Siegbahn." *Physics Today* 32 (February, 1979): 68. This obituary notice, which reviews Siegbahn's entire scientific career, examines his contributions to both the experimental and theoretical aspects of X-ray spectroscopy. It also discusses his great skills as an instrument maker and the large influence he had on the numerous students and foreign visitors who worked with him. It contains a picture of Siegbahn as a young man.

Jaffe, Bernard. *Moseley and the Numbering of the Elements*. Garden City, N.Y.: Doubleday, 1971. Although, as the title indicates, this book is not primarily about

Siegbahn, it may be the most readable discussion of the type of work for which Siegbahn won the Nobel Prize. It is one volume in the Science Study Series and, as such, is accessible to both the student and the layperson. It contains numerous diagrams and several photographs of people and equipment.

Magnusson, Torsten. "Manne Siegbahn." In *Swedish Men of Science, 1650-1950*, edited by Sten Lindroth. Stockholm: Swedish Institute, 1952. This article, by one of Siegbahn's colleagues, is the most detailed discussion of Siegbahn's career and character available. Besides providing information about Siegbahn's scientific work, it gives a firsthand view of Siegbahn's relationships with his many co-workers.

Wasson, Tyler, ed. *Nobel Prize Winners*. New York: H. W. Wilson, 1987. As the title indicates, this book is a compilation of articles on the Nobel Prize winners through 1987. The two-and-one-half-page article on Siegbahn is an excellent review of his work on X rays and the work on which he built. It also includes some biographical information on Siegbahn, a list of his major honors and awards, and a picture of him in middle age.

*Richard K. Gehrenbeck*

# 1925

### Physics
James Franck, Germany
Gustav Hertz, Germany

### Chemistry
Richard Zsigmondy, Austria

### Physiology or Medicine
no award

### Literature
George Bernard Shaw, Great Britain

### Peace
Sir Austen Chamberlain, Great Britain
Charles G. Dawes, United States

# JAMES FRANCK
## 1925

*Born:* Hamburg, Germany; August 26, 1882
*Died:* Göttingen, West Germany; May 21, 1964
*Nationality:* German
*Areas of concentration:* Atomic and molecular physics

*Franck, along with his coworker Gustav Hertz, discovered by careful experimentation how an electron behaves when it strikes an atom. In particular, they verified the revolutionary concept that the energy of the atom is quantized*

## The Award

*Presentation*

In ceremonies held in December of 1926, Professor C. W. Oseen, a member of the Nobel Committee for Physics of the Royal Swedish Academy of Sciences, announced that the 1925 Nobel Prize in Physics was awarded jointly to James Franck and Gustav Hertz. They received their prizes from the hands of King Gustav V.

In his remarks before the presentation of the prizes, Oseen credited Niels Bohr (1885-1962) with the founding in 1913 of the new science of atomic physics. He explained that for a generation, scientists had studied spectra emitted by atoms. (A rainbow is an example of a spectrum. Atomic spectra usually have only some of the colors of the rainbow and are dark where colors are missing.) Scientists had been able to find mathematical relationships between the various colors of light emitted by particular kinds of atoms but had been unable to discover why the atoms emitted light in that fashion. Bohr made the revolutionary assumption that the atom could exist only in certain states called "stationary states." Here, "stationary" does not mean that the atom or its parts are at rest but that certain properties of the atom, such as its energy, remain fixed. Bohr further supposed that an electron could change from one stationary state to another if the electron gave off light of the color corresponding to the difference in energy between the two states.

Oseen said that the experiments of Franck and Hertz had shown Bohr's assumptions to be basically correct. Oseen further concluded that Franck and Hertz had evolved the theory of collisions of electrons with atoms to a point where it could be used as a tool to study the structure of atoms and the even more complex structure of molecules.

*Nobel lecture*

On December 11, 1925, Franck began his lecture, titled "Transformations of Kinetic Energy of Free Electrons into Excitation Energy of Atoms by Impacts," with an explanation of how he and Hertz would divide their report. Franck was to present their work in a historical setting, while Hertz would follow with a discussion of the significance of their work for Bohr's theory of the atom.

Franck noted that it had been his teacher, Emil Warburg (1846-1931), a leading expert in the field of gas discharges in rarefied gases, who had first interested him in the subject. Franck also acknowledged the work of others who had laid the foundation on which he had built. Among them, he cited Sir Joseph John Thomson (1856-1940), who is credited with the discovery of the electron; Sir John Townsend (1868-1957), who studied the movement of electrons and ions through gases; and Philipp Lenard (1862-1947), who analyzed the photoelectric effect, in which light incident on certain metals causes the metals to emit electrons.

One of the experimental devices used by Franck and Hertz was a glass tube resembling a complex light bulb with several wires inside. At one side of the tube was a hot, glowing wire—the filament. Some electrons would actually "boil off" and form a cloud around the filament. A small piece of wire screen was placed a few centimeters from the filament. If the positive terminal of a battery were connected to the screen and the battery's negative terminal to the filament, electrons would be pulled from the cloud toward the positively charged screen. Placing a metal plate beyond the screen caused many of the electrons to pass through the holes in the screen and strike the plate. If the plate were then connected to a meter which measured electrical current, the number of electrons striking the plate could be counted.

In a particularly important experiment, Franck and Hertz introduced mercury vapor into the glass tube. The vapor was at low pressure so that electrons without much energy could flow through it. By adjusting the voltages on the wire screen and metal plate, they were able to measure the energy of the electrons. Surprisingly, they discovered that low-energy electrons passed through the mercury vapor with practically no energy loss, even though they must have struck many mercury atoms. This behavior continued as the physicists increased the electron's energy by increasing the voltage between the filament and screen. The situation suddenly changed, however, when the power reached 4.9 volts. The electrons collected at the plate now had almost no energy. If the voltage were raised higher, the electrons again arrived at the plate with more and more energy. At twice 4.9 volts, the electron energy again dropped suddenly to near zero.

As Franck remarked in his Nobel lecture, the conclusion seemed inescapable: mercury atoms could receive energy from the impacting electrons only in certain amounts. This energy, they realized, must correspond to the energy difference between two of Bohr's proposed stationary states for the mercury atom. These findings were the first experimental proof that Bohr's revolutionary proposals were correct. As Franck explained, the proof was completed by showing that after the mercury vapor atoms were excited by the electrons, the atoms emitted ultraviolet light with a single frequency. This frequency corresponded exactly to the energy of a 4.9-volt electron.

## Critical reception

The popular press barely noted Franck's receipt of the Nobel Prize; the scientific press, however, acknowledged his work to be historic and of fundamental importance. There was no great discussion of the significance of his work, simply because its significance had been accepted years before.

*The New York Times* carried a brief notice announcing the names of the scientific award recipients, including Franck, on November 12, 1926. A month later, on December 11, the paper carried an article about the presentation ceremony. It reported that two thousand persons had attended the ceremony honoring the Nobel recipients of the physics, chemistry, and literature awards. It also noted that the prize was worth about $32,000, but it provided neither a technical description nor a critique of the scientific work. In Franck's case, this reaction was hardly surprising, given the esoteric nature of his experiments.

Watson Davis, the science editor of *Current History*, described Franck and Hertz's work in an announcement of the physics and chemistry awards. He called their work "the first proof of the validity of quantum theory." He also referred to the paper in which some of their work had been presented before the Berlin Physical Society in 1912. In *The Scientific Monthly*, E. E. Slosson wrote a column titled "The Progress of Science." Slosson listed the five "men of science" who had just received Nobel prizes and noted the dominance of Germans, who received as many awards in physics and chemistry in 1926 as Americans had during the twenty-five-year history of the awards. Like Davis, Slosson cited Franck and Hertz's work as "the first proof of the validity of the quantum theory." He then added that after the 1912 Berlin paper had been presented, "Professor Fritz Haber, greatest of the German chemists, is said to have remarked that 'this paper will be fundamental in the progress of physics,' a prediction which has been amply fulfilled."

## Biography

James Franck was born August 26, 1882, in Hamburg, Germany. He was the son of Jacob Franck, a banker, and Rebecca Franck. As a teenager, he attended the Wilhelm Gymnasium, a very demanding college preparatory school. Because of his habit of shutting out the rest of the world while absorbed in a problem, he gained a reputation as a daydreamer. For example, a grease spot on the page of his Greek textbook once captured his attention during class. He puzzled over why the grease made the paper transparent, oblivious to the classroom instruction being conducted around him. His exasperated teacher, like Albert Einstein's, supposed that Franck would never amount to much.

Franck did manage to earn his diploma and was sent to college in Heidelberg to prepare for the family business by studing law and economics. His studies only proved to him that he greatly preferred science. With the encouragement of friends such as Max Born (1882-1970), he persuaded his parents to allow him to study physics. (His parents had opposed him at first because they considered the occupation of scientist menial.) After a year at the University of Heidelberg, he transferred in 1902 to the University of Berlin, the center of physics in Germany. Franck found the atmosphere there tremendously stimulating. He met many of the world's greatest physicists, among them Max Planck (1858-1947) and Einstein (1879-1955), who visited the university. After receiving his Ph.D. in 1906, Franck was immediately appointed to the research staff.

He wed Ingrid Josephson, a Swedish pianist, in 1911. They had two daughters, Dagmar and Lisa. Ingrid died in 1942, and four years later, he married Hertha Sponer, a former coworker.

### Scientific Career

Franck's major professor at the University of Berlin suggested that for his thesis Franck study corona discharge, or the mechanism by which electric fields cause gas to glow. Franck quickly discovered that this type of discharge was complex. He decided that he first needed to study more elementary processes: How do electrons flow through gases? What happens when an electron hits an atom? Does it make a difference if the electron travels quickly or slowly? Over the next several years, Franck devised various experiments to answer these questions.

It was an exciting time to be a physicist, for atomic physics was being born. In 1913, Niels Bohr proposed a new model of the atom. His model, like others, assumed that electrons orbited the nucleus, but he had invented a completely new set of rules to govern the action of the electron. The old theories stated that the electron should radiate energy as it circled the nucleus. Bohr, in contrast, said that the electron does not radiate if it is in a "stationary state." In a stationary state, the values of such things as energy and spin are fixed. Furthermore, electrons can only be in stationary states. If an electron goes from one such state to another, it must emit a quantum (from the Latin for "quantity") of light. This light quantum must have exactly the same energy as the difference in energy between the two stationary states.

Borrowing from Planck's work on heat radiation and Einstein's work on the photoelectric effect, Bohr related the energy of a light quantum, which is now called a photon, with the color of the light. He then showed that the spectra (bands of various colors of light) emitted by hot, glowing atoms could be explained by his theory. It was not clear, however, whether the Bohr model was simply a mathematical tool or whether it represented reality.

By 1914, Franck and Gustav Hertz had become experts on electron collisions with atoms. As explained above, they had found that electrons colliding with mercury vapor atoms could lose energy only in amounts corresponding to 4.9 volts. They concluded, therefore, that Bohr's stationary states must be real and that the first excited state of mercury must be about 4.9 electron volts above the ground state. To complete the experiment, Franck and Hertz measured the energy of the light emitted by the excited mercury atoms; it measured 4.9 electron volts, as predicted by Bohr's theory. Their work made it obvious that Bohr's model of the atom was more correct than any other model.

After an interruption of two years for military service, Franck returned to the University of Berlin. In 1916 he was made an assistant professor, and in 1918, an associate professor. He served as the head of the physical chemistry section of the Kaiser Wilhelm Institute from 1917 to 1921. He first met Bohr during this time.

Continuing his earlier research, Franck and his coworkers studied some particularly long-lived excited states, which they named "metastable states." In 1921, Franck became a professor of experimental physics at the University of Göttingen.

In continuing his research, Franck examined the reverse of the case described in his Nobel lecture, or the case in which an electron strikes an atom which is already in an excited state. He found that the atom could give up its excitation energy directly to the electron, causing it to move off at a higher speed. In 1925, he formulated a guideline to determine which excited states of a molecule were likely to occur. This formula was later expanded by Edward Uhler Condon (1902-1974), one of the Göttingen students, and is now known as the "Franck-Condon principle." Having often studied the light emitted by excited atoms and molecules, Franck next turned his attention to the light they absorbed, which, in turn, led him to study photosynthesis, a study that he would continue to the end of his life.

Another important experimental technique developed by Franck was the accurate determination of how much energy is required to separate the atoms of a molecule completely. He was able to relate certain features of the spectrum emitted by a molecule to this energy. This separation energy is called the "binding energy" and is an important clue to understanding the force which holds a molecule together.

A high point of the time spent at Göttingen was the announcement of Franck's Nobel Prize in 1926. In 1933, this fruitful period of his career came to an abrupt end. The Nazi Party had come to power, and, on April 7, 1926, they announced "The Law for the Restoration of the Professional Civil Service." It stated that non-Aryan persons were not to hold civil service positions. Since German universities were state-supported, their faculties, including the research students, were classified as civil servants. One-fourth of the physics faculties in Germany were Jewish. Although Jewish himself, Franck was exempted from the order because of his meritorious service in World War I. As director of his division, however, Franck was called upon to dismiss Jewish faculty members and students. Outraged, Franck refused. In a quandary about the best course to pursue, Franck visited with Bohr. Bohr insisted that the political actions of societies were ultimately the responsibilities of individuals.

Franck resigned his university position in protest on April 17, 1933. He wrote a public letter to the newspapers detailing his reasons. In turn, thirty-three members of the Göttingen faculty wrote a letter accusing Franck of sabotaging the new Germany. Seeing no future in remaining, Franck took his family to Copenhagen, where he worked with Bohr, and then on to the United States in 1935. Franck had delayed leaving Germany for a while in order to assist younger Jewish scientists; he used his friendships with scientists abroad to find positions for these German refugees. His good friend Max Born also left Germany at this time.

Once settled in the United States, Franck accepted a position at The Johns Hopkins University in Baltimore. Unfortunately, anti-Semitism there prompted him to leave. In 1938 he accepted a professorship of physical chemistry at the University of Chicago. The Samuel Fels Foundation had established a laboratory there for the investigation of photosynthesis. Franck became the director of this laboratory, a position he kept until his retirement in 1949. After he retired, he continued to work there part-time.

During World War II, Franck set aside his other duties and served as the head of the "Chicago Metallurgical Project," the code name for the chemical division of the atom bomb project. The scientists of the project worked quickly, fearing that German scientists would develop the atom bomb before they did. When Germany was defeated, Franck and his coworkers gave thought to how the bomb should be used and whether it should be used at all. Franck headed a committee which made its recommendations in what has come to be called the Franck Report. The report stated that there would be great pressure to use the bomb against the Japanese with the hope of bringing an early end to the war, thereby saving many lives. The committee feared that if this happened, a disastrous arms race between nations would result. Concerned about the moral issues involved and seeking a way to make their voices heard, Franck and others formed a group known as the Atomic Scientists of Chicago. One of their first successes was joining with similar organizations to block an attempt by the military to maintain a monopoly over the nuclear industry after World War II.

After the war, Franck returned to studying photosynthesis. He pioneered methods of preparing chloroplast solutions and of measuring their activity by very sensitive means. For several years, he was frustrated because biologists paid little attention to his results. Gradually, his theories of photosynthesis improved, and at the same time, biologists began to comprehend what he was accomplishing. In 1963, he had the great satisfaction of seeing the participants of a special conference on photosynthesis give serious attention to his ideas and a rousing ovation to him.

In addition to winning the Nobel Prize, Franck was awarded several honorary doctorates, the Max Planck Medal of the German Physical Society, the Rumford Medal of the American Academy of Arts and Sciences, and a Foreign Membership in the Royal Society of London.

In writing about Franck, a remarkable number of authors praise his character. "The great scientist with a conscience . . . a unique example of warmth, goodness, and modest greatness," says Eugene Rabinowitch, editor of the *Bulletin of the Atomic Scientists* and Franck's former coworker. His anonymous Nobel biographer praises his "courage in following what was morally right." Franck's biographer for the Royal Society says that he "loved jokes and could laugh heartily, but his humour was never caustic or at the expense of others." The two characteristics which stand out for Kuhn are Franck's "absolute, natural honesty, both intellectual and moral, and his profound human warmth and kindness."

In his later years, Franck took many trips to Göttingen to visit old friends. It was on one of these visits that he died. He was a remarkable individual, a perceptive scientist whose work was essential to the growth of scientific understanding of the structure of atoms and molecules and the basic processes involved in photography and photosynthesis. He was also a man of great kindness and moral courage.

# Bibliography
*Primary*

PHYSICS: "Über die Erregung der Quecksilberressonanzlinie 253.6μμ durch Electronenstösse," *Verhandlungen der physiologischen Gesellschaft zu Berlin*, vol. 16, 1914 (with Gustav Hertz); "Die Bestätigung der Bohr'schen Atomtheorie im optischen Spektrum durch Untersuchungen der unelastischen Zusammenstösse langsamer Elektronen mit Gasmolekulen," *Physikalische Zeitschrift*, vol. 20, 1919 (with Gustav Hertz); *Anregungen von Quantensprüngen durch Stösse*, 1926 (with Pascual Jordan); "Migration and Photochemical Action of Excitation Energy in Crystals," *Journal of Chemical Physics*, vol. 6, 1938 (with Edward Teller); "Franck Report," *Bulletin of the Atomic Scientists (of Chicago)*, vol. 1, no. 10, 1946 (with Jerome L. Rosenberg); "A Theory of Light Utilisation in Plant Photosynthesis," *Journal of Theoretical Biology*, vol. 7, no. 2, 1964.

*Secondary*

Abro, A. d'. *The Rise of the New Physics: Its Mathematical and Physical Theories.* 2 vols. New York: Dover, 1951. This book is similar to Segrè's book in subject matter, but it is significantly more technical. Those with a good background in science will find d'Abro's book to be a comprehensive summary of the rise of modern physics and of the place of the Franck-Hertz experiment in this history.

Born, Max. *My Life: Recollections of a Nobel Laureate.* Philadelphia: Taylor and Francis, 1978. This book is by one of Franck's closest friends and coworkers. It contains numerous references to Franck and describes the world as Born and Franck encountered it. It is largely nontechnical and is easy to read.

Frisch, David H. "Scientists and the Decision to Bomb Japan." *Bulletin of the Atomic Scientists* 26, no. 6 (June, 1970): 107-115. This article contains a careful discussion of the Franck Report and of other efforts by scientists to influence how the bomb would be used. It lists some of the possibilities for a "demonstration bomb" and attempts to evaluate some of the associated problems.

Kuhn, H. G. "James Franck, 1882-1964." *Biographical Memoirs of Fellows of the Royal Society* 10 (1965): 53-74. This comprehensive article covers Franck's life and discusses his work in reasonably simple terms. Contains a complete bibliography (prepared by R. L. Platzman) of more than one hundred fifty articles by Franck. The later third, mostly about photosynthesis, are in English; the other articles are in German.

Segrè, Emilio. *From X-Rays to Quarks: Modern Physicists and Their Discoveries.* San Francisco: W. H. Freeman, 1985. This books is based on a lecture given by Segrè and was originally published in Italian. Although it refers to Franck and his work, its main value is in establishing the framework of the emerging "modern physics." The reader will better understand Franck's work. Segrè's book contains some technical material, but he concentrates on the scientists' "human side." The lay reader should find it profitable.

*Charles W. Rogers*

# 1925

## Physics
James Franck, Germany
Gustav Hertz, Germany

## Chemistry
Richard Zsigmondy, Austria

## Physiology or Medicine
no award

## Literature
George Bernard Shaw, Great Britain

## Peace
Sir Austen Chamberlain, Great Britain
Charles G. Dawes, United States

# GUSTAV HERTZ
## 1925

*Born:* Hamburg, Germany; July 22, 1887
*Died:* Berlin, East Germany; October 30, 1975
*Nationality:* German
*Areas of concentration:* Atomic and molecular physics

*Experiments by Hertz and his colleague James Franck demonstrated that light emissions from ionized mercury vapor give spectroscopic evidence confirming Niels Bohr's theory of the structure of the atom and its possible "energy states"*

## The Award

*Presentation*

After a year in which no prizes had been officially awarded, the Nobel Prize ceremonies resumed in 1926. Representing the Nobel Committee for Physics of the Royal Swedish Academy of Sciences, Professor C. W. Oseen presented the 1925 Nobel Prize in Physics to Gustav Hertz and James Franck on December 11, 1926. Oseen summarized Niels Bohr's theory of quantized atomic structure and explained how the pioneer electron collision experiments of Franck and Hertz had served to verify Bohr's hypotheses and open the way for new and productive research on atoms, ions, and subatomic particles.

In his presentation, Oseen identified the spectroscopy of glowing bodies as the most fertile recent branch of physics. The field was established, he noted, in 1885 with the publication of a study by Johann Jakob Balmer (1825-1898.) Balmer's experiments with glowing hydrogen gas represented the first investigation into the significance of spectral lines for the internal structure of an element, but questions regarding the large number of spectral lines for each element and the relationships of the wavelengths within each element's spectrum were not satisfactorily answered until 1913, when the Danish scientist Niels Bohr (1885-1962) applied Max Planck's ideas on discrete energy quanta to the study of the oscillation frequencies of light emitted by an atom, concluding that spectroscopic evidence should reveal various predictable stationary energy levels for each element. Although some of Bohr's assumptions were too narrow, his basic hypotheses were proved correct by methods developed by Franck and Hertz. Following the precepts established much earlier by Philipp Lenard (1862-1947) in his work with cathode rays, Franck and Hertz refined practical approaches by which physicists could study actual elastic collisions between electrons and ions, atoms, or molecules.

*Nobel lecture*

"The Results of the Electron-Impact Tests in the Light of Bohr's Theory of Atoms" was the English title of Gustav Hertz's Nobel lecture, which was delivered in German. The lecture, though highly technical, began with an assessment of the general significance of Hertz and Franck's prizewinning work. Hertz said that their contribution lay exclusively in providing "direct experimental proof of the basic assumptions of Bohr's theory of atoms."

The first section of the lecture was devoted to a description of Planck's theory of discrete energy quanta, the mathematical constant used to describe these units, and the significance of Bohr's observation that there exists a connection between internal energy levels of atoms and the wavelength of an oscillating electron emitted from or absorbed by the atom. With diagrams and equations, Hertz outlined the mathematics of spectral analysis of the specific element under consideration, mercury, and proceeded to a discussion of certain improvements made by Hertz and him on Philipp Lenard's techniques for the ionization of a gas (the alteration of the electric charge of a gas's atoms by electron bombardment, which changes the number of electrons in the electron orbits of atoms in the gas).

Bohr's theory of the atom had provided a physicomathematical explanation for the fact, discovered by Lenard, that an electron must possess a specific minimum velocity before it can cause the ionization of an atom: Only discrete quantities of energy (based on relations involving Planck's constant) can be taken up by the atom, whose stationary ground state is changed to one of various stationary but "excited" states in the process. A combination of electrical measurements and the spectroscopic study of mercury gas and alkali metals in a state of "quantum excitation" showed that radiation emitted when an atom returned to its ground state was always the same in energy content and frequency as that of the electron originally absorbed in the collision. In other words, the electron-impact tests of Franck and Hertz yielded observed values which agreed with Bohr's calculated values.

The second half of Hertz's lecture was devoted to discussing the outlook for the future application of electron-impact study to the inert gases as well as the metallic vapors. He concluded with a call for increased study of not only elastic but also nonelastic electron collisions and for determination of "the probability that in a collision between an electron of sufficient velocity and an atom, energy will in fact be transferred."

Hertz made no effort to simplify sophisticated concepts or explain professional terminology for a general audience. His Nobel lecture was virtually indistinguishable in style from his other scientific papers, and in that respect it revealed the kind of scientist he was: a professional practitioner of a specialized branch of physics, an experimenter, a "scientist's scientist." Unlike the more theoretically minded men of this period of rapid scientific advancement, such as Albert Einstein and Werner Heisenberg, Hertz had no real interest in translating physics into popular language or publicly discussing the larger implications of his investigations into the structure of matter.

*Critical reception*

The specialized nature of Hertz's scientific contribution limited any controversy about the selection that might have arisen in the lay press. Moreover, Hertz and Franck's prewar experiments had already been generally accepted as confirmation of the quantized energy levels postulated in Bohr's theory of the atom. The announcements that appeared in the professional journals were matter-of-fact, recognizing the work of Hertz and Franck not for its originality but for its significance as a stepping-stone toward a more profound understanding of the atom. Brief mentions in the major newspapers in Germany and abroad echoed this consensus, and more extensive commentary was reserved for the flamboyant remarks of the Nobel Prize winner for literature of that year, George Bernard Shaw.

More interesting, perhaps, is the coincidental nature of the association of Bohr's model of the atom with the work of Franck and Hertz, who in fact were unfamiliar with Bohr's theory when they were conducting their laboratory work. As Franck would later explain in an interview of January, 1961, he and his colleague had been negligent in reading the literature, since they were convinced—as were most scientists at the time—that spectral line emission theory was still a quite "inconclusive" field with respect to new conceptual models of the atom. Moreover, when Hertz and Franck finally examined Bohr's theory shortly before the publication of their experimental results in 1914, they did not realize the full significance of their own contribution and concentrated instead on a disagreement over the relationship of the energy required for ionization of an atom and that required for mere excitation. In any case, their goal at the time was a kinetic theory of the electrons of gases. Moreover, they were unaware, before the start of their experiments in 1911, of Johannes Stark's important work on spectral lines or of his verification of the Planck-Einstein quantum hypothesis, published in 1907. Thus, the two experimenters had conducted much of their work in a kind of scholarly vacuum, uninformed of salient developments in related fields, but nevertheless destined to enter the annals of science as contributors to the general acceptance of those developments: Planck's notion of discrete energy quanta and Bohr's elaborate model of the atom and its various stationary states.

## Biography

Gustav Ludwig Hertz was born in Hamburg, Germany, on July 22, 1887, a nephew of the famous expert on electromagnetic waves Heinrich Hertz (1857-1894). His parents were Auguste Hertz, née Arning, and the lawyer Gustav Hertz. After attending the Johanneum School in Hamburg, Hertz began his studies at the University of Göttingen in 1906, departing for Munich the following year. After performing his military service, he went in 1908 to Berlin and was graduated from the university there in 1911, after which he began working with James Franck on the experiments that would earn for them the Nobel Prize in 1926.

Hertz entered private industry as a research scientist twice during his career, and he always showed a primary interest in applied physics. In the 1930's, his research began to address problems associated with the actual creation of nuclear energy, such as methods for separating isotopes. Indeed, after World War II he was among the most distinguished German scientists to work for the Soviet Union, which he did until 1954, and he was instrumental in developing the first Soviet atomic weapons.

Hertz's wife of twenty-two years, Ellen (née Dihlmann), died in 1941. They had two sons, both of whom became professional scientists. In 1943, Hertz was married to Charlotte Jollasse. After finishing his researches in the Soviet Union, Hertz became director of the Physics Institute at the University of Leipzig in the German Democratic Republic. He was nearly ninety years old when he died on October 30, 1975.

## Scientific Career

Meticulous laboratory work and cautious analysis of experimental data were Hertz's scientific domain; his contributions did not alter, but rather helped to "fill in," the edifice of modern atomic theory. His scientific career was his life, so to speak, and he managed, despite his racial background and political opinions, to remain in Germany and continue his work during the tribulations of the Nazi period. Moreover, he was able at the end of World War II to arrange for nearly ideal working conditions by casting his lot with the Soviet Union. Unlike his former colleague Franck, who fled Germany as early as 1933 and later worked in the United States on the first atom bomb, Hertz never made known any trepidation he might have felt about the political and ethical implications of a military use of nuclear power.

Hertz seems to have settled on a scientific career early in his life. It is not known to what extent his uncle's example influenced him, if at all, but in any case he embarked on a study of mathematics and physics when he enrolled at the University of Göttingen in 1906. During a semester in Munich, he made the acquaintance of the influential atomic scientist Arnold Sommerfeld (1868-1951). In 1908, after a period of military service, Hertz resumed his studies, this time at the University of Berlin; he earned his degree in 1911 with a dissertation on the infrared absorption spectrum of carbon dioxide. Hertz then began working with one of his dissertation adviser's assistants, a young physicist named James Franck, who was also Jewish and also from Hamburg. Their experiments with electron bombardment of mercury vapor continued until the outbreak of World War I, at which time both entered the army.

Hertz received severe wounds in 1915, and his recovery was slow. In 1917 he returned to the University of Berlin and occupied a position as a *Privatdozent*, or lecturer. He continued his work on the quantized energy exchanges that accompany electron collisions and also experimented with X-ray spectroscopy. In 1920 he was hired to work in the new laboratory at the Philips Incandescent Lamp Factory at Eindhoven in the Netherlands. After five years with Philips, Hertz became director of the Physics Institute at the University of Halle, and three years later he received an invitation to return to Berlin in an equivalent capacity at the Technische Hochschule of Berlin-Charlottenburg. In the meantime, his earlier work with Franck was recognized by the Nobel Committee for Physics in its award ceremony of 1926.

In the early 1930's, Hertz developed a highly successful method for separating gaseous isotopes of helium and neon by diffusion. This technique was known as a diffusion cascade, and it was based on principles applicable to all isotopes. Hertz's successes in this field would become especially important in the following decades, as he and other scientists began to investigate the uses of uranium isotopes in the creation of nuclear energy. Scientists in the United States used the method in constructing the first atom bombs.

Hertz refused to take a Nazi loyalty oath in 1934 and resigned his academic post to accept a position as chief physicist for Siemens Corporation in Berlin. Had it not been for his usefulness to Siemens, his future in Germany—and that of his wife, who was vocally pro-Allies—undoubtedly would have been far gloomier. At Siemens, Hertz continued his work on the separation of isotopes such as heavy neon (neon 22).

Hertz is often credited with leading the team that built Germany's first cyclotron. He wished to use this "atom-smashing" device to extend his early investigations on energy transfer in elastic collisions of electrons and atoms to inelastic collisions, or collisions in which an elementary particle fired at an atom is not "absorbed" but actually causes the breakup of the nucleus. The Nazi government did little to discourage his work in private industry. In time, he made considerable advances in the development of a method for the separation of the volatile isotope uranium 235.

When the Red Army entered Berlin, Hertz agreed to join a research team in the Soviet Union. At first it was reported that he had been coerced by the Soviets, but Werner Heisenberg revealed to the press in February of 1947 that Hertz and about two hundred other German scientists had joined the Soviet project willingly, accepting a stipend of six thousand rubles per month. Hertz and several of his colleagues and former pupils were given a manor house near Stochi on the Black Sea in which they constructed a laboratory for nuclear research and began planning for the production of radioactive isotopes on a large scale. In 1949 and 1950, when the Soviet Union acquired essential technical information for the construction of its own atom bomb, Hertz's skills were employed directly in the construction of nuclear weapons; he did not return to Germany until 1954, when he moved to Leipzig to teach experimental physics and serve as director of the Physics Institute at the university there. By 1957, it was widely known in the West that Hertz was one of the key minds behind the Soviet Union's atomic weapons program, although little was known about the details of his work.

As a teacher at the University of Leipzig, Hertz saw the need for good textbooks on the specialized field of atomic physics and subsequently devoted much of his seemingly limitless energy to consolidating and compiling his knowledge of the structure of the atom. In 1957 he published a book on the principles and methods of nuclear physics (*Grundlagen und Arbeitsmethoden der Kernphysik*), which was followed by a three-volume compendium of nuclear science in 1958-1962 (*Lehrbuch der Kernphysik*). While the scope of these works was more sweeping than anything

Hertz had written before, their style was characterized by the same technical precision and clarity that had been typical of the previous, more specialized, papers and essays. Still, Hertz never stepped out of his professional role as scientist and thus never wrote without assuming a level of training that excludes most laymen from his readership.

Hertz retired in 1961 and was honored by his colleagues with a ceremony and written tribute in celebration of his eightieth birthday in 1967. He was praised for two major contributions: the discovery of laws, as predicted by Bohr, governing discrete energy transfer in electron collisions, and the invention and continuous refinement of methods for separating isotopes, without which the use of nuclear power would have been impossible. In addition to the Nobel Prize he shared with Franck, Hertz had by the end of his life received many other professional awards, including the Lenin Prize of the Soviet Union in 1955. He was a member of most scientific academies in the Eastern Bloc and of the Göttingen Academy of Sciences in the West.

## Bibliography

*Primary*

PHYSICS: Über die Erregung der Quecksilberressonanzlinie 253.$\mu\mu$ durch Electronenstösse," *Verhandlungen der physiologischen Gesellschaft zu Berlin*, vol. 16, 1914 (with James Franck); "Die Bestätigung der Bohr'schen Atomtheorie im optischen Spektrum durch Untersuchungen der unelastischen Zusammenstösse langsamer Elektronen mit Gasmolekulen," *Physikalische Zeitschrift*, vol. 20, 1919 (with Franck); *Grundlagen und Arbeitsmethoden der Kernphysik*, 1957; *Lehrbuch der Kernphysik*, 1958-1962.

*Secondary*

Barwich, Heinz, and Elfi Barwich. *Das rote Atom*. Munich: Scherz, 1967. Though this book is in German, it is a standard work on the otherwise obscure history of atomic research in the Soviet Union following World War II. Also available in a French translation.

Franck, James. "A Personal Memoir." In *Niels Bohr: A Centenary Volume*, edited by Anthony P. French and P. J. Kennedy. Cambridge, Mass.: Harvard University Press, 1985. This bit of autobiographical writing by Hertz's colleague gives an interesting account of the experimental work that earned for them the Nobel Prize. Franck explains why he and Hertz were slow to realize the significance of their results for the tenability of the Bohr theory of the atom.

Heathcote, Niels Hugh de Vaudrey. *Nobel Prize Winners in Physics, 1901-1950*. New York: Henry Schuman, 1953. This valuable collection contains a straightforward treatment of the electron experiments of Hertz and Franck, based on selections from their Nobel Prize lectures.

Hermann, Armin. *The Genesis of Quantum Theory, 1889-1913*. Translated by Claude W. Nash. Cambridge, Mass.: MIT Press, 1971. There is a useful discussion of

Hertz and Franck's contributions to quantum theory on pages 77-78. The author's historical approach is intended not only for the physicist but also for the reader with a basic knowledge of science.

Holton, Gerald. "On the Recent Past of Physics." *American Journal of Physics* 29 (1961): 805-810. This article, published in the year of Hertz's retirement, discusses briefly the work of Franck and Hertz in the course of describing early responses to the Bohr model of the atom.

*Mark R. McCulloh*

# 1926

### Physics
Jean-Baptiste Perrin, France

### Chemistry
Theodor Svedberg, Sweden

### Physiology or Medicine
Johannes Fibiger, Denmark

### Literature
Grazia Deledda, Italy

### Peace
Aristide Briand, France
Gustav Stresemann, Germany

# JEAN-BAPTISTE PERRIN
## 1926

*Born:* Lille, France; September 30, 1870
*Died:* New York, New York; April 17, 1942
*Nationality:* French
*Area of concentration:* Molecular physics

*Perrin's studies of the Brownian motion of particles in an emulsion confirmed the existence of atoms and molecules by a number of independent experimental routes and allowed the calculation of certain basic physical constants*

## The Award

*Presentation*

Professor C. W. Oseen, a member of the Nobel Committee for Physics of the Royal Swedish Academy of Sciences, presented Jean-Baptiste Perrin with the 1926 Nobel Prize in Physics on December 10, 1926, in Stockholm. The award was formally conferred by King Gustav V of Sweden. In his presentation address, Oseen pointed out that matter may be understood in two ways. The first, a phenomenological approach, establishes laws to predict the behavior of matter—to describe, for example, the decreasing density of air with altitude with equations that yield the density at any altitude—without making assumptions about the nature of matter. In the second way, a hypothesis would be adopted to explain air density changes in terms of moving molecules, allowing the consequences of their motion to be tested against known laws of mechanics. The latter was Perrin's method, and his quest was to demonstrate those consequences so thoroughly that molecules would be regarded as real, not hypothetical, entities.

His method was to work with microscopically observable particles of an emulsion of the vegetable gum gamboge. He showed that a collection of these particles would obey the same laws that gases do, and statistical studies of particle distribution allowed him to calculate the important physical constant, Avogadro's number, which is the number of molecules of a substance in so many grams of the substance. In a second study, Perrin confirmed that Albert Einstein's equation for the average distance traveled by an emulsion particle agrees with reality, and he obtained an independent calculation of Avogadro's number. In a third study of the rotational motion of emulsion particles, he obtained yet another confirmation of the number. The agreement among values obtained by different methods gave strong evidence for the existence of molecules. For this evidence, as well as for the determinations of Avogadro's number, Perrin was awarded the Nobel Prize in Physics for 1926.

*Nobel lecture*

The title of Perrin's Nobel lecture, "Discontinuous Structure of Matter," points to the concern that had motivated him for three decades. The work cited in the presentation address was a large part of the evidence that Perrin presented for the discontinuity of matter, and he summarized it in his lecture. To this summary he added work by himself and others which, taken in its entirety, placed the reality of molecules beyond question. Beginning with the age-old question of whether the appearance of continuity of matter persists to submicroscopic levels or resolves to particles in a void, he advanced some evidence for the latter view: the solution and recovery of pure materials; the chemical laws of combining weights and mass conservation; and the X-ray refractions of crystallography, which suggest layers with molecular dimensions. Without a quantitative determination of the size and weight of molecules, however, these observations were only suggestive, not definitive. Values for some constants had been calculated from the kinetic molecular theory of gases developed in the nineteenth century, but these were too imprecise to inspire conviction and came from only one type of determination.

Perrin believed that Brownian motion was a phenomenon that could lead to quantitative information about molecules. Brownian motion is the movement of microscopically small particles in an emulsion; it was described in 1827 by the Scottish botanist Robert Brown, who observed pollen granules in water. The motion of such a particle is rapid and completely random, with short, straight paths and abrupt changes in direction. The motion becomes more violent with decreasing particle size and increasing temperature, and it is therefore attributable to collisions of invisible molecules with the visible particles—collisions that are stronger with more heat energy and more effective with smaller particles. Perrin first proved that a gaslike assemblage of emulsion particles would obey the laws of motion established for gas molecules. He then studied a single aspect of gas and emulsion behavior, the distribution of particles with altitude. Relating an emulsion to a gas, however, which has molecules of uniform size and mass, requires an emulsion with uniform granules. Obtaining such an emulsion with the vegetable gum gamboge and counting numbers of particles in successive layers of the emulsion took Perrin several months. The value he eventually obtained for Avogadro's number was well within the range of values given by gas-law calculations.

Encouraged by this result, Perrin turned to other topics: the compressibility of the emulsion particles separated in the liquid; fluctuations in the distribution of the particles; linear displacement of an individual particle with time; the diffusion of the granules across an imaginary plane surface; and the Brownian rotation of the particles. All the equations describing these phenomena contained Avogadro's number, and the values calculated from the experiments all fell within the range he had already determined. In his Nobel lecture, Perrin cited six further determinations by others and by methods quite different from his. He concluded, "Such a collection of agreements between the various pieces of evidence . . . creates a certitude . . . [that the] *objective reality of molecules and atoms* which was doubted twenty years ago, can today be accepted as a *principle* the consequences of which can always be proved."

Perrin concluded his lecture with a discussion of monomolecular films (soap bubbles and films on water), suggesting that the fact that their thicknesses vary stepwise is direct evidence of molecular size, and a quick sketch of subatomic structure and his valuable findings on the nature of the electron. He also offered his speculations, later confirmed, that the source of energy in the Sun and stars is the fusion of hydrogen nuclei into helium. He reemphasized in his final paragraph, however, that his topic was the discontinuity of matter and not the transmutation of matter.

*Critical reception*

The most enthusiastic response to Perrin's receipt of the Nobel Prize came from the French semipopular journals of science. The *Revue générale des sciences pures et appliquées* called the prize a "long-deserved homage" that was "greeted with great joy in France and abroad." The article reviewed Perrin's Nobel work as well as his other accomplishments. *La Nature* noted in reporting the award that Perrin's work had "revolutionized modern physics" and that his book on atoms was "universally admired for its 'Gallic' elegance, as Max Planck put it." Even the biweekly *Journal des débats*, ordinarily devoted to political and literary pursuits, stated, "No one will be surprised at the presentation of the Nobel Prize in Physics to M. Jean Perrin. The choice is excellent; M. J. Perrin is a physicist of the first order." The English-language journals were less effusive. *Nature* reported on the prize and the work for which it was awarded and concluded by stating that Perrin had been elected a foreign member of the Royal Society in 1918. *Scientific American* ran a large portrait with a brief appreciation by the British physicist Frederick Soddy. *Scientific Monthly* discussed Perrin's prize along with others in chemistry and physics for 1925 and 1926.

The daily press appears to have restricted itself to reportage. *Le Temps* devoted most of its article of November 13, 1926, to the peace prize for that year and merely supplied the winners' names for the chemistry and physics prizes for 1925 and 1926. *The New York Times* described Perrin as "an authority on the transmutation of matter" in its report of November 13, 1926, and gave only his name on December 11. The French weekly *L'Illustration* ran a laudatory article by Perrin's former student René Darbord on November 20, 1926, discussing both Perrin's Brownian-motion work and his recent attempts to bring about nuclear reactions with high-voltage X rays. The accompanying illustrations showed Perrin in his laboratory and one of his photomicrographs of the vertical distribution of emulsion particles. The widespread understanding of Perrin's work and approval of the Nobel Committee's choice was typified by the comment of Anatole France, winner of the 1921 Nobel Prize in Literature, that "what is striking is not that molecules are so numerous, so small, so turbulent, but that M. Jean Perrin has measured them."

## Biography

Jean-Baptiste Perrin was born in Lille, France, in the Department Nord near the Belgian border, on September 30, 1870. His father, an army officer, was killed in the

Franco-Prussian War while Perrin was a baby, and young Jean and his two sisters were reared by their mother. He received his secondary and undergraduate education at Lyons and Paris and entered the École Normale Supérieure in Paris in 1891 after a year in the army. In 1895, he was named *agrégé-préparateur* (graduate instructor) at the École Normale Supérieure, and two years later he received the degree of Docteur ès Sciences. Thereafter, he went to the Sorbonne (the University of Paris) as a professor of physical chemistry; he was so successful in teaching this new discipline that in 1910, a chair of physical chemistry was created for him, which he held until his death in 1942. He was a member of the Solvay Conferences of 1911 and 1921 and of the Conference of the University of Paris in 1921. In 1913 he was an exchange professor at Columbia University in New York. During World War I, he served as an officer in the Engineers. In 1923 he was elected to the Academy of Sciences, Paris. After winning the Nobel Prize in 1926, he moved into French government service, becoming Undersecretary of State for Scientific Research in 1936 and President of the High Council of Scientific Research in 1939. In late 1941, Perrin left France to avoid Nazi persecution for his anti-Fascist views, going to New York, where he worked to generate support for the French government-in-exile of Charles de Gaulle. He died in New York on April 17, 1942, without seeing his country liberated. His remains were returned to France in 1948 and reinterred in the Panthéon in Paris, with memorial addresses by many famous French physicists.

In 1897, Perrin was married to Henriette Duportal. They had two children: a daughter, Aline, and a son, Francis, who became a physicist in his own right. Many honors came to Perrin over the years, among them the French Legion of Honor, the Order of the Commander of the British Empire and the Order of Leopold of Belgium, eight honorary doctorates, and membership in an equal number of foreign academies of science.

## Scientific Career

Jean-Baptiste Perrin devoted his career to the demonstration of the discontinuity of matter and the reality of atoms and molecules. He came of age, scientifically, at a time of great controversy about the molecular theory taken for granted today. In the last quarter of the nineteenth century, chemists and physicists were sharply divided about the reality of atoms, and physicists were further divided about what reality was, if it were not atoms. For the chemists, the answer was simple: They had their combining weights for elements and compounds, the atomic weights and equivalent weights. These figures worked; that is, they allowed prediction of the masses of chemical materials required for exact reaction, and they even allowed the theoretical organization of elements into the periodic table. Whether they were related to atoms and molecules was an interesting speculation, but not important to chemistry.

To physics, however, many hypotheses vied with one another to explain the real underlying structure of matter. The kinetic molecular theory explained gas behavior as the result of particle motion but did not address chemical action; its particles were point masses, or spheres, with no chemical properties. A school of electromagnetic explanation postulated, without resort to atoms, vortexlike motions in the electromagnetic ether that resulted in the phenomena associated with matter. Thermodynamicists argued that since energy flow was all that could be measured, theory should begin with regarding energy as reality; matter was somehow merely a concretion of energy. The thermodynamic view had the advantage of explaining the irreversibility of physical phenomena by reference to the increase of entropy according to the second law of thermodynamics, but it tended to reduce chemical reactions to mere heat-transfer phenomena. The atomist hypothesis was further cast into doubt by the spectroscopists, whose studies of line spectra suggested that atoms had internal vibrations or energy levels, indicating that some ultimate particle smaller than the atom might exist. To this confused theoretical background must be added a peculiarly French situation. The hierarchical structure of French education placed great importance on the views of major scientists, and their opinions influenced the science curricula of the secondary and undergraduate institutions. Thus, the eminent chemist Marcelin Berthelot, an antiatomist, could pronounce that the atomic hypothesis was of no value in teaching (the sole purpose of the Écoles Normales), and the hypothesis was simply not presented.

That was the situation when Jean Perrin began his scientific career in the 1890's. Within twenty years, the controversy would be resolved and the molecular hypothesis would have triumphed, largely because of Perrin's work. The first signs that atomism might be the explanatory key to both physics and chemistry lay in the discovery that atoms are not the ultimate particles of matter: Cathode rays, it was learned, consist of electrons, and the positive fragments given off in radioactive disintegration are much smaller than the atoms from which they come. The existence of positive and negative parts of the atom accounted for the charge attractions that the chemists needed to explain chemical combination; evidence for such parts lent further support to the atomist position. Perrin contributed to these investigations almost from their outset. His first publication appeared in 1895, two years before he earned his doctorate, showing that cathode rays are negatively charged, that equivalent positively charged rays exist, and that their behavior is more consistent with particles than with waves. For ten years, he continued to investigate cathode rays and X rays, examining the electrifying of bodies by the former and discharge by the latter, and the ionization of gases by X rays, all of which suggested the particulate nature of the matter under investigation. He even began the determination of the charge-mass ratio of the electron, but he gave it up when the British physicist Sir Joseph John Thomson obtained the value in his own researches.

A series of thermodynamic studies by Perrin appeared between 1900 and 1907, as did his text *Traité de chimie physique: Les Principes* (1903; treatise on physical chemistry: principles), which arose from his teaching at the Sorbonne. In 1905 he investigated the electrical properties of emulsions, which led him in 1908 to the Brownian-motion studies described in his Nobel lecture. In four years of brilliant work, these experiments were essentially complete. As early as 1909, Perrin reported his conclusion that molecular reality was demonstrated in an article in

*Annales de chimie et de physique* that was published in book form in English and German translations in 1910. In 1911, he presented his findings to the major physicists of Europe at the Solvay Conference of that year; so careful and complete was his presentation that there were no substantive criticisms, and atomism was thereafter accepted in professional circles.

In 1913, Perrin published his enormously popular and influential *Les Atomes* (*Atoms*, 1916), which was widely translated and went through eleven French editions, the last in 1948. Here, he reviewed all the reseach, his own and others', that had led to any quantitative determination of atomic and molecular properties. His conclusion, given in the final chapter, was very like that of the Nobel lecture: "One is seized with admiration before the miracle of such precise agreements coming from phenomena so different . . . this gives a probability to molecular reality really bordering on certitude. . . . The atomic theory has triumphed." The phenomena were truly different. In addition to the values determined through his own Brownian-motion studies, Perrin reported values for Avogadro's number determined from gas viscosities; the distribution of gas molecules; critical opalescence; the blue of the sky; black body radiation; the charge of spherules; and radioactive decay. All the values for Avogadro's number clustered about a mean of $68 \times 10^{22}$ in a standard statistical distribution. Perrin subsequently found that soap bubble films or films of oleic acid on water have thicknesses (measured by the refraction of light from their upper and lower surfaces) that vary stepwise in increments of about 4.5 nanometers. Perrin took this increment to be the thickness of a double layer of oleic acid molecules and thus a direct measure of a molecular dimension and a means of "seeing" molecules. This finding was incorporated into later editions of *Atoms*.

After his service in the Engineers during World War I, Perrin turned his attention to the interactions of matter and light, studying both light emitted by matter, or fluorescence, and chemical reactions induced by light, or photochemistry. These studies, some carried out with his son Francis, furthered Perrin's view that both matter and light are particulate, as expressed in the title of his later book, *Grains de matière et de lumière* (1935; particles of matter and light).

Perrin also interested himself in the infant science of nuclear physics. He presented work on the separation of isotopes at the second Solvay Conference of 1921, and in the same year he put forward the suggestion that the fusion of four hydrogen nuclei into a helium nucleus should be accompanied by a loss of mass. That loss, translated into energy according to Einstein's well-known equation $E = mc^2$, would produce a prodigious amount of energy. Fusion, Perrin proposed, is the energy source in the Sun and the stars, a speculation that was later confirmed.

As he passed his sixtieth year, Perrin found himself increasingly involved in the relation of science to government. He had already been associated with the founding of the Institut de Biologie Physico-Chimique in 1927, which had been funded by Baron Edmond de Rothschild. In 1936, he was made Undersecretary of State for Scientific Research in the Popular Front government of Léon Blum. Knowing from his own research career that state funds were inadequate, particularly for pure research, Perrin set about providing both structure and funding for scientific investigation. His first success was the Service Nationale de la Recherche (National Office of Research), founded in 1936, which organized research scholars and directors throughout France. In the same year, he authorized the establishment of the Observatory in Haute-Provence; in 1937, he arranged the formation of the Institute of Astrophysics in Paris. In 1939, he capped all these accomplishments by founding the Centre National de la Recherche Scientifique (National Center of Scientific Research), the CNRS that today has a worldwide reputation, particularly in particle physics. Perhaps his most interesting innovation was the Palais de la Découverte (Palace of Discovery), a science museum with exhibits that can be manipulated by the visitors and demonstrations by trained technicians, designed to interest and excite students by showing them how scientific procedures are actually conducted. It is still in operation.

When the Germans conquered France in 1940, Perrin was in danger as a prominent government official, a member of the Comité de Vigilance Antifasciste, and a known anti-Nazi. His friends persuaded him to leave for the United States. He arrived in New York shortly before Christmas, 1941, and in the few months remaining to him helped to organize the French University of New York and attempted to inform the American public of French feeling about the collaborationist Vichy government. His last publications were pamphlets on the hope and expectation of France for liberation. He died on April 17, 1942.

## Bibliography

*Primary*
PHYSICS: *Rayons cathodiques et rayons de Röntgen: Étude expérimentale*, 1897; *Traité de chimie physique: Les Principes*, 1903; *Peut-on peser un atome avec précision?*, 1908; *Brownian Movement and Molecular Reality*, 1910; *Sur les preuves de la réalité moléculaire: Étude spéciale des émulsions*, 1912; *Les Preuves de la réalité moléculaire*, 1913; *Les Atomes*, 1913 (*Atoms*, 1916); *Les Élémentes de la physique*, 1929; *Grains de matière et de lumière*, 1935; *À la surface des choses*, 1940-1941; *Œuvres scientifiques*, 1950.

OTHER NONFICTION: *La Recherche scientifique*, 1933; *L'Organisation de la recherche scientifique en France: Discours prononcé au Conseil supérieur de la recherche scientifique*, 1938; *L'Âme de la France éternelle*, 1942; *Pour la liberation*, 1942.

*Secondary*
Broglie, Louis de. "La Réalité des molécules et l'œuvre de Jean Perrin." *Memoires de l'Académie de sciences* 67 (1949): 67-95. The best of the many accounts of Perrin's work to be found in the journal literature. De Broglie, who received the Nobel Prize three years after Perrin for his work on the quantum structure of the atom, was a friend of Perrin and was well placed to evaluate his work. The treatment is brief but complete.

Courtines, Marcel. *La Lumière, principe du monde*. Paris: L'Artisan du Livre, 1926.

A short but fairly complete exposition of Perrin's work, marred by a euphuistic style which fortunately is mostly abandoned in the actual scientific descriptions.

Nye, Mary Jo. *Molecular Reality: A Perspective on the Scientific Work of Jean Perrin*. Canton, Mass.: Watson Publishing International, 1972. The one indispensable study of Perrin's life and work. Nye reviews the nineteenth century scientific background, discusses Perrin's investigations in detail but with a minimum of mathematics, and places them in context by describing their impact on the sciences, both for Perrin's immediate colleagues and for chemists and physicists in more distant fields. She also provides a reasonable biographical account, discussing Perrin's religious and political views, among other topics, and showing how the latter led to many of his public actions. Complete bibliographic apparatus.

_____, ed. *The Question of the Atom: From the Karlsruhe Congress to the First Solvay Conference, 1860-1911*. Los Angeles: Tomash, 1984. A selection of primary source materials from twenty-one scientists preceded by a short but definitive introduction describing the nature of the argument between the atomists and antiatomists. The Perrin selection is the work mentioned above, *Brownian Movement and Molecular Reality*, an account nearly a hundred pages long that describes Perrin's Brownian-motion work but none of the experiments that made *Atoms* so compelling.

Perrin, Jean. *Œuvres scientifiques*. Edited by Francis Perrin. Paris: Centre National de la Recherche Scientifique, 1950. Mentioned above as primary literature, this collection begins with a complete bibliography of Perrin's works, scientific and otherwise, arranged under topic headings in such a way as to give shape to his thinking and output over the years. In addition, there is a brief biographical chronology. The works presented are selections, but they constitute about one-third of his lifetime output in the scientific journals.

*Robert M. Hawthorne, Jr.*

# 1927

### Physics
Arthur Holly Compton, United States
Charles Thomson Rees Wilson, Great Britain

### Chemistry
Heinrich Wieland, Germany

### Physiology or Medicine
J. Wagner von Jauregg, Austria

### Literature
Henri Bergson, France

### Peace
Ferdinand Buisson, France
Ludwig Quidde, Germany

# ARTHUR HOLLY COMPTON
## 1927

*Born:* Wooster, Ohio; September 10, 1892
*Died:* Berkeley, California; March 15, 1962
*Nationality:* American
*Areas of concentration:* X-radiation and optics

*Compton's discovery and interpretation of the change in the wavelength of scattered X rays, which became known as the Compton effect, was the first conclusive experimental proof of Albert Einstein's light quantum hypothesis and led to the creation of modern quantum theory physics*

## The Award

*Presentation*

Professor Karl Manne Georg Siegbahn, member of the Nobel Committee for Physics of the Royal Swedish Academy of Sciences, presented the Nobel Prize in Physics to Arthur Holly Compton at the award ceremonies in December, 1927, on behalf of the Royal Swedish Academy of Sciences and King Gustav V, from whom Compton accepted the prize. The honor was shared with Charles Thomson Rees Wilson (1869-1959) of the University of Cambridge. Siegbahn's presentation surveyed the complementary contributions of Wilson and Compton, for the British scholar in 1923 had offered "the experimental proof of the existence of the recoil electron tracks that had been postulated by Compton for his explanation of the change in wavelength of scattered X-rays." X-radiation, Siegbahn noted, had been a prime concern of physics since the discovery of X rays by the Nobel Prize winner for physics in 1901, Wilhelm Conrad Röntgen (1845-1923). Soon after Röntgen's discovery, it was realized that matter, when exposed to X rays, "emits radiations of different character." In addition to "an emission of electrons . . . there is . . . a secondary X-radiation." English physicist Charles Glover Barkla (1877-1944) investigated X rays and analyzed the X-ray scattering of materials, becoming a Nobel laureate for physics in 1917. Compton "made exact spectrometrical investigations of the secondary X-radiation from matter with small atomic weight" and, after some preliminary work, found "that the scattered radiation consists of two lines, one exactly the same as that of the source of rays, the other with a somewhat greater wavelength." This phenomenon was named the Compton effect. Since the change in wavelength was independent of the matter used but varied with the angle between the incident and the scattered rays, it was clear that Compton "had deduced a new kind of corpuscular theory." Siegbahn viewed this theory as a breakthrough in physics and said that it had paved the way for "the new wave mechanics."

*Nobel lecture*

Compton's Nobel lecture, titled "X-Rays as a Branch of Optics," was delivered on December 12, 1927. It is a succinct and readable summary which places Compton's research in the context of X-ray studies since 1900. Its style, while scholarly, is comprehensible to the layperson. Documented and richly illustrated, the lecture introduces "one of the most fascinating aspects of recent physics research." One can see why Compton was a popular teacher and an effective public communicator.

Compton began his lecture with a statement of one of the goals of physics research at the time: the extension of the laws of optics to the realm of X rays to show a parallelism between the X ray and light. The essential characteristics of light—reflection, refraction, diffuse scattering, polarization, diffraction, emission, absorption spectra, and photoelectric effect—had also been found in X rays. These discoveries had invited research. In what reads like a visit to an early twentieth century hall of fame of modern physicists, Compton summarized the research of his predecessors, the lesser known as well as the famous, including Röntgen, Barkla, William Henry Bragg (1862-1942), Hendrik Antoon Lorentz (1853-1928), and Karl Manne Georg Siegbahn (1886-1978); all these men were also Nobel laureates in physics. Their findings, Compton said, meant that "optical refraction and reflection were extended to the region of X-rays." This extension "brought with it more exact knowledge not only of the laws of optics but also of the structure of the atom."

Compton then focused on the study of the diffraction of X rays. It was believed at the time that most of the properties of X rays could be explained if they consisted of "electromagnetic waves much shorter than those of light." Many scholars had attacked this problem, including the German Victor Schumann (1841-1913) and the American Robert Andrews Millikan (1868-1953), the Nobel laureate for 1923. Difficult and demanding tests had confirmed the suspicion that "the laws which [had] been found to apply in the optical region [applied] equally well to the X-ray region."

To study the scattering of X rays and light was the next step. Experiments followed showing that "secondary X-rays are of greater wavelength than the primary rays which produce them." This answer posed a question of classification: "Are these secondary X-rays of increased wavelength to be classed as scattered X-rays or as fluorescent?" Classical theory did not facilitate a solution. A new understanding of the scattering process was needed. Compton went on to analyze the problem and to show that it could best be solved by the new wave mechanics. He said that his work, and that of his predecessors and peers, had provided important confirmation of the electron theory of dispersion through the study of the refraction and specular reflection of X rays. It was now possible to count with high precision the number of electrons in the atom. Compton concluded that the study of X rays as a branch of optics had led him to see in X rays "all of the well-known wave characteristics of light," but that he had been forced to "consider these rays as moving in directed quanta." This discovery, he said, was largely responsible for the new ideas regarding the nature of the atom and of radiation.

*Critical reception*

Perhaps Compton anticipated the positive reception awaiting his honor in his remarks upon acceptance of the Nobel award, given in Stockholm on December 10, 1927. Recounting a recent trip to China, Compton contrasted the greatness of that nation in the days of Kublai Khan with its ordeals under Sun Yat-sen in the 1920's. Marco Polo, Compton recalled, had shocked Europe with his discussion of Chinese technological achievement. Most regarded that Venetian explorer as utterly insane when he wrote that the Chinese "take two baths daily, one in the morning and another in the evening." "Not only this," he continued, "but the baths are in warm water." Such vast amounts of hot water seemed to be impossible to produce. When Marco Polo explained that heat was obtained not from wood but from "burning black rocks," that seemed "beyond the realm of possibility." In the six hundred years since Marco Polo's death, Compton suggested, a remarkable change had occurred in the Western mentality. A revolution of consciousness had transpired, reversing the roles of Europe and Asia. That great transformation was primarily a result of the scientific spirit, "the eagerness to learn from nature her truths" and "to put these truths to the use of mankind." This attitude—of humility before the complexity of truth, of tenacity of questioning coupled with a certainty of finding answers, and of ardent practicality—altered the human mind forever. "I verily believe that in the advancement of science," he said, "lies the hope of our civilization." The benefits, he contended, would be not simply material but moral. Science not only results in better living through technology but also can unify humanity in the recognition and reception of new truth. Because "the spirit of science knows no national or religious boundaries," it becomes "a powerful force for the peace of the world." Compton, humbly accepting the Nobel Prize as "the highest honor that one can receive," did so with the earnest expectation that both the scientific community and the general public would approve.

Compton's optimism was justified. In part it was based on his own painful process of rethinking the fundamental principles of physics. Along with many other Americans, including his predecessor at the University of Chicago, Millikan, Compton had been initially skeptical of the hypothesis of Albert Einstein (1879-1955), winner of the physics prize for 1921. At the end of World War I, there was still "almost universal skepticism" about the light quantum hypothesis, suggested almost a generation earlier, which held that "high-frequency radiation can exhibit particle characteristics." With Millikan and Owen Willans Richardson (1879-1959), the prizewinner for 1928, Compton was an "agnostic." Later laboratory work, however, compelled Compton to admit that in spite of himself, he had come up with "the first conclusive experimental proof of Einstein's quantum hypothesis." His personal odyssey caused him to be hopeful that other scientists could also experience a "conversion."

Compton's optimism was justified also because initial opposition to his discovery, made in 1923, had been resolved by the time he received his award. That opposition had been twofold: William Duane (1872-1935) and his coworkers at Harvard University had been unable to find the Compton effect experimentally, and Niels Bohr (1885-1962), the 1922 Nobel laureate, and his colleagues in Copenhagen had challenged Compton theoretically. The challenges had ceased, however, by 1927. The complementary work of Wilson, with whom Compton shared the prize, had done much to vindicate his experimental success and had indicated that the theoretical revisions required by the Compton effect were in accord with the new wave mechanics.

Niels Heathcote, writing in *Current Biography*, sums up the personal triumph that the Chicago physicist experienced: "The discovery, made almost at the outset of his career, remains Compton's single greatest achievement, not only on account of its importance in the theory of X-ray scattering, but also because it lends additional support to Einstein's photon theory of light." This analysis by Heathcote also suggests that the discovery of the Compton effect was a vital step in the creation of modern quantum theory in the period from 1924 to 1927 by such notables as Bohr and Werner Heisenberg (1901-1976), the Nobel Prize winner in Physics for 1932. Compton's contribution was immediately recognized, for in 1927 he was elected to the National Academy of Sciences and appointed Charles H. Swift Distinguished Service Professor at Chicago. In his mid-thirties, he had reached the apex of his career.

## Biography

Arthur Holly Compton was born in Wooster, Ohio, on September 10, 1892, the son of Elias Compton and Otelia Catherine Augspurger Compton. His father, a Presbyterian minister, was a professor of philosophy and Dean at Wooster College. Although Compton initially wanted to be a pastor, his father wisely suggested that his service to humanity might best be performed through science, a field for which he had early demonstrated considerable aptitude. An older brother, his closest friend and most trusted scientific adviser, Karl Taylor Compton (1887-1954), was also to be a physicist, becoming a professor at Princeton University and later the president of the Massachusetts Institute of Technology. He inspired Arthur to follow in his footsteps. Another brother, Wilson, was an economist, and a sister, Mary Compton Rice, was a missionary educator in India. Compton finished the Wooster Elementary and Grammar School in 1905 and the Wooster Preparatory School in 1909. He exhibited an interest in various sciences, such as paleontology, astronomy (he photographed Halley's comet in 1910), and aeronautics. He eventually chose physics, receiving his bachelor of science degree from Wooster College in 1913. Following in brother Karl's footsteps, Compton pursued graduate studies in physics at Princeton, obtaining his master's degree in 1914 and his doctorate in 1916. He concentrated on X-ray research.

Upon receipt of his Ph.D., Compton wed Betty Charity McCloskey, a Wooster classmate, on July 28, 1916. They had two sons: Arthur Alan, who became an officer in the U.S. State Department, and John Joseph, who became the head of the philosophy department at Vanderbilt University. From 1916 to 1917, Compton was a physics instructor at the University of Minnesota; then, until 1919, he worked for the Westinghouse Lamp Company, East Pittsburgh, researching the sodium-vapor lamp and developing instrumentation for military aircraft. For the next two years, Compton was a National Research Fellow at the Cavendish Laboratory at the University of Cambridge. He returned to the United States to become the chairman of the physics department at Washington University, St. Louis. There, he continued his experimentation with X rays, making his famous discovery of the Compton effect in 1923, for which the Royal Swedish Academy would honor him in 1927. In 1923, Compton moved to Illinois, becoming a professor of physics at the University of Chicago, where he stayed until 1945.

## Scientific Career

Had Compton done nothing more than the early work completed by his thirty-first birthday while he was teaching at Washington University, he would have been assured a place in the history of modern physics. For almost forty more years, however, Compton would continue to be creative as a scientist, philosopher, and administrator.

Compton entered the field of physics in one of its most exciting eras. His brilliant work with X rays resulted in two classic texts, both published after he had moved to the University of Chicago. *X-Rays and Electrons: An Outline of Recent X-Ray Theory* (1926) was a lengthy book that resulted from lectures delivered at the University of California and at Chicago. In seven chapters, Compton surveyed the discovery and properties of X rays—their scattering, reflection, absorption, and refraction—and various problems connected with the quantum theory of X-ray scattering and diffraction. Within a decade, a second edition was needed; *X-Rays in Theory and Experiment* (1935) was written in conjunction with Samuel K. Allison, a young colleague at Chicago. Admitting that "no field of investigation has contributed more to our knowledge of atomic structure than has the study of X-rays," the authors, in a tightly written text, summarized the state of knowledge in their area as of 1935.

By the 1930's, however, Compton had become interested in "ultra-gamma radiation," or "Hess-rays," or, as Millikan named them, "cosmic rays." With a grant from the Carnegie Institution, Compton deployed about one hundred physicists in nine regions around the globe to measure these cosmic rays with identical equipment. From 1931 until 1934, Compton traveled more than forty thousand miles, from Switzerland to Australia, from the edge of the Arctic to the heights of the Andes, supervising this project and collecting data. The main result of this work was the confirmation of the "latitude effect," suggested in 1927 by the Dutch physicist Jacob Clay, who had theorized that "the intensity of cosmic rays at the surface of the earth steadily decreases as one goes from either pole to the Equator."

Compton's work with X rays and cosmic rays established him as a physicist of global reputation. Many honors were bestowed on him, including the Rumford Gold Medal of the American Academy of Arts and Sciences (1927), the Gold Medal of the Radiological Society of North America (1928), the Matteucci Medal of the Italian Society of Science (1933), the Franklin Gold Medal of the Franklin Institute

(1940), the Hughes Medal of the Royal Society of London (1940), and the United States Government Medal for Merit (1946). More than twenty honorary doctorates were awarded to Compton from universities in the United States and abroad. Educational organizations elected him to high positions, and Compton was President of the American Physical Society (1934), the American Association of Scientific Workers (1939-1940), and the American Association for the Advancement of Science (1942). Industry sought his advice, and he was a consultant for the General Electric Company, Nela Park, Ohio, from 1926 until 1945. A frequent traveler, Compton attended the First International Conference on Nuclear Physics in Rome in 1931; he was George Eastman Visiting Professor, University of Oxford, in 1934-1935; and he became a Regent of the Smithsonian Institution in 1938.

Compton once said, "World War I opened my eyes to the fact that a nation cannot of itself determine to remain at peace." The approach to war in Europe in the late 1930's convinced him that the United States neither could nor should remain neutral. "American to the roots of his being" and "proud to be a man of science," Compton sought ways to be useful to his government in the impending war. By 1941, he was chairing the National Academy of Sciences Committee to Evaluate Use of Atomic Energy in War. As one who strongly urged President Franklin Delano Roosevelt to facilitate nuclear research, Compton became involved in the development of the atom bomb. Later, Compton told the story in a readable recollection, *Atomic Quest: A Personal Narrative* (1956). For Compton, it was essential that the release of atomic energy first be accomplished by a democracy, not a dictatorship. A "strange team," Compton remembers, composed of "military men, captains of industry, scientists, engineers, and competent laborers" took up "the titanic task" of forging the atom bomb. In 1942, as Director of the Metallurgical Laboratory of the Manhattan Project, Compton encouraged Enrico Fermi (1901-1954), the Nobel Prize winner in Physics for 1938, to join him in Chicago. On December 2, 1942, the first self-sustaining nuclear chain reaction was produced.

For four years, Compton directed the U.S. government's Plutonium Research Project, devoting his considerable energies to the production of an atom bomb. Compton himself admitted the irony of this, for his mother's family were Mennonites, and his grandfather, Samuel Augspurger, had been a conscientious objector, refusing to take any part in the Civil War. In the war with the Axis, however, Compton believed that the defense of high ideals demanded the use of every weapon that could be devised. Compton supported President Harry S. Truman's decision to drop the first atom bomb on Hiroshima on August 6, 1945, and a second one three days later on Nagasaki. Wrestling with the military, ethical, and social consequences involved in the release of nuclear energy, Compton contended that the basic question was this: Will it shorten the war and save American and Japanese lives? For Compton, the answer was affirmative.

On more than one occasion, Compton defined his philosophy as "a compassionate Christian humanism." He believed that human endeavor requires not only science, but ethics, art, and philosophy. As a scientist, Compton found himself driven to philosophy. With Albert Einstein, he believed that "concern for man himself must always constitute the chief objective of all technological effort." The goal of science is to better life, but only philosophy, he believed, could determine what was best. For these reasons, Compton was in demand as a philosopher. In 1931, he delivered the Terry Foundation Lectures at Yale University, the Elliott Lectures at Western Theological Seminary, and, four years later, in 1935, the Loud Foundation Lectures at the University of Michigan. His theme was "man's place in God's world." These lectures were published as the book *The Freedom of Man* (1935). Dedicated to his father, the volume explores the relationship of philosophy and science.

Science needs philosophy, Compton contends, to save it from sectarianism. The scientist, furthermore, is obligated to operate within a framework of morality and meaning and to give an intelligible explanation of his labors to the general public. Within this important treatise, Compton explores the implications of Heisenberg's principle of indeterminacy, or uncertainty, for contemporary philosophy, especially its implications for the ancient question of liberty and necessity. "The whole great drama of evolution," he concludes, is "moving toward the goal of making persons with free intelligent wills, capable of learning nature's laws, of seeing dimly God's purpose in nature, and of working with him to make that purpose effective." The book impressed the philosophical community. Part of it, an eloquent argument for human dignity and immortality called "Death or Life Eternal?" was selected by theologian Thomas S. Kepler for inclusion in his collection *Contemporary Religious Thought: An Anthology* (1941).

Respected as a scientist-philosopher, Compton published with the Jewish Theological Seminary of America a treatise titled *The Religion of a Scientist* (1938), and he explored the impact of science on the human condition in *The Human Meaning of Science* (1940). Compton asserted that his motto was that of Pythagoras, the ancient philosopher and physicist, who had said: "Search to find of what and how the world is made, in order that you may find a better way of life." In 1940, Compton was also asked to give the first Garvin Lecture on "The Idea of God as Affected by Human Knowledge" at the Church of Our Father, Unitarian, in Lancaster, Pennsylvania. This lecture was later published in *Man's Destiny in Eternity: The Garvin Lectures* (1949). In the essay, Compton explains his reasons for believing in an intelligent and benevolent deity.

The end of World War II found Compton seeking a new direction for his life. Now in his fifties, Compton decided to become a full-time college administrator. His interest in education was not new. From 1946 to 1948, he had been a member of the President's Commission on Higher Education. Compton also had exercised a major role in establishing the Palos Park (later Argonne National) Laboratory; the Clinton Engineer Works, in Oak Ridge, Tennessee; and the Institutes for Nuclear Studies, Metals, and Microbiology at the University of Chicago. For these reasons, Compton was receptive to an invitation to return to Washington University, St. Louis, to serve as chancellor from 1945 until 1953. During his tenure, he strengthened the science departments and the medical school. Compton also served as a trustee of Wooster College, the Brookings Institution, and Fisk University, and he was a member of the Board of Visitors at the United States Air Force Academy. In 1946, Compton became a member of the United States delegation to the First General Conference of the United Nations Educational, Scientific, and Cultural Organization (UNESCO) at Paris.

"Finding a place to do thinking," Compton admitted, "has been a central problem personally for me." In 1953, he retired from his chancellorship at Washington University to accept the position of professor of natural history. In 1961, approaching seventy, Compton was made professor-at-large. His desire was to devote more of his time to two of his favorite themes: human brotherhood and world peace. "The prime problem faced by this generation," Compton wrote, "is that of preventing major war while at the same time securing the widespread freedom that gives value to life." It was in the pursuit of these ideals that the "tall and rugged" Arthur Holly Compton spent his life. He died in Berkeley, California, on March 15, 1962.

## Bibliography

*Primary*
PHYSICS: *X-Rays and Electrons: An Outline of Recent X-Ray Theory*, 1926; *X-Rays in Theory and Experiment*, 1935 (with Samuel K. Allison); *Scientific Papers of Arthur Holly Compton: X-Ray and Other Studies*, 1973.
OTHER NONFICTION: *The Freedom of Man*, 1935; *The Religion of a Scientist*, 1938; *The Human Meaning of Science*, 1940; "Death or Life Eternal?" in Thomas S. Kepler, comp., *Contemporary Religious Thought: An Anthology*, 1941; *Man's Destiny in Eternity: The Garvin Lectures*, 1949; *Atomic Quest: A Personal Narrative*, 1956.

*Secondary*
Allison, Samuel K. "Arthur Holly Compton, Research Physicist." *Science* 138 (November 16, 1962): 794-797. This tribute by a personal friend, coworker, and successor at the University of Chicago appeared the year of Compton's death. It should be read in conjunction with Allison's later evaluation, "Arthur Holly Compton," in *Biographical Memoirs, National Academy of Sciences* (1963) and compared with Compton's obituary in *The New York Times* (March 16, 1962).
Blackwood, James R. *The House on College Avenue: The Comptons at Wooster, 1891-1913*. Cambridge, Mass.: MIT Press, 1968. In 265 pages, this well-written, illustrated study introduces the talented Compton family: Elias Compton, a Presbyterian minister and professor of philosophy; his wife, Otelia Catherine Augspurger, of Pennsylvania-German Mennonite ancestry; and their four talented children, Karl, Wilson, Mary, and Arthur.
Johnston, Marjorie, ed. *The Cosmos of Arthur Holly Compton*. New York: Alfred A. Knopf, 1967. This 468-page book is the best extant introduction to Compton as a

philosopher-scientist and as a public mentor. Organized into ten units, which in turn are subdivided into forty-five chapters, this volume provides a description of Compton in his own words. Especially helpful is "A Life in Science," an auto-biographical sketch prepared from notes left by Compton.

Kevles, Daniel J. *The Physicists: The History of a Scientific Community in Modern America*. New York: Alfred A. Knopf, 1977. This 489-page volume tells the story of the professional physicists in the United States who came to maturity following World War I. As a study of "the generation that changed the world," it has a double focus: an examination of the academic, industrial, and cultural universe of the physicists and an examination of the individuals in their own right. Kevles' survey helps to place Compton in a historical context.

Stuewer, Robert H. *The Compton Effect: Turning Point in Physics*. New York: Science History Publications, 1975. Stuewer is the recognized authority on Compton's career and contributions. A physicist and historian, Stuewer contends that Compton's discovery did not spring from a sudden insight but rather was the culmination of years of research. Although it surveys developments in radiation theory that preceded Compton's work, the volume focuses on the critical years from 1912 to 1922, concluding with an analysis of the immediate reaction to Compton's discovery and an evaluation of its permanent significance for modern physics.

*C. George Fry*

# 1927

### Physics
Arthur Holly Compton, United States
Charles Thomson Rees Wilson, Great Britain

### Chemistry
Heinrich Wieland, Germany

### Physiology or Medicine
J. Wagner von Jauregg, Austria

### Literature
Henri Bergson, France

### Peace
Ferdinand Buisson, France
Ludwig Quidde, Germany

# CHARLES THOMSON REES WILSON
## 1927

*Born:* Glencorse, Midlothian, Scotland; February 14, 1869
*Died:* Carlops, Peeblesshire, Scotland; November 15, 1959
*Nationality:* British
*Areas of concentration:* Ionizing particles and atmospheric electricity

*Wilson developed the cloud chamber, which renders visible the characteristic tracks of ionizing particles. He also provided experimental confirmation of the Compton effect*

## The Award

*Presentation*

On December 12, 1927, on behalf of the Royal Swedish Academy of Sciences, Karl Manne Georg Siegbahn (1886-1978), a member of the Nobel Committee for Physics and the winner of the Nobel Prize in Physics for 1924, presented the Nobel Prize in Physics to Charles Thomson Rees Wilson and Arthur Holly Compton (1892-1962). In his presentation speech, Siegbahn described the principle behind Wilson's cloud chamber, an apparatus which renders visible the tracks of ionizing particles. According to this principle, when supersaturated air is suddenly expanded, the resulting lowering of temperature below the dew-point facilitates the formation of droplets with charged particles as their nuclei, causing a flow of electricity in the medium. By taking advantage of this fact, Wilson had been able to observe the tracks of ionizing particles and X rays as they passed through a supersaturated medium. The condensations that occur with these ions as nuclei, when suitably illuminated, are easily photographed.

The importance of Wilson's method lay not only in the observation of tracks of ionizing particles, which in itself was a great achievement, but also in the distinguishing of different particles and processes. In 1923, the cloud chamber was instrumental in providing experimental proof of the Compton effect by permitting the observation of recoil electrons. This apparatus, which Wilson had invented long before 1927, had led to numerous important discoveries in the fields of particle and nuclear physics.

*Nobel lecture*

Wilson's Nobel lecture, titled "On the Cloud Method of Making Visible Ions and the Tracks of Ionizing Particles," was characteristic of the quiet, shy scholar. He described every detail of his invention, which had had its origin in 1894. In Wilson's own words:

In September 1894 I spent a few weeks in the Observatory which then existed on the summit of Ben Nevis, the highest of the Scottish hills. The wonderful optical phe-

nomena shown when the sun shone on the clouds surrounding the hill-top, and
especially the coloured rings surrounding the sun . . . greatly excited my interest and
made me wish to imitate them in the laboratory.

In early 1895, Wilson conducted some preliminary experiments based on the work
of John Aitken (1839-1919), Hermann von Helmholtz (1821-1894), and others, with
the sudden expansion of air saturated with water vapor to make clouds. He realized
that even after the removal of "Aitken's dust" from the moist air, clouds appeared if
the expansion-to-contraction ratio of supersaturation exceeded a certain critical
value. Wilson then built a prototype of a quantitative expansion apparatus that later
evolved into an indispensable research tool.

After these initial investigations, Wilson proceeded to improve his apparatus and
his technique of observation. He found that the number of drops formed remained
relatively small, within certain limits of the ratio of expansion to contraction, but
greatly increased with larger expansion. At this juncture, even though the nature of
the atom was not clear, Wilson wondered whether ions could be responsible for the
formation of clouds in the expansion chamber. The studies on conductivity of air
exposed to the newly discovered X rays, carried out in 1896 by Joseph John Thomson (1856-1940), director of the Cavendish Laboratory at Cambridge University,
provided Wilson with an excellent opportunity to use the cloud chamber to advance
his research.

By the autumn of 1898, Wilson had succeeded in confirming his earlier suspicion
that the clouds formed in the expansion chamber were attributable to condensation
occurring around ions and that these ions were produced either by X rays or by
energetic charged particles traversing the supersaturated medium. These findings
were immediately applied by Thomson to the determination of the ionic charge.
During the next ten years, Wilson proceeded methodically to describe his research
activities on atmospheric electrical conductivity at Cavendish Laboratory.

In 1910, Wilson began to experiment with the cloud chamber once again, and by
1912, aided by an improved version of the apparatus, he had published many
exquisite photographs of alpha-particle, beta-particle, and X-ray tracks. In his Nobel
lecture, Wilson carefully described the necessary conditions for securing fine photographs of tracks of ionizing particles: ". . . firstly, the production of the necessary
supersaturation by sudden expansion of the gas; secondly, the passage of the ionizing particles through the supersaturated gas; and finally, the illumination of the
cloud condensed on the ions along the track." The photographs of the tracks were
taken with a stereoscopic camera. With obvious delight, Wilson recalled the appreciation of William Henry Bragg (1862-1942) on seeing the first good alpha-ray
tracks. The cloud chamber had become a most important tool with which to
observe the mysterious world of the atomic nucleus.

After World War I, Wilson resumed his research. The cloud chamber photographs
of electron recoil tracks subsequent to a collision with X-ray photons were published between 1921 and 1923, conclusively proving the existence of the Compton

effect. After illustrating his characteristically thorough and historically accurate account with photographs of the tracks, Wilson concluded his speech, citing the continuing research work of Patrick Maynard Stuart Blackett (1897-1974) and James Chadwick (1891-1974), among others.

## Critical reception

On November 10, 1927,. the Royal Swedish Academy of Sciences announced the winners of the Nobel Prize in Physics for that year. The prize was to be shared by Arthur Holly Compton of the University of Chicago, for the discovery of the Compton effect, and Charles T. R. Wilson of the University of Cambridge, for the discovery of a way to make visible the paths of charged particles by condensation of water vapor. Wilson, who was fifty-eight years old at the time, had already received many coveted awards, among them the Royal Medal (1922) and the Gunning Prize (1921). He was also serving as the Jacksonian Professor of Natural Philosophy at the University of Cambridge. Moreover, at the Cavendish Laboratory, surrounded by brilliant physicists such as J. J. Thomson, Sir William Henry Bragg, and others, he was known among his colleagues as a "scientist's scientist."

Wilson was a keen observer and preferred to work alone, seeking perfection in both his apparatus and his technique. Dedicated to his research at Cambridge, he stayed away from academic intrigues and politics. He had no research students until 1920 and only a chosen few thereafter. The cloud chamber that he invented, which made it possible to observe and systematically explore the nucleus of the atom, could not have been discovered at a more opportune time. Colleagues of Wilson among the select groups of men and women engaged in X-ray and nuclear research received the news with enthusiasm.

Wilson's honors were well deserved. The award bestowed on him by the Nobel Committee received no criticism in the press. *The New York Times* of November 11, 1927, merely published the news with no further comment, indicating an unfamiliarity with the man and his work. Only years later, on November 16, 1959, while announcing his death, did the same newspaper hail him as "the man who opened the window on the atomic world," describing him as one of the unsung "back room boys" in British physics laboratories. Wilson, who had found his calling early in life, had conducted his work with dignity and steadfastness, never the center of any controversy. The stability of his life is apparent from the recollections of his colleagues and students at Cavendish Laboratory.

## Biography

Charles Thomson Rees Wilson was born on February 14, 1869, at Glencorse, Midlothian, near Edinburgh. He was the son of John Wilson, a progressive sheep farmer whose ancestors had lived in the area for generations, and Annie Clark Harper, of a once-prosperous Glasgow family.

At the age of four, Charles lost his father, and subsequently his mother moved to Manchester to be close to her parents. There, from ages nine to fifteen, he attended

Greenheyes Collegiate School, a private school; in 1884 he entered Owens College in Manchester. Intending to become a physician, Wilson obtained a bachelor of science degree in 1887, concentrating mainly on botany, zoology, and chemistry. In 1888, after having studied philosophy, Latin, and Greek for a year, he entered Sidney Sussex College, Cambridge, on a scholarship. It was during the next four years that he became interested in physics, and he was graduated in 1892 as the only physics major at Cambridge in that year. Wilson spent the next two years working as a demonstrator and giving private lessons. Aware of the uncertainty of his future, he briefly filled the position of science master at Bradford Grammar School, only to return to Cambridge at the end of 1895 as Clerk Maxwell Student. When the studentship ended in 1899, Wilson worked on atmospheric electricity problems for the Meteorological Council for a year. He was elected Fellow of Sidney Sussex College and Fellow of the Royal Society and became a university lecturer and demonstrator in 1900.

Wilson, who had begun his work on the cloud chamber in 1895, continued to improve it while conducting research on atmospheric electrical phenomena. At Cavendish Laboratory, he lectured on light and was also in charge of teaching practical physics to advanced students. At the age of thirty-nine, in 1908, he wed Jessie Fraser Dick, the daughter of the Reverend George Hill Dick of Glasgow; the couple had three children, a son and two daughters. In 1918 Wilson was named Reader in Electrical Meteorology; he was elevated to Jacksonian Professor of Natural Philosophy in 1925. He was awarded the Hughes Medal (1911), the Royal Medal (1922), and the Copley Medal (1935) by the Royal Society. In 1927 Wilson shared the Nobel Prize with Arthur Holly Compton and thereafter was honored by numerous institutions of higher learning.

After his retirement from Cambridge in 1934, Wilson moved to Edinburgh and in 1949 took up residence in Carlops, close to his birthplace. During this period, he remained active; in 1956 he published a lengthy paper, "A Theory of Thundercloud Electricity." After a brief illness, Wilson died on November 15, 1959, survived by his wife and children. During his life he had been surrounded by such brilliant men as J. J. Thomson and William Henry Bragg and had directly influenced the work of Lawrence Bragg (1890-1971), Cecil Frank Powell (1903-1969), Patrick M. S. Blackett, and a host of others.

## Scientific Career

Wilson's contributions to physics fall roughly into two areas: his invention of the cloud chamber, which made visible the tracks of ionizing particles and which won for him the Nobel Prize, and his investigation of atmospheric electricity and associated phenomena. His experience during the few weeks spent in the Observatory at Ben Nevis in 1894, related by him in his 1927 Nobel lecture, led him to the invention of the cloud chamber. The experience of having been caught in a severe thunderstorm on the summit of Carn Mor Dearg, as described by Wilson in the article "Ben Nevis Sixty Years Ago," which appeared in the magazine *Weather* in 1954, was the origin of his lifelong interest in atmospheric electricity. He spent the greater part of his research career in the study of condensation phenomena, the conductivity of air, the cloud chamber, and atmospheric electricity. C. T. R., as Wilson was affectionately called by his colleagues at Cavendish Laboratory, was determined and single-minded, carrying out all of his investigations to perfection with a singular originality.

Wilson, while holding the Clerk Maxwell Studentship from 1896 through 1899, published the results of a series of well-designed experiments on condensation nuclei. "Condensation of Water Vapour in the Presence of Dust-Free Air and Other Gases" (1897), "On the Condensation Nuclei Produced in Gases by the Action of Röntgen Rays, Uranium Rays, Ultra-Violet Light and Other Agents" (1899), and "On the Comparative Efficiency as Condensation Nuclei of Positively and Negatively Charged Ions" (1899), which were published in *Philosophical Transactions of the Royal Society*, are among the classics of this period. Wilson constructed several ingenious types of quantitative expansion chambers and also made the fundamental discovery that no cloud formation or condensation would occur unless the ratio of expansion to contraction exceeded 1.252 in dust-free, moist air. He also noted that this critical ratio did not change appreciably for a temperature range of 18 to 20 degrees Celsius. Wilson experimented with different gases to achieve various expansion-to-contraction ratios and by 1897 had concluded that X rays and the rays from uranium produce nuclei which serve as centers of condensation. Later, in 1904, he showed that X rays and uranium rays in the cloud chamber produced ions around which condensation occurred. On the application of an electric field, the drops disappeared, proving that their nuclei were charged particles. This finding was to play a crucial part in the construction of Wilson's cloud chamber.

In 1901, Wilson, with a simple gold-leaf electroscope, began his investigation of the conductivity of air and unwittingly stumbled on the fertile field of cosmic rays. In reporting the findings of his experiments on the conductivity of air, Wilson made the remark, "Experiments were now carried out to test whether the production of ions in dust-free air could be explained as being due to radiation from sources outside our atmosphere, possibly radiation like Röntgen rays or like cathode rays but of enormously greater penetrating power." Although he conducted further experiments with his electroscope in the Caledonian Railway tunnel to prove his point of view, it was not until 1912 that the extraterrestrial origin of cosmic rays was established. Wilson had wondered about the origin of Earth's excess negative electric charge; it is ironic that cosmic rays are all positively charged particles. Wilson's deep and abiding interest in atmospheric electricity stayed with him throughout his productive life.

By 1910, Wilson was seriously considering the feasibility of making the tracks of ions visible by illuminating the condensed droplets and simultaneously photographing them. With the help of his newly constructed cloud chamber apparatus, Wilson published some of the best photographs of alpha-particle, beta-particle, and X-ray tracks in a classic paper of 1912. Construction of the famous apparatus is known to have cost only £5. Cylindrical in shape, the cloud chamber was 16.5 centimeters in diameter and 3.4 centimeters high. Its roof, walls, and floor were made of glass coated on the inside with gelatin. The glass floor was fixed to the top of a thin-walled brass piston which slid freely in an outer bronze cylinder made gastight by a water seal.

By connecting the space under the piston to a vacuum vessel using a rubber valve, Wilson could accomplish the expansion. Actuated by Leyden jars (electric condensers), a capillary mercury vapor spark illuminated the chamber. The apparatus was simply triggered by a falling weight that first opened the valve, then energized the X-ray tube, and finally activated the spark. A stereoscopic camera was used to photograph the tracks made visible by the scattered light.

With the cloud chamber, once described by Ernest Rutherford (1871-1937) as "the most original apparatus in the whole history of physics," Wilson had "opened the window on the atomic world." Because World War I interrupted his work, it was not until 1923 that Wilson published the results of his findings from five hundred stereoscopic pairs of cloud chamber photographs in papers titled "Investigations on X-Rays and β-Rays by the Cloud Method. Part I: X-Rays," and "Part II: β-Rays." The cloud chamber tracks that Wilson called "fish tracks" were identified as the tracks of recoil electrons resulting from the Compton effect, providing conclusive evidence for Compton scattering. Thus, the cloud chamber had opened the door to the possibility of observing an individual photon and identifying a particular particle. It was most fitting that Wilson and Compton shared the Nobel Prize in 1927 for their brilliant achievement.

Wilson's first major study on atmospheric electricity, titled "On the Measurement of the Earth-Air Current and on the Origin of Atmospheric Electricity," appeared in 1906. In 1916 and 1921, Wilson published his major findings on the sign and magnitude of electric discharge in lightning flashes. In 1920 he put forward the suggestion that "the electric fields and currents of fine weather could be maintained by the currents in storms and showers." His pioneering investigations on atmospheric electricity, which were based on his observations using his own simple and well-designed apparatus, were to serve as models for later research.

Wilson moved on to the study of thunderstorms and their dynamics, which culminated in the publication of his last paper, "A Theory of Thundercloud Electricity," in *Proceedings of the Royal Society* three years before his death. He had spent many years of methodical research on this final work, which can be summarized in his own words:

The thundercloud is regarded as a great influence machine, the ionization currents associated with it being the agents by which its electromotive force is developed and maintained. The moving ions which constitute these currents may be intercepted by solid or liquid cloud elements so that it becomes possible for them to be carried against the field and so increase an existing electromotive force. The early stages in its growth are due to ionization currents within the cloud initiated by the earth's fine weather field. Later it is the external currents due to the thunder cloud's own field which are effective. Lightning discharges may themselves contribute to the electromotive force of the thundercloud.

Wilson's theory of thunderclouds is detailed and indicative of many years of careful research. The mechanism he suggested, although not the only one, is currently believed to be operative. This pioneering study, supported by elegant experimental observations, remains as one of Wilson's major contributions to the study of this complex and fascinating phenomenon.

Wilson's research suffered at Cavendish Laboratory, relatively speaking, because he took his teaching duties much more seriously than his colleagues did. His lectures on light were well thought out and original. Lawrence Bragg, who shared the Nobel Prize in Physics for 1915 with his father, William Henry Bragg, and who was one of Wilson's foremost students, recalled that Wilson's series of physics experiments covered the entire field of physics that existed at that time. Bragg said that Wilson's "lectures were the best, and the delivery was the worst, of any lectures" he had ever attended. "He mumbled facing the board, he was very hesitant and jerky in his delivery and yet the way he presented the subject was quite brilliant." Wilson genuinely loved teaching, although the pursuit of scientific perfection prevented him from having more than a few pupils. He invited those who were scientifically associated with him not "merely into his house, but into his home." According to Patrick M. S. Blackett, who won the Nobel Prize in 1948 and who carried on the work on the cloud chamber, "of the great scientists of this age, he was perhaps the most gentle and serene and the most indifferent to prestige and honour; his absorption in his work arose from his intense love of the natural world and from his delight in its beauties."

At a time when nuclear physicists were literally groping in the dark, Wilson, through his powers of observation and his love of natural phenomena, opened numerous avenues leading to countless discoveries. He achieved a high place of honor in the history of physical science, and the lives he touched were honored as well.

## Bibliography

*Primary*

PHYSICS: "Condensation of Water Vapour in the Presence of Dust-Free Air and Other Gases," *Philosophical Transactions of the Royal Society A*, 1897; "On the Production of a Cloud by the Action of Ultra-Violet Light on Moist Air," *Proceedings of the Cambridge Philosophical Society*, 1897; "On the Condensation Nuclei Produced in Gases by the Action of Röntgen Rays, Uranium Rays, Ultra-Violet Light and Other Agents," *Philosophical Transactions of the Royal Society A*, 1899; "On the Comparative Efficiency as Condensation Nuclei of Positively and Negatively Charged Ions," *Philosophical Transactions of the Royal Society A*, 1899; "The Condensation Method of Demonstrating the Ionization of Air Under Normal Conditions," *Philosophical Magazine*, 1904; "On the Measurement of the Earth-Air Current and on the Origin of Atmospheric Electricity," 1906; "On a Method of Making Visible the Paths of Ionizing Particles Through a Gas," *Proceedings of the Royal Society A*, 1911; "On an Expansion Apparatus for Making Visible the Tracks of Ionizing Particles in Gases and Some Results Obtained by Its Use," *Proceedings of the Royal Society A*, 1912; "On Some Determinations of the Sign and Magnitude of Electric Discharges in Lightning Flashes," *Proceedings of the Royal Society A*, 1916; "Investigation of Lightning Discharges," *Philosophical Transactions of the Royal Society A*, 1921; "Investigations on X-Rays and β-Rays by the Cloud Method. Part I: X-Rays," *Proceedings of the Royal Society A*, 1923; "Investigations on X-Rays and β-Rays by the Cloud Method. Part II: β-Rays," *Proceedings of the Royal Society A*, 1923; "On Some α-Ray Tracks," *Proceedings of the Cambridge Philosophical Society*, 1923; "The Electric Field of a Thundercloud and Some of Its Effects," *Proceedings of the Physical Society, London*, 1925; "A Theory of Thundercloud Electricity," *Proceedings of the Royal Society A*, 1956.

OTHER NONFICTION: "Ben Nevis Sixty Years Ago," *Weather*, 1954.

*Secondary*

Blackett, P. M. S. "Charles Thomson Rees Wilson, 1869-1959." *Biographical Memoirs of Fellows of the Royal Society* 6 (1960): 269-295. In the absence of a complete biography of C. T. R. Wilson, this lengthy account of his life and work is the most authoritative and exhaustive that one can find. Blackett, who continued Wilson's work on the cloud chamber and was himself awarded the Nobel Prize in 1948, portrays the man and the significance of his achievements with exceptional insight and understanding.

Crowther, James G. *The Cavendish Laboratory, 1874-1974*. New York: Science History Publications, 1974. The history of the Cavendish Laboratory and the story of some of the men who spent their lives there is perhaps nowhere told better or with greater compassion and understanding. Wilson spent his entire life at the Cavendish, although his final years at Cambridge were of necessity taken up by other duties in addition to the teaching of experimental physics. The reader will be rewarded with insights that he will not find in other works concerning Wilson and his time.

Heathcote, Niels Hugh de Vaudrey. *Nobel Prize Winners in Physics, 1901-1950*. New York: Henry Schuman, 1953. This volume provides a perspective on the life and times of Wilson and the research work that went on immediately before and after his contributions. The scholars with whom he associated were to push the frontier of physics ever further, attaining high honors for themselves.

Larsen, Egon. *The Cavendish Laboratory: Nursery of Genius*. New York: Franklin Watts, 1962. This volume, with a foreword by Sir John Cockcroft (winner of the Nobel Prize in Physics for 1951), centers on the unique "nursery of genius" that nurtured and trained scholars such as Wilson and delves into the background of the people that surrounded these scholars.

Lipsett, W. G. "C. T. R. Wilson, The Inventor of the Cloud Chamber." *Science Digest* 53 (January, 1963): 73-78. This sketch of Wilson gives the reader a condensed view of the Nobel laureate's career. It is obvious that time did not diminish the importance of his work. The article characterizes Wilson's discovery as a "science milestone."

Oxbury, Harold, ed. *Great Britons: Twentieth Century Lives*. New York: Oxford University Press, 1985. This entry is probably one of the briefest, yet clearest, sources concerning C. T. R. Wilson. All the basic information about Wilson is contained in this one sketch.

*V. L. Madhyastha*

# 1928

## Physics
Sir Owen Willans Richardson, Great Britain

## Chemistry
Adolf Windaus, Germany

## Physiology or Medicine
Charles Nicolle, France

## Literature
Sigrid Undset, Norway

## Peace
no award

# SIR OWEN WILLANS RICHARDSON
## 1928

*Born:* Dewsbury, Yorkshire, England; April 26, 1879
*Died:* Alton, Hampshire, England; February 15, 1959
*Nationality:* British
*Area of concentration:* Thermionics

*Richardson investigated and elucidated the emission of electrons from heated metal filaments, a phenomenon for which he coined the term "thermionics"*

## The Award

*Presentation*

Professor Carl W. Oseen, Chairman of the Nobel Committee for Physics of the Royal Swedish Academy of Sciences, presented the 1928 Nobel Prize in Physics to Owen Willans Richardson. His speech reviewed several applications of Richardson's work. First, he discussed telephonic communication, describing a circuitous connection of more than twenty-two thousand kilometers between Stockholm and New York. Its clarity despite this enormous distance was attributed to 166 amplifiers, each containing a glowing filament which emitted electrons.

Oseen next turned to the value of radio in entertainment and exploration; an amateur radio operator heard a distress call from the lost 1928 arctic expedition of Italian explorer Umberto Nobile (1885-1978), enabling Nobile's rescue one month after the crash of his airship near the North Pole. Third, Oseen discussed the ability of X rays, or Röntgen rays (so named for the 1901 Nobel laureate Wilhelm Conrad Röntgen), to combat tuberculosis and cancer. To minimize damage to healthy tissue, the intensity of the radiation must be precisely controlled, Oseen said, as by striking a metal target with an electron stream from an incandescent filament to produce the X rays.

Oseen pointed out that these effects "all have one thing in common. A 'red thread' connects them—the glowing filament." He then sketched the initial findings of several investigators: Charles-François Du Fay (1698-1739), who discovered that air near a glowing object conducts electricity; the prolific German team of Julius Elster (1854-1920) and Hans Friedrich Geitel (1855-1923); and Sir Joseph John Thomson (1856-1940), the Nobel physics laureate for 1906.

Finally, Oseen summarized Richardson's theoretical and empirical contributions. Richardson had had the insight to connect thermionic emission to both electrical conductivity in metals and the free-electron theory of metals, and he had proposed a relationship between the maximum emission current and the temperature for a given metal. As Oseen stressed, however, "knowledge of reality . . . can be obtained only by means of experimental research," and Richardson had verified all the essentials of his theory in twelve years of painstaking testing.

*Nobel lecture*

Richardson delivered his Nobel lecture, titled "Thermionic Phenomena and the Laws Which Govern Them," on December 12, 1929. He began by briefly discussing several predecessors who had studied what he called "the effect of heat on the interaction between electricity and matter." After Frederick Guthrie (1833-1886) had shown that a red-hot ball could retain a negative charge but not a positive one, Elster and Geitel had investigated in detail the charge collected on an insulated plate near hot wires. Sir Joseph John Thomson, discoverer of the electron, proved in 1899 that the charged radiation from a glowing filament consisted of escaping electrons. Finally, Richardson cited the discovery by J. McClelland that the emission from an incandescent carbon filament was almost totally independent of the nature and pressure of the surrounding gas at low pressures. It is curious that Richardson did not mention the discovery made by Thomas Alva Edison (1847-1931) in 1883 that when a metal plate is placed inside a carbon filament lamp, a current flows if the positive terminal of the lamp is connected to the plate but not if the negative terminal of the lamp is connected to the plate.

Richardson said, "These facts seemed to me to be highly significant, and I resolved to investigate the phenomenon thoroughly." He described this inquiry in his lecture, a model of lucid explanation just as the research exhibited was a model of scrupulous experimentation. He related his early conviction that the ejection of electrons was a thermal effect—specifically, that an electron escaped from the surface when its outward motion was sufficient to overcome the electrical attraction of the solid as a whole. The availability of efficient vacuum technology and the difficulty of obtaining thin wires of a reasonably pure metal hindered his early research. Nevertheless, he confirmed his predictions in platinum in 1901 and in sodium and carbon by 1903. After summarizing his findings on the positive ionization often observed, he recounted studies made with Fay C. Brown of the components of the emitted electrons' velocity. The results provided the first experimental substantiation of the law of velocity distributions for any gas, proposed around 1860 by James Clerk Maxwell (1831-1879).

Next, Richardson pursued the analogy of evaporating water; the emission of electrons, like perspiration, cools the emitting body. Collaborating with Hereward Cooke (1879-1946), he established the existence of the cooling effect in 1913. Furthermore, they detected and measured in 1910 and 1911 the inverse process, heating caused by the impact of an electron stream, which is why an X-ray tube requires cooling water. Richardson then explored the possible relationship between thermionic emission and the photoelectric effect, a phenomenon that Albert Einstein (1879-1955), the 1921 Nobel laureate in physics, had explained in 1905 as the ejection of an electron from a metal by a collision with a bundle of electromagnetic energy called a photon. Richardson and Karl T. Compton (1887-1954) confirmed Einstein's photoelectric theory in 1912. With Compton and later with F. J. Rogers, Richardson proved that thermionic emission is a phenomenon distinct from the photoelectric effect.

He then addressed his work's bearing on the theories of metallic conduction propounded by J. J. Thomson; Hendrick Antoon Lorentz (1853-1928), the cowinner of the 1902 physics prize; Paul Drude (1863-1906); and Eduard Riecke (1845-1915). His student Keith K. Smith had investigated emission currents over an enormous range of temperatures as Richardson fine-tuned the theoretical fundamentals of the phenomenon. Eventually, electronic behavior was greatly illuminated when Arnold Sommerfeld (1868-1951) demonstrated that electrons in metals obeyed the statistical distributions given by Enrico Fermi (1901-1954), the 1938 Nobel honoree, and Paul Adrien Maurice Dirac (1902-1984), the 1933 laureate. The electron diffraction experiments performed by Clinton Joseph Davisson (1881-1958) and Lester Germer (1896-1971) corroborated Sommerfeld's concepts.

Richardson was receiving the 1928 Nobel Prize in Physics on the same day that Louis de Broglie (1892-1987) was receiving the 1929 prize. Therefore, it was both fitting and characteristically gracious for Richardson to indicate the connection, suggested in 1928 by Sir Ralph Fowler and Luther Nordheim, between thermionic emission and Broglie's wave theory of matter. Lastly, he explicated the related effect of extraction of electrons from a metal by a strong electric field in the context of the newly proposed wave equation for which Erwin Schrödinger (1887-1961) would be granted the Nobel Prize in Physics three years later.

*Critical reception*

The selection of Owen Richardson by the Royal Swedish Academy of Sciences for the 1928 Nobel Prize in Physics was reported on November 13, 1929, in both *The New York Times* and *The Times* of London. In neither was Richardson mentioned in the lead headline. The former, on page 3, ran a story titled "Thomas Mann Wins Nobel Prize for 1929." Richardson was mentioned in the fourth subheadline, "Professor Richardson and Duc de Broglie get 1928 and 1929 Awards for Work in Physics." Four paragraphs of the article discussed Richardson's contributions. He was described as "instrumental in making possible the development of the radio tube."

*The Times* of London reported the Nobel Prize announcements on page 13. Biochemist Arthur Harden (1865-1940) of the University of London, who was to be knighted in 1936, shared the chemistry prize that year; thus, two London personalities were among the laureates. The headline, however emphasized only that the awards that year were, in monetary terms, the largest to date. Several paragraphs of text reviewed Richardson's life and scientific accomplishments. The following day, *The Times* published, on page 18, small photographs of Richardson and Harden. The stories in both newspapers implied that Richardson unquestionably deserved the recognition.

There also apparently was no doubt about Richardson's qualifications as a Nobel laureate in the mind of Arthur Holly Compton (1892-1962) when, some months after the award, he wrote a segment of the article "Nobel Prize Winners in Physics" titled "Michelson, Millikan, and Richardson." The article appeared in the August,

1931, issue of *Current History*. A student of Richardson at Princeton, Compton had shared the 1927 Nobel Prize in Physics for his discovery of the Compton effect, a shift in frequency for a photon scattered from a free electron. He compared Richardson, the sojourner in the United States, with the first two American Nobel Prize recipients in physics: Albert Abraham Michelson (1852-1931), the 1907 winner, and Robert Andrews Millikan (1868-1953), the 1923 winner. Praising his mentor as "extremely versatile," Compton stated, "There probably is no other living physicist who has to his credit as many important contributions to the scientific journals." He continued, "His prolific writings have shed light on difficult problems covering almost the whole field of fundamental physics."

## Biography

Richardson was born April 26, 1879, in Dewsbury, Yorkshire, England, the only son and eldest of three children of Joshua Henry and Charlotte Willans Richardson. His father came from a middle-class manufacturing family and was a salesman of industrial tools; he strongly supported his son in developing his mathematical and scientific gifts. At age twelve, Richardson was admitted with a full scholarship to Batley Grammar School, where he did work of great distinction. He received an Entrance Major Scholarship to Trinity College, Cambridge, in 1897. Scholarships financed his entire education.

Richardson came to the Cavendish Laboratory, Cambridge, which was directed by the legendary Joseph John Thomson. He earned high honors in botany, which nearly became his major, as well as in physics and chemistry. Invited to remain at Cavendish after completing his undergraduate studies, he began investigating the ejection of electricity from hot metal. In 1901, he announced an empirical rule describing this emission, which, though slightly altered, became known as Richardson's law. A Fellow of Trinity College from 1902 to 1908, he received his doctorate in 1904.

In 1906, Richardson accepted a research professorship at Princeton University, where he completed his prizewinning research. Shortly before leaving for the United States, he was married to Lilian Maud Wilson. Their two sons (one of whom became a physicist also) and one daughter were born in that country. He joined the faculty of King's College, University of London, in 1914, just before he was to become a naturalized American citizen. Knighted in 1939, he continued to work in London until retiring in 1944. Lilian Richardson died in 1945; three years later, Richardson wed Henrietta Rupp, herself an eminent physicist. On February 15, 1959, he died at his country home, Chandos Lodge. He was widely described as a gracious, quiet man with a sharp sense of humor, a discriminating taste in collecting antique furniture and objets d'art, and a deep love of nature.

## Scientific Career

In his presentation address of 1929, Carl W. Oseen referred to Joseph John Thomson as "the Grand Old Man of English Physics of today." At the Cavendish Laboratory around the turn of the century, Thomson had acted as a magnet for scores of other talented physicists. Thus, beginning in 1897, Richardson had the rare opportunity to work and study there in the company of many superlative scientists: Charles Thomson Rees Wilson (1869-1959), who shared the 1927 Nobel Prize in Physics with Arthur Holly Compton for his invention of the Wilson cloud chamber; Ernest Rutherford (1871-1937), the founder of nuclear physics and the recipient of the 1908 Nobel Prize in Chemistry; Paul Langevin (1872-1946), a pioneer in applying electron theory to magnetism; Frederick Soddy (1877-1956), who introduced the concept of isotopes and won the 1921 Nobel Prize in Chemistry; James Jeans (1877-1946), famous for his contributions in the fields of statistical mechanics and stellar dynamics; Francis Aston (1877-1945), who was awarded the 1922 chemistry prize for conceiving the mass spectrograph; and Harold A. Wilson (1874-1964), who progressed from being Richardson's fellow student to being his longtime collaborator and brother-in-law. It is noteworthy that in that era, all work with the atomic nucleus was considered chemistry. Accepting his Nobel Prize, the irrepressible Rutherford commented that he had seen many remarkable transformations in his work with radioactivity, but none more rapid than his own from physicist to chemist.

After receiving a bachelor of arts degree from Cambridge and a bachelor of science degree from the University of London in 1900, Richardson immediately began graduate work at the Cavendish Laboratory, entering the field of research for which he is most remembered. His interest in the emission of charged radiation from heated metals is reflected by the title of the first scientific paper he presented, "On an Attempt to Detect Radiation from the Surface of Wires Carrying Alternating Currents of High Frequency," which he read before the Cambridge Philosophical Society. His second paper, read on November 25, 1901, was titled "On the Negative Radiation from Hot Platinum." Even at the inception of his career, he was making a marked contribution to physics; the second paper contained an early version of what is now internationally referred to as Richardson's law. He displayed tremendous physical and mathematical intuition in developing this equation, which describes the maximum emission current per unit area from a filament of a given metal at a given temperature. Richardson's basic approach was rooted in classical physics, specifically in kinetic theory, not in the quantum physics developed by Schrödinger and others in the 1920's. In spite of that and Richardson's incomplete understanding of the electron gas within the metal, fundamental concept of "evaporating" electrons from heated metal is still considered correct.

Richardson was a Fellow of Trinity College from 1902 to 1908, and a dazzling stream of research publications ensued. That stream would persist year after year until beyond his retirement in 1944, to be seriously interrupted only by two world wars. With Humphrey O. Jones, Richardson investigated questions of chemical physics concerning the dissociation of molecules. Returning to his original field of endeavor with a new perspective, he next pursued the diffusion of hydrogen through metals, attempting to unravel the interior structure of the metals, working either alone or with J. Nicol and T. Parnell. He also worked on ionic recombination at the interface of the outer surface of a metal and a surrounding gas. Many investigators at that time believed that the emission of charged particles from a hot metal was caused by a chemical reaction with the residual gas in the "evacuated" chamber. In his Nobel lecture, Richardson reported that he "often heated a wire in a tube for weeks in succession in order to make sure that the currents observed were stable and not coming from residual gas." Richardson was selected as the James Clerk Maxwell Scholar in 1904, the year in which he received his doctorate from University College, London. He remained at the Cavendish Laboratory until the autumn of 1906, when, at the recommendation of Joseph John Thomson to the dean of Princeton University, Richardson moved to the United States.

Just as he had seen Thomson do several years before at Cambridge, Richardson at Princeton set out to surround himself with brilliant young physicists; he succeeded to a spectacular extent. His students in New Jersey included Arthur Holly Compton and his brother, Karl T. Compton, who succeeded Richardson as the director of physics research at Princeton and served as the president of the Massachusetts Institute of Technology from 1930 to 1949; Fay C. Brown, who matured into the longtime associate director and director of the National Bureau of Standards (later renamed the National Institute of Standards and Technology); Clinton Joseph Davisson, the 1937 Nobel physics laureate, and George Paget Thomson (the son of Joseph John Thomson), famous for their observations of electron diffraction; and rocket pioneer Robert Goddard (1882-1945). Davisson wed one of Richardson's sisters.

Richardson had been hired at Princeton to form the nucleus of an active physics research group which would put Princeton on the map in the world of international physics. As a further indication of the university's commitment to this effort, the Palmer Laboratory was completed on that campus in 1908. The prominent place Princeton has held in the American physics community ever since Richardson began his service there is a measure of his fulfillment of the plan. He delighted in imparting to others his passion for scientific discovery, and it seems that he was as proficient at this activity as he was at actual experimental and theoretical physics.

Thermionics, to use the term Richardson coined for the title of a 1909 paper, occupied the bulk of his attention during his six and a half academic years at Princeton. Before his return to England in December, 1913, thermionic emission would be a firmly established phenomenon. Richardson's collaboration with Hereward Cooke, a former fellow student at Cambridge who was also on the Princeton faculty at that time, was especially fruitful. Yet, he also directed or personally performed research into a wide variety of other topics: alpha particles (the nuclei of helium atoms) and other products of radioactive decay, the photoelectric effect, the ether (a hypothetical medium in which electromagnetic waves, such as visible light, were at that time thought to travel), magnetism, and X rays. It should be mentioned that the line of investigation into the gyromagnetic effect, the connection between magnetism and motion, which Richardson initiated at Princeton bore fruit in 1925 when Samuel Goudsmit and George Uhlenbeck introduced the concept of electron "spin"; this idea led directly to Dirac's development of the relativistic quantum theory of the electron. In all, Richardson's work at Princeton led to the publication of more than thirty papers of which he was author or coauthor.

During this time, he was elected to honorary membership in the American Philosophical Society and participated vigorously in meetings of the American Physical Society. In 1913, he was elected a Fellow of the Royal Society. That was also the year in which he commenced work on his first book, *Electron Theory of Matter* (1914), which was based on his graduate lectures at Princeton. The book, whose second and revised edition was published in 1916, was a standard introduction to the field for many years and remains worthwhile reading.

In 1914, Richardson began his tenure in the Wheatstone Professorship of Physics at King's College, University of London. Shortly after that, World War I erupted. Much of Richardson's ability was consequently allocated to the British Admiralty, for which he explored telecommunications technology. During the war, however, he was able to publish his second book, *The Emission of Electricity from Hot Bodies* (1916). The Royal Society awarded him the Hughes Medal in 1920. In 1921, he served as president of Section A of the British Association.

For several years after assuming the position in London, Richardson dedicated his efforts to such topics as long-wavelength X rays, gravitation, photoelectricity, and the emission of electrons associated with chemical action. Then, in 1924, his first publication scrutinizing the spectrum of molecular hydrogen, written with Tutomu Tanaka, appeared. The spectroscopy of molecular hydrogen was to become the second area in which Richardson assumed international leadership.

The Royal Society appointed him one of three Yarrow Research Professors in 1924. Concurrently, he became the director of research in physics at King's College. In 1926, Richardson, Iakov Frenkel (1894-1952), the versatile and controversial physicist-politician Frederick Lindemann (1886-1957), and Sir Arthur Eddington (1882-1944), director of the observatory at Cambridge from 1914 until his death, pooled their talents to produce a paper titled "Spinning Electrons." President of the Physical Society of London from 1926 to 1928, Richardson participated in the fifth Solvay Conference during 1927 in Brussels, Belgium, frequently cited as possibly the most illustrious gathering of gifted physicists the world has ever witnessed. Eighteen of the participants either had won or would win the Nobel Prize in Physics or the Nobel Prize in Chemistry.

The Royal Society granted Richardson the Royal Medal in 1930. Two years later, he accepted an invitation to return to the United States to deliver the Silliman Memorial Lectures at Yale University. These lectures formed the foundation of his third book, *Molecular Hydrogen and Its Spectrum* (1934). He was knighted in 1939 and acted in the capacity of honorary foreign secretary of the Physical Society from 1928 to 1945. He received honorary degrees from the Universities of Leeds, St. Andrews, and London.

During World War II, Richardson immersed himself in research on radar, sonar, and electronic instrumentation. Historians of that war attribute the survival of

England in the Battle of Britain in large part to the fact that the Royal Air Force, although greatly outnumbered by the Germans, had radar and therefore was much more effective. Hostile action destroyed Richardson's laboratory at King's College, including a superb reflection diffraction grating.

Richardson's retirement from King's College in 1944 did not signal the end of his publications. A paper written with E. W. Foster, on the spectrum of molecular hydrogen, appeared in 1947, and another was published in 1953. Richardson's career spanned more than half a century. Today, picture tubes in television sets and cathode-ray-tube displays in computer systems are constant reminders of thermionic emission. He contributed immensely to the world's store of fundamental scientific knowledge, producing 133 major articles and three books. He also passed the torch to a number of highly capable students and peers whom he had profoundly influenced.

## Bibliography

*Primary*

PHYSICS: Richardson published 133 major articles, listed by William Wilson in "Owen Willans Richardson," *Biographical Memoirs of Fellows of the Royal Society*, vol. 5, and three books: *Electron Theory of Matter*, 1914, revised 1916; *The Emission of Electricity from Hot Bodies*, 1916, revised 1921; *Molecular Hydrogen and Its Spectrum*, 1934.

OTHER NONFICTION: Richardson's manuscripts and memorabilia, along with his personal library of some twenty-seven hundred books, are housed in the Sir Owen Richardson Collection of the Harry Ransom Humanities Research Center at the University of Texas, Austin. In 1967, James H. Leech and Dessa Ewing completed a three-volume catalog of the twenty-five-thousand-item collection: *Letters* (volume 1), *Works* (volume 2), and *Miscellaneous* (volume 3).

*Secondary*

Compton, Arthur H. "Nobel Prize Winners in Physics, I: Michelson, Millikan and Richardson." *Current History* 34 (August, 1931): 699-705. One of Richardson's most famous students profiles three early physics Nobel laureates. He capably shows how the personalities of the three men affected their sizable but diverse contributions to science in the United States.

Davisson, Clinton J. "Professor Owen Willans Richardson, Nobel Laureate." *Scientific Monthly* 30 (March, 1930): 280-283. Davisson, another of Richardson's illustrious students and also his brother-in-law, wrote this article for a journal that merged with *Science* in 1958. Davisson explains how Richardson came to Princeton and elaborates on his enormous impact on American science.

Foster, E. W. "Sir Owen Richardson, F.R.S." *Nature* 183 (April 4, 1959): 928-929. This obituary was written by the collaborator on Richardson's last two papers; he also wrote Richardson's obituary for the London *Times* (February 16, 1959). Few pieces on Richardson have the gentle insight shown here. Foster admired Richardson greatly, evidently not without cause.

——————————. "Sir Owen Willans Richardson." In *Dictionary of National Biography, 1951-1960*, edited by E. T. Williams and Helen M. Palmer. London: Oxford University Press, 1971. Like Foster's writings mentioned above, this article introduces the reader to Richardson the person as well as to Richardson the physicist. It describes, for example, his ability to walk forty miles cross-country per day when a young man, the beauty and hospitality of his home, and his loathing for totalitarianism.

Gambling, W. A. "Sir Owen Richardson, F.R.S.: Nobel Prizewinner in Physics, 1928." *The Radio and Electronic Engineer* 44 (August, 1974): 400-406. Of all the references listed in this section, the interested reader can obtain the most detailed information about the specifics of Richardson's research into thermionics from this essay. Excerpts of Richardson's *The Emission of Electricity from Hot Bodies* are incorporated into a readable survey.

Heathcote, Niels Hugh de Vaudrey. "Owen Willans Richardson." In *Nobel Prize Winners in Physics, 1901-1950*. New York: Henry Schuman, 1953. A distinctive feature of this article is that it incorporates information supplied to Heathcote by Richardson concerning the investigation by Richardson and others into the gyromagnetic effect, or the relation between the magnetization of an object and its rotation.

Nobelstiftelsen, ed. *Nobel Lectures, Physics: Including Presentation Speeches and Laureates' Biographies*. Vol. 2, *1922-1941*. Amsterdam: Elsevier, 1964. This invaluable resource provides the texts of Carl W. Oseen's presentation speech and Richardson's Nobel lecture, as well as a short biography of Richardson. The reader will find Richardson's lecture as interesting as it is informative.

Swenson, Loyd S., Jr. "Owen Willans Richardson." In *Dictionary of Scientific Biography*, edited by Charles Coulston Gillespie, vol. 11. New York: Charles Scribner's Sons, 1975. A reflective and thorough brief biography, this source has strengths which include an emphasis on the interactions of Richardson with his students and peers throughout his career and discussions of each of Richardson's three books.

Whitman, Alden, et al., eds. *Nobel Prize Winners*. New York: H. W. Wilson, 1987. The article on Richardson provides a good concise biography, covering primarily the various research projects undertaken by Richardson. It would be very helpful to a reader interested in an overview of his accomplishments.

Wilson, William. "Owen Willans Richardson." In *Biographical Memoirs of Fellows of the Royal Society*. Vol. 5. London: Royal Society of London, 1959. Wilson contributes to the published information about Richardson from the standpoint of his decades-long friendship with Richardson; he also consulted with Richardson's two sons in the preparation of this work. An interesting portrait of Richardson emerges.

*Clyde J. Smith*

# 1929

### Physics
Louis de Broglie, France

### Chemistry
Sir Arthur Harden, Great Britain
H. von Euler-Chelpin, Sweden

### Physiology or Medicine
Christiaan Eijkman, Netherlands
Sir F. Hopkins, Great Britain

### Literature
Thomas Mann, Germany

### Peace
Frank B. Kellogg, United States

# LOUIS DE BROGLIE
## 1929

*Born:* Dieppe, France; August 15, 1892
*Died:* Louveciennes, Yvelines, France; March 19, 1987
*Nationality:* French
*Areas of concentration:* Quantum physics and wave mechanics

*De Broglie developed a comprehensive theory in which he showed that electrons and other atomic particles may behave like waves*

## The Award

*Presentation*

Professor C. W. Oseen, Chairman of the Nobel Committee for Physics, presented the Nobel Prize in Physics to Louis de Broglie on December 10, 1929. Noting that the question of the nature of light is one of the oldest questions in physics, Oseen briefly reviewed its history. An early view was that light was a stream of tiny particles emitted by a source, such as the Sun. When the particles struck and rebounded from an object, such as a flower, it was thought, they entered the eye and produced the sensation of vision. Sir Isaac Newton (1642-1727) adopted this view. Using it, he was able to explain the effects of lenses and mirrors.

During the nineteenth century, however, it was emphatically established that light must be a wave. When light was allowed to pass through two adjacent slits and then to fall on a screen, a series of light and dark bands appeared. The light bands occurred when the light waves added together (peak to peak); the dark bands resulted from subtraction (wave peak to wave valley). This phenomenon of light waves interacting to produce light and dark bands is called diffraction.

The tide turned once again when the photoelectric effect was discovered; in this case, light behaves exactly as a stream of particles would. Since light behaved both like a particle and like a wave, it was suggested that matter might have a wavelike nature. That notion was quickly rejected by most as ludicrous; there was not a shred of evidence in its favor. De Broglie, however, thought otherwise. He advanced a theory in which particles, under appropriate conditions, would behave like waves. He was vindicated a few years later, when experimenters observed the diffraction pattern formed by a stream of electrons. Matter, it appeared, could assume the guise of waves.

Stating that de Broglie had brought fresh glory to the already honored family name, Oseen invited him to receive the Nobel Prize from the hands of King Gustav V.

*Nobel lecture*

Resuming his studies in 1920 after World War I, de Broglie had no inkling of the honor they were to bring him. Instead, as he explained in his Nobel lecture, "The Wave Nature of the Electron," he

> was attracted to theoretical physics by the mystery enshrouding the structure of matter and the structure of radiations, a mystery which deepened as the strange quantum concept introduced by Planck in 1900 . . . continued to encroach on the whole domain of physics.

At the beginning of the twentieth century, said de Broglie, there had seemed to be a grand division in the physical world. On one side were material particles which obeyed the mechanical laws of Newton; on the other side were various electromagnetic waves, such as light and radio waves. The waves obeyed the wave mechanics established by James Clerk Maxwell (1831-1879) and others. Then, in 1905, Albert Einstein (1879-1955) showed that the photoelectric effect (in which light shone on a metal ejects electrons from that metal) could best be explained by assuming that light had a granular structure. Light consisted of particles, called photons, which could somehow associate themselves with waves.

In 1913, Niels Bohr (1885-1962) proposed that the possible movements of an electron in an atom were quantized, or could have only certain values. Bohr's only justification for this theory was that it could explain the colors of light emitted by atoms. It occurred to de Broglie that if electrons behaved like waves, Bohr's quantum conditions might be understood in terms of the number of electron wavelengths that would fit in the atom.

De Broglie began with the notion that the electron did have a wavelike characteristic. Ingeniously, he applied Einstein's special theory of relativity to show how observers not at rest with respect to the electron wave might perceive it. This procedure allowed him to define a wavelength for the electron which depended on its momentum. This wavelength is now called the de Broglie wavelength. Two of his countrymen, Pierre de Fermat (1601-1665) and Pierre-Louis Moreau de Maupertuis (1698-1759), had formulated powerful principles to determine the paths of light rays (Fermat) and of particles (Maupertuis). De Broglie showed that the path predicted by Maupertuis' principle for an electron was the same as that predicted by Fermat's principle for an electron wave if the de Broglie wavelength was used. Next, he showed that if the electron waves in an atom reinforced each other, or resonated (as the vibrating strings on a piano do), Bohr's quantum conditions followed naturally.

In his lecture, de Broglie then acknowledged the fine work of Erwin Schrödinger (1887-1961), who had developed a complete scheme of wave mechanics based on the work of de Broglie, Bohr, and others. He pointed to the experiments that supported his claims and then finished by saying that the duality of waves and particles would form the foundation for all future developments of this science.

*Critical reception*

The response to de Broglie's receiving the prize was predictable. Neither he nor his work caught the eye of the American public, so *The New York Times* (November 13, 1929) carried only the simple notice that the "1929 Physics Prize was awarded to Duc de Broglie of Paris." Even that brief statement shows inattentiveness, since the proper title was "Prince." De Broglie did not take the title "Duc" until the death of his brother in 1960.

As one might expect, de Broglie was held in higher regard by the scientific community; accordingly, *Scientific American* (March, 1930) printed a photograph of the laureate along with a brief explanation of his work. He was described as a "brilliant French physicist, younger brother of the X-ray physicist, Duc Maurice de Broglie." His accomplishment "was to synthesize brilliantly some of the main concepts of physics which previously seemed contradictory." Finally, it was noted that de Broglie's great-grandfather had fought in the American Revolution as General Lafayette's chief lieutenant.

The French were more effusive, de Broglie being their native son. Some saw de Broglie's award as vindicating French science and the traditional values of religion and the old aristocracy. All these factors can be seen in an article written by Alphonse Berget and published in *The Commonweal* (January 15, 1930). The editors introduced the article by announcing de Broglie's Nobel Prize and claiming that it also represented recognition for a number of other French investigators. (The article mentioned Augustin-Jean Fresnel, Antoine-Henri Becquerel, and Maurice, Duc de Broglie.) The editors also said that the award was "fresh proof that fidelity to religious beliefs is not incompatible with the keenest determination to study the laws of nature."

Offering a "meager skeleton outline" of de Broglie's work, Berget noted de Broglie's "brilliant" scholarship in the field of history and pronounced him a "complete man in every sense." Looking back to the days of the monarchy and the nobility, Berget found in de Broglie's work evidence that the old ways were sound. Berget was

> grateful, in this age of unrestrainable demagogues, for the opportunity to see once again that a descendant of a noble family can achieve distinction in the scientific world—which declaiming politicians had declared closed to all who hold traditional beliefs.

## Biography

Louis-Victor-Pierre-Raymond, Prince de Broglie, was born on August 15, 1892, to Victor, Duc de Broglie, and Pauline d'Armaillé. The de Broglies were a distinguished French family who had served in high government and military positions for generations. The title of Duc de Broglie was granted in 1742 and thereafter went to the eldest living son, all other sons having the title "Prince." When Louis' older brother Maurice decided to study science, grandfather de Broglie prevented it at first, holding that such an activity was beneath the family dignity. Louis de Broglie took up the safe subject of medieval history and received his degree from the Sorbonne in 1909. Instead of entering a government career, however, he became increasingly interested in science and in scientific philosophy.

De Broglie was drawn into his life's work in the following fashion. Paul Langevin (1872-1946) was one of the few French physicists to concern himself with the new quantum theories. He had been one of Maurice de Broglie's teachers and would later teach Louis de Broglie. Langevin selected Maurice to assist him in editing the proceedings of the first Solvay Congress on questions of modern physics, held in 1911 in Brussels. Reading the proceedings and discussing them with Maurice, Louis became so fascinated that he vowed to devote all of his "efforts to achieve an understanding of the mysterious quanta."

De Broglie received a degree in science from the University of Paris in 1913. He was then called for military duty; he served at the radio telegraph station at the Eiffel Tower during World War I. As the operator on duty, it is said, he was the first Frenchman to receive word of the armistice in 1918. After the war, he returned to school and to work in his brother's laboratory. The rest of his life would be spent in seeking an understanding of the mysterious quanta.

After completing his doctoral thesis in 1924 at the University of Paris, de Broglie began to teach at the Sorbonne. Two years later, he was appointed to teach theoretical physics at the Institut Henri Poincaré. In 1932, he accepted the chair of theoretical physics at the University of Paris. Elected a member of the Académie des Sciences in 1933, de Broglie became the organization's permanent secretary for mathematical sciences in 1942. He was awarded the Grand Cross of the Légion d'Honneur and honorary degrees from the Universities of Warsaw, Bucharest, Athens, Lausanne, Quebec, and Brussels. He was also a member of eighteen foreign academies. He died on March 19, 1987, in Louveciennes, France.

## Scientific Career

The story of de Broglie's rise to fame contains several twists and turns. X rays were the chief subject of study at Maurice de Broglie's laboratory; they were used to probe the structure of the atom. According to Niels Bohr's theory, a complex atom, such as gold, contains electrons of various energies, but only certain values, or quanta, of energy are possible. One may understand this situation by considering a slide trombone and a piano. The common piano has eighty-eight keys and can produce eighty-eight distinct tones. Its tones are quantized. The slide trombone can produce many of the same notes that the piano can, but it can also produce a continuous gradation of tones between any two standard notes. The familiar, everyday world is like the slide trombone. For example, a car may go ten miles per hour, twenty miles per hour, or any speed in between. Electrons in an atom, however, are restricted to certain speeds (or, more correctly, certain energies), just as the piano can produce only certain tones.

Alexandre Dauvillier (1892-1979) joined the de Broglie laboratory and developed a way to measure the kinetic energies of electrons. Since X-ray energies could also be measured, the following experiment was performed: X rays were directed at atoms, from which they ejected electrons. The difference between the energies of the incident X ray and the ejected electron represented the energy with which the electron had been bound to the atom. Thus, atomic structure was revealed. The experiment, however, had a surprising result: The entire energy of the X-ray wave seemed to be available to eject the electron. It was as if the energy of the entire wave concentrated itself into a single spot, into an "X-ray particle," which then struck the electron. This case is very similar to that of the photoelectric effect, which was explained by Einstein in 1905.

Having been impressed with the particle nature of X rays, de Broglie had the opposite experience when he considered the radiation emitted by radioactive substances. Radium and its decay products emit three kinds of radiation: alpha, beta, and gamma. Alphas are helium nuclei and therefore particles. Betas are electrons, which are also particles. Gammas are like X rays, but they have higher energy; they are electromagnetic waves. It seemed to de Broglie that all three types of radiation should be similar on some deeper level. Perhaps they were all waves or all particles. Because Einstein had demonstrated the particle nature of light, de Broglie set out to demonstrate the wave nature of particles.

In a series of papers which he later, in 1924, combined into his doctoral thesis, de Broglie advanced his theories of the wave nature of matter. As is often the case in the history of science, many of his initial ideas were later discarded after having served as bridges to more correct concepts. For example, de Broglie supposed that photons had a very small (perhaps zero) mass. This idea was contrary to what is now generally accepted, but he was led to the notion because he accepted photons as real particles. Many scientists of the time (about 1920) regarded them as simply a useful mathematical model.

In trying to imagine how electrons might mimic photons, de Broglie supposed that the electron consisted (in some unexplained fashion) of an "internal wave" which was also associated with what he called a "phase wave." A point where the internal wave and the phase wave were related in a certain way marked the physical location of the electron. Not believing that these waves were well understood, de Broglie left their physical properties vague. He did suggest that the density of the internal wave represented the density of the electron (very much concentrated in the center), and that the phase wave indicated where the electron would go.

Using principles from Einstein's theory of relativity, de Broglie was able to derive a wavelength for his phase wave. This "de Broglie wavelength" is inversely proportional to a particle's mass, so it is of consequence only for very small things, such as electrons. By requiring that integral numbers of electron wavelengths fit into the atomic orbits established by Bohr, de Broglie derived in an unforced fashion the quantum conditions postulated by Bohr (that only certain electron energies are possible).

Another important development was a chapter on the quantum statistics of gases which de Broglie included in his thesis. It supported some of Einstein's work and paralleled some of Schrödinger's work, facts which probably helped them to regard de Broglie's work favorably. Most scientists, however, either ignored de Broglie's thesis or considered it absurd. How could a particle behave like a wave? Besides that, when an electron struck an atom and produced X rays, the wavelength of these X rays was completely different from the de Broglie wavelength predicted for the electron. Two loners, Einstein and Schrödinger, changed the course of history. Paul Langevin recommended de Broglie's thesis to Einstein. Einstein sensed genius at work and recommended it to Schrödinger. Schrödinger read it, and after a few false starts and much hard work, he developed wave mechanics, the framework for almost all of atomic and nuclear physics today.

When submitting his doctoral thesis, de Broglie was asked if there were any experiments which could be done to prove his theory. He suggested that a diffraction experiment with electrons might be possible. An experimental difficulty is that the slits can be only about one wavelength wide if diffraction effects are to be pronounced, and electron wavelengths may be as short as the distance between atoms. It was eventually realized that the sheets of atoms in a crystal could serve as "slits" of the proper size.

Electron diffraction from a crystal was first achieved accidentally. Clinton Joseph Davisson (1881-1958) and Charles H. Kunsman (1890-1970) had bombarded metal crystals with electrons. They had discovered maxima and minima in the intensity of reflected electrons as the reflection angle was changed. Their results were reported in a 1923 journal article. This article found its way into the hands of Walter Elsasser. In 1925, Elsasser was a doctoral student of James Franck in Göttingen. Having recently read a reference by Einstein to de Broglie's work, Elsasser wondered if Davisson and Kunsman's results could be explained in terms of the diffraction of electron waves. It seemed that they could be, and he suggested follow-up experiments.

Because matter waves seemed so absurd, these experiments were not done and reported until 1927. In that year, Davisson and Lester H. Germer, in the United States, and George Paget Thomson and Alexander Reid, in England, obtained unmistakable proof of electron waves in diffraction experiments. It is interesting to note that Joseph John Thomson (1856-1940) pinned down the properties of the electron as a particle in 1897 and his son George Thomson helped to establish the electron's wave nature in 1927.

Acceptance of de Broglie's theory came with the experimental proof of matter waves. De Broglie was awarded the Nobel Prize two years later, in 1929. Today, the existence of de Broglie waves is completely accepted, although concepts and terminology have evolved. Instead of "phase waves" and "internal waves," one speaks today of "wave packets" and "probability densities." Nevertheless, one can still start a lively discussion in a group of physicists by asking, "If I have two slits and I send an electron through one of them, how does it know to go to the proper place on the screen for a two slit pattern? How does it know the other slit is even there?" The answers one gets are many and often profound, showing that de Broglie's work is yet very fertile.

Although de Broglie continued to enjoy some success in his scientific investigations (for example, he predicted the discovery of the neutrino), he is better known for his career as an author and teacher. He taught first at the University of Paris and then at the Henri Poincaré Institute, where he founded a center of studies in applied mathematics. Both Louis and Maurice de Broglie were named to the French High Commission on Atomic Energy in 1945. De Broglie worked to promote the peaceful use of atomic energy but also warned of the perils of nuclear war, including immediate and future harmful effects from radioactive fallout. Besides receiving several other honors, he was awarded the Henri Poincaré Medal of the Académie des Sciences (1929), elected as a foreign member of the Royal Society of London (1953), and named a grand officer of the Legion of Honor (1954). He was described as a polite and unaffected man, one who enjoyed walking, reading, reflection, and games such as chess.

De Broglie was the author of more than twenty technical and popular books on physics and wave mechanics. In 1952 he was awarded the Kalinga Prize from the United Nations "for the work which has most contributed to the popularization of scientific knowledge." He was elected to the French Academy in 1945 for his literary works and was also an honorary president of the French Association of Science Writers.

Among de Broglie's popular works which have been translated into English are *Matière et lumière* (1937; *Matter and Light*, 1939), a discussion of the wave and particle natures of light and electrons; *La Physique nouvelle et les quanta* (1937; *The Revolution in Physics*, 1953), which tells the story of the birth of relativity and quantum mechanics; *Physique et microphysique* (1947; *Physics and Microphysics*, 1955), which contains essays on science, chance, moral values in science, and history; and *New Perspectives in Physics* (1962), which describes some of the then-recent advances in quantum mechanics and includes essays on the interpretation of wave mechanics, the role of the scientist, and the history of science.

## Bibliography

*Primary*
PHYSICS: *Matière et lumière*, 1937 (*Matter and Light*, 1939); *La Physique nouvelle et les quanta*, 1937 (*The Revolution in Physics*, 1953); *Physique et microphysique*, 1947 (*Physics and Microphysics*, 1955); *New Perspectives in Physics*, 1962.

*Secondary*
Fener, Lewis S. *Einstein and the Generations of Science*. New Brunswick, N.J.: Transaction Books, 1982. In a section on the sources of quantum theory, this book has a chapter on de Broglie as an aristocratic revolutionist. Providing a thought-provoking treatment, Fener seeks to show the influence of the philosopher Henri Bergson on de Broglie.
Herbert, Nick. *Quantum Reality*. Garden City, N.Y.: Doubleday, 1985. An essential source for anyone interested in the meaning of particle waves, this volume

discusses all the possible interpretations of the phenomenon, Bell's theorem, the Einstein-Podolsky-Rosen paradox, "Schrödinger's cat," Alain Aspect's experiment, and much more. Contains very little mathematics. A fascinating account that is easy to read.

McCormmach, Russel, ed. *Historical Studies in the Physical Sciences*. Vol. 1. Philadelphia: University of Pennsylvania Press, 1969. Includes an intriguing chapter titled "Why Was It Schrödinger Who Developed de Broglie's Ideas?" Placing de Broglie in his milieu, the authors show why Einstein and Schrödinger were attracted to his work when others were repelled. The book contains little mathematics.

Mehra, Jadish, and Helmut Rechenberg. *The Historical Development of Quantum Theory*. 5 vols. New York: Springer-Verlag, 1982. This five-volume set covers the rise of quantum mechanics from 1900 to about 1926. Although it is a technical work, the nonexpert will find in it much of value, since a considerable amount of history is included between the technical points. Although there are numerous references to de Broglie, his Nobel work is covered in part 2 of volume 1. A bibliography of twenty-one pertinent papers by de Broglie is included.

Wheaton, Bruce R. *The Tiger and the Shark: Empirical Roots of Wave-Particle Dualism*. Cambridge, England: Cambridge University Press, 1983. Accessible to the intelligent layperson, this book is an in-depth treatment of the origins of quantum mechanics. It is perhaps the first such source in which "Louis de Broglie appears less as a surprising intruder than as a person with just the background required to play the role for which he is known" (quoted from the foreword by science historian Thomas S. Kuhn).

*Charles W. Rogers*

# 1930

### Physics
Sir Chandrasekhara Venkata Raman, India

### Chemistry
Hans Fischer, Germany

### Physiology or Medicine
Karl Landsteiner, United States

### Literature
Sinclair Lewis, United States

### Peace
Nathan Söderblom, Sweden

# SIR CHANDRASEKHARA VENKATA RAMAN
## 1930

*Born:* Trichinopoly (Tiruchirapalli), India; November 7, 1888
*Died:* Bangalore, India; November 21, 1970
*Nationality:* Indian
*Area of concentration:* Optics

*Raman discovered that when monochromatic light is directed through a transparent substance and is scattered, the scattered portion contains spectral lines with wavelengths of the original light and weaker spectral lines which differ from those of the original light by constant amounts. These weaker lines, called Raman lines or the Raman effect, are attributable to the loss or gain of photon energy that results from the light's interaction with the molecules of the medium through which it passes*

## The Award

*Presentation*

Professor H. Pleijel, Chairman of the Nobel Committee for Physics of the Royal Swedish Academy of Sciences, presented the Nobel Prize in Physics to Sir Chandrasekhara Venkata Raman at the award ceremonies in December, 1930. Pleijel began his presentation with a discusion of the basic physics of the scattering of light, referring to the work of John Tyndall (1820-1893) and the scattering effect named for him. Pleijel continued his chronological account, mentioning the work of Lord Rayleigh (John William Strutt, 1842-1919) and his observations concerning the scattering effects of sunlight in the atmosphere. It was Rayleigh who had specified that this scattering (and the color of the sky) was attributable to fine particles of dust and water in the sky. Later, in 1914, Cabannes succeeded in showing that dustless gases also scatter light rays. Further investigations of light scattering in solids, liquids, and gases revealed divergences from results predicted by the Tyndall effect.

Pleijel noted that it was at this juncture that Raman began his study of the nature of scattered light. He described Raman's discovery, in 1928, that the scattered light not only showed wavelengths derived from primary light but also "contained other wavelengths, which were foreign to the primary light." To study the properties of these new rays, Raman used a powerful mercury lamp whose light was filtered so that it yielded a single wavelength; using a scattering medium, Raman took a spectrogram, in which every wavelength appears as a characteristic line, and found that the scattered light had produced a series of unexpected lines surrounding the mercury line. The "extra" spectrum appeared even when Raman used another mercury line, and the effect persisted when different scattering media were employed.

Pleijel went on to summarize the explanation for this effect, discovered by Raman, by reviewing the quantum nature of light energy and the atomic origins of Raman's spectral lines in terms of frequencies of emitted energy (quanta) from atoms. The spectral lines that emerge as a result of the Raman effect, previously undetectable, enable structural details of atoms and molecules to be studied through investigation of their characteristic oscillations. Pleijel closed by noting the promise held forth by this new methodology for revealing the chemical constitution of substances and the very structure of matter.

*Nobel lecture*

Lord Rayleigh had set out to answer the question, "Why is the sky blue?" as the basis of his investigations into the scattering of light. Sir Raman opened his lecture, titled "The Molecular Scattering of Light," with a discussion of the foundation of his own investigation: "the colour of the sea." The simplicity of this notion, elucidated at once by Raman, underscores the implicit significance of asking such fundamental questions which, as Raman stated, "has been the starting-point in the development of a new branch of knowledge." It occurred to Raman, on a voyage to Europe in 1921, that "the wonderful blue opalescence of the Mediterranean Sea" was caused by the scattering of sunlight by the molecules of water, similar to the scattering of light by air molecules. Raman and his colleagues set out to determine the specific nature of that observation upon their return to Calcutta in September, 1921.

They began their work by studying the state of polarization of scattered light in fluids, specifically optical anisotropy; a substance is "anisotropic" when it displays properties that differ in value when measured along different axes. The primary purpose of this search was to formulate a method of determining specific properties of substances on the basis of these optical measurements. In April of 1923, while Raman and his coworkers were investigating the scattering phenomenon, a secondary scattering was observed, the magnitude of its intensity being only a few hundredths of the classical Tyndall scattering, and its wavelength being different from that of the primary or incident light. After careful purification of the liquid being studied, the same effect was observed, which led Raman to believe that it was a "characteristic property of the substance studied and not due to any fluorescent impurity."

Coincidentally, Raman's group discovered that light scattered through highly viscous liquids was always different from the incident light and was displaced. Earlier work by Arthur Holly Compton (1892-1962) had revealed that the wavelength of radiation could be degraded in the process of scattering, a phenomenon called the Compton effect. With this in mind, Raman attributed the effect he had observed to an optical analogue of the Compton effect. By mounting a seven-inch refracting telescope in the path of the scattered beams, Raman was able to isolate the weak, scattered light for study.

Using the conservation principle inherent in the Compton effect, which stated that a scattering particle gains energy by an encounter with a quantum and the quantum is deprived of energy and appears as a wave of diminished energy (frequency), Raman deduced that the conservation principle must hold in the scattered light from liquids which he was observing, and that thermodynamically the reverse must also be true. This would account for the spectral lines he had observed. Raman noted that the spectral lines of a gaseous molecule show four different species of energy of four orders of increasing magnitude corresponding to (1) translatory motion, (2) rotation, (3) vibration, and (4) electronic excitation, all but the first expressed as quantum numbers. He pointed out the complex varieties of emission and absorption spectra and that the new lines he had discovered should "rival in . . . complexity the band spectrum of the molecule observed in the emission or absorption of light."

What Raman found, in fact, was the opposite. It was this difference that made the effect so valuable. Said Raman, "The most conspicuous feature revealed by experiment is the beautiful simplicity of the spectra of even complicated polyatomic molecules. . . . It is this simplicity that gives to the study of light-scattering its special significance and value." Raman related the effect to the principle of correspondence, discovered by Niels Bohr (1885-1962), which quantitatively related classical and quantum theories of atomic behavior, including scattering.

Raman noted the significance of the effect was attributable to its universality and the simplicity of the spectra. From the frequency differences, the width and character of the lines, and the intensity and state of polarization, a vast amount of information could be deduced about the nature of the scattering substance. It had opened up a whole new field of spectroscopy, one with "unrestricted scope in the study of problems relating to the structure of matter."

## Critical reception

Chandrasekhara Venkata Raman was the first Indian citizen to win the Nobel Prize. Still a British colony in 1930, the specter of impending independence was more than just rumor. The link between education and civil responsibility was never more strongly felt than by Raman himself, who stated, "Unless the real importance of pure science and its fundamental influence in the advancement of all knowledge are realized and acted upon, India cannot make headway in any direction and attain her place among the nations of the world." This close association of the scientist with his country, the state of impending, dramatic social change, and the social implications of one of the highest honors of science lent this Nobel Prize great symbolic as well as scientific significance.

Raman had received all of his education in India. *The Scientific Monthly* (March, 1931) made pointed reference to that fact, noting, "It speaks well for the development of science in India that Professor Raman apparently owes little or nothing of his eminence to direct contact with physicists in other countries." *Time* (November 24, 1930) noted that the Raman effect was being used as a proof of the "new quantum theory of light." *Time* devoted nearly twice as much space in Raman's introduction and statement of qualifications as it did to describing the discovery itself. *Science Newsletter* (November 22, 1930) duly noted that two Americans had observed the Raman effect soon after Raman had announced his discovery: R. W. Wood, of The Johns Hopkins University, and Alfred L. Loomis, who operated a private laboratory in Tuxedo Park, New York. The publication stated that Dr. Wood had "considerably improved the original apparatus of the Indian scientist and detected the effect in the summer of 1928." The comment, although flavored with conspicuous pomposity, left the intimation at that and went on to ascribe Sir Raman proper credit by giving him a biographical sketch.

Although *Science Newsletter* had offered the unseemly comment, Wood himself stated in *Nature*, "Professor Raman's brilliant and surprising discovery . . . opens up a wholly new field of study of molecular structure . . . which resulted from Professor Raman's long and patient study . . . one of the most convincing proofs of Quantum theory."

## Biography

Chandrasekhara Venkata Raman was born in Trichinopoly (Tiruchirapalli), in the Indian province of Tamil Nadu, on November 7, 1888. He was the son of Chandrasekhara Iyer and Parvathi Ammal. His father was a professor of mathematics and physics at the Society for the Propaganda of the Gospel College. The second of eight children in a family of modest income, Raman spent the early years of his life in the city of Vishakhapatnam of Andhra Pradesh province, where the family had moved after his father had accepted a position at Mrs. A. V. N. College. Raman's brilliance was established early as he finished his secondary education and entered Mrs. A. V. N. College at eleven years of age. Two years later, he entered Presidency College in Madras. Raman finished at the top of his class there, and at age fifteen he received his B.A. with honors in English and physics.

At the turn of the century in India, those who did well academically were typically sent to study abroad, but because of his poor health, the Civil Surgeon of Madras certified that Raman was not well enough to travel abroad. He continued his academics at Presidency College.

In November, 1906, Raman published his first paper, "Unsymmetrical Diffraction Bands Due to a Rectangular Aperture, Observed When Light Is Reflected Very Obliquely at the Face of a Prism" in the English publication *Philosophical Magazine*. In 1907, Raman was graduated at the top of his class, receiving his M.A. with honors.

There were few opportunities for men of science in India in the early 1900's. Hence Raman accepted the only position available to one with his high education: He entered the Indian Civil Service in 1907. There he spent a decade in the Finance Department as an Assistant Accountant General in Calcutta. While in Calcutta, Raman studied stringed instruments and Indian drums, and he was able to sustain his interest in science by working in the laboratories of the Indian Association for the Cultivation of Science. In 1907 Raman wed Lokasundari, an Indian artist.

In 1917, Raman accepted the Palit Chair of Physics at Calcutta University, where he would spend the next fifteen years. Elected to the Royal Society in 1924, he was knighted in 1929. Between 1933 and 1948, he was at the Indian Institute of Science at Bangalore, and thereafter he was director of the Raman Research Institute, which he had established and endowed himself. He would remain active at the institute until his death on November 21, 1970, at the age of eighty-two.

## Scientific Career

During the decade of his civil service, Raman worked intensely in the laboratories of the Indian Association for the Cultivation of Science. Indeed, Raman's work rescued the laboratories from an impending dissolution from neglect and disuse. Working exclusively in his off hours, Raman published relentlessly in such journals as *Nature, Philosophical Magazine*, and *Physical Review*. Thus he earned his scientific reputation while attracting students to study under him.

In 1917, his scientific standing established in India, Raman was offered the post of the newly established Sir Tarakanath Palit professorship of physics at the University of Calcutta. The post required Raman to study abroad, which he refused to do; as a result, Vice Chancellor Asutosh Mookerjee changed the requirements and Raman accepted. Raman resigned his civil service for the professorship, whose remuneration was to be 80 percent less than what he had been earning.

Until his move to Calcutta in 1917, Raman's work had been focused primarily on the physics of stringed instruments and drums. As Raman stated fifty years later, "My call to the professorship at the Calcutta University in July 1917 and the intensification of my interests in optics inevitably called a halt to my further studies of the violin family instruments." In 1921, Raman traveled to the Congress of Universities of the British Empire held in Oxford, England, the first of many trips away from his native India. There he presented a lecture to the Physical Society about his research. It was on his return to Calcutta that he made his fundamental observation on the "wonderful blue opalescence" of the Mediterranean Sea and the observation that the blue was caused by the scattering of light by the water itself, and not by the reflection of the sky.

Raman and his student, K. R. Ramanathan, began detailed observations of light scattering in 1923. It was during these series of observations that the Raman effect, as it would later be called, was discovered: a barely detectable spectral trace, shifted to either side of the primary optical spectra of the media under observation. Raman at first suspected that impurities in the scattering media were to blame, but the effect persisted undiminished even in very carefully purified substances. Attempts were made to analyze these weak "side bands," but they were impossible to test using available methodologies.

By 1927, Raman had discovered that the effect was exhibited by liquids, gases, solids, and crystals. Finally, he used a very intense beam of monochromatic light (light of a single wavelength, in this case that of a mercury arc lamp) for the incident illumination. With such an intense beam, the side spectra were bright enough to evaluate, and Raman was able to study them in detail. He and his colleagues made the momentous discovery on equipment, largely improvised, whose value totaled a mere five hundred dollars.

In 1924, only seven years after joining the faculty at Calcutta University, Raman was elected to the Royal Society of London. The British made him a knight of the British Empire in 1929; the next year he claimed the Hughes Medal from the Royal Society. Sir Chandrasekhara Venkata Raman accepted the Nobel Prize in Physics in Stockholm on December 10, 1930.

This rather meteoric rise to international greatness benefited not only Raman but also his country. For the first time in its history, an Indian scholar, educated entirely in the country, had received the highest honor in science. Raman recognized this honor as an opportunity to promote India's science in several directions. In 1926 he founded the *Indian Journal of Physics*. He began to organize Indian educational institutions, eventually founding the Indian Academy of Sciences (1934) and its publication, *Proceedings*.

In 1934, Raman left Calcutta to accept the directorship of the Indian Institute of Science in the province of Bangalore. Immediately Raman attempted to gather a world-class faculty. But by 1936, he was forced to resign the directorship because of irresolvable conflicts with the institute's board of governors. Nevertheless, he remained at the institute for twelve more years as a professor of physics, continuing his studies in optics and light scattering. To Raman's delight, he discovered an area of research that combined his beloved acoustics and his optical knowledge when he discovered that sound waves in a liquid could diffract light. Raman offered several papers on this topic, defining the intrinsic nature of this unique and surprising effect.

In 1948, Raman retired from the Indian Institute of Science and in 1949 accepted the directorship of the newly completed Raman Research Institute in Bangalore. India had passed from British colony to a new nation on August 15, 1947. Upon independence, Raman had been appointed a National Professor. At the institute that bore his name, Raman continued his studies in optics. He particularly enjoyed, as he had all of his life, studying the scientific basis of natural phenomena. He studied the nature of light reflected from roses that he had grown in his own gardens. Around 1960, he became fascinated with the physical nature of vision, specifically the reaction of cellular components to light and color. In 1968, on his eightieth birthday, his collection of forty-three papers on vision was published as *The Physiology of Vision*. During this period Raman continued to build the institute, to which he frequently referred as "my institute." Here he also continued to nurture his roses and his love of music. For his manifest love of nature and the incorporation of overtly simple observations into full blown scientific investigations, Sir Raman has been described as one of the last true "natural philosophers of science."

The impact Raman had on Indian education and science is incalculable. His designation in 1954 as "Jewel of India"—the highest award bestowed by that nation—was literal: Raman had accomplished more toward the advancement of science in his country than had any other single individual. He was able, through his strong, perhaps somewhat stubborn, personality, to compel other educators and even government bureaucrats to work toward national scientific literacy. In his own words, there was "only one solution for India's economic problems, and that is science, science and still more science." His own contributions attest the truth of that statement. Since the advent of the laser, the Raman effect has experienced a rebirth of interest. With the purity of the laser's monochromatic light—its natural coherency and power—the Raman effect is now used extensively in the study of complex molecular structures, just as Raman had predicted, nearly half a century earlier.

## Bibliography

*Primary*

PHYSICS: "Dynamical Theory of the Motion of Bowed Strings," *Bulletin, Indian Association for the Advancement of Science*, 1914; "On the Molecular Scattering of Light in Water and the Colour of the Sea," *Proceedings of the Royal Society*, 1922; "A New Type of Secondary Radiation," *Nature*, 1928; "A New Radiation," *Indian Journal of Physics*, 1928; *Aspects of Science*, 1948; *The New Physics: Talks on Aspects of Science*, 1951; *Lectures on Physical Optics*, 1959.
OTHER NONFICTION: *The Physiology of Vision*, 1968.

*Secondary*

Blanpied, William A. "Pioneer Scientists in Pre-Independent India." *Physics Today* 39 (May, 1986): 36. This article depicts the lives and professional contributions of six influential physicists in pre-independent India from the late nineteenth century to 1947. It discusses, in historical perspective, the role of science and the scientist in shaping the political affairs of a nation in quest of sovereignty and identity, including the work of Raman.
Jayaraman, Aiyasami, and Anant Krishna Ramdas. "Chandrasekhara Venkata Raman." *Physics Today* 56 (August, 1988): 56-64. This article is the most detailed contemporary biography readily available in English of the Nobel Prize winning physicist. Written by a close associate of Raman and one of his students, it gives an intensely personal view of the physicist and of his important work. The article depicts the physicist in both a private and professional light from Raman's early years to his death. Some details of the scientist's investigations are also revealed.
Mehra, Jagdish. "Chandrasekhara Venkata Raman." *Dictionary of Scientific Biography*, edited by Charles Coulston Gillespie. New York: Charles Scribner's Sons, 1984. This account of Raman's life details the physicist's discoveries in a concise, chronological fashion. Requires some technical expertise to understand abbreviated quantum equations supporting the Raman effect. It is a reference work, however, primarily written for and directed toward the general reader.
Weber, Robert L. *Pioneers of Science: Nobel Prize Winners in Physics*. Edited by J. M. A. Lenihan. Bristol, England: Adam Hilger, 1980. Written for readers of all

backgrounds, this book presents a chronological account of the Nobel laureates in physics to 1980. It provides a biographical sketch of Raman and details the discovery for which he won the Nobel Prize. An excellent source for those interested in how Raman fit into the developing picture of physics during the explosive early twentieth century.

*Dennis Chamberland*

# 1932

### Physics
Werner Heisenberg, Germany

### Chemistry
Irving Langmuir, United States

### Physiology or Medicine
Edgar D. Adrian, Great Britain
Sir C. Sherrington, Great Britain

### Literature
John Galsworthy, Great Britain

### Peace
no award

# WERNER HEISENBERG
## 1932

*Born:* Würzburg, Germany; December 5, 1901
*Died:* Munich, West Germany; February 1, 1976
*Nationality:* German
*Area of concentration:* Quantum mechanics

*Heisenberg's theory of the uncertainty principle led to significant advances in the new field of quantum mechanics. Modern atomic physics was to reach a sound footing as a result of his studies. He provided the groundwork for solutions to some of the problems relating to the rotations of atoms*

## The Award

*Presentation*

H. Pleijel, Chairman of the Nobel Committee for Physics of the Royal Swedish Academy of Sciences, presented the Nobel Prize in Physics to Werner Heisenberg in December of 1933. Although Heisenberg's prize was for 1932, the award was not officially presented to him until the 1933 ceremony. At the same ceremony, Erwin Schrödinger (1887-1961) and Paul Adrien Maurice Dirac (1902-1984) were jointly awarded the 1933 prize.

Pleijel praised all three physicists for their contribution to the development of modern atomic physics. His speech outlined the evolution of atomic theory, beginning with Max Planck (1858-1947), who, in 1900, conceived of light's having atomic properties and determined that the constant $h$, "Planck's constant," was always obtained when the quantity of energy of a photon was divided by the frequency of oscillation of the ray of light. Pleijel went on to say that Albert Einstein had carried Planck's concepts of light further, into the theory of relativity. Later, Louis de Broglie's theory of matter-waves had indicated that matter can change in space. The structure of atoms and molecules was then studied by Niels Bohr (1885-1962), who developed a theory of hydrogen atoms. As an electron transfers paths in an atom, light rays are emitted; Bohr found that Planck's constant was a factor that could be used in determining the frequency of these rays.

Heisenberg's contribution was in the realm of the spectra of atoms and molecules. Pleijel described Heisenberg's theory:

According to quantum mechanics it is inconceivable to determine, at a given instant of time, both the position taken up by a particle and its velocity. Closer study of quantum mechanics shows in fact that the more one attempts to fix exactly the position of a particle, the more uncertain the determination of its velocity becomes, and vice versa.

Pleijel concluded the speech by recalling Heisenberg's success in "predicting that the hydrogen molecules would appear in two forms, which later [was] confirmed."

Commendation was given him for his research in quantum mechanics, which had encouraged the hope of further advances in physics.

*Nobel lecture*

Heisenberg's lecture, "The Development of Quantum Mechanics," posed the problem of a new type of physics which could not be limited by classical mechanics. He traced how Ernest Rutherford (1871-1937), Bohr, and Arnold Sommerfeld (1868-1951) had taken a classical approach to their research and compared the atom neatly to a planetary system, with electrons as the "planets." Such an interpretation of the atom, however, now had to be put aside. Heisenberg suggested that in the atomic spectrum there could be no "visual description of the atom." Observation of the electron within the atom required a microscope of extreme resolution, and with the high-resolution microscope, the field must be illuminated with light of an extremely short wavelength. Such light waves would eject the electron from its path, according to the law named for Arthur Holly Compton (1892-1962), the Compton effect. Therefore, the observer could view only one point on the electron's path at any one moment.

Heisenberg gave credit to Max Born (1882-1970), Ernst Pascual Jordan (1902-1980), and Dirac for expanding the mathematical scheme relating classical physics to quantum mechanics. By means of a mathematical relationship, these physicists could detect in quantum mechanics the laws of classical mechanics, such as "the invariability in time of energy, momentum, and angular momentum." Heisenberg also credited his findings to several other physicists. Schrödinger had created a mathematical equation for wave mechanics, and it was thanks to Max Born that Schrödinger had developed his ideas; Born's wave function and collision theory set the fundamental rules of quantum mechanics. Broglie had proposed the concept of waves occurring in a space-time framework.

Heisenberg discussed the theory of matter-waves in three-dimensional space, which had arisen from the combination of wave and quantum mechanics. He also explained Wolfgang Pauli's principle of the stationary states of atoms. He said that Dirac's success in treating wave phenomena as aspects of quantum mechanics could also be attained with respect to material particles.

Heisenberg next tackled the fundamental problem faced by physicists: the significance of wave mechanics for theories of classical physics. Classical physics pictured the atom as a planetary system or a charged cloud. It sought objective results according to rules governed by standard space-time conditions. Now, however, the physicist had to deal with a new set of rules which provided no objective outcome and no space-time reference. Quantum mechanics required standard phenomena to be determined in a new light, and experimental outcomes had to be hypothesized based on the probability of results.

Disruptions of a system caused by observation were responsible for another factor of quantum mechanics: "[The] fundamentally unverifiable part of the perturbation of the system caused by the measurement itself . . . hampers accurate ascertainment of the classical characteristics and thus permits quantum mechanics to be applied." Elimination of the uncertainty would require incorporating the object, observer, and measuring device into one quantum-mechanical system. Although the statistical nature of the laws of quantum mechanics contributed to the predictability of results, the actual observations could be explained only in terms of probabilities. Heisenberg said that there was "an element of chance" in every experiment.

Heisenberg concluded his acceptance speech with the prediction that quantum theory would be reconciled with the special theory of relativity—which was based on universal laws, not probability—and a call for continued research on the atomic nucleus.

### Critical reception

The reception of Heisenberg's Nobel Prize was muted. The award's one-year delay indicates there was indecision about the winner. When the award was about to be announced, an article in *The New York Times* of October 29, 1933, anticipated the prize's going to Percy Williams Bridgman (1882-1961) of Harvard, who later received the Nobel Prize for 1946. On the announcement of the award, *The New York Times* of November 10 indicated that there was "complete surprise in ordinarily well-informed circles here."

In Germany, the state of political unrest did not help Heisenberg's reception. In 1934 the Nazi regime was on the verge of taking over Germany. When Heisenberg had refused to join the Nationalist Socialist organization and declare his allegiance to the Führer, he had met with criticism. Nevertheless, after he received the prize, his students planned an ovation ceremony for him. The mixed home reception Heisenberg received was only the beginning of future problems he would have with the politics of his country, especially during Adolf Hitler's reign.

Among friends as well as foes, Heisenberg was attacked for receiving the prize. Physicists were embroiled in the quantum mechanics revolution, and some had not yet come to terms with Heisenberg's subjective and mathematical approach. Heisenberg believed that Max Born, who had contributed greatly to his research and ideas, should have shared the prize with him.

### Biography

Werner Karl Heisenberg was born in Würzburg, Germany, on December 5, 1901, to August and Annie Wecklein Heisenberg. When August Heisenberg became professor of classical languages and Byzantine culture at the University of Munich in 1911, the family moved there. Young Heisenberg attended the Maximilian Gymnasium in Munich until 1920. In 1920, he entered the University of Munich to study theoretical physics with Arnold Sommerfeld. After earning his doctorate in physics in 1923 from the University of Munich, Heisenberg took a post at the University of Göttingen (then known as the mathematical center of the world) as Max Born's assistant. In 1927, he moved to the University of Leipzig and became a professor of theoretical physics.

When Heisenberg was twenty-one years old he met Albert Einstein and Niels Bohr at a conference in Göttingen. His friendship with Bohr was to continue for many years, a friendship that generated for the physicists new ideas in quantum mechanics. Heisenberg and Einstein, however, did not see eye to eye on quantum mechanics; Einstein opposed Heisenberg's statistical and subjective approach to physics. For years to come, Heisenberg would consider himself successful whenever he could bring Einstein to agree with his ideas.

Heisenberg's fame as a professor of physics rapidly grew. He was offered appointments at the Universities of Zurich and Leipzig in 1927. He chose Leipzig so that he could remain in his beloved fatherland, despite Zurich's beauty and glamour. During World War II, Heisenberg had many offers to leave Germany, yet he remained loyal to his country. He was called to Berlin's army headquarters to work with a group of physicists on nuclear fission for the war project. Although he did not support the German government's goal of producing an atom bomb, Heisenberg regarded the "uranium project" as presenting the possibility of producing energy from uranium. In 1942, Heisenberg became a professor of physics at the University of Berlin and was appointed director of the Kaiser Wilhelm Institute, the highest scientific research position in Germany. After the war, from May, 1945, to January, 1946, Heisenberg and the German physicists from the Institute were imprisoned in England. The U.S. government hoped to find out about their research on the atom bomb. There was nothing to reveal, however, because Germany had had little financing available to fund such an immense project. From 1946 to 1958, Heisenberg set his sights on restoring the sciences in Germany and building an international community of scientists. He lectured around the world and headed numerous organizations that supported scientific research and funded programs for rising young physicists in the country. In 1952, Heisenberg became chairman of the Commission for Nuclear Physics, and in 1957 he joined a group of physicists known as the Göttingen Eighteen to speak out against the nuclear bomb.

Heisenberg wed Elisabeth Schumacher on April 23, 1932. They had seven children, some of whom followed their father into scientific endeavors. Heisenberg was also known as an excellent pianist. He found great pleasure in playing the piano, reading philosophy, and hiking in the mountains. During these pastimes, he was able to synthesize his ideas about the atom.

## Scientific Career

Heisenberg's first major step in his scientific career was his appointment to the University of Göttingen in 1924 as Max Born's assistant. A prolific career would begin under Born; Heisenberg even attributed to him his early research findings that led to the Nobel Prize.

Although Heisenberg produced many scholarly publications in physics after receiving his doctorate, "On Quantum Mechanics: Parts I and II," his first widely acclaimed paper, was written with Born and Ernst Pascual Jordan and published in 1926. A preceding work on quantum mechanics, "On the Quantum Interpretation of Kinematical and Mechanical Relationships," and the collaboration piece were mathematically based. Heisenberg was aiming for the creation of a new physics, and these works were setting the stage for the formulation of the uncertainty principle. Einstein derisively said, "Heisenberg has laid a big quantum egg."

In 1927, Heisenberg published "On the Evident Contents of Quantum Theory Kinetics and Mechanics." Heisenberg had been exchanging ideas with Bohr for some time as his theory germinated. Bohr and Heisenberg were considered the focus of a new school of thought in quantum mechanics, referred to as the Copenhagen school. According to the Copenhagen interpretation of quantum mechanics, the new physics was characterized by discontinuity, indeterminacy, and statistical constructs rather than causality of space-time concepts of reality. This group, breaking with classical physics, which aims to predict outcomes in a universe of continuity, supported Heisenberg's uncertainty principle and Bohr's principle of complementarity (the idea that light is both a wave and a particle).

In September, Heisenberg delivered a lecture on the uncertainty principle at a conference commemorating the one hundredth anniversary of the death of Alessandro Volta (1745-1827). The principle's proving ground, however, would be the Solvay Congress in Brussels in October of that year. The 1927 Solvay was the first meeting since 1911 of the leading physicists of the world; its theme would be the uncertainty principle, and Heisenberg would attempt to convince Einstein of the principle's validity. The Copenhagen group, namely Born, Bohr, and Heisenberg, were to be tested against Einstein, Planck, Max von Laue (1879-1960), Broglie, and Schrödinger. Although Bohr tried to convince Einstein of the Copenhagen interpretation of quantum mechanics, the father of relativity theory would continue to maintain that there was a firm foundation to reality, determinism was possible, and there was continuity in space and time. The revolution in thought that was spurred by the Copenhagen school, however, catapulted Heisenberg to the Nobel Prize.

Heisenberg's interests turned to the nucleus of the atom. Physicists within the next few years would be discovering neutrons and positive electrons. The nucleus of the atom was a popular topic of research. The theme of the 1933 Solvay Congress, held in Brussels, was the structure and properties of the atomic nucleus. Heisenberg made a presentation on the topic. The paper that appeared in November, "Structure of the Atomic Nucleus," proposed that the proton and neutron, not the electron, were parts of the nucleus. Shortly afterward, on November 9, 1933, Heisenberg received the telegram announcing that he had won the Nobel Prize for 1932.

For the next several years, Heisenberg's research and scientific writings focused on deciphering the atomic nucleus. During the war, Heisenberg was required by the state to investigate the creation of nuclear energy through nuclear fission. He published "The Possibilities of Technically Gaining Energy from the Fission of Uranium" in December, 1939. He directed his research, however, to peaceful uses of nuclear energy. In 1942 the German government was encouraging research toward nuclear weaponry. In February, 1942, there was a conference in Berlin concerning the potential applications of nuclear physics to the development of weapons. In

June, at a secret conference with Albert Speer (1905-1981), a Nazi politician, Heisenberg was able to convince him not to work on the atom bomb. On April 4, 1942, Heisenberg accepted the directorship of the Kaiser Wilhelm Institute in Berlin-Dahlem. At the time, the German Army Ordnance Department was concentrating its efforts on nuclear weapons development at the institute. Thus, when Heisenberg took the position, he was criticized as an opportunist and a collaborator with the Nazi regime. During October, Heisenberg accepted a position at the University of Leipzig as a professor of theoretical physics. The newspapers hailed him as Germany's youngest professor. Heisenberg's plan for exchange centers of physics was taking shape during this period.

From May, 1945, to January, 1946, Heisenberg was imprisoned in England. After his return, he directed his efforts toward reestablishing Germany's reputation as a scientific research center. In March, 1949, he was named president of the new German Research Council, and in 1952, he became chairman of the Commission for Nuclear Physics. Heisenberg placed much importance on attempting to steer nuclear research away from destructive uses. In 1956, he oversaw the constitution of the German Atomic Commission, which recognized the threat of nuclear war and the uselessness of bomb shelters. Heisenberg was among the physicists of the Göttingen Eighteen, who in 1957 presented a manifesto speaking out against the atom bomb. Two of Heisenberg's later books stressed scientists' responsibility to develop mankind's potential: *Das Naturbild der heutigen Physik* (1955; *The Physicist's Conception of Nature*, 1958) and *Der Teil und das Ganze* (1969; *Physics and Beyond: Encounters and Conversations*, 1971).

The unfolding of Heisenberg's study of elementary particles, which he began after winning the Nobel Prize, culminated in his work *Introduction to the Unified Field Theory of Elementary Particles* (1966). The quest for these elementary particles was a truly united effort on the part of many physicists. In 1933, with the discovery of the "positive electron" by Carl D. Anderson (born 1905), the key was found for the theory of elementary particles.

The reverberations of Heisenberg's work were felt beyond the confines of science. The uncertainty principle, interpreted in art and literature after World War II, fostered a sense of insecurity in the culture at large. The reaction was one of fear at the shaking of foundations that had existed for centuries. When Heisenberg proposed that he could not know all the details of the present, that he could not measure the position and velocity of the electron accurately, he had to give up the ability to make firm predictions on the future outcome of an experiment. It seemed to many, especially artists and intellectuals, that there was nothing certain left.

## Bibliography

*Primary*
PHYSICS: "On the Quantum Theory of Molecules," 1924 (with Max Born); "Anomalous Zeeman Effects," 1924; "The Correspondence Principle and the Polarisation of Fluorescence Light," 1925; "On the Quantum Interpretation of Kinemati-

cal and Mechanical Relationships," 1926 (with Born); "On Quantum Mechanics: Parts I and II," 1926 (with Born and Ernst Pascual Jordan); "Fluctuation Phenomena and Quantum Mechanics," 1926; "Spectra of Atom Systems with Two Electrons," 1926; "On the Evident Contents of Quantum Theory Kinetics and Mechanics," 1927; "Quantum Dynamics of Wave Fields," 1929 (with Wolfgang Pauli); *Die physikalischen Prinzipien der Quantentheorie*, 1930 (*The Physical Principles of the Quantum Theory*, 1930); "Theory of Radiation," 1931; "Structure of Atomic Nuclei," 1932; "Structure of Light Atomic Nuclei," 1935; "Universal Length in the Theory of Elementary Particles," 1938; "Atomic Nuclei," 1939; "The Possibilities of Technically Gaining Energy from the Fission of Uranium," 1939; "Observable Quantities in the Theory of Elementary Particles," 1943; *Die Physik der Atomkerne*, 1943 (*Nuclear Physics*, 1953); *Das Naturbild der heutigen Physik*, 1955 (*The Physicist's Conception of Nature*, 1958); *Physics and Philosophy: The Revolution in Modern Science*, 1958; *Das Naturgesetz und die Struktur der Materie*, 1964 (*Natural Law and the Structure of Matter*, 1970); *Introduction to the Unified Field Theory of Elementary Particles*, 1966; *Der Teil und das Ganze*, 1969 (*Physics and Beyond: Encounters and Conversations*, 1971); *Schritte über Grenzen*, 1971 (*Across the Frontiers*, 1974).

## Secondary

Buckley, Paul, and F. David Peat. "Werner Heisenberg." In *A Question of Physics: Conversations in Physics and Biology*. Toronto: University of Toronto Press, 1979. This book is a collection of interviews with several leading scientists of the twentieth century. The interview conducted with Heisenberg was held at the Max Planck Institute in Munich. Heisenberg discusses his background research leading to the uncertainty principle and the negative reception from those who did not agree with the language of the interpretation, namely Planck, Einstein, and Laue. He elaborates on the problem of dealing with quantum physics in the terms of classical physics, such as position, velocity, energy, and temperature. He concludes the interview with a discussion of the elementary particle theory, noting that when science arrives at the fundamental unit of the universe, it will need to be explained in a new way.

Cassidy, David, and Martha Baker Cassidy. *Werner Heisenberg: A Bibliography of His Writings*. Berkeley: University of California, Office for History of Science and Technology, 1984. This bibliography provides 1,059 entries of Heisenberg's scientific and nonscientific publications from 1922 through 1983. The posthumous works listed are reprints or reproductions of earlier works.

Heisenberg, Elisabeth. *Inner Exile: Recollections of a Life with Werner Heisenberg*. Translated by S. Cappelari and C. Morris. Boston: Birkhäuser, 1984. Heisenberg's wife provides insight into his personal life. She explains his reasons for remaining in Germany during the war and describes his subsequent conflicts with the Nazi Party. What becomes most evident throughout the biography is Heisenberg's desire to bring to fruition his plan for a world community of scientists.

Hermann, Armin. *The New Physics: The Route into the Atomic Age*. Bonn, West Germany: Inter Nationes, 1979. Hermann's history of modern physics illuminates Heisenberg's contribution to the evolution of quantum mechanics. His overview of the major physicists of the period places the scientific advances in the context of changing culture and technology.

——————. *Werner Heisenberg: 1901-1976*. Bonn, West Germany: Inter Nationes, 1976. The intricacies of Heisenberg's career are cataloged in this biography, with emphasis placed less on Heisenberg's personal life and more on the political and scientific aspects of his career.

Pauli, Wolfgang. *Wolfgang Pauli: Scientific Correspondence with Bohr, Einstein, Heisenberg, A.O.* Edited by Armin Hermann et al. Vol. 1. New York: Springer-Verlag, 1979. This source contains correspondence for the period 1919-1929 among these important physicists, who, with the exception of Einstein, were part of the Copenhagen school of quantum mechanics. The collection contains facsimiles of letters, a chronology of events from 1919 to 1929, and indexes of letters by chronology, correspondent, and subject. The most significant period in the development of quantum mechanics is viewed through the words of these physicists, who shared their ideas with one another.

Price, William C., and Seymour S. Chissick, eds. *The Uncertainty Principle and Foundations of Quantum Mechanics: A Fifty Years' Survey*. New York: John Wiley & Sons, 1977. This book comprises a collection of essays on quantum mechanics by scientists from around the world. It was published to mark the fiftieth anniversary of Heisenberg's formulation of the uncertainty principle. The book was organized with the help of Heisenberg before his death and includes an article by him, "Remarks on the Origin of the Relations of Uncertainty." Heisenberg died as the book went to press.

*Caroline G. Porcari*

# 1933

### Physics
Erwin Schrödinger, Austria
Paul Adrien Maurice Dirac, Great Britain

### Chemistry
no award

### Physiology or Medicine
Thomas Hunt Morgan, United States

### Literature
Ivan Bunin, France

### Peace
Sir Norman Angell, Great Britain

# ERWIN SCHRÖDINGER
## 1933

*Born:* Vienna, Austria; August 12, 1887
*Died:* Vienna, Austria; January 4, 1961
*Nationality:* Austrian
*Areas of concentration:* Atomic theory and wave mechanics

*Schrödinger advanced the de Broglie-Einstein wave theory of electron movement by applying the mathematics of geometrical optics to the mechanics of light particles emitted from gases. Schrödinger's famous "wave equation" accounts for the mechanical possibilities and properties not only of electrons but also of protons, atoms, and even molecules*

## The Award

*Presentation*

Erwin Schrödinger was introduced at the 1933 Nobel Prize ceremony on December 12 by H. Pleijel, Chairman of the Nobel Committee for Physics of the Royal Swedish Academy of Sciences. In his presentation speech, Pleijel announced that the physics awards for 1932 and 1933 were "devoted to the new atomic physics" and named as founders of that field the recipient for 1932, Werner Heisenberg (1901-1976), and the recipients for 1933, Paul Adrien Maurice Dirac (1902-1984) and Erwin Schrödinger (1887-1961).

Pleijel sketched the history of quantum theory from Max Planck's first ruminations in 1900 on the nature of energy as universally quantized in discrete amounts — that is, in multiples of a specific constant $h$. Yet, it was clear that the old controversy concerning the corpuscular theory versus the undulatory or wave theory of light energy had not been resolved, and that the concept of light quanta, later called photons, did not explain the phenomenon of light propagation by waves. Louis de Broglie (1892-1987) in the early 1920's had applied some of Albert Einstein's ideas to developing the next step toward a solution, which was the theory of "matter-waves." De Broglie held that the motion of matter, like that of energy radiation, was to be conceived as a representation by many waves, mostly out of phase, that form a crest, which in turn propagates itself at a velocity completely different from that of the many component waves. Could this noncorpuscular, nondurable character of matter be reconciled with the idea of definite and discrete energy quanta?

Pleijel continued, explaining how in 1913 Niels Bohr (1885-1962) had first hypothetically connected the oscillating frequencies of an element's spectrum with the quantized energy levels within the atom. In 1925, Heisenberg, Dirac, and Schrödinger, working from different scientific starting points, fashioned convincing comprehensive explanations. Schrödinger's solution was closely related to de Broglie's viewpoint, whereas Heisenberg rejected on empirical grounds all models for the atom and worked from the perspective of the whole, the oscillating system. Dirac also developed a wave equation for the motion of matter and in addition proposed the idea of the "positron," the positive counterpart of the negatively charged electron.

Schrödinger's contribution was the creation of a new mechanics of matter-waves "which also holds good for motion within the atoms and molecules." Assuming the electrons within the atom to be the source of wave phenomena, Schrödinger developed a "wave equation for the motions executed by the electrons which would define these waves in the same way as the wave equation which determined the propagation of light." His accurate physicomathematical description of matter linked wave phenomena with the specific discrete energy values within the atom, as determined by Planck's constant.

## Nobel lecture

Schrödinger followed Werner Heisenberg in delivering his acceptance speech before King Gustav V and the assembled Royal Swedish Academy. Titled "The Fundamental Idea of Wave Mechanics," the lecture is an excellent example of Schrödinger's compelling literary style, which gives ample evidence of the author's perspicuity, his love of intellectual history, and his desire to speak to all educated men and women, not merely to the experts.

He began, as Einstein often did in his papers, not with a reference to some arcane, specialized problem described in the jargon of physicists but with a familiar physical phenomenon: changes in the direction of light rays by refraction or reflection. He described in general terms mankind's historical preoccupation with the phenomenon. He then illustrated Pierre de Fermat's principle of the shortest light time by comparing the movement of a light ray to the forward advance, over rough terrain, of a rank of soldiers, all of whom are grasping firmly the same long rod and attempting to march as quickly as possible. Now and again, the left or the right will be slowed by the terrain, creating a sort of undulation, but the important thing is that the overall trajectory of the advancement will be curved. The Irish mathematician Sir William Rowan Hamilton (1805-1865) noted this tendency of light to seek not the shortest but the quickest path, as when a ray of sunlight entering the atmosphere does not move in a straight line but remains for a time in the upper atmosphere, where resistance is lower. The light travels in a curved line, and thus covers a greater distance, but it still arrives on Earth more quickly than if it had traveled in a straight line through the atmosphere. Hamilton applied the idea to mechanics and proposed that an analogous principle governs the movement of "mass points" in a field of forces. Hamilton's notions did not seem viable during his lifetime, since observable phenomena such as "a planet on its orbit around the sun or . . . a stone thrown in the gravitational field of the earth" exhibited little evidence to confirm the idea that matter behaved in an undulatory fashion, as does light. At a more elementary level of physical reality, however, Hamilton's ideas might be useful, Schrödinger thought. Indeed, he described in his lecture how he had extended certain nearly forgotten concepts from Hamilton's geometrical optics to what he called the "inner life" of the atom, arriving at a new theory that was not really novel, but "a completely organic development" of Hamilton's idea that mathematically defined "mass points" show properties similar to those of light waves.

The lecture's next section was devoted to an explanation of certain diffraction phenomena that result from the wave nature of light—that is, the interference of light waves. In this portion of the speech, Schrödinger was leading up to the "salient point of the whole matter," which was that "the diameters of the atoms and the wavelength of the hypothetical material waves are of approximately the same order of magnitude." This equivalence is no accident. The atom, Schrödinger suggested, should be understood as a reflex of the diffraction caused by an electron wave "captured" by the atom's nucleus.

Still, Schrödinger had to conclude that his new wave mechanics could not entirely replace the old corpuscular, or "point," mechanics but could account for only one aspect of reality. Light propagation, from which his understanding of subatomic phenomena was derived, retained a dual nature. For Schrödinger, light propagation appeared to be composed of particles in a "longitudinal" sense, whereas a "transversal" perspective evinced light's wave nature. He believed, however, that there must be a unifying principle. In a pointed reference to the empirical convictions of Heisenberg and his school, Schrödinger grudgingly accepted the idea that science is best suited only for describing what is observed in specific cases. Nevertheless, he questioned whether "from now on we shall have to refrain from tying description to a clear hypothesis about the real nature of the world." For him, the advance of science required the challenge of explanation.

## Critical reception

As *The New York Times* reported on November 10, 1933, "well-informed circles" were surprised by Schrödinger's selection. Harvard professor Percy W. Bridgman had been expected to receive the award for 1932, for which Werner Heisenberg was named, and many assumed that Auguste Piccard would be next in line for the 1933 award by dint of his stratospheric explorations.

The press in Schrödinger's homeland of Austria welcomed the news of his prize with enthusiasm, whereas the German press tended to emphasize the simultaneous announcement of Heisenberg's selection for the 1932 prize. The nationalistic daily paper *Berliner Tageblatt* on November 10, 1933, lauded Heisenberg, thirty-two, as the youngest Nobel Prize winner, even printing a portion of an essay by the young physicist. Schrödinger was not mentioned at all in the paper until November 19, when pictures of both scientists appeared in its Sunday magazine. In the meantime, the National Socialists were elected by a large majority to the Reichstag, a fact that convinced Schrödinger, then at Oxford, to remain abroad.

Schrödinger himself was irritated that his award came at the same time as Heisenberg's, for he had begun to regret having had anything to do with the advancement of the new quantum mechanics, which to his increasing dismay relied on statistical probability and the concept of "indeterminacy." Even more abhorrent was the philosophical conviction of Heisenberg, Dirac, and others that all reality is predicated on the act of observation. Schrödinger would comment extensively on his objections to physics' new direction in his book *Science and the Human Temperament* (1935).

Despite some ambivalence in the foreign press, the critical reception of Schrödinger's work was on the whole positive, since professional colleagues generally recognized his work as an extension of advancements made by de Broglie and saw his wave equation as a singularly brilliant achievement of lasting value for physics. Furthermore, there was a consensus that Heisenberg and Schrödinger, though basing their work on conflicting tenets, had reached by different means solutions in agreement with one another.

## Biography

Erwin Schrödinger was born on August 12, 1887, in Vienna. His father, Rudolf, ran the family oilcloth factory but was mainly interested in botany (he published several papers on plant phylogeny), Italian painting, and chemistry. Schrödinger, an only child, considered his father a great friend and teacher and was indelibly marked by his father's wit and inquisitiveness. An additional influence was his grandfather on his mother's side, the professor of chemistry Alexander Bauer. Schrödinger also benefited immeasurably from the cultural ambience of Vienna itself, for the city was in the midst of its richest flowering of science and literature while he was growing up, and such were his interests.

Schrödinger did not attend school until he entered the *Gymnasium* in 1898, from which he was graduated first in his class in 1906. He was interested in all the subjects of the humanistic curriculum, but he detested rote memorization and scholastic dissection of great poetry and drama. Not until his third semester at the University of Vienna did Schrödinger actually begin the formal study of physics under Friedrich Hasenöhrl, who had been chosen to replace his own teacher, Ludwig Boltzmann (1844-1906). Schrödinger completed his doctorate in 1910 and began laboratory work with another of Boltzmann's pupils, Franz Exner.

At the outbreak of World War I, Schrödinger entered military service as an artillery officer. He returned to his position in Vienna after the war and soon met Annemarie Bertel, whom he wed on April 6, 1920. Within the year, but only after several brief sojourns at other universities, Schrödinger finally settled into a full professorship at the University of Zurich. Schrödinger's marriage was not without its crises, but the childless couple would manage to stay together, and Annemarie was in the end a most devoted companion.

Schrödinger's work on the famous wave equation was completed by the end of 1926, and for his efforts he received the Nobel Prize, along with P. A. M. Dirac, seven years later. In the meantime, he had moved to Berlin to serve as Max Planck's successor in 1927. He left Germany for the United States, then England, on Adolf Hitler's ascension to power in 1933, but he returned, homesick for Austria, to a position at the University of Graz in 1936. With the *Anschluss* of 1938, he fled to

Erwin Schrödinger

Italy. He was given a position at the University of Dublin for the remainder of his career, and he returned to Austria in semiretirement in 1956. Even during a difficult illness that began in 1957, he made an effort to accept the numerous honors offered him, and he returned to Vienna to occupy a professorship for a time. He died on January 4, 1961, and was buried in his beloved Tirolean village of Alpbach.

## Scientific Career

The course of Schrödinger's career is unusual for a modern physicist of note. He has been rightly called a "polymath." Indeed, Schrödinger was one of the few scientists in the twentieth century with the agility of mind and depth of knowledge to combine universal interests with distinctive achievement in almost every field he investigated. He was not merely an accomplished physicist who attempted to make developments in his field comprehensible to the general public; he was a philosopher, a biologist, a historian of ideas, and a scholar of literature and languages. His parents had provided him with a broad and rich cultural education, and he grew up speaking both German and English, a fact that explains the ease with which he wrote many of his books in the latter language, beginning in the mid-1930's.

When Schrödinger, in the second year of his studies at Vienna, settled on physics as his major subject, his talent was quickly recognized by his teachers. In his fourth year of study, 1910, he completed his doctorate under the direction of Ludwig Boltzmann's successor Friedrich Hasenöhrl and then began work as Franz Exner's laboratory assistant. His first publication was the result of collaboration with K. W. F. Kohlrausch on atmospheric radioactivity. At the end of World War I, Schrödinger began to receive numerous job offers, the first of which, at the University of Czernowitz, did not materialize as a result of the ceding of that Austro-Hungarian city and its region to the Ukraine in the aftermath of the war. Schrödinger was invited to teach at Jena in 1920, where he remained only briefly before accepting a position at the Technische Hochschule in Stuttgart. He removed to Breslau the following year but soon accepted the prestigious chair in physics at the University of Zurich, once held by Albert Einstein and Max von Laue. During his six years at Zurich, Schrödinger explored many scientific subjects, including optics and the phenomenon of color blindness, but he concentrated primarily on statistical thermodynamics, a field pioneered by Boltzmann.

It was the work of the French scientist Louis de Broglie that led to the insights that would make Schrödinger internationally famous. De Broglie had first suggested in his doctoral thesis and in several subsequent publications of 1924 that matter, like light, had a dual nature, exhibiting the properties of both waves and particles. The behavior of electrons could only be understood by applying the mathematics of undulation, and de Broglie showed that this wave concept could be reconciled with Niels Bohr's notion of quantized electron orbits around a nucleus. Einstein lent his support to the theory in a 1925 article on quantum theory and "ideal" gases. His ideas captured Schrödinger's interest and led him to explore the de Broglie concept in depth. Thus, the way was paved for Schrödinger to show the connection between the frequency of spectroscopic emissions from an electron and the corresponding frequency of the "wave crest" that describes the electron even in its role as particle orbiting the nucleus of that atom. Schrödinger's progress was slowed, however, by his initial inability to understand the spin of the electron, a problem which would be addressed by P. A. M. Dirac, who shared the Nobel Prize with Schrödinger in 1933.

Intuition instead of reason, Schrödinger would later say, led to the final insight that produced the famous wave equation in 1926. He had for a time abandoned a relativistic model, and had joined with his colleague Hermann Weyl in addressing the mathematics of a wave description of matter. The result was a series of four papers in the German journal *Annalen der Physik*. Beginning with the second paper, Schrödinger developed his thinking on the basis of mathematical calculations introduced in the previous century by William Rowan Hamilton, in which the methodology of geometrical optics provided a model for a mechanical description of nature. These papers are the source of several of Schrödinger's best-known contributions other than the wave equation itself, such as the concept of the electron as the manifestation of the "crest" of a "wave group."

Schrödinger found himself at odds with the ascending school of physicists represented by Heisenberg and his colleagues at the University of Göttingen, who looked to Niels Bohr and Ernest Rutherford (1871-1937) for their basic principles as they formulated a new "matrix mechanics" to describe empirically identifiable occurrences at the atomic level. Schrödinger, on the other hand, insisted—as did Einstein—on theoretical order and direct causation, not to mention "naturalness," or a kind of aesthetic integrity which demanded that one explain, not merely describe, phenomena. He quickly became restless about the discontinuity inherent in the view that came to be known as the "Copenhagen interpretation," despite the mathematical agreement of wave mechanics and the matrix approach, which Schrödinger himself had taken considerable pains to prove.

The subtle and complex argument among physicists continued, with Max Born (1882-1970) further (though unintentionally) insulting Schrödinger by interpreting the wave equation along the lines of statistical probability in 1927. Schrödinger rejected absolutely the discontinuous or corpuscular conclusions of his opponents and continued to develop his wave conception of matter. He felt vindicated, to some extent, when he was offered the chair in theoretical physics at the University of Berlin, which was to be vacated by Max Planck (1858-1947), the venerable originator of the "quantum" idea. Schrödinger's years in Berlin were to be pleasant enough, especially because of the continued presence of the great teacher Planck as a professor emeritus, but he missed the Alpine landscape. As the years progressed, the Nazi Party gained more and more power and was able to effect the dismissal or voluntary departure of numerous talented scientists; in 1933 Schrödinger accepted a temporary position at Oxford and left the country himself, expecting the worst for Germany. It was in England that he received the news that his previous work on wave mechanics had earned for him the Nobel Prize in Physics.

His exile was short-lived. By 1936 he had composed and published several books on scientific subjects in English; he seemed quite acclimated but in fact longed to return to his homeland. The University of Graz offered him a position that same year and he went back to Austria, only to be forced to flee with his wife to Rome after the *Anschluss* in 1938. The prime minister of Ireland, Eamon de Valera, managed in the autumn of 1938 to engage Schrödinger's services for the newly founded Dublin Institute for Advanced Studies, where, with the exception of an early period at the University of Ghent, Schrödinger remained until 1956. During this time, he pursued his well-known studies of genetics (*What Is Life?*, 1944) and other projects in physics and became immersed in the Celtic language and culture. He explored oriental philosophy, probably influenced by earlier studies of the philosopher Arthur Schopenhauer. One of his last writings, *Meine Weltansicht* (1961; *My View of the World*, 1964), attempts to construct a comprehensive philosophy based in Eastern wisdom as well as in modern science.

Some of Schrödinger's more ambitious theoretical work at Dublin during World War II and after did not receive lasting recognition. His theory of the nature of genetic material (the hypothetical "aperiodic crystal") was an early attempt to define genes as complicated molecules, but it was replaced by James Watson and Francis Crick's "double helix" concept in 1953. Similarly, Schrödinger's 1947 announcement of a complete solution to the electromagnetic and gravitational problems of Einstein's unified field theory failed to receive a response from Einstein and was soon forgotten.

The early 1950's saw continued debate on the Copenhagen interpretation of quantum physics, and Schrödinger continued to express his dissatisfaction with principles that seemed to him to have become dogma far too quickly. He questioned everything from the idea of "quantum jumps" to Heisenberg's uncertainty principle. He and Einstein believed that the new school had made a serious mistake in abandoning the deterministic worldview for a probabilistic or statistical description of nature. Ironically, Schrödinger's wave equation had in the meantime become an integral part of the apparatus of quantum mechanics and was used to draw probabilistic conclusions that were anathema to him.

Since the end of World War II, efforts had been made to obtain Schrödinger's agreement to return to Austria for good. In 1956, after the Soviet occupying forces withdrew, he agreed to accept a professorship at the University of Vienna, where he taught for two more years before retiring. His honors during that time were many, including the endowment of a science prize in his name, to be administered by the Austrian Academy of Sciences. He spent much of his retirement in Alpbach, a favorite Tirolean village. He lived for three years after suffering a critical illness in 1957 but finally died on January 4, 1961.

## Bibliography

*Primary*

Physics: Important early papers that won for Schrödinger the Nobel Prize can be found reprinted in *Abhandlungen zur Wellenmechanik*, 1927. They also appeared in English as *Collected Papers on Wave Mechanics*, 1928. His major books on physics are *Statistical Thermodynamics*, 1944; *Space-Time Structure*, 1950; *Studies in the Non-Symmetric Generalization of the Theory of Gravitation*, 1951; *Science and Humanism: Physics in Our Time*, 1951; *Expanding Universes*, 1956.

BIOLOGY: *What Is Life?*, 1944.

OTHER NONFICTION: *Science and the Human Temperament*, 1935; *Nature and the Greeks*, 1954; *Mind and Matter*, 1958; *Meine Weltansicht*, 1961 (*My View of the World*, 1964).

## Secondary

Fischer, Ernst Peter. "We Are All Aspects of One Single Being: An Introduction to Erwin Schrödinger." *Social Research* 51 (Autumn, 1984): 809-835. An excellent summary of the unifying principles and essential themes in Schrödinger's approach to physics, biology, and cosmology. This article characterizes the major writings of Schrödinger with a finely tuned sense for his humanism and his continual search for truth within the limitations of mankind's quite recent attempts to establish a disinterested, or objective, worldview. Fischer hints at Schrödinger's quintessentially German monism.

Gribbin, John. *In Search of Schrödinger's Cat: Quantum Physics and Reality.* New York: Bantam Books, 1984. The author of this lively and fascinating book is a British physicist who has written on other compelling subjects in modern science. As the title indicates, he is mostly concerned with the philosophical implications of Schrödinger's positions on quantum mechanics, as illustrated by the famous "cat in the box" problem that Schrödinger invented to expose the absurdity of probabilistic physics. The book has charts and drawings and is designed for the average reader.

Hermann, Armin. "Erwin Schrödinger: Eine Biographie." In *Die Wellenmechanik.* Stuttgart: Battenberg Verlag, 1963. Much of this rather brief biography, prompted by the lack of a comprehensive autobiography from Schrödinger's pen at the time of his death, can be found in English in Hermann's entry for Schrödinger in the *Dictionary of Scientific Biography*, vol. 12. Hermann was a classmate of Schrödinger at Vienna and a longtime friend.

Kilmister, C. W., ed. *Schrödinger: A Centenary Celebration of a Polymath.* Cambridge: Cambridge University Press, 1987. This ambitious collection of essays addresses Schrödinger's achievements in the various fields in which he worked, from wave mechanics to unified field theory to microbiology. Although the book contains a useful bibliography and several articles of interest to the layman, some papers are far too technical for the average undergraduate.

Mehra, Jadish, and Helmut Rechenberg. *The Historical Development of Quantum Theory.* 5 vols. New York: Springer-Verlag, 1982. Many consider this five-volume work the definitive historical study of the field in which Schrödinger played so great a role. The text is thorough and concise but at times quite technical; it will appeal primarily to the serious student of the history of physics.

Prizbaum, Karl, ed. *Letters on Wave Mechanics*. Translated by Martin J. Klein. New York: Philosophical Library, 1967. The lively and sometimes emotionally charged correspondence of Schrödinger and his elders shows the human side of the development of a new and indispensable concept in the new physics. More information on Schrödinger's correspondence with various figures can be found in *Sources for History of Quantum Physics: An Inventory and Report*, by Thomas Kuhn et al. (Philadelphia: University of Pennsylvania Press, 1967).

Scott, William T. *Erwin Schrödinger: An Introduction to His Writings*. Amherst, Mass.: University of Massachusetts Press, 1967. This is the most useful overview of Schrödinger's thought available in English. It is a critical study of medium length with a bibliography which, though now outdated, can be supplemented by an examination of Kilmister's *Centenary Celebration*, mentioned above.

*Mark R. McCulloh*

# 1933

### Physics
Erwin Schrödinger, Austria
Paul Adrien Maurice Dirac, Great Britain

### Chemistry
no award

### Physiology or Medicine
Thomas Hunt Morgan, United States

### Literature
Ivan Bunin, France

### Peace
Sir Norman Angell, Great Britain

# PAUL ADRIEN MAURICE DIRAC
## 1933

*Born:* Bristol, Gloucestershire, England; August 8, 1902
*Died:* Tallahassee, Florida; October 20, 1984
*Nationality:* British
*Area of concentration:* Quantum mechanics

*Dirac's formulation of a relativistic wave equation showed that electron spin properties were a direct consequence of this new account of wave mechanics rather than a hypothesis added in order to account for experimental results concerning alkali spectra. His division of the wave equation into two parts led to the hypothesis of a new particle, the positron, whose existence was confirmed experimentally*

## The Award

*Presentation*

On December 12, 1933, Paul Adrien Maurice Dirac was presented the Nobel Prize in Physics by H. Pleijel, Chairman of the Nobel Committee for Physics of the Royal Swedish Academy of Sciences. Dirac shared the award with Erwin Schrödinger (1887-1961), who was responsible for the first wave mechanical formulation of the quantum theory. Pleijel's presentation speech outlined some of the major developments in physics, beginning with the quantum hypothesis of Max Planck (1858-1947). Planck's discovery had provided an account of the atomic properties of light which emphasized that matter could absorb or create light only in quantities of energy that were multiples of a specific unit called a "quantum." This quantity divided by the frequency of the oscillation of the light ray yielded a constant, $h$, which came to be known as "Planck's constant." Pleijel went on to describe the analogy first proposed by Louis de Broglie (1892-1987) between light waves, which carry light particles (photons), and matter waves, which carry particles of matter; the central idea was that the motion of matter and light results from the propagation of waves. The experimental corroboration of de Broglie's theory suggested that matter was composed of changeable particles in space.

In 1913, Niels Bohr (1885-1962) developed a new model of the atom which incorporated Planck's constant as the determining factor for movements within the atom and for the absorption and emission of the light waves that produce atomic spectra. The remarkable agreement between Bohr's model and the observed spectrum of hydrogen not only showed the significance of Planck's constant but also marked the end of classical mechanics in the atomic realm.

Pleijel outlined further developments in the quantum theory, including Schrödinger's wave mechanics and Werner Heisenberg's matrix mechanics, and gave a brief account of Dirac's contributions. Building on Schrödinger's wave equation, Dirac had introduced relativistic constraints which confirmed the existence of electron spin and of a new, positively charged electron, the positron. The speech concluded with a summary of some of the conceptual changes resulting from quantum mechanics, including the abandonment of causality at the micro level.

*Nobel lecture*

Like most of his technical and nontechnical writing, Dirac's Nobel lecture, "Theory of Electrons and Positrons," is a model of clarity. Dirac described in detail the reasoning that led to his formulation of the relativistic wave equation for the electron and the consequences of that account, including the spin hypothesis and the theoretical motivation behind the theory of the positron. The lecture began with a discussion of elementary particles and what could be inferred about them solely on the basis of theoretical considerations. Because the nature of protons and neutrons was not well understood at the time, Dirac dealt almost exclusively with electrons and positrons.

The quantum mechanics of Schrödinger and Heisenberg could be applied to particles with small velocities, Dirac said, but was invalid in cases where velocities approached that of light—cases where relativity effects needed to be considered. When quantum mechanics was subjected to these relativistic constraints, certain restrictions on the properties of particles arose, and from these theoretical considerations, inferences could be drawn about the nature of these particles. Dirac first considered electron spin. He outlined some of the mathematical details and isolated the variables necessary for producing the relativistic version of the wave equation. Using general principles of quantum mechanics, he said, one can deduce that it is exactly these variables that are responsible for giving the electron a spin angular momentum and a magnetic moment (a measure of the magnetic strength of an electron resulting from the angular momentum of the electron in its orbit).

Dirac then described the theoretical discovery of the positron. In classical relativistic mechanics, the equation connecting the kinetic energy $W$ of a particle with its momentum allows $W$ to be a positive or negative quantity. These results also hold in the quantum mechanical formulation of the equation. Because the kinetic energy of a particle is always positive in practice, one is left with a kind of motion that results in faster-moving electrons having energy that is inversely proportional to their speed. Hence, energy must somehow be added in order to bring them to a rest state. The problem cannot be solved by simply ruling out the existence of this latter kind of motion in practice, for it is a consequence of the theory that by disturbing electrons the experimenter can cause a transition from a positive to a negative energy state of motion. Therefore, said Dirac, some interpretation had to be given to this discrepancy between theory and experimental practice.

An examination of these negative energy states in an electromagnetic field revealed that they corresponded to the motion of an electron with a positive rather than a negative charge, or a positron. That still did not solve the problem, however; observed positrons did not have negative energies. Using the exclusion principle of Wolfgang Pauli (1900-1958), which states that there can be only one electron in any one state of motion, Dirac assumed that nearly all the negative energy states for electrons are occupied, each by one electron—an event that is unobservable. Any unoccupied state, however, is observable. Because there is a lack of negative energy in these unoccupied states, or holes, they will have a positive energy. These holes are just like particles and can be identified with positrons, which are the mirror images of electrons.

The lecture concluded with a brief description of electron-positron annihilation and creation and some speculations about the existence of negative protons based on the symmetry between positive and negative charge.

## Critical reception

On November 10, 1933, it was announced in *The New York Times* that Paul Dirac had won the Nobel Prize in Physics along with Erwin Schrödinger, a German physicist who was then teaching at Oxford. The 1932 prize, which had not been awarded the previous year, was also announced: the winner was Werner Heisenberg of Leipzig, chosen for his creation of quantum mechanics. Both announcements came as a complete surprise to the ordinarily well-informed sources in Stockholm. In the October 29 edition of *The New York Times*, it was reported from Stockholm that Auguste Piccard of Belgium was expected to win the 1933 physics prize for his exploration of the stratosphere. It was also expected that the 1932 prize would go to Percy Williams Bridgman of Harvard. Surprise about the actual award was not documented in any of the other announcements. *The Times* of London, on November 10, gave a short summary of Dirac's work, as did the November 18 issues of *Science* and *Nature*; no mention was made of the reaction of the physics community.

The only negative response that was made public concerned the validity of Dirac's electron theory, not his receipt of the prize. The criticism came from Robert Andrews Millikan (1868-1953) of the California Institute of Technology. A report was carried in the November 26 edition of *The New York Times* of a meeting of the National Academy in Cambridge, Massachusetts, at which Millikan had provided experimental evidence that challenged Dirac's account of the positron. Carl Anderson (born 1905), who was responsible for the first experimental discovery of the positron, had been part of the team at Millikan's lab. According to Dirac's theory, photons (gamma rays) can be converted into pairs of positrons and electrons. In other words, there is a direct connection between energy and matter. Millikan, who had studied fourteen hundred photographic tracks made by the flying debris of lead atoms struck by gamma rays, concluded that positrons and electrons are simply knocked out of the nucleus of an atom by gamma rays. On the basis of his observations, Millikan also concluded that of the 10 percent of the tracks caused by direct hits of the nucleus, only 40 percent yielded positrons and electrons; the remaining 60 percent yielded only positrons. This finding was in direct contradiction to the Dirac account, which claimed that there ought to be as many positrons as electrons. Despite this challenge, however, further theoretical and experimental evidence showed the superiority of Dirac's theory.

## Biography

Paul Adrien Maurice Dirac was born on August 8, 1902, in Bristol, England. His father, Charles Adrien Ladislav Dirac, was Swiss, and his mother, Florence Hannah (née Holten), was English. He was educated at Merchant Venturer's Secondary School in Bristol, which was closely associated with the University of Bristol; there, he received a bachelor of science degree in electrical engineering in 1921. He remained at Bristol to study mathematics until 1923, when he received a grant to study at the University of Cambridge and enrolled at St. John's College as a research student in mathematics. He received a doctorate in 1926 and the following year became a Fellow of St. John's College. In 1930 Dirac was elected a Fellow of the Royal Society and was awarded the Society's Royal Medal.

Dirac's work dealt mainly with theoretical and mathematical aspects of quantum mechanics; he published his first paper on the subject while still a student at Cambridge. Many of his early papers, which extended some of Werner Heisenberg's mathematical ideas, were published in the *Proceedings of the Royal Society*. His most notable contributions include his 1928 paper "Theory of the Electron" and the 1930 "Theory of Holes," which introduced the positron; these developments won for him the Nobel Prize.

In 1932 Dirac was named Lucasian Professor of Mathematics at Cambridge, a chair once held by Isaac Newton. He remained there until he retired in 1969. After his retirement, he moved to Tallahassee, Florida, where he became a professor of physics at Florida State University; he held the post until his death in 1984.

Dirac was extremely fond of travel and was a visiting lecturer at several American universities, including Wisconsin, Michigan, Miami, and Princeton, where he was a member of the Institute for Advanced Study in 1934 and 1935. In 1929, having spent five months in the United States, he traveled around the world and together with Heisenberg visited Japan, returning to England by way of Siberia. Dirac was married to Margit Wigner, sister of the famous physicist Eugene Wigner (born 1902); they had two daughters.

## Scientific Career

Dirac originally went to Cambridge with the intention of studying relativity theory but was assigned to Ralph H. Fowler (1889-1944), who was working on developments in quantum physics. Consequently, Dirac turned his attention to this subject and published several papers on problems in quantum theory between 1923 and 1925. Dirac received a proof copy of Heisenberg's famous paper on quantum mechanics from Fowler, and he soon recognized that the noncommutative algebra used by Heisenberg to represent physical quantities provided the foundation for a general theory of quantum mechanics. From there, Dirac developed his own ideas about the structure of quantum mechanics, introducing his characteristic notation, much of which is still widely used. Most of his work was directed at combining the approaches of Schrödinger and Heisenberg into one common system using the methods of what is now known as "transformation theory." In the process, Dirac developed the bracket notation and claimed in his doctoral dissertation that "the whole of classical dynamical theory, insofar as it can be expressed in terms of P[oisson] B[racket]'s instead of differential coefficients, may be taken over immediately into the quantum theory." The Poisson bracket was the analogue of the commutator, and using Heisenberg's noncommuting theoretical variables, Dirac formulated a new kind of dynamics that would replace classical mechanics as a description of atomic phenomena. Fowler was so impressed with Dirac's results that he had him write them up and immediately contacted the Royal Society, urging them to give priority to Dirac's paper. "The Fundamental Equations of Quantum Mechanics" was received on November 7, 1925, and published in the *Proceedings of the Royal Society* on December 1. During 1925 and 1926, Dirac made several contributions to quantum mechanics, establishing a formal correspondence between this new physics and classical mechanics. One important development was his introduction of q numbers, a new kind of variable which does not satisfy the commutative law of classical mathematics.

By 1927, Dirac believed that the quantum theory could now be considered a fairly complete theory of dynamics. Because Niels Bohr's atomic model necessitated a departure from classical electrodynamics, however, some account of this subject within the context of quantum mechanics was required. The problems in this area were especially difficult, because at the quantum levels, forces propagate at the speed of light, requiring that relativistic constraints be applied. In addition, the moving electron sets up an electromagnetic field which, in turn, affects the electron itself.

Dirac was successful in overcoming these theoretical difficulties; he provided the first account of emission and absorption of radiation as well as of dispersion (the decomposition of a beam of white light into colored beams which spread out and produce spectra). These results, he believed, provided even more evidence for the superiority of his general methods and interpretation of the quantum theory over the Bohr-Heisenberg (sometimes called the "Copenhagen" or "Orthodox") account. He further pointed out that some difficulties inherent in competing interpretations were the result of using classical formulas to describe radiation. These methods, he argued, were limited in scope, because they were not applicable in cases that did not have classical analogues. Because Dirac's general transformation theory had a definite basis distinct from classical physics, it could successfully describe phenomena for which there existed no classical counterpart. One such phenomenon was the magnetic electron.

Dirac had been unhappy with previous attempts to derive the properties of the electron from the quantum theory; they either violated relativity theory or used methods for which there was no justification within the boundaries of general quantum theory. By introducing relativistic constraints into the Schrödinger wave equation, Dirac developed a quantum mechanical account of a relativistic electron and submitted it to the Royal Society on January 2, 1928. The paper was published in the February 1 issue of the *Proceedings*. Although Dirac's equation agreed with the observed data, it met with one fundamental difficulty: To give a complete calculation of the solutions, one had to admit negative energy values, a notion which, in the light of then-current theories, seemed rather suspicious if not altogether meaningless.

Despite this vexing problem, the theory had some remarkable successes. It gave correct solutions for scattering and bound state problems and, without the addition of any further parameters, allowed the deduction of specific properties of the electron, such as its spin and magnetic moment. Spin properties had been ascribed to the electron in 1925 by Samuel A. Goudsmit (1902-1978) and George E. Uhlenbeck (born 1900) by means of a special hypothesis used to account for empirical results concerning the nature of alkali spectra. In addition to revealing electron properties, the Dirac equation, unlike Schrödinger's and de Broglie's wave mechanics, gave results which agreed with observations of the hydrogen spectrum. (Spectral lines are the empirical manifestation of energy levels within the atom.)

In an attempt to account for the problem of negative energy states, Dirac formulated what came to be known as the "hole theory" and submitted this new interpretation to the Royal Society on December 6, 1929. His resolution of the problem contained three steps. First, he used the Pauli exclusion principle to argue for the assumption that most states of negative energy are occupied. Next, he assumed that a uniform filling of these states is unobservable. Any unoccupied negative energy state, however, because it departs from this uniform picture, can be observed. Dirac maintained that the unoccupied states, or "holes," would move like positively charged particles with positive kinetic energy. This hypothesis led him to conclude that the holes were in fact protons. Dirac later modified his views about the nature of the holes and published his new ideas in the *Proceedings* later in 1931. By this point, he had recognized that the hole had the same mass as the electron and therefore could not be a proton after all; consequently, the hole became known as the "antielectron." According to Dirac's theoretical account, one should expect an electron with positive energy to drop into a hole in the otherwise uniformly filled negative energy states. Once this hole was filled, the kinetic energy of the electron would be freed in the form of electromagnetic radiation. This process could be characterized as one in which the electron and the antielectron, or the positron, annihilate each other. Conversely, one should be able to create an electron and a positron from electromagnetic radiation.

In 1932 Dirac was named Lucasian Professor of Mathematics at Cambridge. (Theoretical physics was regarded as part of mathematics.) Scientists at the famous Cavendish Laboratory at Cambridge, including Dirac himself, were skeptical about the possibility of observing the antielectron. In fact, several famous physicists, including J. Robert Oppenheimer (1904-1967), expressed skepticism about Dirac's hole theory in general. In September of 1932, Carl Anderson, who was then working at Robert Millikan's laboratory at the California Institute of Technology, announced his observation of a positively charged particle having a mass comparable to that of the electron. He named his discovery the "positron" but did not connect it to Dirac's theory until September, 1933, after several others had reported similar findings. Patrick M. S. Blackett (1897-1974) and his collaborator Giuseppe Occhialini were the first to present the evidence for Dirac's theory. They studied the production of positive electrons from nuclei and, on the basis of further experimental results obtained from Irène Joliot-Curie (1897-1956) and her husband, Frédéric Joliot (1900-1958), in France and from Lise Meitner (1878-1968) and her colleagues Phillip and Kunze in Germany, presented a forceful argument at the 1933 Solvay Conference for the experimental confirmation of Dirac's theory. Their argument was strongly supported by Bohr. In addition to this evidence, the work of Enrico Fermi (1901-1954) on beta decay, which made use of Dirac's electron theory and the creation and annihilation operators, further confirmed the relativistic quantum dynamics. For these outstanding contributions to the development of the quantum theory, Dirac was awarded the Nobel Prize in 1933.

After 1933, Dirac continued to work on applications of quantum mechanics, and in conjunction with Fermi, he developed the famous Fermi-Dirac statistics that govern the distribution of certain elementary particles among various possible energy levels. Some of Dirac's original ideas, such as the prediction of the existence of magnetic monopoles (hypothetical magnetic particles analogous to electrical particles such as the electron and proton but with a magnetic charge of either north or south), were never confirmed. Others, however, were developed in important and interesting ways; one example is an idea briefly mentioned in his *Principles of Quantum Mechanics* (1930), which contained the origins of Richard Feynman's famous path integral method, used widely in quantum electrodynamics.

Dirac remained at Cambridge until he retired in 1969. Up until that time, he visited and lectured frequently in the United States and was a member of the Institute for Advanced Study at Princeton, New Jersey, in 1934-1935, 1946-1948, and 1958-1959. From 1968 to 1972, he was a member of the Center for Theoretical Studies at the University of Miami. In 1971 Dirac accepted a post as professor of physics at Florida State University, in Tallahassee, where he remained until his death in October, 1984.

Dirac was the recipient of many awards and distinctions, including the first Oppenheimer Prize, which was awarded to him in 1969 by the Center for Theoretical Studies. His acceptance speech was published in 1971 as *The Development of Quantum Theory*. The book traces the history of his ideas and their impact on quantum physics in a clear and nontechnical way. A set of lectures delivered at the University of Miami was published in 1970 under the title *Spinors in Hilbert Space*; it contains a highly mathematical updating of *Principles of Quantum Mechanics*. The latter continues to be a much-used source in the field and has been reprinted and revised several times. In 1973 Dirac received the Order of Merit, one of the most distinguished British honors for intellectual achievement.

## Bibliography

*Primary*
PHYSICS: Dirac published more than one hundred scientific papers. The more tech-

nical ones, including most of his early writings, appeared in the *Proceedings of the Royal Society*. He also published in *Physical Review*, *Reviews of Modern Physics*, and *Nature*. A paper titled "The Evolution of the Physicist's Conception of Nature," published in *Scientific American* 208, no. 5 (1963), is an excellent presentation of some of Dirac's ideas. His books are *The Principles of Quantum Mechanics*, 1930; *Lectures on Quantum Mechanics*, 1964; *Lectures on Quantum Field Theory*, 1966; *Spinors in Hilbert Space*, 1970; *The Development of Quantum Theory*, 1971.

*Secondary*

Kursunoglu, Behram N., and Eugene P. Wigner, eds. *Paul Adrien Maurice Dirac: Reminiscences About a Great Physicist*. New York: Cambridge University Press, 1987. The book was originally planned as a festschrift for Dirac's eightieth year, but because of his death, it was produced as a memorial volume. It has three sections, one describing Dirac's early days at Cambridge and his life in Florida, and contains a portrait of Dirac sketched by Richard Feynman. There are contributions from many of Dirac's close friends, including his wife, Margit, and her brother, the physicist Eugene Wigner. The other two sections deal with Dirac's scientific ideas and the impact he and his work had on other physicists in the field. The volume also contains an entry by Dirac titled "The Inadequacies of Quantum Field Theory" and a detailed chronology of his life.

Mehra, Jagdish. *The Physicist's Conception of Nature*. Dordrecht, Netherlands: D. Reidel, 1973. This source contains the proceedings of a symposium held at the International Center for Theoretical Physics in Miramare, Trieste, Italy, on September 18-25, 1972, to honor Dirac's seventieth birthday. It contains articles by Dirac and by numerous other contributors, including Heisenberg, on a variety of topics, such as space, time, and geometry; the development of quantum theory; and some of quantum theory's philosophical foundations. It concludes with an essay on Dirac titled "The Classical Mind" by the famous novelist C. P. Snow.

Mehra, Jagdish, and Helmut Rechenberg. *The Historical Development of Quantum Theory*. Vol. 4. New York: Springer-Verlag, 1982. This volume presents the most detailed account of Dirac's contributions to quantum mechanics available. It describes Dirac's intellectual development, tracing his student years at Bristol and Cambridge, his early research on the problems of quantum theory, his formulation of the relativistic wave equation, and his development of the algebra of q numbers. The book benefits from Mehra's personal conversations and meetings with Dirac.

Moyer, Donald Franklin. "Origins of Dirac's Electron, 1925-1926." *The American Journal of Physics* 49 (October, 1981): 944-949.

_____. "Evaluations of Dirac's Electron." *The American Journal of Physics* 49 (November, 1981): 1055-1062.

_____. "Vindications of Dirac's Electron." *The American Journal of Physics* 49 (December, 1981): 1120-1125. This three-part article traces Dirac's early work on quantum mechanics to the final experimental confirmation of the famous hole theory. It provides details of the arguments found in the early papers and describes how the members of the physics community reacted to the consequences of Dirac's relativistic generalization of quantum mechanics. The papers also describe many of the specifics of the experimental work done in connection with the positron.

Salam, Abdus, and Eugene Wigner. *Aspects of Quantum Theory.* New York: Cambridge University Press, 1972. This volume was dedicated to Dirac on his seventieth birthday; it commemorated his contributions to quantum physics. It contains a complete bibliography of Dirac's writings up to 1971, an early portrait, and a portrait taken at a Solvay Conference in the late 1960's. There are a number of technical papers on some of Dirac's mathematical contributions to quantum mechanics, such as the delta function, Poisson brackets, and the Fermi-Dirac statistics. There are also papers on the electron, a piece on Dirac's work from 1924 to 1933, and some reminiscences of Dirac's days at Cambridge and his travels through the Rocky Mountains.

*Margaret C. Morrison*

# 1935

## Physics
Sir James Chadwick, Great Britain

## Chemistry
Frédéric Joliot, France
Irène Joliot-Curie, France

## Physiology or Medicine
Hans Spemann, Germany

## Literature
no award

## Peace
no award

# SIR JAMES CHADWICK
## 1935

*Born:* Manchester, England; October 20, 1891
*Died:* Cambridge, England; July 24, 1974
*Nationality:* British
*Areas of concentration:* Atomic and nuclear physics

*Chadwick experimentally established the existence of the neutron, which had been theoretically predicted by Ernest Rutherford in 1920. He established that the neutron has essentially the same mass as the proton. In the process of doing so, he devised a new method of calculating the mass of a nucleus*

## The Award

*Presentation*

On December 12, 1935, H. Pleijel, Chairman of the Nobel Committee for Physics of the Royal Swedish Academy of Sciences, presented James Chadwick to King Gustav V, who awarded him the Nobel Prize in Physics. In his presentation, Pleijel put Chadwick's research and discovery into historical and scientific perspective and also noted the close connection between Chadwick's work and the research of Frédéric Joliot (1900-1958) and Irène Joliot-Curie (1897-1956), winners of the 1935 Nobel Prize in Chemistry.

Pleijel noted that prior to Chadwick's discovery of the neutron, it had been known that electrons and protons were present whenever radioactive material decayed or atoms disintegrated. This finding had led to the theory that atoms were made up of one or more electrons orbiting a much heavier nucleus made up of protons and enough electrons to make the entire atom electrically neutral. At first, this theory seemed to agree with experience, but the continued study of the energy conditions when atoms disintegrated showed that the model was seriously deficient. In 1920, Lord Ernest Rutherford (1871-1937) suggested that these problems would be eliminated if there existed neutral particles with the same weight as a proton; Chadwick discovered that these theoretical particles were real. This discovery paved the way for the theory that atoms are made of electrons orbiting a nucleus made up of protons and neutrons. The discovery of the neutron also made possible a satisfactory explanation for isotopes. Pleijel also pointed out that the electrically neutral neutron could be a powerful tool for the future study of the atom.

*Nobel lecture*

Chadwick's Nobel lecture consisted of three parts: In the first part, he described how his discovery had come about; in part two, he described the nature of the neutron; and in the last part, he explained how his discovery had changed the model of the atom and the theories concerning the radioactive transmutation of atoms from one element into another.

Chadwick claimed no originality for the idea that there may be fundamental particles with no electrical charge. He specifically mentioned Walther Hermann Nernst (1864-1941) and Lawrence Bragg (1890-1971) and quoted Rutherford on neutrons. Rutherford believed that such a body would be extremely difficult to detect, yet he also believed that just such a neutral particle was needed if scientists were to explain the evolution of the heavier elements from hydrogen. Chadwick recalled that several attempts had been made to find this neutral particle and that all, including his early attempts, had failed.

Chadwick credited the experimentation that Frédéric Joliot and Irène Joliot-Curie had done with beryllium radiation, a radiation that induces paraffin to emit large numbers of high-speed protons, with setting him on the path to the discovery of the neutron. Chadwick believed that these high-speed protons could best be explained by viewing the beryllium radiation as made up of particles rather than of an X-ray-like radiation, as had previously been supposed. He therefore began to study the beryllium radiation proton effect, using the counter, the expansion chamber, and the high-pressure ionization chamber. The expansion chamber produced the evidence needed to show that proton emission from irradiated paraffin was indeed the result of a particle's striking the nucleus of a hydrogen atom and knocking it out of the paraffin.

Chadwick then presented evidence and an argument to show that this particle was not a proton-electron couplet, as Rutherford had suggested, but rather a new fundamental particle. He said:

> A structure of this kind [a proton-electron couplet] cannot be fitted into the scheme of the quantum mechanics, in which the hydrogen atom represents the only possible combination of a proton and an electron. Moreover, an argument derived from the spins of the particles is against this view. The statistics and spins of the lighter elements can only be given a consistent description if we assume that the neutron is an elementary particle.

Chadwick then described how he had used a new method to determine the mass of the neutron. He studied the energy in the disintegration process in which a neutron is liberated from a deuterium, or heavy hydrogen, nucleus. Calculations showed that a neutron's mass is 1.0085 and a proton's mass is 1.0081. In the last part of his lecture, Chadwick demonstrated how his neutron fit into what was known about the radioactive decay and transmutation of an atom of one element into an atom of another. He also showed how his theory simplified the model of the atom by having the nucleus consist of protons and neutrons rather than of protons and enough electrons to make the atom electrically neutral. He suggested that further studies would be needed to determine just what held together the particles that composed the nucleus of an atom.

## Critical reception

The public reaction to the announcement that James Chadwick had been awarded the Nobel Prize in Physics for his discovery of the neutron was positive yet, for the most part, subdued. In most cases, the award was given two or three paragraphs in which not much more was said than that he had discovered the neutron. The technical reasons for the award were generally not mentioned. That is understandable, considering that the study of nuclear physics was less than fifty years old. More scientifically sophisticated articles appeared in *Nature*, an English scientific journal; *New Outlook*, an Australian science news magazine; *Scientific Monthly*, an American science journal; and *Newsweek*, an American news weekly.

The November 23, 1935, issue of *Nature* praised Chadwick as a scientist of first rank and, as such, one who was worthy of the award. His research and that conducted with Lord Rutherford had "laid the foundation on which the new science of nuclear physics was built." The article went on to state that "the importance of the discovery of the neutron may best be realized when it is remembered that it changed completely and simplified our ideas of the structure of nuclei."

News reports in *New Outlook* of June, 1936, besides describing how Chadwick had "trick[ed] the radiation to reveal itself," also noted the neutron's future use as "a new and valuable bombarding particle which can penetrate electrical fields with impunity." On November 23, 1935, *Newsweek* reported this same feature in a more picturesque fashion: "Neutrons' lack of electrical charge made them ideal projectiles with which to smash atoms in the laboratory. . . . They could dart through the electrical shield surrounding each nucleus the way a wooden toothpick can penetrate a magnetic field where a steel pin can not."

The American physicist Robert A. Millikan (1868-1953), the Nobel Prize winner in physics for 1923, commenting on the 1935 Nobel Prizes in physics and chemistry in the January, 1936, *Scientific Monthly*, wrote, "Never have two Nobel Prizes been more richly deserved." He believed that to be so because "it was Chadwick who marshaled the old evidence for the existence of neutrons, then predicted new results on the assumption of their existence, and checked the prediction by unambiguous experimental proof."

## Biography

James Chadwick was born on October 20, 1891, near Manchester, England. He was the son of John Joseph Chadwick and Anne Mary Knowles. He was educated in Manchester, England, and in 1911 was graduated from Manchester University, where he majored in physics. He did postgraduate work under Ernest Rutherford, studying various problems dealing with radioactivity. He earned his master of science degree in 1913. That year, he was awarded a scholarship that enabled him to travel to Berlin to study under Hans Geiger (1882-1945), who is best known for his invention of the Geiger counter. Unfortunately, World War I erupted while Chadwick was in Berlin, and he was held as an enemy alien until the war ended in 1919.

After World War I Chadwick returned to England, where he again studied under Rutherford, at Cambridge University. He later was Rutherford's associate at Cambridge's Cavendish Laboratory. He was elected a Fellow of Gonville and Caius College and was assistant director of research in the Cavendish Laboratory from

1923 to 1935. In 1925 he wed Aileen Stewart-Brown of Liverpool; they later became the parents of twin daughters. In 1932, he discovered the neutron, for which he was awarded the Nobel Prize in Physics in 1935. That same year, Chadwick accepted the position of professor of physics at the University of Liverpool, where he remained for eight years. From 1943 to 1946, he worked in the United States as the head of the British mission attached to the Manhattan Project, which developed the atom bomb. In 1948 he retired from active research to become master of Gonville and Caius College, a position he held until his retirement in 1959. From 1957 to 1962, he was a part-time member of the United Kingdom's Atomic Energy Authority. He died in Cambridge on July 24, 1974.

## Scientific Career

Chadwick's discovery of the neutron placed him in noble company and gave him a notable part in the scientific revolution of the twentieth century. For thousands of years, the atom was thought to be a featureless, indivisible sphere. This view rapidly changed with the discovery of radioactivity by Antoine-Henri Becquerel (1852-1908) and Pierre and Marie Curie (1867-1934), a discovery that gave physicists the tool they needed to study the atom in detail. The awareness that certain elements gave off radiations excited many scientists, notably Ernest Rutherford, Chadwick's professor of physics at the University of Manchester. Their professor-student relationship blossomed into a professional association that lasted beyond Rutherford's death until Chadwick edited Rutherford's papers for publication in the 1960's. He and Rutherford were colleagues at the Cavendish Laboratory from 1923 to 1935. It was in this laboratory that Chadwick discovered the neutron, allowing the refinement of Rutherford's nuclear model of the atom. This model pictured the atom as being made up mostly of space, in which electrons orbit about an atomic nucleus of protons and neutrons.

In the 1920's, only two subatomic particles were known: the electron, discovered by Sir Joseph John Thomson (1856-1940) in 1897, and the proton, which was discovered in 1914 by Rutherford, Thomson's student. Herein lay the problem. If atoms were neutrally charged, as they are, and if only protons made up the nucleus, then the atoms were too massive for their charge. For example, the helium nucleus has a mass equal to four protons and a positive charge equal to two electrons. Thus, it was thought that the nucleus must also contain two electrons to neutralize the two extra protons. It was even suggested that these weightless electrons might also be the glue that held together the protons, which should be repelling each other.

There were theoretical reasons relating to quantum mechanics which led Rutherford to suggest that instead of the helium nucleus consisting of four protons and two electrons, it would be simpler if it were made up of two protons and two neutral particles of the same mass as a proton. In 1920, Rutherford, Chadwick, and others tried to isolate this particle. They failed, not because the particle was nonexistent but because suitable technology for the task was not yet available.

The years between 1920 and 1930 were spent by Rutherford, Chadwick, and other associates at the Cavendish Laboratory bombarding various elements with alpha particles (helium nuclei), causing the elements to disintegrate into lighter elements. They studied the scattering of alpha particles by hydrogen and heavier nuclei and from these experiments determined the law of force around atomic nuclei. These two types of experiment led to the publication of *Radiations from Radioactive Substances* (1930), by Rutherford, Chadwick, and Charles Ellis, and Chadwick's book *Radioactivity and Radioactive Substances: An Introduction to the Study of Radioactive Substances and Their Radiations* (1921).

These years were also spent in identifying the positive charges, or atomic numbers, of various elements' nuclei. This work was done to prove that Henry Moseley (1887-1915) had been correct in arranging the elements into a periodic table by atomic number, or the number of protons in an element's nucleus. Previous periodic tables had arranged the elements in order of increasing atomic weight. Unfortunately, Moseley did not live to see his idea vindicated, as he was killed while serving in the British army during World War I. While Chadwick was occupied with this important research, which laid the foundations for the study of nuclear physics, related research was being done in Europe which was instrumental in setting him on the path to his momentous discovery.

It had been well established that when certain light elements such as nitrogen and aluminum are bombarded with alpha particles (atomic particles, having the size and charge of helium nuclei, which are emitted from radioactive polonium), they are transmuted into heavier elements and in this process give off a proton. For example, when the nucleus of a nitrogen atom, of atomic weight 14, is bombarded by an alpha particle, it momentarily fuses into a particle with a mass of 18 which then splits into a fast-moving proton and a new type of oxygen with an atomic weight of 17. In other cases, nothing of this kind happens. In 1930, Walther Bothe (1891-1957) bombarded beryllium with alpha particles and was surprised that rather than observing the expected transmutation process with the emission of a proton, or observing no change at all, he found that the experiment produced an unexpected radiation. He believed that this radiation was a type of electromagnetic radiation that had been discovered by Rutherford in his early work on radioactivity. Bothe therefore did not pursue the phenomenon.

In 1932, Frédéric Joliot and Irène Joliot-Curie expanded on Bothe's work by using a stronger radiation source. They reported that beryllium, when bombarded by fast alpha particles, gave off a very penetrating radiation which had several unusual properties for gamma radiation. They noted that this radiation was much more penetrating in one direction than in another and that it had the ability to knock protons out of a paraffin block that they had placed in the path of this radiation in order to determine its strength. They, like Bothe, interpreted these results as being caused by an unusually high-energy type of gamma radiation. They also did not pursue the matter.

Chadwick read the Joliot-Curie reports with interest. He believed that their results could be more easily explained if the radiation was assumed to consist of particles instead of electromagnetic waves or gamma radiation. The high penetrating power caused him to suspect that this radiation contained the elusive neutron for which he had been searching. Chadwick therefore duplicated the experiments of Bothe and Joliot-Curie. He concentrated on the high-energy radiation instead of on the artificial radioactive material produced. He directed this high-energy radiation into hydrogen, nitrogen, argon, air, and other materials. In each case, the beryllium radiation ejected protons from the substance's nuclei. If these protons were being ejected by a gammalike radiation, Chadwick realized, their kinetic energies could be calculated using quantum mechanics. Chadwick made the calculations, and the result did not agree with his measurements. He therefore concluded that the beryllium radiation was made up of neutral particles about the same size as a proton.

To prove this theory, Chadwick and his associates ran an extensive series of experiments in 1932 to gather conclusive evidence of the neutron's existence. The one that finally brought success was an elaborate apparatus comprising a powerful alpha source (pure polonium) to irradiate beryllium, a separate ionization chamber, an amplifier, an oscilloscope detector, and a photographic device to record the oscilloscope trace. After calibrating his instruments, Chadwick placed a lead sheet capable of stopping gamma- and alpha-type radiation between the source of radiation and the counter. The sheet caused no decrease in the count, showing that the beryllium radiation being studied was indeed very penetrating and not a gamma ray but rather a neutral particle, the neutron.

When paraffin sheets were substituted for the lead, the deflection rate doubled, just as the Joliot-Curies had reported in their research on artificial radioactivity. All these findings taken together convinced Chadwick that the best way to explain the phenomena was to suppose that alpha particles were knocking neutral particles out of the beryllium nuclei and that these neutral particles were in turn knocking protons out of the paraffin. The rest of the physics community agreed that he had indeed demonstrated the existence of the elusive neutron.

The discovery of the neutron rapidly modified the nuclear model of the atom. Werner Heisenberg (1901-1976) was quick to point out that a nucleus made up of protons and neutrons was, from a theoretical point, much more satisfying than one made up of a certain number of protons and a smaller number of electrons. He also pointed out that isotopes of elements, discovered by Frederick Soddy in 1913, could be easily explained if each isotope contained the same number of protons but a different number of neutrons. Thus, one isotope of chlorine could be thought to consist of seventeen protons and eighteen neutrons; the other, of seventeen protons and seventeen neutrons. The neutron proved most useful for initiating nuclear reactions. In 1938, Otto Hahn (1879-1968) and Lise Meitner (1878-1968) were to show that it was Chadwick's neutron that caused uranium to fission.

In 1935, Chadwick left the Cavendish Laboratory to become the Lyon Jones Professor of Physics at the University of Liverpool. There, he embarked on the construction of a 36-inch cyclotron, or "atom smasher." This instrument was completed just before World War II, so at the outbreak of the war, Chadwick took up the study of nuclear chain reactions based on the fission of uranium. He, along with Otto Robert Frisch (1904-1979), informed the British government in the spring of 1940 that an atom bomb could probably be produced if enough uranium 235 could be concentrated in a small enough space.

During this part of Chadwick's career, he served primarily as the elder statesman of British nuclear physics. His reaction to the discovery of the possibility of atomic chain reactions in uranium was eagerly sought. At first he was skeptical, but as more and more research became known, he changed his mind. Chadwick was quick to recognize that plutonium also had characteristics that made it suitable for the production of an atom bomb. He was influential in getting the British and American scientific, military, and political communities to cooperate.

In 1943, Chadwick recruited a small but powerful British team of scientists to work in Los Alamos, New Mexico, and Berkeley, California, as part of the Manhattan Project team that developed the atom bomb. He and his family moved to Washington, D.C. From there, he supervised the British research efforts and coordinated them with those of the United States. Chadwick was instrumental in getting Niels Bohr (1885-1962) to join the project and in procuring a supply of uranium from central Africa. In due course, both the uranium and plutonium atom bombs were constructed and detonated against Japan, bringing a rapid end to World War II in the Asiatic theater. For his effort, Chadwick was awarded the Medal of Merit by President Harry S. Truman in 1946.

With the end of the war, the joint operation of the British and American scientists was disbanded and Chadwick returned to Liverpool, virtually unhonored and unsung by his countrymen. He spent the remainder of his scientific career involved in nuclear energy developments in Great Britain and pure research in nuclear and particle physics. To promote the latter, he started construction of a larger cyclotron capable of producing 300-megavolt protons to replace the obsolete cyclotron he had originally built at the University of Liverpool.

In 1947, Chadwick spent a short time in New York City as an adviser to the British delegation to the United Nations. While there, he was taken aback by the notion, held by many, that matters of atomic energy ought to be left entirely in the hands of nuclear physicists. Chadwick realized that these issues were not only scientific in nature but also of political and social concern. He believed that nuclear physicists should provide essential, expert advice but not decide the issue alone. This view made him unpopular with scientists who had worked with him during the development of nuclear power. Perhaps that explains the following statement by Sir Harrie Massey and Norman Feather in a biographical memoir written on the occasion of Chadwick's death in 1974:

> It would be hard to overestimate Chadwick's contribution to the development of atomic energy from all angles, scientific, technical, managerial, diplomatic, political, and social. Few men are possessed of all the qualities which are required to make this possible. It is surprising how little recognition he was accorded for this work.

# Bibliography

*Primary*

PHYSICS: *Radioactivity and Radioactive Substances: An Introduction to the Study of Radioactive Substances and Their Radiations, the Nature of Radioactivity and the Bearing of Radioactive Transformations on the Structure of the Atom*, 1921; *Radiations from Radioactive Substances*, 1930 (with Ernest Rutherford and C. D. Ellis); "Possible Existence of a Neutron," 1932; "Existence of a Neutron," *Proceedings of the Royal Society of London*, vol. 136, 1932; *Papers on the Neutron*, 1932 (with Norman Feather and P. I. Dee); "Evidence for a New Type of Disintegration Produced by Neutrons," 1934 (with Feather and W. T. Davies).

EDITED TEXT: *Collected Papers*, 1962-1965 (by Ernest Rutherford).


*Secondary*

Feather, Norman. "Chadwick's Neutron." *Contemporary Physics* 15 (1974): 565-572. A firsthand account of the history of the discovery of the neutron as told by one of Chadwick's associates at the Cavendish Laboratory at the time the discovery was made.

Gowing, Margaret. *Britain and Atomic Energy, 1939-1945*. New York: St. Martin's Press, 1964. This three-volume work, the official history of the United Kingdom's Atomic Energy Authority, details the early history of atomic research in Great Britain. As a result, one must comb through the work to find references to Chadwick. Part of this history concerns the cooperation between the United States and Great Britain, which is described from a British perspective. In the first volume, Gowing, historian and archivist for the Atomic Energy Authority, recalls the important part Chadwick played in this cooperation as a coordinator of the British effort and diplomatic liaison between British scientists and Major General Groves, head of the Manhattan Project of the U.S. Army Corps of Engineers.

Massey, Sir Harrie, and Norman Feather. "James Chadwick, 20 October, 1891-24 July, 1974." *Biographical Memoirs of Fellows of the Royal Society* 22 (1976): 11-70. This biographical memoir is the most complete account of the life and works of James Chadwick written to date. It is the personal account of two men who knew Chadwick well, both professionally and personally. The memoir ends with a quite complete bibliography of the published scientific writings of James Chadwick.

Rhodes, Richard. *The Making of the Atomic Bomb*. New York: Simon & Schuster, 1986. A very detailed history. Although it does not focus on Chadwick alone, it traces his part in the story, from his discovery of the neutron to his observation of the first test blast of an atom bomb. That Chadwick is mentioned in some thirty parts of the book shows that he was in the thick of the action. Nevertheless, his name is not often connected with the project, nor is his work as well-known as that of J. Robert Oppenheimer, Edward Teller, Niels Bohr, and Albert Einstein.

Segrè, Emilio. *From X-Rays to Quarks: Modern Physicists and Their Discoveries*. San Francisco: W. H. Freeman, 1980. The title of this book is a good description of its contents. James Chadwick plays a prominent part in chapter 9, "The Wonder Year 1932: Neutron, Positron, Deuterium, and Other Discoveries." It concentrates on the early part of Chadwick's professional career and the discovery of the neutron rather than on his contribution to the harnessing of atomic energy.

Shamos, Morris H. *Great Experiments in Physics*. New York: Henry Holt, 1959. This book supplies the background for twenty great experiments in physics and reprints the original scientific report of each experimenter. The papers are annotated for the general reader by Shamos. The twentieth experiment is the one that led to the discovery of the neutron by James Chadwick.

*Theodore P. Aufdemberge*

# 1936

### Physics
Victor Franz Hess, Austria
Carl David Anderson, United States

### Chemistry
Peter Debye, Netherlands

### Physiology or Medicine
Sir H. H. Dale, Great Britain
Otto Loewi, Germany

### Literature
Eugene O'Neill, United States

### Peace
Carlos Saavedra Lamas, Argentina

# VICTOR FRANZ HESS
## 1936

*Born:* Waldstein Castle, near Graz, Styria, Austria; June 24, 1883
*Died:* Mount Vernon, New York; December 17, 1964
*Nationality:* Austrian
*Area of concentration:* Cosmic radiation

*Hess won the Nobel Prize for his surprising discovery of cosmic radiation, which came from the depths of space far beyond Earth, the solar system, and possibly the galaxy, and for his skillful experiments which proved that these cosmic rays had a penetrating power far surpassing any previously known radiation*

## The Award

*Presentation*

Professor H. Pleijel, Chairman of the Nobel Committee for Physics, presented the Nobel Prize in Physics for 1936 to Victor Franz Hess on behalf of the Royal Swedish Academy of Sciences on December 10, 1936. Pleijel reviewed the discoveries, made just before and after the turn of the century, of surprising types of radiation which marked a new direction in physics. Wilhelm Conrad Röntgen (1845-1923) had discovered X rays; Antoine-Henri Becquerel (1852-1908), the radioactive rays that led Marie (1867-1934) and Pierre (1859-1906) Curie to discover radium. His search for the sources of radioactivity led Hess to the discovery of a new and more puzzling type of radiation, cosmic rays.

These newer radiations could not be shielded from a sensitive detector by any practical thickness of lead plates, which suggested that the source of these rays was not within Earth or in the atmosphere. In 1911 and 1912, Hess made a series of balloon ascents more than three miles high which showed that the new rays doubled in intensity at the top of the ascent. Later investigations by Hess's successors showed that the intensity increased further, until the rays were forty times as intense at an altitude of five and one-half miles as they were at the surface.

Pleijel noted the decade of skepticism which had passed before the existence of cosmic rays was generally accepted. Later, Hess had found that these cosmic radiations came from all directions of space, day and night. Very precise measurements made by Hess showed very small daily and seasonal variations which correlated with the motion of the Milky Way. The rays came neither from Earth nor from the Sun, but possibly from a source beyond the galaxy.

*Nobel lecture*

Hess's Nobel lecture, "Unsolved Problems in Physics: Tasks for the Immediate Future in Cosmic Ray Studies," delivered in German, summarized his own contributions and those of others to this then-new field of research. With keen foresight,

Hess pointed to the mystery of the origins of cosmic rays as one of the main unsolved problems in physics at that time and called for greater funds with which to attack the problem.

Hess had already demonstrated by 1912, in a series of daring balloon flights, that the new radiations decreased in intensity near Earth but increased noticeably above three thousand feet. Hess recounted how he had undertaken a new balloon ascent to ten thousand feet during a solar eclipse on April 12, 1912, and had found no reduction in the intensity of the rays as the Sun disappeared from view. That eliminated the Sun as a major source of the cosmic rays.

With determination, Hess sought other means over the years to solve the puzzle. In the fall of 1931, he set up an observatory at seven thousand feet on the Hafelekar mountain at Innsbruck, Austria. Data from the observatory revealed a small daily fluctuation which indicated a slight atmospheric influence on the rays as they passed through the high atmosphere. A still smaller fluctuation, related to stellar time, moved Arthur Holly Compton (1892-1962) to propose that the rays originated in galaxies beyond the Milky Way.

In his Nobel lecture, Hess proposed a number of ways to pursue the study of cosmic-ray composition and origin. These methods included perfecting automated balloons and stratospheric flights, pursuing studies deep in shafts and mines, and recording data simultaneously by all available techniques. Hess emphasized the need for greater funding to make decisive progress. Finally, Hess noted that studies of cosmic rays in strong magnetic fields had led Carl David Anderson (born 1905) to discover the positive electron. Anderson was corecipient of the Nobel Prize with Hess, and he predicted the discovery of still other unknown particles in the future.

*Critical reception*

The week in which Hess delivered his Nobel lecture was an ominous week for the world. World War II was soon to begin. Rebel aircraft were flying over Madrid as the Spanish Civil War continued. Benito Mussolini had just abolished all civil and criminal courts in Italy, replacing them with tribunals. French prices had risen 20 percent in one month. A new dust bowl threatened the Great Plains of the United States, and 3.5 million Americans were still on relief as the Great Depression lingered. Germany and Japan had just signed a military alliance.

The ominous world events muted the reception of the Nobel prizes that year. National newspapers, understandably, gave wider coverage to their own recipients. *The New York Times* on November 13, 1936, carried a front-page story on the awarding of the Nobel Prize in Literature to Eugene O'Neill and the physics prize to Carl Anderson, merely noting that the Austrian Hess was Anderson's corecipient. Yet, even in the lay press, there was recognition of Hess's pioneering effort. On the editorial page the following day, while summarizing Anderson's discovery of the positron (the electron's positively charged twin), *The New York Times* characterized Hess as the man who established the extraterrestrial origin of the cosmic rays and "who must therefore be regarded as their Columbus."

The real connection between Hess's work and the discovery of the positron was made clear to the public by Anderson himself the following week. On arriving at Newark Airport on November 29, on his way to Norway and the Nobel Prize presentations, Anderson lavishly praised Hess's work on cosmic rays, saying that it was in cosmic-ray debris that he had found his evidence for the positron. Anderson concluded, "All of our knowledge of interstellar space must for some time continue to proceed from further exploration of the cosmic ray."

## Biography

Victor Franz Hess was born on June 24, 1883, in Waldstein Castle, near Graz, Styria, Austria. His father was a forester who served an Austrian prince. Hess was educated at Graz Gymnasium and Graz University; he obtained his doctoral degree in 1910. From 1910 to 1920, he served as assistant at the Institute of Radium Research of the Viennese Academy of Sciences and also lectured on physics at the Vienna Veterinary College. It was during this time, in his late twenties, that Hess undertook ten difficult and courageous balloon flights which determined the extra-terrestrial origin of cosmic rays. World War I brought a temporary interruption to Hess's activities.

After receiving the Leiben Prize in 1919 for his research on cosmic rays, he was appointed Extraordinary Professor of Experimental Physics at his alma mater, Graz University. The Extraordinary Professorship is a special position for promising researchers, who assist the Ordinary Professor heading the laboratory. Hess's career was now well under way. The next year, he wed Mary Bertha Warner.

Hess now developed interests well beyond his homeland. On a leave of absence from Graz, he traveled to the United States, where he established the Research Laboratory of the U.S. Radium Corporation in Orange, New York, and also took on a consulting position with the U.S. Department of the Interior at its Bureau of Mines. He returned to Graz in 1923 and in 1925 was appointed to the Ordinary Professorship. In 1931, in his late forties, Hess became a professor at Innsbruck University at the new Institute of Radiology and, that autumn, established the famous cosmic-ray observatory on Hafelekar mountain. A year later, he received the Abbe Medal of the Carl Zeiss Institute. His career was capped by the Nobel Prize in 1936, but World War II loomed.

Hess returned to Graz in 1937 but lost his professorship during the Nazi occupation of Austria. He was a staunch Catholic, and his wife was Jewish. In 1938, Hess was offered the position of professor of physics at Fordham University, in New York. He accepted the position and remained in the United States, becoming a naturalized citizen in 1944. His wife of thirty-five years died in 1955. Later that year, he was married to Elizabeth M. Hoenke, who had nursed his wife during her illness. The next year, he retired from Fordham University, becoming professor emeritus. On December 17, 1964, he died in Mount Vernon, New York, at the age of eighty-one. He had no children of his own.

Hess spoke excellent English in a hoarse whisper, the result of a throat operation performed in the 1930's. He was a gentle and humble man who made little of his awards.

## Scientific Career

Victor Hess's entire career was intimately connected with cosmic rays. At the turn of the century, scientists had puzzled over a strange fact. If a vessel was tightly sealed with a measured amount of air, a small amount of electrical charge soon appeared. The charge appeared even when the most stringent efforts were made to prevent any electrical leakage and to remove all sources of radiation which might produce the electrical charge. As with most scientific discoveries in the making, it was hard to determine whether the problem was simply a nuisance that would go away with better technique or was indeed the first glimpse of a new, possibly important, discovery.

The nuisance would not go away. Very thick shielding did diminish the effect slightly, indicating that a very penetrating radiation produced the free charges by colliding with the air atoms in the container. The effect, however, was found over sea as well as on land, eliminating the known radioactivity of rocks on land as the source of the penetrating rays. Preliminary altitude measurements, including tests made atop the Eiffel Tower and on primitive balloon flights, were inconclusive. In 1910, Victor Hess tackled the problem. Hess had earned his doctorate at the University of Graz in 1910. He had originally intended to study the science of light, but his prospective professor committed suicide before Hess could begin. Hess now committed himself to understanding the strange charging effects and joined a group under Franz Exner and Ergon von Schweidler working on atmospheric electricity.

At that time, the basic instrument for studying electrical charges was the electroscope. It was then known that air contained electrons and that if these electrons were removed when air was sealed in the electroscope, electrons soon reappeared, producing the puzzling electrical conduction. Hess undertook studies of the problem using electroscopes and enlisted aid from both the Austrian Academy of Sciences and the Austrian Aeroclub to settle the question of whether the effect changed with height.

Hess knew that balloon flights were needed. Before his flights, he calculated the height at which ground radiation would not affect the results. The height was about one and one-half times the height of the Eiffel Tower. His flights would have to be much, much higher if he were to distinguish a source different from the ground radiation. He designed electroscopes to withstand the very low temperatures and pressures to be encountered in the empty skies above. Finally, he enlisted companions daring enough to help in the flights.

At six in the morning of August 7, 1912, Hess and two companions ascended near Aussig, Austria. The balloon rose for two and one-half hours as Hess tended his three electroscopes while the others checked altitude and temperature and navigated the craft. The balloon settled at a frigid altitude between thirteen thousand and sixteen thousand feet and drifted with the air for another hour. The descent came near noon, bringing the three companions to the ground at Pieskow, Germany, 30 miles east of Berlin and 125 miles from the launch site. Hess had found that the response of his electroscopes at the highest altitude was four times the response on the ground. Hess went on to make a total of ten flights, half at night. In November of that year, he summarized his conclusions in a German journal of physics: "The results of my observations are best explained by the assumption that a radiation of very great penetrating power enters our atmosphere from above."

Hess found that the unknown radiation decreased with distance close to Earth's surface but that above five hundred feet, the radiation increased; at three miles, the radiation strength was several times greater than it was at the surface. The effects of the radiation were the same day or night and were unaffected when the Sun was blotted from view in flight during a solar eclipse. Hess was satisfied that the rays came from beyond the Sun. Later, in 1913, W. Kohlhorster ballooned to almost six miles and measured a twelvefold increase in intensity. Nevertheless, there were many scientist skeptics who doubted Hess's and Kohlhorster's results and especially the interpretation of them as evidence for rays from outer space. As with many new theories, acceptance was slow in coming.

Hess proceeded with his work. In 1913 he set up a meteorological station at Hoch Obir, 1.25 miles high, to obtain continuing data on the radiations. World War I halted these studies. At its end, Hess received his appointment as assistant at Graz and traveled to the United States while on leave. He returned to Austria in 1923 and in 1925 was made full professor at Graz and head of his own laboratory. That same year, Robert Millikan (1868-1953), the 1923 Nobel laureate in physics, termed the radiations "cosmic rays," and the theory's acceptance was complete. There was still, however, much to learn about the rays.

Hess continued his high-altitude investigations in several locations in the Alps. In 1931, with international assistance from the Rockefeller Foundation, the Austrian Academy of Sciences, the Prussian Academy of Sciences, and the Emergency Society for German Sciences, he set up the famous Hafelekar cosmic-ray observatory near Innsbruck, 1.5 miles above sea level. The data obtained from this laboratory became a standard for reliable monitoring of cosmic-ray intensity. A small daily variation in cosmic-ray intensity was established, indicating that the Sun contributed a very small component to the cosmic rays. In addition, data were accumulated pointing to an extragalactic origin for the rays.

The Nobel Prize came in 1936. Hess's return to Graz in 1937 promised further accomplishments and rewards, but on March 11, 1938, Adolf Hitler's troops marched into Austria and annexed the country. Hess had served as a representative of the sciences in the independent Austrian government, was a strict Roman Catholic, and had a Jewish wife; consequently, in March of that year, Hess was dismissed from his post at Graz. A sympathetic Gestapo officer warned the Hesses that they might be placed in a concentration camp, so they fled to Switzerland. Fortunately, Hess was offered the position of professor of physics at Fordham University in New York City. He accepted, traveled to the United States, and remained. He continued his cosmic-ray studies, but the main advances in the field passed to others.

Hess pursued other research in the United States, as well. In 1946, he and Paul Luger of Seattle University performed the first radioactive fallout tests, and in the next year, Hess developed a sensitive test for detecting very small amounts of radium in the human body. In the 1950's, he served on a U.S. Air Force team which studied radioactive fallout from atom bomb tests; they found that perhaps fifty years would have to pass before the effects of fallout radioactivity could be correctly assessed. As a result, Hess strongly opposed atomic testing. He knew well the consequences of radioactive poisoning; his thumb had been amputated after an accident with radioactive material in 1934.

Hess had many honors in addition to his Nobel Prize. He was a member of the Austrian Academy of Sciences, held honorary doctorates from Fordham University, Loyola University, and the University of Innsbruck, and was awarded the 1959 Austrian Medal of Science and Arts. In 1962, two years before his death, Hess was inducted into the Pontifical Academy of Science in Rome.

After World War II, new techniques for detecting cosmic rays were developed rapidly. Geiger counters had been in use since the late 1920's, and fast photographic emulsions and cloud chambers were added to the experimentalists' tools. The post-World War II era saw the widespread use of instrumented balloons and rockets, already foreseen by Hess. Present-day physicists use scintillation detectors in association with particle detectors to sort out the various components of cosmic rays.

It now appears that most cosmic rays are generated by supernovae, the explosions of massive stars at the end of their lives. Particles in the rays have energies of up to $10^{20}$ volts, and it is this huge energy that gives the discovery of cosmic rays such lasting significance. Only high energies can reveal the secrets of the subnuclear regions that physicists seek to explore. Thus, in discovering cosmic rays, Hess not only opened a door to the vast depths of space beyond the solar system and the galaxy but also pointed to a pathway descending into the smallest secret realm of nature.

## Bibliography

*Primary*

PHYSICS: The vast majority of Hess's published works are in German, and the Austrian Academy has a list of more than 130 of his articles. Two of his major works are *Die elektrische Leitfähigkeit der Atmosphäre und Ihre Ursachen*, 1926 (*The Electrical Conductivity of the Atmosphere and Its Causes*, 1928); *Die Weltraumstrahlung und ihre biologischen Wirungen*, 1940 (with Jacob Eugster; *Cosmic Radiation and Its Biological Effects*, 1949).

*Secondary*

Auger, Pierre. *What Are Cosmic Rays?* Rev. ed. Chicago: University of Chicago Press, 1945. A translation from the French, this popular book presents a fascinating history of the early investigations of cosmic rays. Where needed, the physics is presented clearly. Hess's contributions are discussed in chapter 1.

Hillas, A. M. *Cosmic Rays*. New York: Pergamon Press, 1972. This text is for readers with a background in physics. The first chapter presents a review without mathematics, but thereafter the writing becomes more technical. Hess's contributions are discussed, and in the book's second half, there is a fairly readable translation of part of his 1912 paper reviewing his balloon results. Also includes original papers by other workers.

Pasachoff, J. M. *Contemporary Astronomy*. Philadelphia: W. B. Saunders, 1977. An excellent undergraduate text in astronomy, requiring no knowledge of mathematics or physics. It includes a general review of scientists' knowledge of the stars, the solar system, the galaxy, and the universe as a whole. Chapter 8 has a section on cosmic rays, their nature, and their probable origins in supernovae.

Rossi, Bruno. *Cosmic Rays*. New York: McGraw-Hill, 1964. A readable and authoritative book by a well-known physicist who worked with cosmic rays. The first chapter provides interesting details on Hess's measurements and his ballooning. The physics of cosmic rays is explained for the nonspecialist. Some details are out of date, but the book is a good introduction to the topic.

*Peter J. Walsh*

# 1936

### Physics
Victor Franz Hess, Austria
Carl David Anderson, United States

### Chemistry
Peter Debye, Netherlands

### Physiology or Medicine
Sir H. H. Dale, Great Britain
Otto Loewi, Germany

### Literature
Eugene O'Neill, United States

### Peace
Carlos Saavedra Lamas, Argentina

# CARL DAVID ANDERSON
## 1936

*Born:* New York, New York; September 3, 1905

*Nationality:* American
*Area of concentration:* Particle physics

*While investigating cosmic radiation, Anderson identified the positron—an elementary particle possessing a mass identical to that of the electron but with a positive charge instead of a negative one. The achievement contributed materially to the understanding of elementary particles*

## The Award

*Presentation*

On December 10, 1936, Carl David Anderson became a corecipient, together with Victor Franz Hess, of the Nobel Prize in Physics. In presenting the two scientists to the King of Sweden, Professor H. Pleijel, Chairman of the Nobel Committee for Physics, explained the connection between their works. Hess, in 1911 and 1912, had discovered that cosmic radiation had its source in deep space; Anderson, between 1930 and 1932, had engaged in definitive investigations of the nature of this radiation and in the process had produced some incontrovertible evidence concerning the existence of the positively charged electron. Moreover, the discovery had given empirical support to Paul Dirac's relativistic theory of the electron.

Anderson had constructed a Wilson cloud chamber and immersed it in an extremely strong magnetic field. Since the tracks of positively charged particles moving downward could have been misinterpreted as the tracks of negatively charged particles moving upward, Anderson inserted horizontally into the cloud chamber a thin lead plate. A particle traversing the plate, he reasoned, would lose some of its energy, with an attendant decrease in the radius of curvature of its track, and would reveal the direction of its motion. Several photographs culled from the thousands shot manifested tracks that Anderson identified as those of particles with the electron's mass but a positive charge—or positive electrons—which he named "positrons."

Experiments that he and a number of other scientists subsequently performed revealed that gamma radiation emitted by a thorium plate enclosed entirely within the chamber led to the single-center production of electron-positron pairs in a nearby lead plate. This process, known as pair creation, was linked to the action of gamma radiation interacting with the nuclei of the thorium atoms, and as such, it added further credibility to Dirac's theory.

*Nobel lecture*

On December 12, 1936—in his Nobel lecture, "The Production and Properties of

Positrons"—Anderson made an irrefutable case for the existence of the positive electron. He briefly summarized the background for his experimentation, with an allusion to the work of Dmitri Skobelzyn, who in 1927 published the first set of photographs of the tracks of cosmic radiation, and the plans in 1930 of Robert Andrews Millikan and Anderson to design and build a cloud chamber for their investigations. Subsequently, he cited the works of scientists, notably Giuseppe Occhialini and Patrick M. S. Blackett, at the University of Cambridge, who in early 1933 had built a more efficient positron detector and confirmed his discovery. Finally, he gave a synopsis of the theoretical basis for the positron, as formulated by Dirac in his relativistic theory of the electron.

In its design, the cloud chamber is a pumplike apparatus, with a piston and a facing glass wall. Supersaturated moist air which fills the pump can be brought to condensation when the piston is quickly withdrawn and the pressure lowered adiabatically. Anderson's apparatus measured 17 by 17 by 3 centimeters and was mounted vertically along its long dimension. The device was placed between the poles of an electromagnet which could maintain a uniform field of 24,000 gauss. Energy measurements which had hitherto been limited to 15 million electron volts were extended by Anderson during the course of the summer of 1931 to 5 billion electron volts, a thirtyfold increase.

Measurements of specific ionization, obtained from the density of condensed droplets, indicated that the radiation penetrating the chamber was composed of particles of unit charge. The negatively charged particles were identified as electrons, and initially, the positive ones were identified as protons; however; as Anderson's measurements of energy determination became more accurate, certain anomalies began to appear, and the earlier picture of electrons and protons as the sole constituents of charged cosmic radiation began to appear somewhat muddled.

Charged particles are deflected in a magnetic field, but other conditions determine by how much they are deflected: their mass, their speed, and their direction of approach relative to the magnetic field. If two oppositely charged particles were moving downward in the magnetic field, and the negatively charged particle curved to the right, the positively charged one would curve to the left. A negatively charged particle moving upward in the field would also curve to the left, however, and from its track, it could be misconstrued as a positively charged particle. In order to ascertain whether the particles were moving upward or downward, Anderson inserted horizontally into his cloud chamber a lead plate 6 millimeters thick. The energy loss in a particle traversing the plate manifested itself in a decrease in the radius of curvature of the particle's track. Among the figures Anderson presented during his Nobel lecture was a cloud chamber photograph showing a particle with the proper requirements of a positive charge. If it had been a proton, the radius of curvature of its track, in a region where the magnetic field measured 15,000 gauss, would have given it an energy of 200,000 electron volts. With that energy, a proton would have had a range of only 5 millimeters. On the other hand, a positron track of the same radius of curvature would have called for an energy of 63 million electron volts and a much greater range—the observed 5 centimeters.

Anderson cited the investigations by Occhialini and Blackett at the Cavendish Laboratory at Cambridge in which a triple-coincidence of Geiger counters surrounded the cloud chamber. That removed the hit-or-miss aspect in the detection of positrons that had encumbered Anderson's own work. In addition, a new phenomenon was reported by Occhialini and Blackett involving the production of positrons in the alpha particle bombardment of beryllium. Finally, Anderson referred to his work with a colleague, and the work of James Chadwick, Blackett, and Occhialini, in which evidence for the pair-creation phenomena was observed. In the latter process, gamma radiation emitted by thorium interacted with the nuclei of lead and produced electron-positron pairs.

*Critical reception*

Anderson's announcement of the discovery of the positron was greeted by skepticism from almost all quarters. His mentor Millikan suggested that the particle track that Anderson identified as belonging to a positron must have been caused by secondary radiation scattered by cosmic radiation from the walls of the chamber; the particle, no doubt, had been an electron traveling in the wrong direction. With the introduction of the lead plate into the chamber and a new round of photographs, however, the directions of the particles were properly ascertained, and Millikan accepted Anderson's claim. In fact, he pressed Anderson to send a note to *Science* immediately. According to Daniel Kevles, at a meeting at the Cavendish Laboratory in the fall of 1933, Millikan himself reported on the positron. He met a wall of resistance, a number of those in attendance coldly suggesting that it had to be interpretive error. Niels Bohr evidently dismissed the possibility of a negative electron altogether.

There were, however, two promising sources of support for the positron. The first was experimental in nature and came from the Cavendish's resident expert on cloud chambers, Blackett. With his research assistant Occhialini, Blackett had been engaged in cloud chamber investigations of his own. By 1933, the two physicists had found particle tracks which agreed with Anderson's conclusions and had published a paper in the *Proceedings of the Royal Society* announcing their discovery.

The second source of reinforcement was theoretical in nature: Paul Dirac, in formulating his "hole theory," had predicted such a particle some years earlier. In deriving a wave equation that was in concert with the special theory of relativity, Dirac had been forced to replace Erwin Schrödinger's equation with a four-component equation. When he solved the problem for the free electron, his equations had yielded four eigenvalues (energy values): two corresponding to positive energy and two to negative. These solutions gave not only the electron's spin-up and spin-down possibilities (properties which had been suspected for electrons but which had not been explained theoretically) but also a positively charged conjugate particle's spin-up and spin-down possibilities. In a time when the electron and proton had become fixed in scientists' minds as the only two elementary particles existing in nature, it was difficult for Dirac to accept the notion of the existence of a positive electron, especially since it had not been detected yet. He surmised initially that this conjugate particle was probably the proton; however, on physicist Hermann Weyl's encouragement, he decided to take seriously the symmetry apparent in his mathematics and to announce that the particle in question had to be the positive electron.

Subsequent investigations by Blackett, Occhialini, Chadwick, Irène Joliot-Curie, Frédéric Joliot, Lise Meitner, Anderson, and others pointed to the validity of Anderson's original claim and, too, the validity of Dirac's.

## Biography

Carl David Anderson was born to Swedish immigrant parents, Carl David Anderson and Emma Adolfina Ajaxson, in New York City on September 3, 1905. While still a child, he moved with his family to Los Angeles, where his father was to provide a modest living for the family by managing small restaurants. The year Anderson won the Nobel Prize, the *Los Angeles Times* quoted Mrs. Anderson's modest comment about her son: "If he has special ability, I don't know where he got it."

Unable to afford a college education out of town, Anderson attended the California Institute of Technology (Caltech), where he earned a bachelor's degree in physics. Having compiled an excellent undergraduate record, he received a fellowship to do graduate work at Caltech. Indeed, the institution was to become his lifelong employer. In 1946 he was married to Lorraine Elvira Bergman, with whom he would have two sons, Marshall David and David Andrew.

Anderson spent a total of fifty-four years at Caltech. He was an undergraduate student, a graduate student, and a postdoctoral research fellow, and finally he ascended through the ranks of the faculty, becoming an assistant professor, an associate professor, and a full professor. In 1977, he received the title of professor emeritus.

## Scientific Career

Carl Anderson's graduate work at Caltech was financed by a Coffin Graduate Fellowship. A memorable experience of his graduate school days was the quantum mechanics course he took from J. Robert Oppenheimer. Its rigor had driven even the theorists among the students to desert the course en masse, but the experimentalist Anderson heeded Oppenheimer's plea and stayed on. For his doctoral thesis, Anderson studied the space distribution of photoelectrons scattered by X rays incident on various gases, and in 1930 he received his doctorate magna cum laude.

It would be Anderson's first scientific endeavor beyond graduate school that would earn for him the Nobel Prize. At the behest of Robert A. Millikan, he stayed at Caltech as a postdoctoral fellow to help in the investigation of cosmic radiation. Millikan had become convinced that this radiation consisted of high-energy photons, or gamma radiation, and that by investigating their absorption by matter, one could measure their energies and ascertain their source. He therefore asked Anderson to join him in designing and constructing a cloud chamber along with a powerful magnet which would be applied to it. His hypothesis, paradoxically, was fueled by a mystical belief that atoms had been born in interstellar space and that cosmic radiation represented the "birth cries" of the process.

A discussion of Anderson's involvement in this project would be incomplete if his powerful mentor were not described. Millikan embodied a number of incongruous traits: He simultaneously possessed deep scientific insight, a remarkable gift for public relations and fund raising, a predilection for self-promotion, and an affinity for the spiritual and mystical—a style perhaps evocative of Tycho Brahe, who lived three hundred years earlier. Millikan's reputation as a scientist had been assured when he successfully measured the charge of the electron in his celebrated "oil drop experiment" and subsequently collected the 1923 Nobel Prize in Physics. With his assets, he had turned Caltech into a preeminent institution for scientific research. His less salutary qualities, however, were also frequently on display. On one occasion, when reverent zealots had left on a Caltech wall the message "Jesus saves," irreverent students added their own postscript: "and Millikan takes credit!"

In accepting Millikan's offer, Anderson had followed a pattern not uncommon in the history of science: He had undertaken a rather unattractive project to propitiate a superior, without whose help he could not hope to find suitable employment, only to discover that the fruits of his labor would become seminal in the field. Only six years earlier, Erwin Schrödinger, at the University of Zurich, had been asked by his department chairman, Peter Debye, to evaluate a doctoral thesis concerning a matter-wave hypothesis. The degree candidate was a young man named Louis de Broglie who was at the Sorbonne. The task had originated with a request from the Sorbonne physics chairman, Paul Langevin, to the visiting Albert Einstein. Einstein, in turn, had transmitted it to Debye. Debye, in deflecting the problem to Schrödinger, had commented to the young assistant professor, "I don't understand these matter-waves. What kind of waves are these anyway without a wave equation?" Schrödinger, in accepting the proposal (with no great zeal), had promised to try to write a wave equation. Within a week, he had indeed produced the equation, and he discussed the matter-wave hypothesis at the weekly departmental seminar—this time, with a modicum of enthusiasm. Apprised of Schrödinger's analysis, Einstein communicated to Langevin a message concerning de Broglie's thesis: "I would give him the degree. He can't do much damage with a Ph.D. in physics." Meanwhile, Schrödinger's wave equation was becoming a harbinger of the quantum mechanical revolution. In 1924, de Broglie received his doctorate, and five years later, he won the Nobel Prize. Schrödinger shared the 1933 Nobel Prize with Dirac.

From the time that Anderson accepted a postdoctoral appointment at Caltech in 1930, his research focused on cosmic-ray physics. In 1933 he became an assistant professor at Caltech. In 1936 he won the Nobel Prize for the discovery of the positron. Soon thereafter, Caltech promoted him to the level of associate professor.

In 1935 the Japanese physicist Hideki Yukawa had postulated the existence of a particle with a mass somewhere between two and three hundred times that of the electron which mediated the exchange force between nucleons, the neutrons and protons that constitute the nucleus. The particle's mass, intermediate between the electron's and the proton's, eventually gained for it the name "meson" (from the Greek word for "intermediate"). In Yukawa's theory, the meson served the same function as the photon, which mediates the coulomb force between charged particles. To search for Yukawa's meson, a particle accelerator was needed that could produce energies of around 100 million electron volts, and although Ernest Orlando Lawrence, of the University of California at Berkeley, envisioned building such an accelerator, the largest extant was his new cyclotron of 16 thousand electron volts. Other physicists proposed searching for the meson in cosmic radiation.

In 1937, Anderson and his Caltech colleague and former student Seth Neddermeyer, unaware of Yukawa's theory, were conducting cloud chamber exposures at the high elevations of Pike's Peak in Colorado when they discovered a new particle. Their particle had a negative charge and a mass intermediate between that of the electron and the proton. By 1938 its mass had been identified as somewhere between 130 and 240 times the mass of an electron, and that made the particle an obvious candidate for being Yukawa's exchange particle. Indeed, it was christened the "mu-meson," although the name was generally shortened to "muon." Unfortunately, the muon failed to satisfy the properties required of Yukawa's meson— namely, to participate in the strong nuclear force and to decay with an exceedingly short lifetime. With a mass 207 times that of the electron, the muon was something like a massive electron. Unlike the electron, however, it is unstable, and it decays with a mean-life of 2.2 microseconds, which is much too long for the lifetime expected of Yukawa's particle. The pi-meson (or pion), discovered in England in 1947 by Cecil Powell and Giuseppe Occhialini, was found to be the proper Yukawa meson; it too was found in cosmic radiation, but the researchers used photographic emulsions rather than the cloud chamber.

Shortly after the discovery of the pion, another of Anderson's former students, Donald Glaser, invented the bubble chamber, which was, in a sense, the antithesis of the Wilson cloud chamber. Superheated fluid (often liquid hydrogen) filling the chamber, when suddenly relieved of confining pressure, was found to develop bubbles along the tracks of charged particles traversing the chamber. It represented a substantial improvement over the cloud chamber, in that the much greater density of its fluid made the device a more efficient detector of high-energy particles.

In early 1938, the German physicists Otto Hahn and Fritz Strassmann discovered the fission reaction in uranium, and the prospect of a superbomb was relayed through a network involving Lise Meitner, Niels Bohr, Eugene Wigner, Leo Szilard, Edward Teller, Einstein, and, ultimately, President Franklin D. Roosevelt. The discovery led to the establishment of the Manhattan Project, which was to develop the atom bomb. The project was assigned to U.S. Army general Leslie Groves, who decided, in turn, to hire a scientist to direct the research. He envisioned his candidate as a man with manifest management abilities, an experimental physicist, and distinguished in his field—preferably a Nobel laureate. Heading his list of candidates for the position were Ernest Lawrence and Carl Anderson. He decided not to ask Lawrence, because the great Berkeley physicist, he believed, was essential for the magnetic separation project necessary to the enrichment of uranium 235. Anderson turned Groves down, for his own reasons, although Neddermeyer, with whom he had discovered the muon, accepted a position in the project and went on to make indispensable contributions. The directorship of the project's Los Alamos Laboratory went to the theorist Oppenheimer, who had taught Anderson quantum mechanics. During the McCarthy era, Oppenheimer became entangled in controversy because of his earlier opposition to the creation of the hydrogen bomb, and in the early 1950's, he lost his security clearance. He nevertheless reached a pinnacle of sorts, becoming the director of the Institute for Advanced Study in Princeton, New Jersey. Meanwhile, in 1939, Anderson was promoted by Caltech to the rank of professor; he remained there until his retirement in 1976. During the period from 1962 to 1970, he served as the chairman of the Division of Physics, Math, and Astronomy.

The year 1932 has been called *annus mirabilis*, or miracle year, an expression that historians of science invoke infrequently. That year saw a wealth of contributions from a group of physicists focusing on nuclear structure and laying the groundwork for the investigation of elementary particles. John Cockcroft and Ernest Walton, with their particle accelerator, and Lawrence with his, the cyclotron, had reached unprecedented particle energies. Before, researchers investigating nuclear structure had had to rely on the emissions of radioactive elements. In the same year, Harold Urey had discovered deuterium; Sir James Chadwick, the neutron; and Anderson, the positron. Werner Heisenberg and Wigner had launched themselves into fundamental theoretical techniques to understand nuclear structure, and Dirac was hard at work establishing the connections between the antimatter particles of his hole theory and Anderson's positron.

In later years, the discovery of a new particle "would not have ruffled the sensibilities of physicists," as pointed out by Daniel Kevles, but in a year in which the discovery of the neutron had tied up some loose ends, the discovery of the positron had initially managed to muddle the picture. What emerged in time, however, was a much clearer understanding of elementary particles and a revolution in which Caltech played a significant role. During Anderson's tenure as division chairman, one of the stars of the institution, Murray Gell-Mann, formulated his "eightfold way" and introduced quarks as the constituents of hadrons (mesons and hyperons).

Anderson's honors and awards are legion. He has received honorary degrees from Temple University (1948), Gustav Adolphus College (1963), and Colgate University (1977). Besides the 1936 Nobel Prize in Physics, he received the Gold Medal of the American Institute of the City of New York (1935), the Elliot Cresson Medal of the Franklin Institute (1937), the Presidential Certificate of Merit (1945), and the John Ericsson Medal of the American Society of Swedish Engineers (1960). He is a

Fellow of the American Physical Society and a member of the National Academy of Science, the American Philosophical Society, Sigma Xi, Tau Beta Phi, and the American Academy of Arts and Sciences.

## Bibliography

*Primary*

PHYSICS: "The Positive Electron," *Physical Review*, vol. 43, 1933; "The Production and Properties of Positrons," in Nobelstiftelsen, ed., *Physics*, 1936; "Early Work on the Positron and Muon," *American Journal of Physics*, vol. 29, 1961.

*Secondary*

Davis, Nuel Pharr. *Lawrence and Oppenheimer*. New York: Simon & Schuster, 1968. This book, focusing on the association between the two great American physicists in the title, is an exposition of the politics of high-powered research during the 1930's and 1940's. The book contains a rare allusion to General Groves's interest in hiring Lawrence, and then Anderson, as the director of the Los Alamos Laboratory.

Dirac, Paul A. M. *Directions in Physics*. New York: Wiley, 1978. A transcription of lectures given in Australia by one of the creators of modern quantum mechanics. In reading the book, one senses the remarkable intuition and unassailable logic of a mind that could predict the existence of antimatter several years before it was observed. The book is written in Dirac's precise and laconic manner.

_____. *The Principles of Quantum Mechanics*. 4th ed. New York: Oxford University Press, 1958. Dirac's legendary monograph, written with the author's characteristic conciseness and precision. In one chapter is an account of relativistic quantum mechanics and the emergence of hole states, positrons, and quantum mechanical spin. It is still a mainstay of any physicist's quantum mechanics library, even though it was published in 1930. Unhappily, it is much too technical for the nonscientist.

Kevles, Daniel J. *The Physicists: The History of a Scientific Community in Modern America*. New York: Alfred A. Knopf, 1977. A superb history of the emergence and development of physics in America. Kevles bases most of his account of Anderson and his times on interviews with Anderson himself. Kevles, who has training in physics, is a professor of the history of science at Caltech. His book is written with the authority of someone who knows physics, Caltech, and, in this context, Carl Anderson.

Schwinger, Julian. *Einstein's Legacy*. New York: W. H. Freeman, 1986. An elementary exposition of Einstein's contributions to physics, written by a Nobel laureate. The energy-mass equivalence relation, a major consequence of the special theory of relativity, is illustrated with a description of electron-positron creation and annihilation phenomena.

Segrè, Emilio. *From X-Rays to Quarks: Modern Physicists and Their Discoveries*. San Francisco: W. H. Freeman, 1980. Like C. P. Snow's book, this work covers the achievements of European physicists as well as American. Segrè, the discoverer of the antiproton, is a Nobel Prize winner himself. The book makes for easy reading and, as a bonus, offers many of the author's own photographs.

Snow, C. P. *The Physicists: A Generation That Changed the World*. Boston: Little, Brown, 1981. This book is not as scholarly as Kevles' book and is suitable for all readers. Snow died before the book was completed, and it was published from a first draft. Some of the errors in the book are pointed out in an excellent book review by R. E. Peierls, Professor Emeritus at the University of Oxford, who was a participant in the heroic age of physics of the late 1920's and 1930's (*The New York Review of Books*, 1981). Snow's book does little justice to Anderson's work; however, it does contain an excellent collection of photographs of many of the physicists of Anderson's day.

*Bulent I. Atalay*

# 1937

### Physics
Clinton Joseph Davisson, United States
Sir George Paget Thomson, Great Britain

### Chemistry
Sir Walter Haworth, Great Britain
Paul Karrer, Switzerland

### Physiology or Medicine
Albert Szent-Györgyi, Hungary

### Literature
Roger Martin du Gard, France

### Peace
Viscount Cecil of Chelwood, Great Britain

# CLINTON JOSEPH DAVISSON
## 1937

*Born:* Bloomington, Illinois; October 22, 1881
*Died:* Charlottesville, Virginia; February 1, 1958
*Nationality:* American
*Area of concentration:* Electron physics

*Davisson's discovery of the peculiar pattern in which a beam of low-energy electrons is scattered from the surface of a single crystal of nickel, and his subsequent detailed investigation of the precise nature of this pattern under a wide variety of parameter variations, led him to conclude that electrons are diffracted much as X rays are, and thus that they exhibit wave properties as predicted by the theories of Louis de Broglie*

## The Award

*Presentation*

Professor H. Pleijel, Chairman of the Nobel Committee for Physics of the Royal Swedish Academy of Sciences, presented the Nobel Prize in Physics to Clinton Joseph Davisson on December 10, 1937, on behalf of the Swedish Academy and King Gustav V, from whom Davisson accepted the prize. Pleijel's presentation, in English, began with a review of work carried out by Davisson and his collaborator Charles Kunsman in 1922, prior to the theoretical investigations performed by Louis de Broglie (1892-1987) in 1923. Pleijel then described how these early, puzzling results had later been extended by Davisson and another collaborator, Lester Germer, in a much more definitive manner because of the availability of de Broglie's theory.

Pleijel described how, before Davisson's work, the question of the nature of X rays had been decided by Nobel Prize winner Max von Laue (1879-1960) when he obtained diffraction patterns by directing X rays at crystals, which have a much finer spacing than do the ruled gratings used for similar studies in optics. Building on this analogy, Pleijel described how Davisson and Germer had directed beams of electrons of specified velocities on the face of a cubic nickel crystal and obtained interference patterns from those electrons scattered back by the atoms in the different layers of the crystal. By comparing the known crystal spacings with the electron wavelengths calculated according to the de Broglie theory, Davisson and Germer had obtained convincing evidence for the wave nature of electrons and, by inference, of all matter. Pleijel further pointed out that by confirming the wave nature of the electron, Davisson had also provided a powerful tool for the continuing investigation of metal surfaces and the effects of various mechanical, thermal, and chemical treatments on them.

*Nobel lecture*

Davisson's Nobel lecture, titled "The Discovery of Electron Waves," is a review of the critical steps taken by several investigators that led to proof of the dual wave and particle nature of radiation and matter. It is also a fascinating account of how Davisson was able to contribute to that discovery in a rather remarkable way. Davisson began by noting that the wave-particle controversy in the case of light had been a battle spanning more than two centuries. Recalling that Sir Isaac Newton's seventeenth century corpuscular concept had given way in the nineteenth century to the wave theory of Thomas Young, Davisson pointed out that the surprising experimental evidence amassed by Owen Richardson, Karl Compton, Arthur Hughes, and Robert Millikan at the beginning of the twentieth century had cried out for a return to corpuscular concepts according to ideas reluctantly proposed by Max Planck (1858-1947) in 1899. He noted, however, that it was not until Niels Bohr (1885-1962) proposed his quantized orbital model of the atom in 1913, and Arthur Holly Compton (1892-1962) added his X-ray collision evidence in 1922, that a seeming solution to the riddle of radiation and matter was at hand. Even then, the joy was premature; significant problems remained, and it seemed that a deeper principle was needed.

It was at this point, Davisson noted, that a crucial step was taken; de Broglie proposed, in his doctoral thesis, the idea that matter might have the same dual nature as light—that electrons might possess wave properties even as radiation possesses particle properties. De Broglie's ideas, however, and their subsequent extension into a comprehensive system of quantum mechanics by Erwin Schrö-dinger (1887-1961), were at first applied only to atomic systems; was there also experimental evidence to warrant extending these ideas to free electrons? It was here that Davisson's contribution was crucial.

In a most fascinating manner, Davisson described how he and his colleagues, working in an industrial laboratory, actually had begun to uncover the evidence that was needed without at first realizing just what they had done. It was not until after Davisson happened to visit England during the summer of 1926 that he became aware of the potential significance of the evidence he was uncovering. Armed with the new theoretical tools of quantum mechanics, Davisson was able, during the fall of 1926 and the winter of 1927, to compare systematically the predictions of the new theory with the evidence of his elastically scattered electron beams. Using graphs to compare his data with the theoretical predictions, he showed that he had indeed obtained near-perfect agreement, indicating with little room for doubt that free electrons do indeed behave like waves and that material particles therefore exhibit the same dual nature as electromagnetic waves. Ever modest, Davisson insisted that he share the credit for this brilliant piece of scientific investigation with his collaborators Kunsman and Germer, and he thanked his superiors at the Bell Telephone Laboratories for the farsightedness they had displayed in allowing this work to take place in a busy industrial laboratory.

In closing, Davisson praised the work of George Paget Thomson (1892-1975), the corecipient of the 1937 prize, who, using an entirely different experimental approach, had also demonstrated electron diffraction and thus verified de Broglie's formula. Davisson also remarked on the later success of Otto Stern and Immanuel Estermann in extending the observations to atomic hydrogen.

## Critical reception

Reaction in the popular and professional press to the awarding of the Nobel Prize to Davisson and Thomson was uniformly favorable. Indeed, one gets the distinct impression that there was little surprise at the announcement; it seems to have been regarded as an expected step in the sequence of awards recognizing the developments that had been occurring in atomic and nuclear physics in the preceding decades. Since the wave-particle duality had become such a fundamental hallmark of the new physics, the recognition of Davisson's and Thomson's roles in its confirmation for electrons was seen as appropriate.

Besides the acclamation given Davisson's and Thomson's work as one of the cornerstones of the new physics, there was considerable comment on the current and future uses of electron diffraction techniques as means of investigating the structure of very thin films of materials and the surfaces of materials. It was pointed out that the widely used X-ray diffraction techniques were too penetrating for close scrutiny of thin films and surface structures and that the less penetrating electron beams were more suitable for this purpose. It was predicted that many new uses would be found for these techniques in the future.

*Science News Letter* of November 20, 1937, made Davisson's Nobel Prize the subject of its cover article, featuring a picture of Davisson and his colleague Germer holding the vacuum tube they had used during their principal investigations of 1927. Despite the prominence it gave to the award, however, the journal mistakenly attributed high-speed electron scattering to Davisson and low-speed scattering to Thomson, when just the opposite was the case. *Science*, in its issue of November 19, 1937, did the same. *Nature*, the journal in which both Davisson and Thomson had published their initial results in 1927, included, in its issue of November 20, 1937, an informative summary of the results leading up to the discovery which ended by calling the electron diffraction camera "an indispensable unit in the well-equipped chemical or physical laboratory."

*The New York Times* of November 12, 1937, proud of the honor Davisson had brought to New York City's Bell Telephone Laboratories and to the city itself, featured the award in a bold headline and story on page 1 and included a picture of the winners in a continuation of the article on page 16. The article traced the controversy of the wave-particle duality back to Newton's seventeenth century corpuscular ideas and stressed the importance of Davisson's work by quoting an excerpt from a letter which de Broglie had written to Davisson when de Broglie had received the Nobel Prize in 1929: "I know very well that if I have received the Nobel Prize, it is because your splendid research has provided confirmation of the ideas I had developed."

## Biography

Clinton Joseph Davisson was born in Bloomington, Illinois, on October 22, 1881, the son of Joseph Davisson, a contract painter and paperhanger, and Mary Calvert Davisson. His only sibling, Carrie Louise, two extra years younger, remembered the home as "a happy, congenial one—plenty of love but short on money." Davisson, frail of health and stature throughout his life, took two extra years to finish his schooling; he was graduated at the age of twenty from Bloomington High School. His academic record, however, enabled him to enter the University of Chicago in the fall of 1902 with a full tuition scholarship. Unfortunately, this scholarship lasted only one year, and Davisson was forced to interrupt his undergraduate studies five times in order to earn the necessary funds to complete his bachelor's degree, which he was awarded in 1908.

Davisson went from Chicago, where his principal mentor had been Robert Andrews Millikan (1868-1953), the 1923 Nobel laureate, to Princeton University, where he came under the influence of Owen Willans Richardson (1879-1959), the 1928 winner. Davisson later attributed his success in physics to "having caught the physicist's point of view—his habit of mind—his way of looking at things" from men such as Millikan and Richardson. Davisson wed Richardson's sister, Charlotte Sara, in 1911, the year Davisson completed his doctoral degree. They had four children.

From 1912 to 1917, Davisson served as an instructor in physics at the Carnegie Institute of Technology in Pittsburgh, a position which did not seem to suit him well. Refused by the U.S. Army when the United States entered World War I in 1917, he obtained a summer position in war-related research in the engineering department of the Western Electric Company in New York City. At war's end, he turned down a promotion and a chance to return to Carnegie Tech in order to stay on at Western Electric, where he found the promise of a somewhat flexible schedule in electron research to be highly attractive. Davisson remained in the engineering department of Western Electric, which became the Bell Telephone Laboratory in 1925, until his retirement in 1946. He spent his last years working with Jesse Beams at the University of Virginia until his death in 1958.

## Scientific Career

Davisson's professional life was almost exclusively devoted to electron emission and electron beam research at the Western Electric Company/Bell Telephone Laboratory. It may not seem at all strange now for pure research, culminating in a Nobel Prize, to take place in a large industrial laboratory, but that was not the case in the early years of the twentieth century. Davisson was the first Nobel laureate from Bell Labs, and it was his example that helped to set the pattern for commercial laboratories' providing opportunities for pure research.

Davisson was not a bold pathfinder in new areas of research. Rather, his forte as a physicist was his willingness to pursue, to great lengths and with great care and thoughtfulness, lines of research begun by others. His mentor at Princeton, Owen Richardson, had given Davisson his initial impetus in electron physics, and he remained in this field thereafter. Unable to establish any effective research program during his short tenure at the Carnegie Institute of Technology, Davisson responded eagerly and effectively to the challenges afforded him at Western Electric, where the problems of electron emission were of great concern to the parent company, American Telephone and Telegraph (AT&T), in its bid to construct long-distance telephone networks. It was this work that ultimately led Davisson to his Nobel Prize-winning investigation.

One of the issues that was of great interest to AT&T was whether positive ion bombardment played any significant role in the emission of electrons from oxide-coated cathodes, a key component in the triode amplifiers employed in long-distance lines. Davisson's first major assignment was to settle this issue, which he did in 1920; positive ion bombardment, he found, made no important contribution. In pursuing the related question of secondary electron emission from grids and plates, Davisson discovered the phenomenon of elastically scattered electrons—that is, electrons that rebound from a target surface with the same energy they had when they struck it. Having become deeply interested in the questions of atomic structure then facing the physics community, he decided that he might be able to use these elastically scattered electrons to investigate the electronic structure of the atom in much the same way that Ernest Rutherford (1871-1937), the 1908 Nobel laureate in chemistry, had used alpha particles to explore its nucleus.

During the next three years, Davisson and his assistant, Charles Kunsman, carried out an extensive investigation of electron scattering from several metals in the hope that they would be able to shed some light on the arrangement of the electrons around the nucleus. Although they published several papers which included a theoretical model based on their experimental results, they were not convinced that they had made much progress on the recalcitrant problem. They did, however, develop the technique of electron beam research to near-perfection, particularly with respect to the high vacuums required for reliable measurements.

In late 1924, after having completed several studies on thermionic emission, Davisson, with a new assistant, Lester Germer, was anxious to return to the electron scattering experiments. Not long after the resumption of these studies, an accidental break in the electron beam tube resulted in a new type of scattering pattern, one with a number of irregular peaks and valleys that Davisson eventually linked to a change in the crystalline structure of the nickel target. This event suggested to Davisson that his electron beam investigations might be more useful as crystal structure probes than as atomic structure probes.

Davisson and Germer's next attempt included a specially prepared, single-crystal nickel target. To their consternation, the new scattering patterns revealed no clear information about the crystal structure. At this point, however, fate again intervened; Davisson and his wife made a trip to England to visit Mrs. Davisson's relatives, one of which was her brother, Owen Richardson, who had been Davisson's research adviser at Princeton. While there, Davisson attended with Richardson the meeting of the British Association for the Advancement of Science, and there he learned of the new quantum mechanics that had just been developed by Erwin Schrödinger out of Louis de Broglie's electron-wave hypothesis. Talking with colleagues at the meeting Davisson became convinced that his electron beam results might be evidence for a wave interpretation of the electron.

In the months after Davisson's return to Bell Labs, he and Germer were able to modify their experiment in such a way that they could test the major predictions of the de Broglie theory. Having been struck by the intense interest shown in his work while at the scientific meeting in England and fearful that others might be doing similar experiments, Davisson rushed a short article to *Nature* in March, 1927. The article, published in April, made known to the world for the first time that there was experimental evidence for the idea that electrons behave like waves when scattered from a metal crystal.

Davisson did not stop there. In the succeeding months, he and Germer pursued an exhaustive investigation of the scattering of electrons from nickel. In their most famous paper, "Diffraction of Electrons," published in the December, 1927, issue of the *Physical Review*, they gave the results of a very careful and systematic review of their experimental results, a feat which had been greatly complicated by the presence of occluded gas atoms on the surface of the nickel target. The fact that they were able to sort out these effects in a satisfactory way and at the same time make adjustments for an unknown "contraction factor" of the crystal (which was not truly clarified until Hans Bethe showed, a year later, that the electrons had been accelerated through a potential difference of 15 volts upon entering the crystal) is a testimony to their ingenuity, thoroughness, and tenacity.

During the next three years, Davisson continued his investigations into the details of electron diffraction. In one set of experiments, he was able to show that electrons are reflected from the surface layers of a crystal in a manner very similar to the way X rays are; these experiments also enabled him to confirm the suggestion that Bethe had made regarding the surface potential of a metal. In another set of experiments, he tried to determine whether a beam of low-energy electrons can be polarized; by examining the intensity of an electron beam that is reflected by two successive targets and using a highly sophisticated statistical analysis of the results, he showed that the polarization effect was zero within the limits of uncertainty of the measurements, a conclusion to which other investigators eventually came as well (although reluctantly, for it seemed to spoil the symmetry between light waves and electron waves). Besides these experimental investigations, Davisson was very busy preparing and delivering numerous papers on the wave properties of electrons, for the scientific community was extremely anxious to learn all the details of his and Germer's definitive work and the implications thereof.

In the 1930's, although Germer continued working with low-energy electron diffraction—a technique which has, since the 1960's, become one of the most powerful for investigating the surfaces of materials—Davisson shifted his emphasis to electron optics. He was a pioneer in the field of sharply focusing electron beams, developing analytical procedures for understanding how they behave and designing and constructing many devices for testing these ideas experimentally. Outgrowths of this work included the development of electron microscopes and of test equipment used to evaluate the quality of signals passing through the coaxial systems of early television transmitters. During the early years of World War II, Davisson's expertise in electron optics was especially valued by Bell Labs when it was called on to help with the development of the multicavity magnetron. From 1943 to 1946, Davisson helped with the design and development of quartz crystal plates for a multitude of electronic circuit applications, another war-related project. He retired from Bell Labs in 1946 and accepted a position as visiting professor at the University of Virginia in Charlottesville, where he lectured occasionally and did experimental work with Jesse Beams on high-speed centrifuges. He retired from the University of Virginia in 1954 and remained at home in Charlottesville until his death in 1958.

Davisson wrote no books; his publications consist exclusively of his scientific papers, some fifty in number, of which slightly more than half are in the areas of electron scattering, electron diffraction, and the interpretation of electron wave phenomena. He published nearly twenty papers in his other two major areas of investigation, thermionic emission and electron optics, and published a handful of other papers on miscellaneous topics. A complete list of his writings appears in *The Bell System Technical Journal* (October, 1951).

In the commercial environment of AT&T, Western Electric, and Bell Labs, where many of Davisson's scientific colleagues went on to become scientific administrators or managers, Davisson remained a research scientist to the end. Probably partially as a result of his frail physical makeup, he was always somewhat cautious and conservative in his approach to problems, but he compensated for any lack of boldness or initiative with the thoughtfulness, care, and thoroughness he brought to his research. Davisson was highly regarded by his colleagues not only for his own scientific contributions but also for the advice and counsel he gave them in their own research efforts; he was often put in charge of young scientists newly hired by Bell Labs, and he helped them to make the transition from academia to industry. This willingness to help others undoubtedly cost much time which might otherwise have advanced his own work, but it was valued highly by his superiors and contributed greatly to the overall excellence of scientific research at Bell Labs.

## Bibliography

*Primary*
PHYSICS: "The Scattering of Electrons by a Single Crystal of Nickel," *Nature*, vol. 119, 1927 (with L. H. Germer); "Diffraction of Electrons," *Physical Review*, vol. 30, 1927 (with Germer); "The Diffraction of Electrons by a Crystal of Nickel," *Bell System Technical Journal*, vol. 7, 1928; "Reflection of Electrons by a Crystal of Nickel," *Proceedings of the National Academy of Sciences*, vol. 14, 1928; "Are Electrons Waves?" *Journal of the Franklin Institute*, vol. 205, 1928; "A Test for Polarization of Electron Waves by Reflection," *Physical Review*, vol. 33, 1929.

*Secondary*
Calbick, Chester J. "The Discovery of Electron Diffraction by Davisson and Ger-

mer." *The Physics Teacher* 1 (1963): 66. This valuable article, written by a junior associate of Davisson and Germer's during the last stages of the period that led to the discovery of electron diffraction, is of considerable help in offering insight into the day-to-day workings of the laboratory and the interactions among the principle participants.

Darrow, Karl K. "The Scientific Work of C. J. Davisson." *The Bell System Technical Journal* 30 (October, 1951): 786. This article, written by a colleague and close friend of Davisson at Bell Labs, is both a personal and a professional examination of Davisson's work and character. Darrow, a gifted writer of semipopular science books and articles, knew Davisson during his entire tenure at Bell Labs, much of the time sharing an office with him. This issue of the *The Bell System Technical Journal* is dedicated to Davisson on the occasion of his seventieth birthday and contains another recollection of Davisson's work by Mervin J. Kelly of Bell Labs (see below). It also provides a complete bibliography of Davisson's publications.

Gehrenbeck, Richard K. "C. J. Davisson, L. H. Germer, and the Discovery of Electron Diffraction." Ph.D. dissertation, University of Minnesota, 1973. This source is the only complete study of Davisson's scientific work, and it includes considerable biographical information on both Davisson and Germer based on extensive use of correspondence and visits with the scientists' families. It develops in considerable detail all Davisson's work leading up to the discovery of electron diffraction, both the false starts and the successes, and attempts to determine why Davisson and Germer were ultimately successful in this effort whereas others, working at approximately the same time, were not. A summary of this work appears in *Physics Today* (January, 1978), and another article based on it appears in the book *Fifty Years of Electron Diffraction* (1981; edited by Peter Goodman).

Germer, Lester H. "Low Energy Electron Diffraction," *Physics Today* 17 (July, 1964): 19-23. This article, written by Davisson's coworker during most of the time the experiments on electron diffraction were in progress, is a fascinating case study of the problems inherent in trying to reconstruct scientific history from memory alone. Although it provides irreplaceable insights into the proceedings, it also is misleading at certain points, as the laboratory notebooks clearly show. It also offers an excellent introduction to the development of low-energy electron diffraction as a modern research tool.

Kelly, Mervin J. "Clinton Joseph Davisson." *Biographical Memoirs, National Academy of Sciences* 36 (1962): 51-62. Mervin Kelly arrived at Bell Labs only a few months after Davisson, and the two were associates and fast friends until Davisson's death. This article provides rare insights into both Davisson's personal and his professional life and includes a complete listing of his published works. The fine article by Karl Darrow listed above, which discusses all Davisson's scientific work from his days at Princeton University until his death, follows Kelly's.

Thomson, George P. *The Inspiration of Science*. London: Oxford University Press, 1961. This delightful book—by the person who discovered electron diffraction independently of, and almost simultaneously with, Davisson and Germer— provides excellent insights into the scientific method in general and into the circumstances surrounding the discovery of electron diffraction in particular. It heaps praise on Davisson for the remarkable feat he accomplished with low-energy electron beams at a time when high-vacuum technology was not generally well developed.

*Richard K. Gehrenbeck*

# 1937

## Physics
Clinton Joseph Davisson, United States
Sir George Paget Thomson, Great Britain

## Chemistry
Sir Walter Haworth, Great Britain
Paul Karrer, Switzerland

## Physiology or Medicine
Albert Szent-Györgyi, Hungary

## Literature
Roger Martin du Gard, France

## Peace
Viscount Cecil of Chelwood, Great Britain

# SIR GEORGE PAGET THOMSON
## 1937

*Born:* Cambridge, England; May 3, 1892
*Died:* Cambridge, England; September 10, 1975
*Nationality:* British
*Area of concentration:* Electron diffraction

*Thomson shared the prize with Clinton Joseph Davisson. Their similar, though independent, experiments supported the wave theory of matter proposed on theoretical grounds by Louis de Broglie, the winner of the 1929 Nobel Prize in Physics. They showed that beams of electrons could be diffracted like light and thus demonstrated the electron's wavelike character*

## The Award

*Presentation*

Because of illness at the time of the award ceremony, Thomson was not present. His prize was received by the British Minister to Sweden on December 10, 1937. In his presentation address, Professor H. Pleijel, Chairman of the Nobel Committee for Physics, noted that the first work on electron diffraction had been done some fifteen years earlier by Clinton Joseph Davisson (1881-1958) and his coworkers. The importance of the experiments, which were aimed at showing the wavelike behavior of what had formerly been considered a particle, became more apparent after Louis de Broglie (1892-1987) had proposed his wave theory of matter.

Pleijel described how recent work with X rays had demonstrated their essentially wavelike character. They had been shown to be, like light, waving electric and magnetic fields. All waves had long been known to diffract, or bend, around obstacles and to spread out through openings. Waves can also be made to interfere with each other when they arrive at the same place after diffraction through small openings. Interference patterns formed by X rays had recently been photographed, thus confirming that X rays consist of electromagnetic waves (though with much shorter wavelengths than light). Physicists believed that if particles, such as electrons, could be represented as waves, they too should display these diffraction and interference effects. De Broglie also postulated the connection between a wave's characteristic wavelength and the corresponding particle velocity: the greater the velocity, the smaller the particle's associated wavelength.

Thomson's experiment consisted of allowing a stream of electrons to fall on extremely thin films of gold, platinum, or aluminum. These substances are crystalline and have regularly spaced rows of atoms in their structures. It was hoped that when the regular openings between atoms were presented to the incident electron "waves," they would cause the same kind of interference patterns that had been seen with X rays. According to calculations based on de Broglie's theory, Thomson's electrons had extremely short wavelengths, and it was expected that interference patterns would be seen only if the atoms' spacings in the crystal were comparable in size to those wavelengths. As he had hoped, Thomson's photographs showed the characteristic rings of a diffraction pattern. From a ring's measured diameter, with the crystal's atomic spacings known, the electron's wavelength could be calculated. Thus, the experiments provided striking confirmation of the de Broglie hypothesis. They also verified the wavelength-velocity relation.

Thomson's findings had further significance. If a crystal whose atomic structure and spacing were unknown was now used in the experiment, the observed sizes of the interference rings, together with the known electron wavelength, would permit the determination of the crystal's structure. Surface impurities, such as corrosion, could also be studied. A powerful new tool for the structural analysis of crystals had been created.

## Nobel lecture

As noted above, Thomson did not receive his prize in person. His Nobel lecture was given in the following year, on June 7. In his talk, titled "Electronic Waves," Thomson began by pointing out that a scientific concept rarely springs from a single mind; most often, ideas mature and become generally accepted as a result of input from many individual sources. He traced the origin of the notion of the electron as a charged "atom" of electricity to the end of the nineteenth century, when it was regarded as an entity possessing both charge and mass—and therefore as a particle in the ordinary sense—that is present in all matter. In fact, it was Thomson's father, Sir Joseph John Thomson (1856-1940), who in 1897 had measured the ratio of the electron's charge to its mass. Others had also demonstrated the necessity of incorporating the notion of spin, which required the electron to rotate on its axis like a top. Yet there had appeared still other experimental evidence concerning the electron's behavior that these combined properties were inadequate to explain.

The new theory, known as quantum mechanics, that would overcome the deficiencies of the old one was yet in its infancy. Thomson acknowledged the advances made in that new theory of matter by Erwin Schrödinger (1887-1961) and Paul Adrien Maurice Dirac (1902-1984). He also cited the pioneering experiments of Davisson and Lester Germer (1896-1971), the first to demonstrate the wave nature of the electron, and went on to describe briefly his own experimental setup. He indicated that his experiments had agreed, within 1 percentage point, with the electron wavelengths predicted by the de Broglie theory.

Thomson concluded his talk with a detailed discussion of the new wave ideas as applied to matter, noting the difficulty that contemporary physicists had in adjusting their thinking to the strange new concepts. The new wave mechanics dealt only with probabilities for finding a particle at a given place at a given time, whereas the old, deterministic, classical theory, which had applied so well to the motion of ordinary objects, was unable to interpret the interference experiments at all.

Thomson ended by remarking that the new field of electron diffraction held great promise for practical applications, especially for studying surface effects, and commented that the practical relevance of this outcome of pure science was characteristic of all physical science.

*Critical reception*

The Times of London made a brief announcement of the physics prize on November 11, 1937, saying it had been awarded for Thomson's and Davisson's "discovery of the interference phenomena in the irradiation of crystals by electrons." The following day, *The New York Times* placed the Nobel citations on its front page and gave an account of the experimental work done by Davisson and Germer at Bell Telephone Laboratories in New York and independently by Thomson. The article noted the "great practical importance" of Thomson's work for discovering the structure of thin metallic surfaces subjected to various kinds of treatment. The correspondent went on to review the peculiar dual status of particle and wave conferred on the electron by the experiments and compared this strange state of affairs to a controversy that had existed in Sir Isaac Newton's day over the nature of light. Newton believed that light consisted of tiny, luminous particles. Experiments done early in the nineteenth century, however, by Thomas Young (1773-1829), were the first to show interference patterns and thus support the wave theory of light. James Clerk Maxwell (1831-1879) provided the full supporting theory for the wave view in the 1860's. The situation was again disturbed, however, by Einstein's work in 1905 on the light quantum, an idea that suggested a particle-like quality for light, a characteristic that was subsequently confirmed by experiments. In a similar way, *The New York Times* concluded, the nature of the electron had now been fully revealed in the diffraction experiments to be a duality which exactly paralleled the dual nature of light. The importance of the new work for the status of the fundamental theories of physics was clear.

A supplement to the journal *Science* carried a brief note on the awards and described the awardees' experiments. The expected usefulness of Thomson's new electron diffraction technique for surface studies—perhaps for exploration of the thin membranes which separate animal and human cells—was also mentioned.

## Biography

George Paget Thomson was the son of one of the most famous physicists at the turn of the century, Sir Joseph John Thomson. The elder Thomson was Cavendish Professor of Physics at the University of Cambridge at that time, and his wife was the daughter of another distinguished academic in the university. The young Thomson was reared in a family setting in which his inquisitive nature was fostered and he was encouraged to develop his talents. His formal education began in a private school, where, in addition to a broad-based education, he acquired a lifelong interest in model ships and sailing. Finally, he entered Trinity College, Cambridge, as a scholar, and after earning a degree in physics he started research under his father. Within a few years, he was appointed lecturer in mathematics, a post that was interrupted by his wartime service, which lasted from 1914 to 1918. He served with the Royal Flying Corps, and at the end of the war worked for a short time in the aircraft industry. His first text, a work on aerodynamics, was written then.

Thomson resumed his work in physics at Cambridge in 1919, but shortly thereafter he was appointed to a professorship at the University of Aberdeen, Scotland. There, he was married to Kathleen Smith, a daughter of the University's president. Their union would produce four children. Some of Thomson's most creative work in physics was completed at Aberdeen. It was during this period that he learned of the work being done on electron diffraction at Bell Laboratories and was able with great speed to carry out the diffraction experiments that would bring him the Nobel Prize.

In 1930, after election to the Royal Society, Thomson was appointed to head the physics department at the Imperial College of Science and Technology, London University, a post he held until 1952. He was knighted in 1943. The last decade of Thomson's professional life was spent as Master of Corpus Christi College, Cambridge. In 1962, he retired.

## Scientific Career

The 1920's and 1930's were an exciting time for physicists. The nuclear atom model was by then generally accepted, and the radically new, but highly mathematical, ideas of the quantum theory were finding increasing support as experimentalists explored with considerable ingenuity the inner structure of the atom. Thomson had a head start. His physicist father, J. J. Thomson, had confirmed the electron's particle character; he had shown that the electricity flowing in wires is not some kind of continuous fluid, but rather is a property possessed by tiny particles of matter. He had actually measured the amount of electricity carried by each electron per unit of weight, though at that time the particulate concept of electricity was so novel, the elder Thomson reported that some of his colleagues believed he was "pulling their legs."

It is important to note that improvements in vacuum technology had taken place in earlier decades, and those advances proved crucial for experimental work at the atomic level. Unless air molecules could be substantially removed from the experimental apparatus, the tiny objects being investigated, often in beams, would soon be lost in collisions with those molecules. Experiments on these elusive fragments of atoms were being conducted in major laboratories throughout the world at that time.

Thomson's electron diffraction experiments were done at Aberdeen. By his own account, he became very interested in the possibility of demonstrating the wave characteristics of the electron when, in 1926, he attended a physics meeting at the University of Oxford. He and others were greatly influenced by the attention being aroused among physicists by de Broglie's ideas on matter waves. Thomson, whose earlier work had acquainted him with the so-called cathode rays (beams of electrons generated by heating a filament in an evacuated glass enclosure), and whose students were then engaged in studying them, asked his assistant to try allowing cathode rays to fall on a thin film of celluloid. Celluloid's structure was unknown, but Thomson thought that its molecules might be of the right kind and structure to show interference effects with electrons. The first results were not dramatic, for the photographs were extremely faint, but it seemed that the faint halos produced by the electrons did indeed possess the wavelengths predicted by the de Broglie theory. Publication of the results in the journal *Nature* followed by only a few months Davisson and Germer's first reports of electron diffraction.

Because metals are crystalline, with the kinds of regularities in their structures that are necessary if interference effects are to be seen, Thomson began working with thin metal films. He knew that if the metal were too thick, the electrons would be quickly absorbed and the diffraction not seen. Therefore, he first needed to find out how to form very thin sheets, sheets much thinner than a piece of paper. With the skillful help of his workshop technician, Thomson soon had acquired suitable films of aluminum and gold, had measured the spacings of their atomic planes with X rays, and had obtained clear and striking photographs showing the dark concentric ring patterns whose spacing enabled him to calculate the electron's wavelength using de Broglie's formula. By late 1927, a mere month or two after his American colleagues, he was able to publish results on the wave properties of the electron. Hence, the remarkable efforts of these several individuals at last confirmed that particles such as electrons really do behave like waves. It seemed strange to physicists at the time that matter could conform to two quite different modes of description, but these descriptions are now an accepted part of physics and have been demonstrated to hold for other particles, such as neutrons and protons, also.

Soon after after joining the faculty of the Imperial College of Science and Technology, Thomson became interested in the problem of nuclear fission. The first splitting of the nucleus was achieved in Germany in 1939 by the physicists Otto Hahn (1879-1968) and Fritz Strassman (born 1902). They noticed that when the element uranium was bombarded with neutrons (the electrically neutral particles that are in the nuclei of atoms, together with protons), the element barium was produced. Barium is a much lighter element, and the conjecture was that the absorption of a neutron led to an instability in the uranium nucleus which caused it to split into two lighter nuclei.

Physicists were quick to calculate that enormous amounts of energy might be released in these reactions if relatively large numbers of uranium nuclei could be split at the same time. The potential for devising a potent weapon, an atom bomb, utilizing the uranium fission reaction was obvious. Thomson persuaded the government to purchase a ton of uranium oxide for experimental work on the process. He wanted to know if a fast chain reaction could be made to occur, for there were varying estimates at that time of the likelihood of such a process' succeeding. Time was critical. Germany had set World War II into motion in September, 1939, and the importance of Great Britain's acquiring a nuclear weapon before the enemy did, if indeed such a weapon was technically feasible, was uppermost in the minds of scientists such as Thomson.

The experiments soon led him to the conclusion, however, that a self-sustaining chain reaction would not occur in uranium oxide and that pure samples of uranium metal probably would be required if the reaction were to proceed with a large release of energy. Soon, Thomson was charged with the supervision of a committee of scientists whose function was to inform the government on the nuclear weapon issue. For a fast reaction to occur, they found, a neutron must not only cause fission but also result in the release of more than one additional neutron so that the fission process can multiply and move rapidly through the mass of uranium. Furthermore, if the mass of the uranium is less than a certain critical mass, the neutrons released will quickly fly out from the uranium without colliding with other nuclei and thus be lost from the reaction. It was believed that a bomb might be feasible if two roughly equal, subcritical pieces of uranium could be joined together so rapidly that the supercritical mass created would fission quickly and completely before it was actually blown apart. Thomson's committee reported to the government in 1941 that a uranium weapon was technically possible, and as a result, Great Britain committed its main scientific effort to the support of the American Manhattan Project. The team succeeded in creating the first nuclear weapon.

During his remaining tenure in London, Thomson became involved in a series of experiments on nuclear fusion (a process whereby light nuclei are joined together to form heavier ones, with considerable energy release). The objective was to achieve a fusion reaction that would proceed in a controlled fashion and produce power, as does a nuclear power reactor, in a moderately slow and usable way. Thompson's group worked closely with scientists at Great Britain's Atomic Energy Research Establishment, but they did not succeed in achieving their goal of building a fusion reactor.

There is no denying the importance of Thomson's work in electron diffraction and its role in establishing the fundamental principles of quantum mechanics. Today, the theory of quantum mechanics—or wave mechanics, as it was known earlier—is basic to every branch of physics; scientists no longer question the necessity of using the wave approach in fields that range from subatomic particle physics to superconductors to the behavior of the semiconductors that are commonly found in electronic devices. Quantum mechanics is the fundamental theory of physics, and Thomson is appropriately honored for his contribution to that theory.

In addition to his research papers, Thomson wrote several books. The first, on aerodynamics, is now of historical interest only. His most important book is undoubtedly the two-volume work that he wrote in collaboration with his father, *Conduction of Electricity Through Gases* (1928-1933). For a long time it was a standard reference work. Another work of interest to physics students and professionals is his *The Wave Mechanics of Free Electrons* (1930), which contains a summary of lectures that he gave during a brief tenure as visiting lecturer at Cornell University the preceding year. A work that is of special interest to anyone wishing to hear firsthand accounts of some of the momentous discoveries in the field is Thomson's short book *The Inspiration of Science* (1961). In it, he attempts to draw a picture of what it is like to do research in pure science and to show the special ways in which scientists are trained to think about nature and the problems that interest them. The book contains some anecdotal material about famous scientists, many of whom were known personally to the Thomsons, and embraces a wide range of scientific topics, from the discovery of the atom's constitution to concepts of space and time.

## Bibliography

*Primary*
PHYSICS: "Diffraction of Cathode Rays by a Thin Film," *Nature*, vol. 119, 1927 (with A. Reid); "The Diffraction of Cathode Rays by Thin Films of Platinum," *Nature*, vol. 120, 1927; "The Waves of an Electron," *Nature*, vol. 122, 1928; "Experiments on the Diffraction of Cathode Rays," *Proceedings of the Royal Society A*, vol. 117, 1928; "Experiments on the Diffraction of Cathode Rays II," *Proceedings of the Royal Society A*, vol. 119, 1928; *Conduction of Electricity Through Gases*, 1928-1933 (with Joseph John Thomson); "Diffraction of Cathode Rays III," *Proceedings of the Royal Society A*, vol. 125, 1929; "A Camera for Electron Diffraction," *Proceedings of the Royal Society A*, vol. 128, 1930 (with G. J. Fraser); *The Wave Mechanics of Free Electrons*, 1930; "Production of Neutrons by the Fission of Uranium," *Nature*, vol. 140, 1939; *Theory and Practice of Electron Diffraction*, 1939 (with William Cochrane); *The Foreseeable Future*, 1955; *The Inspiration of Science*, 1961.

*Secondary*
Crease, Robert P., and Charles C. Mann. *The Second Creation: Makers of the Revolution in Twentieth Century Physics*. New York: Macmillan, 1985. A general account of the revolution in twentieth century physics in which the Thomsons were engaged, this book's main purpose is to tell the story of subatomic particles. It begins with the accidental discovery of radioactivity and concludes with the search for a grand unification theory. The authors write in a casual, almost colloquial, style, and much of what they have to say comes directly from interviews with physicists working on the outer fringes of physics research today. Consequently, their account has a journalistic flavor which will convey to the average reader much of the excitement of research in physics.
Crowther, James G. *The Cavendish Laboratory, 1874-1974*. New York: Science History Publications, 1974. A book written for those who wish to gain some sense of the importance of the Cavendish Laboratory and its role in British physics research. Significantly, some twenty-two physics Nobel laureates started or completed their work there. No work is more authoritative, or more insightful, on the sociological aspects of institutional research or on the interactions among some of the chief engineers of modern physics. It is very readable, with an extensive bibliography on the leaders of the Cavendish, including J. J. Thomson, and several recollections by his son, George.

MacKinnon, Edward M. *Scientific Explanation and Atomic Physics*. Chicago: University of Chicago Press, 1982. Written by a philosopher, this work is an important contribution to the philosophy of science. The author's principal interest is in elucidating the ways in which science reaches a consensus in its modes of explaining the physical world. It is a profound work, and therefore not an easy one, but its relevance is particularly marked in its treatment of the birth of wave mechanics, including the crucial, if somewhat fortuitous, step of de Broglie, whose ideas Thomson tested. Extensive references and end notes.

Moon, Parry. "George Paget Thomson." *Biographical Memoirs of Fellows of the Royal Society* 23 (1977): 529-556. In the absence of any other critical biography of Thomson, this work is extremely important. It is based in part on an autobiographical study that is now in the collection of the library at Trinity College, Cambridge. The article is by a former colleague and junior member of the World War II uranium fission project committee. It covers in authoritative detail the main developments in Thomson's professional life. There is a comprehensive bibliography.

Snow, C. P. *The Physicists*. Boston: Little, Brown, 1981. This work is useful for placing Thomson's work within the milieu of British science of the period.

Weber, Robert L. *Pioneers of Science: Nobel Prize Winners in Physics*. Bristol, England: Adam Hilger, 1980. This book, which was sponsored by the British society for physics, provides brief accounts for the layperson of physics Nobel Prize winners and their work. The individual entries run through 1979. They are concise, and the main emphasis is on the physics, which is presented in simple terms. There is a bibliography.

*David G. Fenton*